STUDIES IN EVANGELICAL HISTORY AND THOUGHT

Evangelical Identity and Contemporary Culture

A Congregational Study in Innovation

STUDIES IN EVANGELICAL HISTORY AND THOUGHT

A full listing of all titles in this series
appears at the close of this book

STUDIES IN EVANGELICAL HISTORY AND THOUGHT

Evangelical Identity and Contemporary Culture

A Congregational Study in Innovation

Mathew Guest

Foreword by David Martin

WIPF & STOCK · Eugene, Oregon

Wipf and Stock Publishers
199 W 8th Ave, Suite 3
Eugene, OR 97401

Evangelical Identity and Contemporary Culture
A Congregational Study in Innovation
By Guest, Mathew
Copyright©2007 Paternoster
ISBN 13: 978-1-55635-806-7
Publication date 1/15/2008

This Edition published by Wipf and Stock Publishers
by arrangement with Paternoster.

Paternoster
9 Holdom Avenue
Bletchley
Milton Keyes, MK1 1QR
Great Britain

STUDIES IN EVANGELICAL HISTORY AND THOUGHT

Series Preface

The Evangelical movement has been marked by its union of four emphases: on the Bible, on the cross of Christ, on conversion as the entry to the Christian life and on the responsibility of the believer to be active. The present series is designed to publish scholarly studies of any aspect of this movement in Britain or overseas. Its volumes include social analysis as well as exploration of Evangelical ideas. The books in the series consider aspects of the movement shaped by the Evangelical Revival of the eighteenth century, when the impetus to mission began to turn the popular Protestantism of the British Isles and North America into a global phenomenon. The series aims to reap some of the rich harvest of academic research about those who, over the centuries, have believed that they had a gospel to tell to the nations.

Series Editors

David Bebbington, Professor of History, University of Stirling, Stirling, Scotland, UK

John H.Y. Briggs, Senior Research Fellow in Ecclesiastical History and Director of the Centre for Baptist History and Heritage, Regent's Park College, Oxford, UK

Timothy Larsen, McManis Professor of Christian Thought, Wheaton College, Illinois, USA, a Fellow of the Royal Historical Society, and Visiting Fellow, Trinity College, Cambridge, UK

Mark A. Noll, McAnaney Professor of History, University of Notre Dame, Notre Dame, Indiana, USA

Ian M. Randall, Deputy Principal and Lecturer in Church History and Spirituality, Spurgeon's College, London, UK, and a Senior Research Fellow, International Baptist Theological Seminary, Prague, Czech Republic

*Dedicated to my parents,
John and Kathleen Guest*

Contents

Foreword by David Martin xiii

Acknowledgements xv

Prologue
First Encounters xvii

Chapter 1
Evangelical Christianity in a Post-Christian World 1
Modernisation and the Homeless Mind 4
Conservative Religion and the Project of Resistance 7
Cultural Accommodation 9
Engaged Orthodoxy 13
Congregational Studies and the Sociology of Community 17
A Note on the Structure of the Book 21

Chapter 2
Growth and Change: The Evangelical Movement Since the 1960s 23
Relative Growth 23
Congregational Growth 27
The Changing State of English Evangelicalism 32
Ecumenism 35
Social Action as Evangelism 37
The Embrace of Popular Culture and the Arts 42
Alpha 45
Post-Evangelicalism 47
Comment: Accommodation and Resistance 50

Chapter 3
St Michael-le-Belfrey: Blazing the Trail 54
Local Context 55
Past and Present, Growth and Change 56
Growth and Decline 62
Who Goes to St Michael's? 66
Community and Commitment 70

Chapter 4
Holding the Many Strands Together: Community and Diversity 76
'St Mike's is a bit liberal for me...' 76
What it Means to be Liberal 78
Scriptural Authority 81
Salvation 87

The Role and Status of Women..91
Capitulating to Modernity?..94
Negotiating the Boundaries of the Faith 95
Sermons: Trends in Public Teaching 98
Public Tensions and the Avoidance of Conflict...102

Chapter 5
Taming the Spirit: Charismatic Experience after the Third Wave 105
The Charismatic Movement: The Story So Far 109
The Charismatic Identity of St Michael-le-Belfrey.......................................112
Personal Narratives 114
Subjectivity in Ritual Forms 120
The 'Turn to Life'..127
The Ritualisation of Life..129
Cynicism Towards the Charismatic 131

Chapter 6
Innovations at the Margins: The Post-Evangelical Pathway.........134
'Warehouse': A Project in Friendship Evangelism.......................................135
Participants: Core and Periphery...139
'Defusing' Authority 142
Mobilising the Aesthetic..147
The Reconfiguration of Shared Attitudes 150
Explanations for Change..157
Cultural Distance: *Visions* within the Context of St Michael's 158
The Wider Context..162

Chapter 7
Small Group Fellowship: The Experience of Community............168
Community Beyond the Congregation...169
Family and Community Congregations 173
Small Groups in St Michael's...175
Small Group in *Visions*...181
Small Groups and Collective Identity 190

Chapter 8
The Bigger Picture...196
Evangelical Networks and Markets..197
Subjectivity, Community and Culture..205
Changes at the Margins 209
Conservative Resurgence...212
Evangelical Growth and Vitality..217

Epilogue
St Michael-le-Belfrey Revisited in 2006...222
Bringing In ... .222
Building Up ... .224

Sending Out 227

Appendix 1
Research Methods 231

Appendix 2
Visions Sung Creed 241

Bibliography 243

Index 257

Foreword

I suppose most people are aware that Evangelical movements inside and outside the Anglican Church have been comparatively resilient over recent decades of decline in active Christianity in Britain, along with some decline in Christian belief and identification. The recent book by Kelvin Randall *Evangelicals Etcetera* (2005) has documented the extent of Evangelical influence within the Anglican ministry, and it has also shown something of the range of positions within Evangelicalism, including the presence of liberalizing tendencies. It is as if one wing of the Established Church has expanded to take over much of the old centre. It is also as if what used to be Nonconformity is now operating within the Establishment, perhaps because the divisive social conditions behind denominationalism have largely disappeared. At the same time the Methodist and Baptist Churches find that new wine is straining at the old containers of traditional Nonconformity, so that different kinds of spirituality take over particular local churches. However these local churches are responding to movements of renewal that are national and transatlantic in scope. Pentecostalism is one such movement, but there are many others and they come in successive waves which are difficult to chart. There are, for example, the numerous groups analyzed by William Kay in his new study *Apostolic Networks in Britain* (2007), also published in this series. I speak for myself when I say it is easy to lose your bearings in a market place where there are so many marginally differentiated products, if the economic metaphor will be forgiven.

Mathew Guest's clear, careful and insightful study of one highly successful Evangelical church in York, and of its innovative 'post-modern' offshoot, presents us with a microcosm of much that is happening in today's Church. Moreover, he sets his study in the context of an extensive theoretical literature, running from the major reference point provided by Peter Berger to the important work of James Davison Hunter and Christian Smith. The literature on Evangelicalism is very extensive, and even those who read this literature professionally will be glad of the kind of critical guide provided by Mathew Guest. He provides something of the global setting as well as the fascinating detail of one remarkable local experiment. In particular he documents the varied and alterative ways a movement often seen as a mode of cultural resistance uses the culture it resists. Those who want to understand this dialectic of incorporation and resistance as it has worked out in a highly mobile and well educated context could hardly do better than read Mathew Guest's book.

David Martin
Professor Emeritus
London School of Economics

Acknowledgements

This book has been long in the making, and I have many individuals to thank in helping me bring it to completion. The original research was conducted for a doctorate in sociology at Lancaster University between 1998 and 2001. I would like to thank the Economic and Social Research Council for providing the funding for this, and my supervisors, Nick Abercrombie, Paul Heelas and Linda Woodhead, for their support, sound advice and encouragement. I have benefited from guidance offered by numerous friends and colleagues during the doctoral study and in subsequent years, and I would especially like to thank Gordon Lynch, Simon Coleman, Grace Davie, Martin Stringer, David Martin, Bernice Martin and Kieran Flanagan. Douglas Davies has been a continued source of sage advice and infectious enthusiasm as teacher, colleague and friend.

The requirement of anonymity prevents me from naming parishioners from St Michael-le-Belfrey, York, whose indomitable kindness and hospitality will, nevertheless, not easily be forgotten. A few individuals should, however, be singled out as their contribution was so significant: the vicar, the Revd Roger Simpson, who, despite a demanding schedule, was kind enough to allow me four lengthy and invaluable interviews; Sue and Malcolm Wallace, who offered extensive and instructive feedback on my interpretation of the *Visions* group; Helen Lawrence, who provided an ear for my worries and a voice of impeccable common sense; Joel Payne, for his generosity and friendship; Julian and Anne Gray, for debate and the greatest warmth over beer, crisps and speaker cables; Mark Rance, for tireless practical support with the questionnaire and other hard data well beyond the call of duty; and Naomi Smith, a great house mate and inspiring conversationist on the spiritual path.

Outside of York, I benefited from the advice of Paul Roberts, who kindly shared his thoughts on the 'alternative' worship scene. The Revd Graham Cray (now Bishop of Maidstone) showed immense generosity in giving me over two hours of his time to talk about his experiences with St Michael's and *Visions* during the 1980s. Thanks also to The Borthwick Institute of Historical Research at the University of York, for access to their archive and to Christian Research, who provided further information on church attendance. Hugh McLeod, of the University of Birmingham, confided to me his thoughts on the religious crisis of the 1960s and I am indebted to him for his magnanimity and scholarship.

In recent years, I have benefited enormously from the warm and supportive environment of the Department of Theology and Religion at Durham University. My gratitude goes out to my colleagues for their gracious welcome and continuing encouragement.

While all of the individuals mentioned above have had a significant impact on this volume, I must, naturally, take full responsibility for the final product.

On a more personal note, I could not have completed this project without the unwavering support of a few individuals, most of all my parents who, as ever, have been unending in their love and encouragement. This book is dedicated to them.

Mathew Guest
Durham University
August 2007

PROLOGUE

First Encounters

Despite its imposing structure, the sixteenth-century Anglican church stands as a warm and welcoming presence on this cold January evening. The church is well lit, bustling with activity, and like every Sunday, over 300 worshippers are busy making their way into the pews. Many of them arrive in groups, and a huddled queue develops as people are welcomed in and greeted by familiar faces as they enter the church building. As we enter, we are greeted by a young couple, each standing on either side of the doorway. They smile warmly, hand us a copy of the weekly notice sheet and welcome us to the church of St Michael-le-Belfrey.

Inside the doorway, a small foyer is packed full of people, flicking through leaflets, browsing through the bookstall, and chatting with familiar parishioners. A couple of middle aged churchwardens stand nearby, watching with interest, and make sure that everyone can find a seat. Any newcomers are taken aside, greeted and escorted to a free space in the pews. The church nave is large and cavernous, capable of seating some 700 in its traditional wooden pews and in the balcony overhead. Its largely white-washed interior is for the most part devoid of visual artistry, that is, apart from the two colourful banners embroidered with enigmatic proclamations: 'Jesus, Light of the World' and 'His Spirit Lives in Me'. A painted reredos of the adoration of the shepherds is also situated behind the altar, although this has faded and darkened with time. However, there is a strong sense of colour throughout the building – shining forth from the vivid stained glass as much as from the keen activity of the congregation.

While the grey stone memorials and solemn altar evoke a sense of tradition, the bright lights and casual style of interaction create a more informal atmosphere. All age groups appear to be represented: large groups of undergraduate students gather in the side pews, long-attending families arrive and sit together, while elderly parishioners greet old friends and make their way to their usual seats, some of them praying quietly alone as they prepare to worship. Some people take this time to skim through the church notice-sheet, or to browse through the other items of promotional paperwork which are placed along the pews: leaflets about the Alpha course, fliers advertising a new youth mission event, and application forms for a forthcoming Lent prayer course. But the majority are engaged in eager conversation, some warmly embracing one another as they meet, their broad smiles conveying an overwhelming sense of shared enthusiasm.

The beginning of the service is signalled by an elderly man who stands at the lectern and announces today's notices. The congregation listen intently in silence. He encourages newcomers to become members of the church by filling in a 'welcome card', asks existing members to bring along non-Christian friends to the forthcoming Alpha course, and urges us all (there is no distinction made between members and non-members) to attend the imminent monthly church prayer meeting, to worship and pray together as a church.

Sung worship features heavily in the service, and is accompanied by a band, consisting of guitars, keyboards, drums, some brass and several leading singers. All are amplified through a central PA system, necessary not only because of the size of the building, but also as a means of achieving sufficient volume over the rousing singing of the congregation. Indeed, many sing along with an expressive confidence that is accompanied by a raising of arms held aloft and open, a recognised gesture of praise. Some close their eyes and shake their heads, smiling in expressions of adoration as they sing. Others save any gestured expression for the rousing chorus. As is commonplace in present-day evangelical churches, popular choruses – with catchy melodies and lyrics which stress the simplicity of the divine–human relationship – are preferred over traditional hymns. However, St Michael's appears to have found a compromise in also offering contemporary, lively arrangements of time-honoured hymnody, and the congregation appears to respond equally well to rousing anthems as it does to sentimental ballads.

If impassioned lay participation is a feature of sung worship, it is also in evidence at more formalised points of the service. While the liturgy of the confession and absolution are led by the lay service leader and the sermon is given by the vicar, normal members of the congregation are instrumental in performing more peripheral, but no less visible, roles. The Bible readings, composition and offering of the weekly prayers, administration of the collection, welcoming at the church doors, running the book store, operating the PA desk – all are performed by different parishioners. Again, all age groups are represented in these tasks, and the leadership appear to have no trouble finding volunteers. If there is an effort to regularly mobilise lay leadership, it is one embraced by the congregation at large.

The day's Bible readings are given, on this occasion especially selected by the preacher rather than taken from the Church of England lectionary. Following this, the vicar approaches the pulpit in preparation for the sermon. His name is Roger Simpson, a clergyman recently appointed to St Michael's who has been received warmly by the congregation. Simpson is in his late forties and is this evening dressed in a dark suit, striped shirt and tie. His tone is warm but assertive, his delivery both measured and steady. The theme for the whole service is the empowerment of others within the church, and the sermon addresses this theme with special reference to the New Testament reading from Paul's letter to the Ephesians. Simpson's preaching is very much in the style of an expositor; he works from a specific biblical passage, moving towards what he takes to be its principal message, before outlining the practical implications of this for the church today. The absolute centrality of the scriptures is evident not only in Simpson's preaching, but also in the way his parishioners eagerly follow his references using the Bibles set in the pews. The reference (and also often the page number) to each cited verse is clearly stated from the pulpit so that congregants may follow the teaching in the printed text before them. Most are keenly attentive to the sermon, some even taking notes.

Simpson speaks about how the members of a living church should relate to one another as a community, and invokes clear biblical guidelines. He refers repeatedly to his chosen passage (Ephesians 4.1-16), stressing two key qualities: unity and holiness,

> This new community that God is calling into existence is to be completely distinct from the secular culture in which it is part, it is to be set apart, holy – that's what holiness means, to be set apart – to belong to God.

Listening to his words, I am reminded of the common tendency within evangelicalism to distance itself from matters of 'the world' in favour of a kind of spiritual purity, but Simpson's message is not so simple. He suggests that our unity in Christ is strengthened by the diversity of human gifts within the church. Simpson disagrees with the traditional understanding, derived from 1 Corinthians, that there are nine spiritual gifts. He says that every person has a gift from God and that this gift is given so that they may serve the church. Throughout his sermon he emphasises this paradox: the strength of the church in its diversity, and its status as set apart from a corrupt 'secular culture'. Indeed, it is through its diversity, argues Simpson, that the church may cope with the problems of the contemporary world.

> ... the New Testament envisages the evangelists, and the pastors and the teachers, equipping and empowering others to do this work to enable the people of God to be a servant people, actively but humbly, according to their gifts, in a world of alienation and pain.

Only with the active lay ministry of the congregation can the church hope to develop and grow for the future. He urges the congregation to encourage each other in the faith, and exist together in relationships of support and mutual learning. He reflects on his own experience as a 'new Christian' when he was a young student, mentioning the important guidance of one of his peers, a young man who mentored him and supported him in his Bible study when his faith was in most need of nurture and growth. The message here is that it is only through the strength of its community that the church – both St Michael's and the wider Christian communion – may hope to withstand the pressures and temptations of modern life.

After the sermon, the elderly service leader approaches the lectern, and says that there are some people who have come forward with things they believe God wants to say to the church tonight. Three 'words of knowledge' are then offered, delivered to individuals from the congregation but spoken to us by the service leader, who reads them from written notes he has been given. After each he offers a response. One of them concerns someone who is thinking about becoming a full member of the church, but who see themselves as a small part and feel that they will be crushed by the enormity of the congregation. The service leader responds with a message from God.

The Lord wants to say to them, the big body is made up of lots of little bodies ... and as all the little parts meet together and fuse together, you become part of one big body – an important part and a useful part, and the thing that is seen is not the foot, but the head, who is Jesus.

The congregation sing the final two songs in succession, *Hallelujah Sing to Jesus* and *We're Looking to Your Promise*. Following the final chorus, the vicar moves to the centre at the front of the church, and gives the blessing. He moves alongside the service leader, and they walk up the centre aisle before approaching the door of the church. There they will stand as they greet people, one by one, as they leave. The band strike up again at this point, and play an instrumental version of the last song. People take their seats, chat with friends close by, and then begin to move around the church – around and among the social networks forged in and through the church community. They will socialise for another thirty minutes or so, before the last stragglers leave, onward home or else to their favourite local pub, where they will join other friends from the church and conclude their Sunday over drinks and conversation.

***

Dating from the mid-fifteenth century, St Cuthbert's is named after its patron, the bishop of Lindisfarne. A parish church in its own right for many years, the building became the administrative centre of St Michael-le-Belfrey in 1973, and later housed the offices of the extensive St Michael's staff, as well as being used for functions and church youth meetings. The *Visions* group have used the building for their services since they first began in 1991.

Although the church structure dates back some 500 years, its interior is partially transformed by twentieth-century technology for the purposes of this evening's event. At the far end of the church, in the old sanctuary, the space has been converted into a small even-sided hall. As is standard practice for *Visions* events, the lighting is heavily dimmed. Any limited illumination is provided by small spot lights carefully positioned high in the ceiling rafters, and the colours emanating from the various slide projections shine more vividly out of the darkness. The intense and evocative scent of incense is immediately present upon entering the building, evoking a sense of ritual, reverence and sacred space.

The entire east wall, which stretches to a height of about twenty-five feet, is covered by a suspended white sheet. This effectively acts as a screen for various images, which are projected onto it from a series of slide projectors, positioned at the back of the room. The images are striking by their apparent incongruity: a foetus in the womb, a circus performance of men riding bicycles across tightropes. The dominant image depicts a large crowd of people who appear to be watching a football match, blending into a crowded scene on a city street. The images form a complex whole, a collage rather than a collection of discrete icons. There are no boundaries between the images and their vivid juxtaposition and tendency to merge into one another is both striking and evocative. It is a symbolism that challenges any

Prologue: First Encounters

straightforward preconceptions one might have about art, church and the 'message' of a ritualised event.

There are a series of TV screens scattered around the room. Two have been placed on what was once an altar table, an old and disused artefact now shrouded in black cloth. All the TVs face inwards, towards the centre, where people are beginning to gather. They each display an identical series of rapidly changing video images. These are mixed and controlled live by a young teenaged girl who stands before a mass of technological gadgetry, tapes and video recorders. Moving images are shown without cessation throughout the service, as well as both before and after the event has apparently concluded, a policy which effectively blurs the boundaries of the service. The images vary considerably – some express an aesthetic love of nature (the constant flow of a waterfall; images of a bud opening into a flower). Others suggest revolution (the tumbling Berlin Wall; soldiers raising rifles triumphantly into the air as they march over a silhouetted hill). Other images combine traditional Christian symbolism with elements from other traditions, or with images drawn from dance or pop video culture (a large cross shines behind lines from a native American poem about the sacredness of the land; a stone cross revolves in 3D as shining stripes of colour emanate from its centre). The images progress rapidly, sometimes appearing to reflect the themes addressed in the service, and sometimes not. The most striking thing about the use of visual simulation is that it is constant and present at every side, the TVs positioned so that images constantly bombard our vision from all angles.

At the very front of the room, positioned behind the video equipment, is a sound desk, and behind this stands the DJ. The music is managed by a man in his early thirties, whose long hair complements his beard. The music played throughout the service is based around the styles of ambient trance and up-beat techno, reflecting the group's affinity with the dance culture. Music plays constantly throughout the event, and punctuates the developing activities and rituals of the service. The majority of the pieces are instrumental, although some feature vocal backing tracks which are used to complement the lines sung by the congregation during the service. The words of these songs, as well as any instructions to participants and liturgy, are projected onto the centre of the east wall. While in St Michael's, the overhead projector allows hymn-book-free hands to be raised in praise, here, it is deployed differently, most notably as a channel of rhetorically expressed order amidst visual chaos.

At the beginning of the service, several tables are positioned around the periphery of the room, each surrounded by chairs. There are fifteen of us present, including those involved in facilitating the service, and we each collect food from a small buffet at the back of the room before joining others at the various tables. Those present are aged between fifteen and forty-four, and most are regular participants in *Visions* services. We collect our food, consisting of salad, cold meats, crisps and cake, and chat while we eat. The conversation is casual, not surprisingly considering that most of those present are well known to one another. Those not engaged in light conversation are busy viewing the video playing on all of the TV screens with sound: a feature film about Oscar Romero, the martyred Roman Catholic priest from El Salvador. Most of those present seem familiar with his story.

After about thirty minutes, while we are still seated, we are welcomed to the service by a young woman named Rebecca, who stands at the front with a microphone. We are told that this is a 'High Tea' service, and that our theme for today is 'Leaps of Faith'. Without any further explanation, she says that we are to begin with our readings. A young teenaged girl begins with an excerpt from Genesis – the story of the calling of Abram – which she reads from a piece of paper by candlelight at the front of the room. She is followed by a woman aged about thirty, who reads from the letter to the Hebrews. We are not told the exact references, nor are we given Bibles in order that we might follow the text.

After the two readings, Rebecca moves to the front once more and introduces a video clip. It is taken from *The Matrix*, the Hollywood feature film released the previous year. She tells us briefly about the character in the clip, Neo, who is about to make a leap of faith, something 'we have all probably had to do at some point'. The clip is played, and the characters of Neo and Morpheus are watched intently on all of the TV screens as they discuss the option of the blue or the red pill. The exchange is not about religion as such, but there are implicit themes of trust and faith that have obvious parallels with Christian understandings of the human relationship with God.

The service moves on, without explanation, to address the figure of Abram once more. Steven, in his mid-thirties and dressed casually with long hair tied back in a ponytail, approaches the front of the room. He gives us a brief synopsis of Abraham's life story,[1] told in historical terms, and paying attention to factors such as his family life and the environment in which he lived. Although clearly basing this on written notes, Steven skims over the details casually and humbly, giving the impression that he intends to give descriptive detail and information: the background to a story, rather than the structure of an argument. If I encounter exposition in St Michael's, here I am offered suggestion and food for thought.

Rebecca takes the floor once more. She says she is going to talk about how we might know God in our lives: we might have strange inner feelings, but how do we know that this is God, and not something else, like indigestion! Speaking briefly and casually, her delivery betrays a nervous hesitancy that suggests she is speaking from the heart. She offers fragments of advice about how we might discern a divine presence or guidance in our lives. We might talk to wise friends whom we trust. We might appeal to our intuition – if it feels wrong then it may well not be right. She asks us to consider our conscience – does our feeling sit well with our conscience? Despite her uncertain tone, she ends on a note of optimism: we can rest assured that God is behind it all – whatever the circumstances, we can be assured of this. Her talk is distinctive in discussing religious experience at a 'Christian' event, but without

---

[1] The two names of 'Abram' and 'Abraham' are both used here, as references to this figure during this service referred both to the original calling of Abram, and to his life after his covenant with God, at which he is renamed Abraham, the 'father of many'. See Genesis 12.1-3; 17.

using biblical language or mentioning Jesus, or the Holy Spirit. Her language is suggestive of a far more vaguely defined notion of experience – real, and yet ultimately mysterious.

Rebecca then introduces the next feature. We are going to say a prayer that helps us to concentrate on God. It is based on the final piece of dialogue from the film, *Bladerunner*, where the female 'replicant' is forced to make a decision of whether to trust the main character, Deckard, to take her safely away from danger. 'Do you love me?', he asks her. 'I love you', she replies. 'Do you trust me?' 'I trust you.' These words are projected onto the large screen before us and a steady dance track begins to play. Over the music is played a haunting recording of a man and a woman speaking the two lines from the film, over and over. Rebecca invites us, 'if we feel comfortable doing so', to say these words to ourselves in prayer.

This exercise lasts around five minutes, and most people can be seen either mouthing the words or else sitting silently in prayer. Although many participants exhibit an intense concentration, few conventional prayer gestures are apparent. Hands are not held aloft, few heads are bowed, and several pairs of eyes remain open. All appear united, however, in facing directly forward, towards the front wall awash with colour and dazzling image, and towards the large, mantra-like words of the prayer before them.

As the backing track fades away, Rebecca re-emerges to introduce 'our period of sung worship'. We are told to feel free to dance and sing as we want to, to feel free to worship God. At this point the dance track becomes louder and begins to ascend into a crescendo of thudding beats before settling into a continuous steady rhythm. Several people stand up and begin to dance near to their seats, clapping to the rhythm and raising their hands in a fashion reminiscent of night clubs and youthful celebration. One or two voices can be heard above the pounding backing track, including the high, impassioned singing of the service leader, whose words are amplified through large speakers while she dances and praises God, facing the stunning front wall as her focal point of vision.

More people get up to dance as new tunes emerge from the speakers. Some songs are based on popular chart tracks, which have been adjusted to include lyrics of a Christian or at least vaguely spiritual character. All follow a fast dance beat and are skillfully sandwiched between instrumental pieces which develop and punctuate the key songs through a deft blending of rhythmic progressions. Dry ice occasionally pours out of two smoke machines positioned at the far corners of the room. They hiss loudly as they emit a white vapour that temporarily engulfs the dancers and adds a renewed sense of mystery and awe to an event already saturated with sensory stimulation from every angle. Here, technology and the sacred appear hand in hand, with each feeding into the other in an intense moment of celebration.

Eventually, after about twenty minutes of dance and sung worship, there is a marked reduction in volume and the music gradually develops into a steady, ambient track – a soothing, relaxing piece that signals the conclusion of the service. Steven steps forward once more and tells us that this is the end of the service, but asks everyone to stick around for coffee and a chat. The group will also retire to the pub later on, and everyone is welcome to join them.

The microphone is switched off, people begin to talk once more, and hot drinks are brought into the hall on a tray. As those present discuss the success of the service and chat to each other about more personal issues, they help themselves to tea or coffee and finish off the rest of the buffet. After about thirty minutes many of the occasional attendees have left, leaving the *Visions* regulars, who proceed across the road to The Black Swan where they will stay until it closes. Several of them will then return to St Cuthbert's to pack away the equipment, a task that will take another hour. However, boredom will be relieved by playing loud dance music through the PA system while cables are coiled, TVs lifted, and huge sheets are taken down to reveal drab stone work where there had, only an hour before, been brilliant colour.

A Study in Evangelical Cultures

These two accounts are of services that I attended during January and March 2000 respectively, some months into a period of ethnographic fieldwork. I had originally become interested in the *Visions* group as a site of 'alternative' worship (or 'alt.worship', as is their preferred label), the multi-media based movement that had swept through many churches since the emergence of the Nine O'Clock Service (NOS) in Sheffield during the late 1980s. Intent on studying the movement *via* a case study, I began researching various UK groups on the internet. Entering the *Visions* site, I was struck by the group's attempt to articulate its identity: 'We're a collective of people with major interests in the visual arts, dance music, technology, and Christian spirituality.'[2]

The site was notable for an evident desire to remain within Christian tradition, but also by an additional appeal to an unusually varied range of other religious and non-religious resources. The site mentioned evangelicalism, liberalism, charismatic renewal, Roman Catholicism, Orthodoxy and Creation Spirituality, post-modernism, environmental concerns such as recycling and nuclear testing, and the spiritual virtues of the Celtic tradition. Most other alt.worship sites had been far less eclectic, and had given much less space to the articulation of a collective position on theological and social issues. I was drawn to the site because of a certain thoughtfulness of language, and by the sense of spiritual openness suggested by its unusually diverse spectrum of influences.

Bearing in mind these initial impressions, I was understandably intrigued to discover that the church to which the *Visions* group were attached had been a major centre of evangelical revival. St Michael-le-Belfrey has been at the vanguard of evangelical growth and vitality since the 1960s, and continues to enjoy a congregation which is exceptionally large and abnormally active, at least compared with most UK churches. St Michael's is also seen as something of an exemplar

---

[2] See http://www.visions-york.org/ (website originally accessed Autumn 1998).

within the evangelical world and is commonly associated with effective church growth, charismatic revival and evangelical integrity. This was something of a surprise; the last thing I expected of an evangelical church was a progressive worship group which appeared to embrace social activism, critical thinking and a liberal, almost 'New Age' embrace of spiritual diversity. What I was about to learn was that *Visions* had constructed itself as a progressive Christian collective, and defined its initiatives as a measured response to the mainstream charismatic worship represented in its parent church. At first sight, this response was virtually asymmetric. Typical services exhibited a series of oppositional trends: words versus images, exposition versus suggestion, clarity versus ambiguity. But at the same time, patterns of continuity – for example a stress on subjective experience and on shared leadership – implied a more complex picture. Moreover, the comments about culture and diversity in Roger Simpson's sermon reflect a process of negotiation with contemporary culture whose implications have radiated throughout the church. The effort to embrace human diversity and creativity alongside maintaining a robust community set apart from the world emerged as a motif relevant to the faith journeys of most of those counting themselves within St Michael-le-Belfrey, including the *Visions* group. And while *Visions* clearly embodied a critique, *but also a progression* of core evangelical ideas, other, ostensively mainstream elements of the church were engaging with similar questions, which took them in different, but not wholly unrelated, directions. Binding them all was an ongoing attempt to relate their evangelical faith to the culture in which they live.

Any simple opposition is also complicated by the local context. In formal, administrative terms, the two services described above represent two different congregational gatherings worshiping under the auspices of a single Anglican parish church. As such, they share the same leadership, church buildings and function within the same organisational structure. They have emerged out of a common history, shaped by parochial factors and by the broader evangelical movement in the UK.

This book is about congregational cultures, based around an extended period of ethnographic fieldwork among the St Michael-le-Belfrey congregation, the specific details of which are given in Appendix 1. It is about the norms of belief and practice dominant in a church community which has for so long been known for its creativity and innovation. The descriptions offered above are not intended to signal two divergent directions of evangelical development; rather, they are meant to illustrate a range of ideas and experiences which are currently changing the course of evangelical Christianity. This book is about the social consequences of these innovations for evangelical congregations. It is a topic that relates to two other questions: first, how do processes of change and radical creativity affect the *experience* of evangelical community for those involved, and second, what do such processes tell us about the changing relationship between evangelicalism and contemporary culture? In focusing on St Michael-le-Belfrey, the book presents a rather peculiar case study. St Michael's is far from representative of the wider evangelical movement in the UK. Indeed, its size, history, reputation and level and range of activity make it both exceptional and socially complex. And yet its unique status makes it an illuminating object of analysis, not simply because it is a novelty, but because it presents us with a hub through which every major change in evangelical Christianity has passed over the past forty years, from charismatic renewal, to creative evangelism, radical community living, Christian dance and drama, alternative worship, the Toronto Blessing and the Alpha course. Indeed, it has played a major part in instigating several of these developments and served as an inspiration for the rest of the evangelical world. As such a centre of activity, it presents an ideal case study for analysing the social consequences of these innovations for the life of an evangelical congregation. Aside from this, it is a highly successful church by UK standards, and there is a need for further reflection on church growth and decline in the UK which takes proper account of congregational cultures. All too often old arguments about secularisation are rehearsed without an attempt to address how churches actually function as social phenomena. I hope this book will make some small contribution to this still live debate.

The innovations that have characterised the life of St Michael-le-Belfrey over the past forty years have been shaped by the ongoing attempts of the church to relate effectively and fruitfully to its cultural context, however this is conceived. In taking account of this process sociologically, we are faced with a rich body of literature. Indeed, the task of exploring the relationship between conservative Protestantism and the modern age is one that has been pursued by a variety of thinkers over the past 100 years and more. We turn to their work in our initial chapter, in seeking to establish a firm theoretical basis for our study.

CHAPTER 1

Evangelical Christianity in a Post-Christian World

Peter Berger has noted that, of the world's religions, it is Protestant Christianity that has had the most 'intense and enduring encounter with the modern world'.[1] Indeed, previous examinations of this relationship have focused on a number of affinities. Ernst Troeltsch charted the role of sectarian Protestantism in the emergence of modern social democracy.[2] Max Weber famously argued that Calvinistic Protestantism was instrumental in the rise of the capitalist system in Europe.[3] More recently, David Martin has mapped the ways in which Protestantism reflects broader processes of social differentiation, drawing complex connections between Protestant revivalism and the development of modern states.[4] Protestantism and modernity clearly enjoy a complicated and multi-faceted relationship.

Taking up the phenomenon of Protestant evangelicalism – associated with the centrality of scripture, strict moral codes and a passion for the conversion of others – many recent scholars have spoken in terms of movements of resistance and protest. According to this paradigm, which shapes much of the literature, evangelical groups emerge and thrive in so far as they form a response to a perceived breakdown in the moral order of contemporary society. They offer meaning and consistency in a context of cultural chaos. Bernice Martin expresses the argument well in her discussion of Pentecostal revivalism in South America:

> The argument that Pentecostalism offers middle-range solutions to these problems owes something to a Durkheimian view of religion as a hedge against anomie, both the anomie of social and institutional disorder and the normlessness accompanying suddenly expanded horizons, mass mobility and the decay of older systems which

---

[1] Peter Berger, *The Heretical Imperative. Contemporary Possibilities of Religious Affirmation* (London: Collins, 1980), p. xii.

[2] Ernst Troeltsch, *Protestantism and Progress. A Historical Study of the Relation of Protestantism to the Modern World* (Boston, MA: Beacon Press, 1966).

[3] Max Weber, *The Protestant Ethic and the Spirit of Capitalism* (New York: Scribner's, 1958).

[4] David Martin, *A General Theory of Secularisation* (London: Basil Blackwell, 1978) and *Pentecostalism: The World their Parish* (Oxford: Blackwell, 2002).

had held the individual tightly within familial, communal, class and patronage frameworks.[5]

Martin's comments reflect a common trend, whereby Protestant evangelicalism is *both explained and defined* in terms of its resistance to 'the world'. Movements and churches are made sense of as self-conscious reactions to a set of social problems, problems for which evangelical groups promise to have the solution. This certainly rings true within many western contexts, in which the impassioned voices of evangelical Christianity have achieved the status of an often jarring but persistent minority. In the USA, this minority is highly significant, not merely because it represents a significant proportion of the population (25-30%[6]), but also because evangelicals are exerting an increasingly powerful influence over the national moral and political agenda. The resistance of US evangelicals to 'the world' has been understood within the context of the 'culture wars' between conservatives and liberals, a struggle for the religious and moral identity of America.[7] If there is a struggle on this side of the Atlantic, then it is far quieter and draws in far fewer participants, not least on account of the heavily secularised nature of western European societies. The UK is no exception, and some have argued that the detachment of the majority of the population from the traditions and values of the church makes the UK a post-Christian nation. This is not the same as saying the UK is a secular nation; statistical evidence counts against a resurgence of secularism and the number of respondents to attitudinal surveys who tick the boxes against atheism or agnosticism is still significantly low.[8] No, the post-Christian thesis specifically refers to the indifference with which the Christian churches are regarded by most of the population. While we may characterise the early twentieth century as a period when, even among non-churchgoers, the institutions of the churches were respected and revered as guardians of morality, symbols of local, ethnic or national identity and trusted purveyors of public ceremony, they are now largely ignored, especially by the younger generations, who simply fail to see them as significant aspects of their lives.

This picture is challenged by some on the grounds that while institutional engagement with the churches has diminished, the pursuit of what they stand for has

---

[5] Bernice Martin, 'From Pre- to Post-Modernity in Latin America: The Case of Pentecostalism', in P. Heelas (ed.) *Religion, Modernity and Postmodernity* (Oxford: Blackwell, 1998), p. 127.

[6] While figures which are cited obviously vary, this approximation is commonly cited as a gauge of evangelical popularity in the contemporary USA. For a discussion of the current situation in the US, see Christian Smith, *Christian America? What Evangelicals Really Want* (Berkeley and London: University of California Press, 2000).

[7] James Davison Hunter, *Culture Wars: The Struggle to Define America* (New York: Basic Books, 1991).

[8] According to the Soul of Britain survey of 2000, for example, 8% of the population said they were 'convinced atheists' while there was a figure of 10% for agnostics. See Steve Bruce, *God is Dead: Secularization in the West* (Oxford and Malden, MA: Blackwell, 2002), p. 193.

not. There remains a strong interest in the spiritual, and proponents of this perspective focus upon various dimensions in building up an alternative account: the role of the churches in maintaining a vicarious form of religion on behalf of the wider population, the mass of unchurched Christians apparently identified by the 2001 UK census, or the enthusiasm for alternative spiritualities which more successfully cater to widespread interest in human experience as a site of spiritual significance. Such developments fall between institutional orthodoxy and post-Christian indifference, highlighting the grey areas of the UK's religious landscape. And yet there remain significant flashes of colour (some might say blocks of shade), reflected in religious movements whose doctrinally conservative, vehemently defended beliefs are constructed in opposition to a vision of western culture as morally and spiritually bankrupt. These movements are not interested in the grey areas, and do not see culture as a potential source of spiritual nourishment, but construct it over and against their own set of fiercely held religious convictions. In recent years, we have come to associate such a passion for religious purity with radical Islam, and with the fundamentalism that inspires acts of terrorism. But the opposition to contemporary culture associated with these groups is also passionately affirmed, if often expressed differently, by some Christians, many of whom call themselves evangelical. They recognise the post-Christian nature of contemporary UK culture and engage with it as a spiritual challenge, a reason to pursue their mission to turn the tide and change things for the better, in accordance with God's plan. In theological terms, this orientation is so pervasive as to be almost an evangelical universal; however, it is pursued in such a variety of ways and with such varied results that the evangelical engagement with culture remains but a foundation for a far more complex analysis.

In so far as contemporary evangelical Christianity may be understood with reference to its passionate engagement with 'the world', the paradigm of resistance described earlier on is a useful sociological starting point in making sense of precise contours of change. While this paradigm may be traced to theological disputes deeply embedded in the chronicles of Christian history, within contemporary sociological discussion, it depends upon a more recent set of ideas. Simply put, it depends upon the commonplace argument that modernity has brought with it differentiation, complexity and a consequent breakdown of traditional social order, including the elevation of the individual and the dissolution of community. This is classically associated with thinkers such as Emile Durkheim, Max Weber and Karl Marx, who have shaped over a century of discussion. One influential account which draws from all three, and which will be described here in detail, is that offered in Peter Berger's *The Homeless Mind: Modernization and Consciousness* (co-written by Birgitte Berger and Hansfried Kellner), which was first published in 1974.[9] Berger's book is especially illuminating as it complements his other highly influential publications on religion and has been taken up by numerous subsequent commentators analysing

---

[9] Peter Berger, Brigitte Berger and Hansfried Kellner, *The Homeless Mind: Modernization and Consciousness* (New York: Vintage Books, 1974).

the fate of religion within the contemporary context. Berger's account is also a straightforward, simplified description of a process often rendered more opaque by other authors.

Modernisation and the Homeless Mind

Berger and his colleagues do not conceive of modernity as a fixed state or era, but rather speak of 'societies more or less advanced in a continuum of modernization'.[10] In isolating key features of the modernisation process, they follow Weber and begin with economic factors, and the influence of technology and bureaucracy upon social institutions. They refer to these as 'primary carriers' of modernisation. Pluralism is identified as a 'secondary carrier', but one which is nonetheless viewed as highly significant. However, Berger et al do not discuss social change in terms of structural factors alone. Building on Berger's own work with Thomas Luckmann,[11] they address how changes in the social structure affect the ways in which people define their social reality. In this respect, they are concerned with questions traditionally associated with the sociology of knowledge.

Berger et al isolate technology, bureaucracy and pluralism as the dominant features of modernity, and argue that, while each of them is embedded in social institutions such as the state, education and the workplace, each also has a 'corollary at the level of consciousness'.[12] That is, they all contribute to the construction of what is called the 'symbolic universe' of modernity.[13] The dominance of technological production generates a sense of the divisibility of reality into components and sequences, which are inter-related. Additionally, it tends to foster a problem-solving attitude towards life and an orientation focused on progress. Bureaucratisation encourages the idea that society may be organised as a system, and that one's affairs are to be carried out in a 'regular and predictable fashion',[14] ideas developed in George Ritzer's later book about the McDonaldization of society.[15] These orien-tations are originally generated on the basis of encounters the individual has with technology and bureaucracy within key social institutions, but there is an inevitable migration, according to Berger et al, into their overall perception of reality.

Whereas many other commentators have drawn attention to the importance of technology and bureaucracy to the modernisation process, not least Max Weber on

---

[10] Berger et al, Homeless Mind, p. 9.

[11] Peter Berger and Thomas Luckmann, *The Social Construction of Reality. A Treatise in the Sociology of Knowledge* (London, Fakenham and Reading: Penguin, 1967).

[12] Robert Wuthnow et al, *Cultural Analysis: The Work of Peter L. Berger, Mary Douglas, Michel Foucault and Jurgen Habermas* (London, Boston, MA, Melbourne and Henley: Routledge and Kegan Paul, 1984), p. 56.

[13] Berger et al, Homeless Mind, p. 99.

[14] Wuthnow et al, Cultural Analysis, p. 57.

[15] George Ritzer, *The McDonaldization of Society: An Investigation into the Changing Character of Contemporary Social Life* (Thousand Oaks: Pine Forge Press, 1996).

the Protestant Ethic and Marshall McLuhan with his work on the mass media,[16] Berger could lay claim to some originality in his focus upon pluralism. Accelerated social differentiation – nowadays intensified by mass communications and advanced technology – engenders a situation in which individuals are exposed to a plurality of lifeworlds. They are forced to deal with the fact that many different sets of values – relating to religion, morality, politics and lifestyle – co-exist, even though they may clash or contradict one another. Berger contrasts this feature of modernity with pre-modern or traditional societies, arguing that the latter offered sufficiently unified and stable value systems to foster social cohesion and secure a sense of meaning for their citizens. Modernity renders this process impossible. For Berger, the pluralism of modernity undermines social cohesion because the disparate elements of reality can no longer be integrated into a single symbolic universe.[17]

Although ostensively a descriptive account of the modernisation process, Berger *et al*'s *Homeless Mind* includes a decidedly negative evaluation, captured in their comments on the discontents of modernity. For the authors, the transformations bound up in modernisation undermine the cohesive power of social institutions; their 'identity defining power' is weakened.[18] The increasing influence of technology brings about experiences of alienation, frustration and anomie. An absorption in bureaucracy fosters abstraction and anonymity in the workplace. Both engender a sense of formality and a dispassionate, scientific outlook on life which fails to cater to the emotional, subjective dimensions of the human condition. Social differentiation also leads to a pluralisation of lifeworlds which undermines any cohesiveness offered in the institutional sphere: '...institutions then confront the individual as fluid and unreliable, and in the extreme case as unreal'.[19]

Consequently, the individual has to fall back on his or her own subjective resources for a sense of identity. In this, Berger follows Arnold Gehlen's argument that modernity generates a turn inward, a *subjectivisation*.[20] The self becomes the centre of the meaning-making process. However, because of the essentially social nature of humankind, this is a very precarious situation. Social identities require affirmation and maintenance from durable agencies outside of themselves, i.e. from institutions and traditions, and these are required to sustain some consistency of form over time. Without these systems of support, humanity stands in a state of existential uncertainty, or homelessness.

Berger *et al*'s account of modernity is now over thirty years old and numerous other accounts of contemporary culture, many of them claiming to trace a shift from modernity into postmodernity, have appeared in subsequent years. However, it is described here in detail for two main reasons. First, it defines and contextualises

---

[16] Marshall McLuhan, *Understanding Media: The Extensions of Man* (London: Routledge, 2001 [original 1964]).

[17] Berger *et al*, *Homeless Mind*, p. 109.

[18] Berger *et al*, *Homeless Mind*, p. 86.

[19] Berger *et al*, *Homeless Mind*, p. 85.

[20] See James Davison Hunter, 'Subjectivisation and the New Evangelical Theodicy', *Journal for the Scientific Study of Religion* 20:1 (1982), pp. 39-47.

several of the conceptual categories which will occupy us later in this book in exploring the changing state of evangelical Christianity. As we shall see, the evangelical engagement with contemporary culture cannot be fully accounted for without some reflection on the nature of rationalisation, subjectivisation and the social consequences of a perceived breakdown in institutions. Subsequent chapters will discuss how these sociological insights illuminate aspects of evangelical belief and practice. Second, it paints in broad theoretical brush strokes a picture of modernity which is useful in understanding contemporary British society. This will be described in greater detail in chapter two, but for now it is worth noting that if technology, bureaucracy and pluralism were dominant forces in the 1970s, they are even more so now, as testified in the massive influence of the internet, increasingly centralised control over systems of accountability, both in the public and private sectors under a New Labour Government, and the multiplication of traditions and worldviews available to the population. For some, the latter process has been intensified to the point of creating a postmodern cornucopia, with traditions reduced to the status of life choices, often treated as commodities available for consumption within the economic, social, moral and spiritual marketplace. The self is fragmented indeed, and appears to have even less in the way of external resources to depend on than when Berger and his colleagues were first formulating their arguments. Working with this analysis, Berger's comments about the discontents of modernity have not lost their relevance nor their urgency, and like his work on religion, remain pertinent to an examination of contemporary evangelicalism as a religious force which sees itself as responding to these problems.

Berger's understanding of contemporary culture – emphasising moral and symbolic anomie – resonates with many other analyses of late modernity which focus on the common quest for sources of certainty and meaning, sources which promise what Zigmunt Bauman has called 'safety in an insecure world'.[21] One solution is religion, and Berger's work on sacred canopies has steered numerous discussions of how religious groups and movements offer order and respite from the discontents of the world. Given its apparently oppositional stance towards contemporary culture, it is not surprising that evangelical Christianity has often been singled out in this debate as representing a form of religious identity especially suited to fending off the dangers of modernity. Berger's work has been highly influential in the ensuing debates, and his arguments have shaped a paradigm which has dominated much of the sociological work on evangelical religion in recent decades. While there have been those who have dissented from Berger's position, his work remains axiomatic, and even those who do not agree with his arguments about the possibilities of religious affirmation may nevertheless find themselves drawing from aspects of his description of modern culture and its dominant forces. For this reason, Berger's work has not been superseded as such, but has generated a debate, with three identifiable trajectories emerging from the discussion, each representing a

---

[21] Zigmunt Bauman, *Community: Seeking Safety in an Insecure World* (Cambridge: Polity, 2001).

different understanding of the relationship between evangelical Christianity and contemporary western culture. These may be summarised as resistance, cultural accommodation and engaged orthodoxy, and I will take each in turn, for together they furnish us with the proper sociological context for the analysis that is to follow.

Conservative Religion and the Project of Resistance

Many have followed Berger's lead in viewing conservative religious movements as both responses and effective antidotes to the fragmentation and existential instability of the modern condition. They offer certainty in a context of perpetual uncertainty and tend to self-consciously identify this uncertainty as a product of secular modernity. It is not surprising, therefore, that the relationship between evangelicalism and modernity is often characterised as antagonistic. Moreover, their often vociferous effort to maintain moral and symbolic – if not spatial – distance from modern norms, serves as an ongoing strategy by which conservative religious groups shape their subcultures and forge the boundaries of their identity.[22]

The claim that conservative Christian groups seek distance from modernity is not a novel one. Berger himself picks up on an existing trend represented by, among others, Richard Niebuhr[23] and Bryan Wilson,[24] which makes sense of certain sectarian developments as movements of resistance against the modern world. Berger has taken this further, however, in claiming that these groups *need* to sustain distance in order to survive in modern contexts. Conservative groups subscribe to what Berger calls a 'deviant body of knowledge'.[25] That is, their belief systems are antithetical to the dominant norms and values of modern culture. Frequently voiced in hyperbolic polemic from either side, communalism is set against individualism, the embrace of strict moral codes defined in contrast to moral libertarianism, and patriarchal structures of authority are asserted over western norms of gender and sexual equality. It is the ideological boundaries which separate these value claims that, according to Berger, need to be accentuated lest conservative enclaves capitulate to modern influence, fragment and decline. In effect, they are best suited to fend off the onslaught of modernity by existing as a kind of counter-community, fostering homogeneity, solidarity among members and a clearly defined set of boundaries that set them apart from the outside world.[26] While Berger was previously pessimistic about their chances, in later work he has acknowledged the recent success of evangelical and fundamentalist Islamic movements, explaining their significant

---

[22] Dale McConkey, 'Whither Hunter's Culture War? Shifts in Evangelical Morality, 1988-1998', *Sociology of Religion* 62:2 (2001), pp. 149-174.

[23] H. Richard Niebuhr, *Christ and Culture* (London: Faber, 1952).

[24] Bryan R. Wilson, 'An Analysis of Sect Development', in B.R. Wilson (ed.) *Patterns of Sectarianism. Organisation and Ideology in Social and Religious Movements* (London: Heinemann, 1967), pp. 22-45.

[25] Peter Berger, *A Rumour of Angels. Modern Society and the Rediscovery of the Supernatural* (London: Penguin, 1969), pp. 31-2.

[26] Berger, *Rumour of Angels*, p. 32.

resurgence in terms of his earlier position. That is, they thrive by keeping modernity out.[27]

This position has been most forcefully advanced in recent discussions of fundamentalism, which in the Christian tradition emerged as a deliberate and self-conscious counter response to the liberal modernist trends of the early twentieth century. Steve Bruce focuses upon the fragmentation of life, societalisation,[28] rationalisation and egalitarianism (particularly of gender roles), as aspects of modernity which challenge those who wish to preserve a purity of tradition, and provoke the ire of fundamentalist groups.[29] In focusing upon these 'evils' of modernity, these groups shape their own identities as projects of resistance. Similar arguments are advanced by Manuel Castells,[30] Gilles Kepel[31] and by Zigmunt Bauman, who sees fundamentalism as the quintessential religious form within post-modernity, on account of the fact that it is a direct and combative counter response to the experience of existential uncertainty characteristic of the postmodern condition.[32]

Many discussions of conservative or evangelical Christianity have similarly emphasised the ability of these groups to forge effective barriers against modernity, for the most part through what Bryan Wilson has called 'values of protest'.[33] In his influential assessment of growth and decline among US churches, *Why Conservative Churches Are Growing*, Dean Kelley advances an argument that owes much to Berger's work. Observing general patterns of growth among conservative churches and a comparative decline throughout more liberal denominations, Kelley explains this by arguing that it is religions which have strict, clear and exacting demands which fair best. According to Kelley, the main business of religion is to explain the ultimate meaning of life, and systems of meaning are more convincing than others not because of their content, but because of their strictness, seriousness, costliness and bindingness.[34] The churches Kelley identifies as growing emphasise evangelism, promote a distinctive lifestyle and morality, and disallow individualism in belief, hence affirming Berger's argument for the importance of homogeneity and strict

---

[27] Peter Berger, 'The Desecularization of the World. A Global Overview', in P. Berger (ed.) *The Desecularization of the World. Essays on the Resurgence of Religion in World Politics* (Washington, DC: Ethics and Public Policy Centre; Grand Rapids, MA: Eerdmans, 1999), pp. 1-18.

[28] The process whereby life is increasingly organised not locally, but societally, with that society most often the nation state. See Bruce, *God is Dead*, pp. 12-14 (drawing from the work of Bryan Wilson).

[29] Steve Bruce, *Fundamentalism* (Cambridge: Polity, 2000).

[30] Manuel Castells, *The Information Age: Economy, Society and Culture, Vol. III: End of Millennium* (Malden, MA, and Oxford: Blackwell, 1998).

[31] Gilles Kepel, *The Revenge of God: The Resurgence of Islam, Christianity and Judaism in the Modern World* (University Park, PA: Pennsylvania State University Press, 1994).

[32] Zigmunt Bauman, *Postmodernity and its Discontents* (Cambridge: Polity, 1997).

[33] Wilson, 'Analysis of Sect Development', p. 22.

[34] Dean Kelley, *Why Conservative Churches are Growing* (New York: Harper and Row, 1972), p. xxii.

community boundaries. In other words, it is by virtue of erecting firm boundaries of faith that religious groups are able to effectively fend off the inevitably secularising forces of modernity. In fact, Kelley is more optimistic than Berger in that he associates strength with a conviction that leads to mission, and therefore social engagement with the outside world, an engagement that is not indicative of accommodation, but which is robust enough to generate growth. In adopting this orientation, conservative groups may not only sustain the integrity of their value systems, but will actually thrive, as an effective counter force against modern western culture.

Despite his later reservations about Berger's work,[35] Stephen Warner makes similar claims within the context of his ethnographic study of an evangelical church in California. Warner argues that conservative religions engender solidarity among their members because they embrace clear teachings which are not open to a wide range of interpretations, and justifies this with reference to his observations of how beliefs are nurtured and sustained within a congregational context.[36] In other words, conservative religions re-affirm and preserve the boundaries that are dissolved or undermined by modern change.

The resistance element within Berger's writing clearly remains influential, and Bauman's work in particular illustrates how the thinking behind this has entered into debates about the nature of postmodernity and the place of religion within it. However, in focusing on resistance to modernity, scholars have been criticised for allowing their interpretative schema to mask important empirical trends on the ground, developments which suggest a greater blurring of boundaries between evangelical Christianity and the culture in which it finds itself. Those concerned with this problem have also built on Berger's work, but as the starting point for a different set of claims, less focused on resistance, more on cultural accommodation.

Cultural Accommodation

Of the recent studies that have found evangelical Christians accommodating to modernity, James Davison Hunter's work stands out as the most influential. Hunter has conducted several empirical studies of evangelical Christian attitudes in the USA and his work, though not uncritical, can be read as an empirical verification of Peter Berger's claim that an absence of boundaries against modernity leads to an erosion of traditional values. Put briefly, Hunter argues that the forces of modernisation have, over the course of the twentieth century, penetrated the boundaries of evangelical religion and have initiated a liberalisation of attitudes. Hunter finds a shift away from an understanding of the Bible and evangelical tradition as external, non-negotiable

---

[35] R. Stephen Warner, 'Work in Progress Toward a New Paradigm for the Sociological Study of Religion in the United States', *American Journal of Sociology* 98:5 (1993), pp. 1044-93.

[36] R. Stephen Warner, *New Wine in Old Wineskins. Evangelicals and Liberals in a Small-town Church* (Berkeley, CA and London: University of California Press, 1988).

authorities. Instead, evangelicals are becoming more tolerant of non-Christians, less rigid in their readings of the scriptures and more open to possibilities of change within the evangelical worldview.[37]

Hunter acknowledges that there are elements of resistance *and* accommodation within the evangelical movement, arguing for a persistent tension between these two powerful forces:

> There is extraordinary pressure to resist these transformations because they [evangelicals] have too much at stake to simply give in. Likewise there is extraordinary pressure to accommodate because, again, they have too much at stake to simply withdraw into an isolated cultural ghetto. Therefore, ideological tension between these two polar responses remains deeply rooted in the world of contemporary Evangelicalism. It is inherent in the faith as it is now lived and experienced.[38]

However, while this pervasive tension undermines any simplistic account of evangelical development, Hunter's evidence indicates a persistent underlying trend. This trend moves in the direction of cultural accommodation, as the values and attitudes of evangelicals increasingly reflect those of the general populace and the symbolic boundaries of conservative Protestantism are eroded.

These changes, according to Hunter, are a result of evangelicals becoming increasingly exposed to the forces of modernity, through higher education and upward mobility, and increased contact with people of other traditions, something endorsed by church sponsored ecumenism. He also points to the fact that the cultural system of evangelical Protestantism, and its associated definitions of moral propriety and familial responsibility, held significant influence over the imagination of the American public right up until the late nineteenth century. In the twentieth century, this changed. First, the fundamentalist controversies caused irreparable damage, and the emerging divisions undermined the prominence the evangelical theological vision had previously enjoyed within American culture. Later on, the cultural revolutions of the 1960s challenged received understandings of sexuality, the family, the beginnings of life and the status of public education. Henceforth, the symbolic boundaries established by conservative Protestantism ceased to exert such strong influence over American culture, which, therefore, no longer provided a context in which the teachings of the evangelical churches appeared so plausible in the eyes of the general population.[39]

Hunter's findings are anticipated in the work of Richard Quebedeaux[40] who, in the 1970s, charted changes in the US evangelical movement, speaking of a new breed of

---

[37] James Davison Hunter, *Evangelicalism: The Coming Generation* (Chicago, IL and London: University of Chicago Press, 1987).
[38] Hunter, *Evangelicalism*, p. 196.
[39] Hunter, *Evangelicalism*, pp. 191-2.
[40] Richard Quebedeaux, *The Worldly Evangelicals* (San Francisco, CA: Harper and Row, 1978).

worldly evangelicals. Writings on the British movement have also identified parallel changes, David Bebbington remarking on a diversification and broadening of perspective[41] and Ian Hall finding a new 'moderation' in evangelical convictions.[42] David Smith sees among late twentieth-century British evangelicals an openness to liberal ideas, to other traditions and a concerted effort to relate the gospel to contemporary culture.[43] An orientation characterised by resistance has apparently been superseded by one that seeks a more positive engagement with modernity.

Hunter is sympathetic to Dean Kelley's model for understanding why conservative churches grow, but is not so optimistic about what this means for American evangelicals. For, as Hunter argues, if Kelley is right, that it is religions with clear, strict and exacting demands which are most robust, and if Hunter's own evidence is reliable, and the symbolic boundaries of evangelicalism have suffered from significant erosion since the end of the Second World War, then the trajectory one would expect to see would be one of decline. Indeed, Hunter examines membership figures among conservative denominations and finds his suspicions confirmed; while absolute numbers between the 1940s and 1980s have increased, when general population changes are taken into account, this increase is not dramatic, and growth rates among conservatives have actually decreased. What little expansion there was in the 1970s Hunter puts down to denominational switching rather than revival.[44] For Hunter, the cultural accommodation of evangelical Christianity has engendered a significant secularisation of the movement.

However, not everyone agrees with Hunter's argument, and he has been challenged on a number of grounds. For example, James Penning and Corwin Smidt attempted a re-examination of Hunter's survey data compared with a repeat survey of a similar college population, producing a longitudinal analysis which tested the persistence of the trends identified by Hunter in his earlier work. While they found that some of these continued into the 1990s, others did not, suggesting that if a capitulation to modern culture has occurred, it has been selective rather than general. Moreover, they found that evangelicals with some college education were much more likely to express certainty in their beliefs than those with none, therefore challenging Hunter's thesis that education generates liberalisation.[45]

More profound challenges to Hunter's and Berger's work have questioned their underlying assumption that cultural accommodation inevitably engenders erosion in the evangelical worldview, leading ultimately to decline. For example, Mark Shibley

---

[41] David Bebbington, *Evangelicalism in Modern Britain. A History from the 1730s to the 1980s* (London: Unwin Hyman, 1989), p. 267.

[42] Ian Rodney Hall, 'The Current Evangelical Resurgence: An Analysis and Evaluation of the Growth of Contemporary Evangelicalism in Britain and the USA' (PhD thesis, University of Leeds, 1994), p. 301.

[43] David Smith, *Transforming the World? The Social Impact of British Evangelicalism* (Carlisle: Paternoster Press, 1998).

[44] Hunter, *Evangelicalism*, pp. 205-6.

[45] James M. Penning and Corwin E. Smidt, *Evangelicalism: The Next Generation* (Grand Rapids, MI: Baker Academic, 2002), pp. 165-7.

has proposed what has been called the 'southernization' thesis, i.e. the argument that evangelical growth in the northern states of the US must be explained with reference to the migration of many southerners during the Great Depression and after the Second World War. Many of these migrants established their own churches, and while at first they offered a spiritual home for other evangelicals from the south, eventually they realised that, in order to thrive, they would have to adapt their separatist style and broaden their appeal. The contemporary inheritors of this tradition, such as the Vineyard churches and Calvary Chapel, have grown rapidly because they have embraced the dominant surrounding culture, including an attitude of tolerance and openness to forms of expression, organisation and community drawn from a wider pool of influences than evangelical Christianity. Contra Kelley, these churches have not thrived by defending clear and strict boundaries, but by adapting to the cultural context in which they find themselves.[46]

In his study of evangelical 'new paradigm' churches, Donald Miller also finds a significant engagement with wider cultural forces, and rejects the Bergerian approach for the additional reason that it is overly cognitive.[47] Instead, Miller focuses on subjectivity, on the importance of an ongoing, intimate relationship with God, which caters to a need for 'life-changing, affective religious experience'.[48] According to Miller, new paradigm churches such as the charismatic Vineyard fellowship thrive in part because they successfully meet this need, a need which is widespread in a society characterised by technology, bureaucracy and a lack of connectedness between people. New paradigm Christians are theologically conservative, often biblical literalists, but are progressive in their ecclesiology – fostering loose organisational structures and encouraging lay leadership. Members affirm that knowledge is not just rational, but also has an important experiential element. They are firm believers in miracles, God's guidance of specific individuals and the charismatic element of worship. In other words, churches of the new paradigm embrace a kind of subjectivisation, a turn inwards, to the complexities of personal experience[49] and in so doing exemplify a creative – and in numerical terms, apparently successful – negotiation with modernity, exhibiting movements of resistance and accommodation concurrently.

In this way Miller's new paradigm reflects developments across the evangelical charismatic movement, whereby human experience becomes a source of religious knowledge or a source of empowerment. It also reflects a widespread focus upon the religious life of the self as both site for the sacred and centre of evangelical responsibility. Together, the various aspects of subjectivisation may be seen as a response to the weakening of institutional sacred canopies and capitulation to modern individualism, in accordance with Berger's vision of modernity, but which also mark

---

[46] Mark Shibley, *Resurgent Evangelicalism in the United States. Mapping Cultural Change since 1970* (Columbia, SC: University of South Carolina Press, 1996).

[47] Donald E. Miller, *Reinventing American Protestantism: Christianity in the New Millennium* (Berkeley, CA: University of California Press, 1997), p. 75.

[48] Miller, *Reinventing American Protestantism*, p. 25.

[49] Hunter, 'Subjectivisation and the New Evangelical Theodicy', p. 40.

an accommodation whose consequences for the evangelical worldview and for the robustness of evangelical community are far from predetermined. As Miller demonstrates, the relationship between evangelicalism and contemporary culture is complex and discriminate, and the dynamic that emerges between them may owe as much to the specifics of local religiosity as to the logic of modern social change.

Engaged Orthodoxy

While many treatments of evangelicalism may be conveniently organised into the above two trends – emphasising resistance and accommodation respectively – it would be untrue to suggest that Peter Berger's work only allows contemporary evangelicals two stark options from which to choose. Indeed, in their critique of Hunter's work, Penning and Smidt point out that in his later writings, Berger speaks more of gradations of resistance and accommodation that evangelical groups may exhibit in their ongoing struggles with modernity. Within the context of this nuanced account, Berger actually highlights four basic options which are available to religious traditions faced with the values of modern society. Cognitive bargaining involves the retention of some beliefs and the discarding of others, and hence some, albeit selective, capitulation to the doubt engendered by secular modernity. Cognitive surrender goes one step further; after acknowledging that modernity is correct in denying transcendence, groups may then attempt to salvage something of what Christian tradition may mean in light of this. Cognitive retrenchment, on the other hand, takes two forms, both based on a denial of the validity of secular modernity and a re-affirmation of the whole of a traditional belief system as it stands. In a defensive form, it requires a withdrawal from society, and the creation and maintenance of a closed religious subculture, preserved from the wider society by separation. In an offensive mode, cognitive retrenchment seeks to re-conquer secular society, actively opposing its values in an attempt to convert both the masses and the polity to its way of thinking.[50] This last option reflects many recent descriptions of contemporary fundamentalism, especially those movements associated with radical Islamism and the New Christian Right, both of which respond to what they see as a corrupt society by attempting to overhaul the social order, either by revolution or reform.

Penning and Smidt claim that Berger's account of the various options described above demonstrates the subtlety of his work, that he 'realizes that responses to modernity do not fall along a neat, single continuum that connects two polar ends'.[51] And yet there remains throughout Berger's work a certain unquestioned assumption that conservative religion and modernity represent two almost diametrically opposed forces in the contemporary world. While movements like evangelicalism may converse with modern culture and survive, maybe even thrive, this is only possible

---

[50] Penning and Smidt, *Evangelicalism*, pp. 36-7, drawing from Peter Berger, *A Far Glory. The Quest for Faith in an Age of Credulity* (New York: The Free Press, 1992), pp. 41-5.

[51] Penning and Smidt, *Evangelicalism*, p. 37.

if they affirm and sustain a mode of engagement characterised by a thorough denial of modernity's values and an uncompromising defence of their own boundaries. Mutual survival is possible, but only at the cost of struggle, and there are strong suggestions in Berger's later work that the religious groups which emerge triumphant do so because they successfully fend off those influences most centrally associated with western modernity.

An alternative perspective, which challenges this basic assumption in Berger's work, has emerged in the work of Christian Smith, who characterises contemporary evangelicalism as an 'engaged orthodoxy'. This is the term that Smith uses to describe the approach to Christian faith expressed by the so-called neo-evangelicals who reacted against fundamentalist separatism in the USA during the 1940s. These men, including Carl F. H. Henry, Charles Fuller and Billy Graham, came to have an enormous influence over the development of evangelicalism through the later twentieth century, and distinguished themselves from their fundamentalist forebears by remaining

> ...fully committed to maintaining and promoting confidently traditional, orthodox Protestant theology and belief, while at the same time becoming confidently and proactively engaged in the intellectual, cultural, social, and political life of the nation.[52]

They remained committed both to orthodoxy and to cultural engagement at the same time, and in this distinguished themselves from liberal Protestants on the one hand, and from the increasingly sectarian fundamentalists on the other. As the neo-evangelicals gained strength, not least through the National Association of Evangelicals and Fuller Theological Seminary, but also through various other seminaries, missions, periodicals and publishing houses, so they came increasingly to shape the contours of the US evangelical movement, so that the 'spirit of engaged orthodoxy' became 'incarnate in one giant, national transdenominational network of evangelical organizations'.[53]

Smith's aim in his book *American Evangelicalism: Embattled and Thriving* is to examine what has become of the engaged orthodoxy of the evangelical movement after the years of social, religious and political upheaval which followed the ascendancy of the neo-evangelical agenda. He builds on an ambitious national survey of US evangelicals and produces an account that challenges the work of both Berger and Hunter on empirical and theoretical grounds. On the former, Smith attempts to demonstrate the vitality of contemporary US evangelicalism, thus putting to rest notions of its encroaching demise or liberalisation in the face of a dominant modernity. He does this by appealing to a variety of factors, all of which, he argues, are important in gauging the strength of a religious movement, and compares their levels among evangelicals with those among fundamentalists, mainline Christians,

---

[52] Christian Smith, *American Evangelicalism. Embattled and Thriving* (Chicago, IL and London: The University of Chicago Press, 1998), p. 10.
[53] Smith, *American Evangelicalism*, p. 13.

liberals and Catholics. On all factors, including robustness of faith, group participation, commitment to mission and retention and recruitment of new members, Smith finds that evangelicals show levels of commitment and activism comparable to, but in many cases well above, those of Christians falling within the other categories.[54] He also finds no evidence to suggest younger evangelicals are less orthodox than the older generations, therefore challenging the liberalisation argument grounded in Hunter's work.[55]

So why does US evangelicalism show so many signs of relative vitality? Here Smith makes a significant break with sociologists who have preceded him, specifically in arguing that it is, in part, the engaged nature of evangelical orthodoxy that makes it such a strong religious movement. Directly opposing the Bergerian position, Smith finds no evidence that suggests evangelicals thrive because of their relative distance from the forces of modernity, citing the high numbers of evangelicals who have benefited from higher education, who have a relatively high income, and who are participants in the paid labour force.[56] He also finds that there is no difference between the major American Protestant traditions in their degree of encapsulation in Christian friendship and associate networks, thus undermining the argument that evangelicals fend off the social consequences of modernity by forging closed social groupings at the local level.[57] Furthermore, he finds reason to question Kelley's strictness theory, as the fundamentalist Christians in his sample show significantly lower levels of religious strength than the evangelicals.[58]

In seeking an alternative explanation, Smith turns to the insights associated with the influential work of Stephen Warner, who formulates a distinction between the old, Bergerian account of encroaching secularisation, with religious groups thriving in so far as they successfully ward off the forces of the modern world, and the 'new paradigm', which seeks to explain the vitality of religion in terms of its place within a pluralistic spiritual marketplace.[59] Some associate the old paradigm with Western Europe and view the new paradigm as quintessentially North American, not least in being grounded in a grassroots free market that owes much to the separation of church and state. Smith finds much of value in the new paradigm competitive

---

[54] Smith, *American Evangelicalism*, pp. 20-66.

[55] Smith, *American Evangelicalism*, p. 26. While impressive for the way it takes into account a variety of salient dimensions that moves beyond many previous studies, Smith's analysis of evangelical vitality arguably relies a little too uncritically on a particular notion of Christian orthodoxy. His understanding of what is 'theologically orthodox' is most reflective of a stereotypically evangelical model (e.g. on human nature as sinful, on p. 22), so that when commitment to orthodoxy is used as one gauge of religious strength in demonstrating evangelical vitality, there is a risk that one aspect of the argument may have some circularity to it (e.g. see pp. 22, 26, 52).

[56] Smith, *American Evangelicalism*, pp. 75-6.

[57] Smith, *American Evangelicalism*, p. 82.

[58] Smith, *American Evangelicalism*, p. 85.

[59] Warner, 'Work in Progress'.

marketing theory associated with scholars like Roger Finke and Rodney Stark,[60] especially as it acknowledges the significance of religious activism, entrepreneurialism and empowerment that has clearly been so crucial to the historical vicissitudes of the US evangelical movement. However, rather than focus on how evangelicals relate to their competitors, Smith attempts to develop the new paradigm by offering an account of the orientation of evangelical Christians to the '*sociocultural pluralistic world* they inhabit',[61] and refers to this in explaining their relative vitality.

For Smith, key to the evangelical response to modernity is the impulse to draw clear symbolic boundaries, thus distinguishing believers from relevant 'outgroups', including secular culture and other religious traditions. In this he is perfectly consistent with Berger's spectrum of responses, from cognitive retrenchment to cognitive surrender, but while Berger, and Hunter in his work, tends to paint religion as a relatively passive force, fending off the forces of modernity from a defensive position, Smith highlights the drives internal to evangelicalism which foster an orientation characterised by *active engagement* with the world. Moreover, this active engagement – which Smith finds both in the mission projects of evangelical organisations as well as in the lives of ordinary evangelicals he interviewed – appears to include a capacity for a strategic re-negotiation of collective identity, in light of the changing socio-cultural environments that evangelicals confront. In other words, evangelicals *do* accommodate their position in response to cultural change, but part of this process of accommodation involves a revitalisation of evangelical identity, not least by focusing on new sources of opposition. Smith contrasts the anti-communism and anti-Catholicism of previous generations with the opposition to moral relativism and homosexual rights in more recent decades. An adjustment is evident, but a strong sense of evangelical identity boundaries remains firmly intact.

Moreover, modernity's pluralism offers evangelicals a favourable environment in which to thrive because it 'creates a situation in which evangelicals can perpetually maintain but can never resolve their struggle with the non-evangelical world'.[62] It is this struggle, which previous commentators have often interpreted as an index of weakness, which Smith argues actually generates vitality, at the same time reinforcing evangelicalism's boundaries while continually creating opportunities for engagement with a wider culture in need of redemption. Smith summarises his position thus,

> American evangelicalism, we contend, is strong not because it is shielded against, but because it is – or at least perceives itself to be – embattled with forces that seem to oppose or threaten it. Indeed, evangelicalism, we suggest, *thrives* on

---

[60] E.g. see Roger Finke and Rodney Stark, *The Churching of America 1776-1990. Winners and Losers in Our Religious Economy* (New Brunswick, NJ: Rutgers University Press, 1992).

[61] Smith, *American Evangelicalism*, p. 88 (original emphasis).

[62] Smith, *American Evangelicalism*, p. 150.

distinction, engagement, tension, conflict, and threat. Without these, evangelicalism would lose its identity and purpose and grow languid and aimless.[63]

Congregational Studies and the Sociology of Community

In fully accounting for this dynamic, Smith argues that we need to move beyond structural and ecological factors alone, and develops a theoretical approach to evangelical collective identity that builds on subcultural identity theory, useful in part because it 'compels us to analyze the cultural content of religious discourse, subcultural narratives, and theological rationales for this-worldly action'.[64] In other words, it highlights the importance of taking into account factors emerging from the evangelical worldview itself, and not just external forces impinging on it, in explaining how evangelicals cope with contemporary culture. This is why Smith places such great emphasis on engaged orthodoxy, which he presents as an orientation with theological roots that has profound sociological consequences. It is in the social application of their orientation that evangelicals demonstrate their capacity to thrive in the modern world, a world that is both an object of mission and a site of perpetual struggle.

Smith's approach to evangelicalism and its relationship to the modern world has much to recommend it, especially within the context of this book, and for two main reasons. First, it offers a method of dealing with plausibility that moves beyond the constraints of a traditional Bergerian sociology of knowledge. Evangelical communities are not presented as inevitably beleaguered enclaves, capitulating to the modern world simply by virtue of engaging with it. Rather, the very nature of that engagement is taken seriously, and it is allowed to be flexible, creative and entrepreneurial, a potential source of vitality, rejuvenation and change. As well as thereby providing a theoretically more potent and ultimately more illuminating method, Smith's perspective is also more aligned with the realities of evangelicalism as reported by historians of its development.[65] Second, Smith's subcultural approach lends itself well to an analysis of interaction and community on a smaller scale, and may therefore be a useful tool in congregational studies.

Congregational studies has emerged as an identifiable field across various disciplines during the past twenty years or so, with numerous studies bringing a variety of methods to bear on the nature, status, social and theological significance

---

[63] Smith, *American Evangelicalism*, p. 89 (original emphasis).
[64] Smith, *American Evangelicalism*, p. 151.
[65] E.g. see Nathan Hatch, *The Democratisation of American Christianity* (New Haven, CT: Yale University Press, 1989); Mark A. Noll, David W. Bebbington and George A. Rawlyk (eds), *Evangelicalism. Comparative Studies of Popular Protestantism in North America, the British Isles, and Beyond, 1700-1990* (New York and Oxford: OUP, 1994).

of Christian congregations.[66] Some, such as those by James Hopewell[67] and Al Dowie,[68] have used ethnographic methods from the social sciences to access the identity or culture of specific congregations, and then used the emerging insights in probing theological questions. Such an approach can be particularly fruitful in arriving at an empirically informed understanding of tricky ecclesiastical issues, such as the authority of leaders, or in reflecting on the possibilities of pastoral ministry in light of the power dynamics of a particular congregation. Other congregational studies have been concerned with more traditionally sociological questions, and have examined specific congregations in order to arrive at a better understanding of how they function as communities and what studying them tells us about the broader religious landscape. This was the preoccupation of Nancy Ammerman's large scale study *Congregation and Community*, which studied the life of twenty-three North American congregations located in social contexts which were in some way engaged in a process of transition.[69] Her aim was to examine how congregations respond to social change, and in order to do this, she adopted what she calls an 'ecological' approach, viewing the local congregation as part of a complex network of human forces, shaped by and shaping salient processes of economic, ethnic, social and cultural change.

This study is not primarily concerned with the local networks in which St Michael-le-Belfrey is embedded because it is a church whose historically and geographically distant linkages are arguably more important, as will be discussed in the following chapters. However, I do follow Ammerman in treating this particular congregation as a living network of 'meaning and activity, constructed by the individual and collective agents who inhabit and sustain [it]'.[70] In this sense my study is a sociological one, concerned with issues of collective identity, changing belief and the nature of community. As suggested above, St Michael's may be viewed as relatively self-contained with respect to its immediate geographical context, but it exists within a network of connections, memories and reputations which renders the congregation especially exposed to the cultural flows of secular modernity, thus evoking the well-trodden theoretical paths of Berger *et al*, as detailed above. My key question in this book may be summarised as, how do members of the St Michael's congregation relate such forces to their individual and collective identities as evangelicals? This inevitably provokes the questions of resistance and accommodation described earlier, but I would argue that in addressing the reality of these processes within a congregational setting, one is dealing with them not as

---

[66] For a survey of the field, see Mathew Guest, Karin Tusting and Linda Woodhead (eds), *Congregational Studies in the UK. Christianity in a Post-Christian Context* (Aldershot: Ashgate, 2004).

[67] James F. Hopewell, *Congregation. Stories and Structures* (London: SCM Press, 1988).

[68] Al Dowie, *Interpreting Culture in a Scottish Congregation* (New York: Lang, 2002).

[69] Nancy T. Ammerman *et al*, *Congregation and Community* (New Brunswick, NJ: Rutgers University Press, 1997).

[70] Ammerman *et al*, *Congregation and Community*, p. 346.

purely individual matters, but as issues pertinent to an understanding of evangelical community. This is in perfect keeping with Berger's position, which implies that cultural accommodation leads to secularisation through the fragmentation of religious communities. More precisely, the shift to a set of positions which rely upon the diffuse standards of culture, rather than the defined standards of a closed religious group, compromises the possibilities of sustaining cohesive and durable collectives.[71] Accommodation to modernity is also associated with individualism, with the primacy of choice and autonomy, rather than on inter-dependence and long-term commitment to organised groups, least of all religious ones. Modernisation and community are, apparently, inversely related and world-accommodating evangelical groups are doomed to fragmentation and decline.

As we shall see in the following chapters, this argument is highly problematic, not least because it fails to take account of the precise way in which a religious community might engage with modernity, a question at the heart of Smith's subcultural perspective. Moreover, the symbolic construction of community within a congregation is far more complicated than this account allows, drawing from local history, norms of leadership and, as Smith acknowledges, discourses internal to that congregation. Smith focuses on engaged orthodoxy as a pan-tradition quintessential to evangelicalism; I will explore how this is manifest in the culture of St Michael's, but also draw attention to other internally constructed discourses, shared traditions which have exerted a significant influence over the life of the congregation and over how it has related to the culture in which it is situated. The prologue which preceded this chapter has already illustrated how the public life of this congregation is both diverse and complex; what I want to argue in the following chapters is how such complexity constitutes a response to internal discourses and external forces, and how these express shifting perceptions of evangelical authenticity. Moreover, following Smith, I want to highlight how modes of cultural engagement adopted by this congregation have shaped changing understandings of evangelical identity. In this sense, my overall intention is to explore how modernity both shapes evangelical tradition, while simultaneously offering new channels for its reinvention in the lives of believers.

One further note needs to be made about method, and that relates to my approach to the congregation as an object of study. My interest is in the culture of the congregation, and this I take not to be something that is separable from its everyday life, but as emerging from the processes of interaction that occur between its members. Here I draw from approaches to community popularised in anthropology, particularly the work of Anthony Cohen. Cohen conceives of community as a collection of people united in their attachment to a common body of symbols, symbols which may be iconic or material, but may just as well be social or elusive. But while these individuals are united in the symbols to which they are attached, they may nevertheless relate to those symbols in a variety of different ways; such is to acknowledge the very real commonality at the heart of community, but also the

---

[71] Bruce, *God is Dead*, p. 239.

diversity of human experience.[72] The same insight can be applied to congregations, and with the same implications, namely, that any suggestion that their identity is based on consensus is a misplaced reification of something far more complicated, and that symbols, as the main building blocks of community, are malleable, imprecise and multivocal. They may mean many things to many different people. This reflects my approach to evangelicalism in this book, as a common body of symbols, which is open to a range of interpretations and patterns of embodiment. In terms of a definition, I follow David Bebbington, who conceives of evangelicalism in terms of

> ...the four qualities that have been the special marks of Evangelical religion: *conversionism*, the belief that lives need to be changed; *activism*, the expression of the gospel in effort; *biblicism*, a particular regard for the Bible; and what may be called *crucicentrism*, a stress on the sacrifice of Christ on the cross. Together they form a quadrilateral of priorities that is the basis of Evangelicalism.[73]

Bebbington's fourfold scheme has the advantage of tallying with numerous other attempts at defining evangelicalism,[74] whilst also drawing attention to *activism*, thus distinguishing practical as well as substantive theological dimensions. Bebbington's scheme is also sufficiently loose to allow for changes in emphasis over time and in different contexts, highlighting key axes rather than a fixed set of credal statements. Conceiving evangelical priorities as axes – or, using Cohen's language, as a common body of symbols – from which social manifestations radiate – emerging, evolving and interacting with other elements and contexts – allows for a much richer appreciation of evangelical identity and evangelical culture. Treating the congregation as a key context for the negotiation of this culture allows us to address a malleable tradition within identifiable communal boundaries.

It is important not to adopt Cohen's insights ahistorically; these interpretations of evangelical tradition are not unconstrained and, as the following chapter will show, this openness among evangelicals has taken on particular patterns during the twentieth century, shaped by a recent history of cultural accommodation. But Cohen's theory of community does allow one to treat congregations in a very particular way, and in fact allows the tension and struggle that Christian Smith identifies at the heart of evangelical tradition to achieve a more prominent place in the story of the individual congregation.

---

[72] Anthony P. Cohen, *The Symbolic Construction of Community* (Chichester: Ellis Horwood, 1985).

[73] Bebbington, *Evangelicalism in Modern Britain*, pp. 2-3.

[74] For example, see definitions in George Marsden, 'Evangelicalism and Fundamental Christianity', in Mircea Eliade (ed.), *The Encyclopedia of Religion, Vol. 5* (New York: Macmillan, 1987), pp. 190-7; Richard Quebedeaux, *The Worldly Evangelicals* (San Francisco, CA: Harper and Row, 1978), p. 7; Mark Shibley, 'Contemporary Evangelicals: Born Again and World Affirming', *Annals of the American Academy of Political and Social Science* 558 (1998), pp. 67-87.

First, it is necessary to look closer at that tradition, specifically, at how it has evolved in the British context in recent decades, for this provides the context for the local developments explored in later chapters.

A Note on the Structure of the Book

Now that I have discussed the theoretical debates in which this study will be embedded, and stated the key research questions, the remainder of this book will be occupied with exploring these questions within the context of the empirical data gathered on the life of St Michael-le-Belfrey, which the author studied in 1999-2000 as part of an extended period of ethnographic fieldwork. An account of this process is provided in appendix one.

Chapter two examines the relationship between modernity and the evangelical movement in Britain, charting developments from the 1960s onwards. In this respect it explores ideas dealt with in more abstract terms in this chapter, but as they have been expressed in the lives of British evangelicals during the latter half of the twentieth century. Following this examination of the national picture, chapter three offers an introduction to the case study, exploring trends in growth and decline, and key demographic features. The aim here is to explore the ways in which St Michael-le-Belfrey is caught up in processes of change characteristic of contemporary British culture and of the broader evangelical movement. Chapters four and five take two emerging issues and address them in detail, exploring how internal diversity and subjective expressions of identity are socially manifest among the St Michael's congregation. Questionnaire data is used alongside interview transcripts and ethnographic description to explore the ways in which the beliefs of individuals are negotiated in light of shared public discourses, and how this impacts on a sense of unity and collective identity. Chapter five also addresses charismatic phenomena such as glossolalia and words of knowledge, seeking to examine how the personal experiences of congregants are expressed through public rituals.

Chapter six is devoted to the *Visions* group. I present an analysis of the ways in which *Visions* continues to reconfigure and rebuild the core aspects of its evangelical heritage, focusing on how authority is defused, on the mobilisation of the aesthetic and on the reconfiguration of shared values. This discussion is set within the context of wider debates about the nature of post-evangelicalism and the so-called 'emerging church'. Chapter seven examines the use of the small group meeting across the life of the St Michael's congregation, with a special focus upon how shared cultures are defined and sustained in communal meetings. After examining the ways in which members of various groups demonstrate practical commitment and an ongoing contribution to networks of support, I relate the emerging experiences of community to the patterns of shared belief and value addressed earlier. The concluding chapter relates the local findings presented to broader debates about the future of evangelical Christianity.

Throughout the book, lengthy quotations from literature, interview transcripts, from my field journals or field notes, are set apart from the text in normal type. All of the church members I refer to or quote in the following pages have been given pseudonyms, for obvious ethical reasons, aside from recent incumbents of St Michael-le-Belfrey, whose names are given as the name of the church is given also (see appendix one for an account of the reasons for this). I have done my utmost to remove details which might make individuals easily identifiable, without sacrificing important contextual information. Quotations from the Bible all refer to the New International Version (NIV) as this version is favoured by St Michael's parishioners and is the one set in the pews each Sunday.

CHAPTER 2

Growth and Change:
The Evangelical Movement since the 1960s

Relative Growth

Evangelical Christianity is far less popular in the UK than it is in many other nations, partly in reflection of the heavily secularised nature of the country generally. Drawing from the 1997 Angus Reid Group's World Survey, Mark Noll claims that 35% of the US population may be counted as 'evangelical'. The figure is 38% for the Philippines, 33% for South Africa, 25% for Brazil, 15% for Canada and just 7% for the UK.[1] However, there are signs that the British tradition has achieved some growth during the post-war period, relative to other Christian parties within the UK context. Moreover, this growth has meant a greater expansion into a broader cultural remit, in turn exposing evangelical churches to new ideas and previously alien traditions. Consequently, an analysis of their encounter with modernity must begin with a consideration of evangelical growth.

Growth has occurred in recent years against a dominant cultural movement towards religious decline. While some sociologists trace the roots of secularisation to the Reformation and beyond,[2] my concern here is with the 1960s onwards. It was during this time that a process of sudden and steep decline began among the UK churches. While the post-war period had been characterised by a general stability in levels of church involvement,[3] the 1960s initiated significant and inexorable falls in confirmations, ordinations, membership and attendance. By 1969, the national ratio of confirmations had dropped by 32% over a six year period, and ordinations had dropped by 25% in five years.[4] Anglican membership fell by 35% in between 1960 and 1970, and the number of Easter communicants dropped by 43% during the same period.[5] This was a pattern generally echoed across the denominations and steady decline has persisted during subsequent decades. In 1975 18.5% of the UK adult

---

[1] Mark A. Noll, *American Evangelical Christianity. An Introduction* (Oxford and Malden, MA: Blackwell, 2001), pp. 39-41.

[2] E.g., see Peter Berger, *The Sacred Canopy. Elements of a Sociological Theory of Religion* (Garden City, NY: Doubleday, 1967), pp. 126-7.

[3] Adrian Hastings, *A History of English Christianity, 1920-1985* (London: Fount Paperbacks, 1987), p. 551.

[4] Hastings, *History*, p. 551.

[5] Paul Chambers, 'Factors in Church Growth and Decline (with Reference to the Secularisation Thesis)' (PhD thesis, University of Wales, 1999), p. 4.

population were members of a church. By 1980 this had fallen to 16.9% and by 1990 to 14.7%.[6] Total Sunday service attendance in England fell by 13% during the 1980s and by 22% during the 1990s.[7]

Scholars differ as to whether this signals a decline or transformation of religion, a drop in interest or a change of form. However, a change of fortunes for the worse is undeniable as far as the institutional life of the Christian churches is concerned. Indeed, the evidence is so stark that Peter Brierley, analyst of attendance statistics, has recently described the UK churches as 'bleeding to death'.[8]

Existing across the Protestant denominations, the evangelical movement has been embroiled in movements of institutional decline. However, the period distinguished by an acceleration in general church decline coincided with a movement into a period of strength and transition for the evangelicals. By the 1950s, evangelicalism was growing in popularity, flourishing in its subculture and achieving a more prominent public presence. David Bebbington claims there was even talk of a 'new evangelical revival'.[9] This transformation in fortunes can be traced to a number of key shifts, and three of the most important are addressed here, beginning with the emergence of the evangelical crusade.

During the 1950s, mass evangelical rallies took place for the first time in modern England, often drawing impressive numbers and always achieving media exposure. In 1954, Billy Graham's 'Greater London Crusade' took place in Harringay and drew over 1,300,000 people over a three month period. After ten months, 64% of the previous non-churchgoers who had put themselves forward as 'enquirers' – i.e. those expressing an interest in the Christian faith – were still attending their new churches.[10] Graham's impact was apparently more than a flash in the pan. In 1966 he returned, this time to Earl's Court, preaching to over 40,000 people either live or *via* closed-circuit TV. Sponsored by the Evangelical Alliance, the 'Mission England' crusade of 1984 was said to have reached well over 1 million people, with over 100,000 'enquirers' seeking further contact with churches after the event.[11]

Historian Callum Brown suggests that it is easy to overstate the importance of the evangelical crusades as, for many, they were merely public spectacles and few

---

[6] Peter Brierley and Heather Wraight (eds), *UK Christian Handbook, 1996/7 Edition* (Bromley: Christian Research, 1995), p. 240.

[7] Peter Brierley, *The Tide is Running Out. What the English Church Attendance Survey Reveals* (London: Christian Research, 2000), p. 32.

[8] Brierley, *Tide*, p. 27.

[9] David Bebbington, 'Evangelicalism in its Settings: The British and American Movements since 1940', in M.A. Noll, D.W. Bebbington and G.A. Rawlyk (eds), *Evangelicalism. Comparative Studies of Popular Protestantism in North America, the British Isles, and Beyond*, 1700-1990 (New York and Oxford: OUP, 1994), p. 367.

[10] David Bebbington, *Evangelicalism in Modern Britain. A History from the 1730s to the 1980s* (London: Unwin Hyman, 1989), p. 259.

[11] Ian Rodney Hall, 'The Current Evangelical Resurgence: An Analysis and Evaluation of the Growth of Contemporary Evangelicalism in Britain and the USA' (PhD thesis, University of Leeds, 1994), pp. 246-7.

attendees were actually converted.[12] Similarly, while the 1971 'Nationwide Festival of Light' raised the issue of moral permissiveness in society, it did not succeed in mobilising change in a way comparable to parallel innovations across the Atlantic.[13] However, the emergence of mass rallies in the 1950s signalled a new age in which evangelicals would achieve a greater presence in the broadcasting and print media. The mass meeting was later fostered as a medium for the Christian festival, with the 1970s giving birth to 'Spring Harvest' and 'Greenbelt' as centres of renewal and celebration. The former saw its annual attendance levels increase thirty times over during the 1980s, to 60,000 in 1988, and has achieved attendances of up to 80,000 since the 1990s.[14] If new conversions have been negligible – and the available statistics are inconclusive – the crusades set evangelicalism on a broad stage, achieving media coverage and public visibility. And while the gospel was seen to be at work, both clergy and lay-people were given fresh opportunities to offer practical contributions to mission.

If the evangelical crusades marked a shift in the kinds of media evangelicals could use to promote their message, the British universities generated new networks through which this message was spread and new members recruited. The evangelical Inter-Varsity Fellowship (IVF) has dominated Christian culture in the universities since the post-war period, overshadowing the more liberal Student Christian Movement (SCM) from the 1950s onwards.[15] The universities also helped to forge links with the US evangelical movement, partly through American graduate students wishing to study under prestigious evangelical scholars like F.F. Bruce.[16] Growth and expansion has continued in subsequent years: in 1948, the IVF had 2,400 members; by 1990, more than 15,000 British students were taking part in regular IVF (by then UCCF) activities.[17]

The IVF was renamed the University and Colleges Christian Fellowship (UCCF) in 1975 and continues to maintain a strong influence within the individual university Christian Unions. At the turn of the millennium, every university Christian Union

---

[12] Callum Brown, *The Death of Christian Britain* (London and New York: Routledge, 2001), p. 173.

[13] Bebbington, 'Evangelicalism in its Settings', p. 377. On the Nationwide Festival of Light, see John Capon, *...And There Was Light. Story of the Nationwide Festival of Light* (London: Lutterworth Press, 1972).

[14] David Smith, *Transforming the World. The Social Impact of British Evangelicalism* (Carlisle: Paternoster Press, 1998), p. 104; Rob Warner, 'Autonomous Conformism: The Paradox of Entrepreneurial Protestantism (Spring Harvest: a case study)', in L. Woodhead and A. Day (eds) *Religion and the Individual* (Aldershot: Ashgate, forthcoming).

[15] Bebbington, *Evangelicalism in Modern Britain*, pp. 259-60; Steve Bruce, *Firm in the Faith* (Aldershot: Gower, 1984), pp. 75-6. On the reasons for the relative decline of the SCM from the Second World War onwards, see Douglas Johnson, *Contending for the Faith. A History of the Evangelical Movement in the Universities and Colleges* (Leicester: Inter-Varsity Press, 1979), pp. 215-7.

[16] Noll, *American Evangelicalism*, pp. 19-20.

[17] Christopher Sinclair, 'Evangelical Belief in Contemporary England', *Archives de Sciences Sociales des Religions* 82 (1993), p. 174.

in the UK except two was affiliated to UCCF,[18] thereby committing them to its conservative doctrinal statement, which stresses the Bible as inspired and infallible and Christ's final condemnation of the unrepentant.[19] Inter-Varsity Press continues to publish in the evangelical field, and remains closely linked to UCCF, which also publishes a journal, *Themelios*, aimed at providing academic guidance for Christian students of theology and religious studies. Since the early twentieth century, IVF/UCCF has served as an important channel through which young and talented leaders have embraced the Christian faith and developed their pastoral and leadership skills before passing into the evangelical churches.

Expansion of evangelicalism has also occurred through clerical networks. As early as 1957, Maurice Wood, chairman of the Islington Clerical Conference, pointed out that among ordination candidates in the Church of England, evangelicals were more highly represented than any other church party.[20] In 1969, 31.2% of ordinands considered themselves to be 'evangelical' in churchmanship. By 1977, this had risen to 44.7% and, by 1986, to 51.6%.[21] This corresponds to a fall in the proportion of ordinands attending theological colleges traditionally seen as catholic or tractarian, from 29.3% in 1969 to 17.2% in 1986.[22] While the ordination of women in the Church of England post-1992 may have revitalised some catholic parties (both for and against), a study of students in theological colleges in 1997 still found that those identifying with an evangelical label (48%) exceeded those falling within all of the other categories available.[23]

From the 1960s, the popular National Evangelical Anglican Congress (NEAC) provided a forum for debate and consolidated a sense of common identity among these clergy, as did the Eclectics network, established by John Stott. It was Stott who claimed that all of the speakers at the 1967 NEAC conference at Keele had been conservatives, implying the welcome decline of liberalism within the churches.[24] The Second NEAC meeting in 1977 further mobilised evangelical leaders, and was attended by 2,000 delegates, representing every evangelical parish in Britain.

There has also been a notable expansion of evangelicals among senior Anglican clergy. In 1987, while more than half of all clergy claimed an evangelical affiliation, less than 16% of diocesan bishops did so. By 1993, this had risen to 30%.[25] In 1975, both archbishops – Coggan at Canterbury and Blanch at York – claimed

---

[18] Information gathered directly from UCCF by the author.

[19] See http://www.uccf.org.uk/resources/general/doctrinalbasis/doctrinalbasis.php (accessed 17 November 2006)

[20] Bebbington, *Evangelicalism in Modern Britain*, p. 250.

[21] Hall, 'The Current Evangelical Resurgence', p. 225.

[22] M. Saward, *The Anglican Church Today. Evangelicals on the Move* (Oxford: Mowbrays, 1987), p. 34.

[23] Sophie Gilliat-Ray, 'The Fate of the Anglican Clergy and the Class of '97: Some Implications of the Changing Sociological Profile of Ordinands', *Journal of Contemporary Religion* 16:2 (2001), p. 213.

[24] Bebbington, *Evangelicalism in Modern Britain*, p. 250.

[25] Hall, 'The Current Evangelical Resurgence', p. 256.

allegiance to the evangelical camp. In 1991 the Church of England would even be admitting a charismatic evangelical into the archiepiscopacy, George Carey. These changes signal a more amenable relationship with church officialdom and a new found public confidence. Moreover, an expansion throughout these networks has enhanced the power and influence of the evangelical cause more generally.

Finally, it is worth noting the increased exposure of evangelicalism within the popular media in recent years. This has been driven by both positive and negative forces. For example, as institutional religion and the ideological certainties it is often taken to represent have become less prominent, so they have become more exotic in the eyes of a secularised population. Evangelicals achieve media exposure precisely because they are seen as socially marginal, especially when they are perceived as adopting unpopular positions on moral issues. More positively, it is possible to attribute a discernible growth in the public exposure of evangelical churches from the 1980s onwards to Clive Calver's leadership of the Evangelical Alliance (1983-97). One could point to his recruitment of young, energetic leaders who were theologically conservative but socially aware, and who nurtured ambitious plans for evangelism within British society. These leaders have demonstrated an ability to adapt to a mass media age, making use of television, radio and the internet to promote their beliefs and projects.

This leads us to another aspect of evangelical growth worthy of note: the distinctively middle class character of the networks through which it has expanded. Most crucial has been the effective evangelical presence in the universities and the upper-middle class backgrounds of prominent evangelical preachers. Influential evangelists like David Watson and John Stott have personified the image of the Oxbridge educated English officer – morally upright, intellectually reflective and embodying a quintessentially British social conservatism. Their social identities have inevitably shaped their presentation of the gospel from the pulpit, attracting those from similar social circles, and the predominance of the middle classes among white English evangelicals is well documented.[26] More recent high fliers, like Nicky Gumbel – another Oxbridge graduate and former barrister – also embody middle class qualities, while advancing a more genteel, tactile approach. As we shall see, the largely middle class constituency of English evangelicalism is a significant factor in shaping the construction of evangelical culture within local congregations, informing both public discourse and the shared values of members.

Congregational Growth

Alongside a heightened degree of public exposure, expansion through university networks and through church hierarchies, there have been signs of comparative

---

[26] E.g., see Sinclair, 'Evangelical Belief in Contemporary England', p. 171; David Martin, *Pentecostalism. The World their Parish* (Oxford: Blackwell, 2002), p. 46. Note also Peter Brierley's data, which reveals that two of the only three regions that experienced evangelical growth in between 1989 and 1998 were Greater London and the South East (the other being the West Midlands). See Brierley, *Tide*, p. 65.

growth on the ground. On the level of the individual parish church, it has been the evangelicals who have enjoyed most success, especially after charismatic renewal in the 1960s. Stories circulated of churches which had grown from a handful of the faithful to a congregation of hundreds. Adrian Hastings offers the examples of Holy Trinity, Brompton, St Aldates, Oxford, and St Michael-le-Belfrey in York, charismatic evangelical churches in which congregations were so considerable 'that the clergy could hardly cope'.[27]

While stories of notable renewal persisted, precise statistics did not become available until the 1980s.[28] For a longitudinal analysis, and for figures of evangelical activity across the denominations, we must turn to Peter Brierley's English Church Attendance Survey, which has now been administered four times, in 1979, 1989, 1998 and 2005. While Brierley's figures are confined to England, they will be discussed here as they provide an appropriate context for our case study.[29] From 1989 onwards, Brierley has asked clergy respondents about the 'churchmanship' of their congregations, working with seven categories: evangelical, catholic, liberal, broad, low church, Anglo-Catholic, and 'other' (allowing for an open response). It is assumed that the majority of each congregation will agree with the description offered by their minister, an assumption defended with reference to the Congregation Attitudes and Beliefs Survey, which apparently suggests that 'about two-thirds of a congregation usually support the churchmanship of the minister of the church'.[30]

In his 1989 survey, Brierley asked respondents to reflect on the growth or decline of their church during the latter half of the 1980s. Based on their estimations of change, he arrives at a total picture that spans the last twenty years or so. Given only four data points, we may observe general trends, though not precise fluctuations over time. Working with Brierley's figures for growth among different branches of 'churchmanship', we arrive at the following picture (see Fig. 1).

'Catholics', a group that includes Roman Catholics but also those churches affirming a 'catholic' churchmanship,[31] exceeded the evangelicals during the 1980s, but experienced a massive decline of 48% during the 1990s, and another 13% since

---

[27] Hastings, *History*, p. 615.

[28] E.g., see Leslie J. Francis and David W. Lankshear, 'The Comparative Strength of Evangelical and Catholic Anglican Churches in England', *Journal of Empirical Theology* 9:1 (1996), pp. 5-22.

[29] Patterns of evangelical growth in other regions of the UK have been dealt with elsewhere. See Peter Brierley, *Turning the Tide. The Challenge Ahead; Report of the 2002 Scottish Church Census* (London: Christian Research, 2003); and Paul Chambers, *Religion, Secularization and Social Change in Wales. Congregational Studies in a Post-Christian Society* (Cardiff: University of Wales Press, 2005).

[30] Brierley, *Tide*, p. 51. The precise results of the Congregation Attitudes and Beliefs Survey have never been published.

[31] A label most associated with those members of the Church of England who favour a high liturgy and support the centrality of bishops to Anglican identity, as opposed to evangelicals, who have often stressed word over ceremony. The Anglo-Catholic designation is reserved for those even closer to the Roman Catholic church in their understanding of ecclesiology, priesthood and liturgy.

1998. During the 1990s, evangelicals overtook 'catholics' as the most numerous category of churchmanship in England, and now constitute 40% of all churchgoers. However, although evangelicals have sustained significant strength where other groups have struggled, they have not achieved significant growth either. Indeed, their numbers, after a 3% rise during the late 80s, have now fallen back to what they were in 1985, i.e., just under 1.3 million.

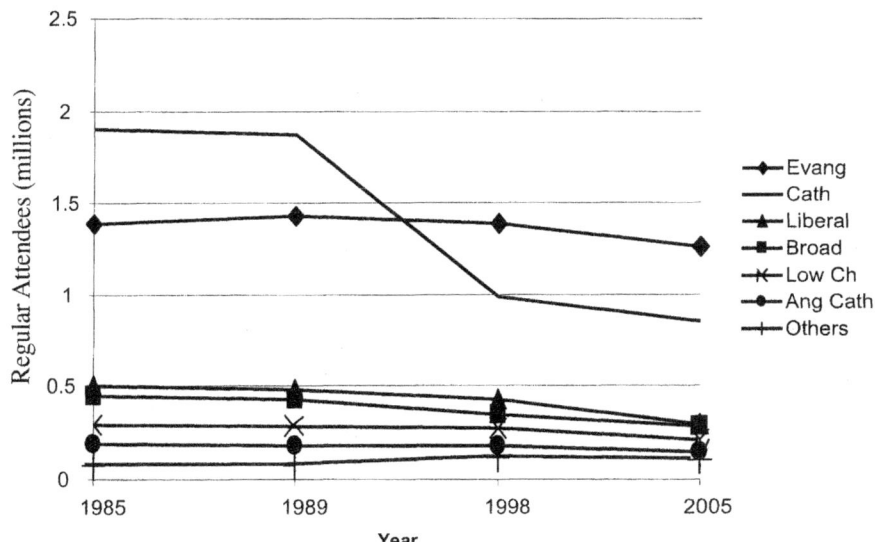

Figure 1: Levels of Regular Church Attendance among English churchgoers by churchmanship, 1985-2005[32]

The average size of an English congregation in 2005 was eighty-four people. If one excludes Roman Catholics, because of the distorting effect of their large inner city churches, one arrives at a figure for all Protestant churches of sixty-seven (down 32% since 1979). The average for evangelicals was eighty-five – above the overall average and well above the average for Protestant churches. As with all churchmanship categories, this number has declined in recent years – from 105 in 1989, and ninety-six in 1998. However, this is an overall decline of 19%, less than the decline in the national average (32%), in the Protestant average (23%), and less than the decline for other churchmanship categories (47% for Anglo-Catholics and

---

[32] Data adapted from Peter Brierley, *Christian England: What the 1989 English Church Census Reveals* (London: MARC Europe, 1991), p. 161; *Tide*, p. 51; *Religious Trends 6* (London: Christian Research, 2006), p. 5.15. Straight lines are used to connect data points for convenience; they do not represent a linear correlation, as, of course, attendances may have fluctuated between the years when the surveys were conducted. This also applies to Figure 2.

Catholics, 22% for broad and liberal churches).[33] When broken down into categories relative to degrees of growth between 1998 and 2005, Brierley also finds that of all of the churches that have grown during this period, almost half – 46% – are evangelical churches.[34]

In summary, Brierley's figures suggest that evangelical churches are the most numerous in England, have the largest congregations, and are most likely to be growing. Although they have not increased their overall net membership in recent years, they demonstrate a greater resilience to decline than non-evangelical churches. Indeed, non-evangelicals declined 'ten times as much' as evangelicals during the 1990s, and twice as much as evangelicals between 1998 and 2005.[35] In conclusion, although the evangelicals cannot be said to be bucking the trend of general church decline in England, they demonstrate signs of vitality that outshine their non-evangelical peers in every discernible respect.

However, a demonstrable robustness has been accompanied by significant changes internal to the evangelical movement. In terms of denomination, the largest proportion of English evangelicals remains in the Anglican Church (23%, almost unchanged from 1998 figures). More notable is the growth among the Pentecostals, which has increased their relative size within English evangelicalism from 14.3% of the total in 1998, to 22% in 2005. Baptists now make up 18% of the movement (almost unchanged from 1998) and the Methodists 4% (down from 9.6% in 1998). In 1998, 15.5% of English evangelicals were in the 'New Churches' (formerly known as 'house churches'), a 30% rise from 1989, due to an absorption of many former independent evangelical churches into the 'New Church' networks. By 2005, this proportion had declined slightly to 12%, although a strong presence among the independent churches, whose boundaries with the 'new churches' are often somewhat blurred, remains (also at 12% of the total of English evangelicals).[36]

Available figures for attendance levels within the evangelical camp also suggest that different styles of evangelicalism have faired differently. Brierley differentiates between 'mainstream', 'broad' and 'charismatic' evangelical churches, and figures are available again for 1985-2005 (Fig. 2).

The high proportion of charismatics reflects how this movement was well entrenched by the mid-1980s, especially among Free Church evangelicals.[37] However, significant decline during the following decades – by 16% during the 1990s and another 5% since 1998 – indicates a change of fortune. Conversely, mainstream evangelicals grew by 2% during the late 1980s, and then by a massive 68% during the 1990s, although they experienced a 10% decline between 1998 and

---

[33] Figures calculated on the basis of Brierley's figures in *Pulling Out of the Nosedive. A Contemporary Picture of Churchgoing* (London: Christian Research, 2006), pp. 43, 64.

[34] Brierley, *Pulling Out of the Nosedive*, p. 195.

[35] Brierley, *Tide*, p. 65; *Pulling Out of the Nosedive*, p. 98.

[36] Figures drawn from Brierley, *Pulling Out of the Nose Dive*, p. 62, and *Tide*, pp. 43, 151.

[37] Brierley, *Christian England*, pp. 164-5.

2005. The 'broad' evangelical category has consistently faired the worst, with a 47% decline during the 1990s and a further 20% since then. These figures suggest several processes of change within the evangelical movement, some of which will be explored below. Not least, we note the apparent shift away from the charismatic to a more centrist position during the 1990s. Moreover, the consistent decline of the 'broad' category suggests that those evangelicals who abandoned the charismatic camp were uncomfortable aligning themselves with a label that has liberal, inclusivist connotations. This reflects a trend that had already taken hold among Anglican evangelicals during the late 1980s, when charismatics declined by 6% and the mainstream category expanded by 15%.[38] The figures suggest the charismatic camp is now showing some signs of recovery, and is declining less rapidly than the mainstream churches, mainly due to the notable success of the black Pentecostal churches, especially in Greater London. However, the situation in the predominantly white, middle class evangelical churches is quite different, and suggests a reconfiguration of charismatic identity that, one could argue, has its roots in the changes of the 1990s.

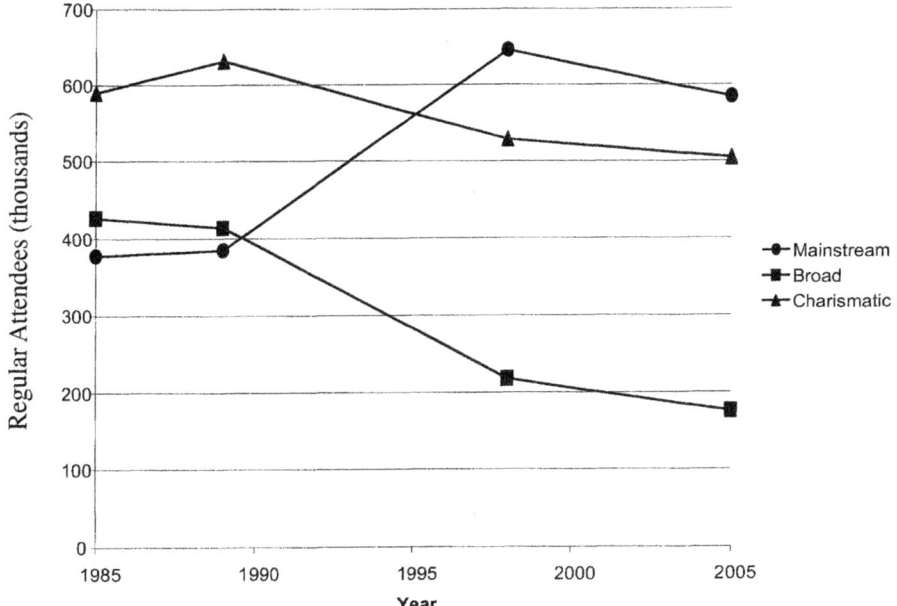

Figure 2: Changes in Attendance Levels among Different Branches of Evangelicalism in England, 1985-2005[39]

---

[38] Brierley, *Christian England*, pp. 164-5.
[39] Data adapted from Brierley, *Christian England*, p. 161; *Tide*, p. 54; *Pulling Out of the Nosedive*, p. 56.

Evangelicalism is clearly not a static phenomenon and has experienced significant transformations in recent years. To explore this issue further, we must turn to historical sources.

The Changing State of English Evangelicalism

The relative vitality of evangelical Christianity in recent times suggests that it has to some extent *successfully* negotiated with the forces of modernity. But negotiation implies some degree of capitulation and it is clear that, as it has enjoyed congregational growth and a greater public presence, UK evangelicalism has become exposed to a broader range of cultural forces. It is important to ask, therefore, how recent changes within the evangelical camp reflect an accommodation to contemporary cultural values. The period of the 1960s presents itself as an obvious focus of cultural and ecclesiastical change.

To argue for change at the axis of the 1960s, it is first necessary to provide some indication of what evangelicalism was like prior to this period. For this we may turn to David Bebbington, who offers an enlightening image of evangelicalism in 1940s Britain. Evangelicals were 'unworldly, diligent in attendance at weekly prayer meetings, meticulous about quiet times, suspicious of the arts, missionary minded, hostile to new liturgical ideas'.[40] One could add to this a defensive Protestantism, the anti-institutionalism of which fostered a suspicion of ritual adornment and of ecclesiastical hierarchy. Evangelicals were austere and traditionalist, both severe in their theology and morals, and in their manner. They were 'firm in their faith' and impervious to change. The 1960s was to change all of this. By the end of the decade, all of these characteristics had either been abandoned or reconfigured by British evangelicals in a way that left the movement enduringly and irretrievably refashioned.

The period of the 1960s has been repeatedly conceived as one of cataclysmic change, and while recent work has documented how such change was rooted in earlier developments, it was undoubtedly a period in which numerous cultural shifts reached maturity and began to leave a dramatic mark on British society.[41] The counter-culture carried with it a libertarian spirit, characterised by an anti-establishment ethic and an antipathy towards previously dominant traditions. But the revolts of the sixties were existential as well as political, driven by the values of freedom of movement and identity, individual self-expression and a romantic turn towards emotional and subjective needs. The cultural revolution was in part as much against technocracy and rationality as it was against political dominance and militarism. Revivals in leftist politics occurred alongside new quests to recover the natural and primitive

---

[40] J. King, cited by Bebbington, *Evangelicalism in Modern Britain*, p. 263.

[41] I am here indebted to Hugh McLeod's astute and sensitive analysis of the culture of the 1960s, which, he argues, 'provided the context in which much older ideas could come fully into their own. Gradual processes of change over a much longer period of time provided the long-term preconditions for the more rapid changes in that decade.' See *The Religious Crisis of the 1960s* (Oxford: OUP, 2007), p. 20.

aspects of human existence. Most radically, personal fulfilment became associated with having the freedom to 'do one's own thing'.[42] Such values were disseminated and given fresh impetus by the expansion of higher education in England, with fourteen new universities established in the 1960s and more to follow, by the freedom afforded by full employment and economic growth, the consequent expansion of consumer culture, and the growth of religious and moral pluralism, which gave British citizens more life-options from which to choose.

At the same time great unrest ensued in some quarters. New-found prosperity and a shortage of labour after the Second World War had attracted immigrants, most from the former colonies, with 260,000 Caribbeans entering England between 1955 and 1962.[43] This caused tension in some areas, occasionally spiralling into violence, and prompting Enoch Powell's 'Rivers of Blood' speech in 1968. Some expressed concern at a growing moral laxness, especially among young people, as abortion and homosexuality were both legalised in 1967 and divorce legislation was reformed by the Wilson government in 1969, allowing for legitimate marital breakdown on the basis of a broader range of factors than merely adultery.[44] The latter was particularly significant, as it marked an official endorsement of new understandings of marriage and the family, no longer conceived as necessarily fixed and permanent, but subject to the changing fortunes of human relationships. Some radicals wished to push the changes further and railed against the system, as with the student rebellions of 1968 or the emerging feminist movement. In spite of a significant conservative backlash, a general liberalisation of values took place across British culture, which had individualism and the respect for individual freedoms at its centre. But alongside this, political upheaval on both sides of the Atlantic – epitomised in the Cold War and Vietnam – meant that idealism often gave way to disillusionment and a cynicism towards received traditions.

All of these changes generated specific challenges for the churches. An anti-establishment ethic, liberal morals and a turn to individualism all counted against the authority and cultural norms of Christian tradition, especially as interpreted by evangelicals. Austerity, deference to one's elders and leaders, as well as moral restraint, were anathema and thus points of alienation. A turn to subjectivity reflected a yearning for new experiences, fostering an experimentalism which scoffed at convention and consistency – the mainstay of the religious establishment. And while these cultural shifts are perhaps most applicable to the youth of the time – now known as the baby boomer generation – they capture changes which had implications across the population. Moreover, just as these changes signalled a turn away from traditional religious forms and conventions of religious observance, they also generated what Robert Ellwood has called a new 'religious imagination', that is, a fresh way of conceiving religion in the light of new cultural conditions. According

---

[42] Robert S. Ellwood, *The Sixties Spiritual Awakening. American Religion Moving from Modern to Postmodern* (New Brunswick, NJ: Rutgers University Press, 1994), p. 335.

[43] Hastings, *History*, p. 510.

[44] Brown, *Death of Christian Britain*, p. 176.

to Ellwood, this imagination reconceived religion in terms of egalitarian community, 'concerned with subjectivity' and 'driven by feeling rather than highly consistent doctrine'.[45]

The evangelical response to these changes was double-edged. On the one hand, its conservative wing was gaining in popularity after a period of relative insignificance, to the detriment of traditionally liberal branches of the movement. This was due to a number of factors. Firstly, the liberal evangelical wing had lost much of its vigour. The Anglican Evangelical Group Movement, which had channelled liberal voices from the Church of England and Methodism, lost support as key figures died or were elevated to senior positions which kept them from engaging with sectional movements. More persistent strains of liberalism tended to be less evangelical or were absorbed into wider secular perspectives, including those militant factions who identified with the counter culture or with Marxist revolutionary politics.[46]

Secondly, developments in post-war theology were more sympathetic to conservative concerns. Of particular significance was the neo-orthodoxy represented by Karl Barth, which stressed an existential encounter with Christ that was more congenial to conservatives than liberals. Thirdly, the emergence of radical theology, despite achieving some recognition among intellectuals, held less sway on the ground, and triggered a conservative backlash. John Robinson's *Honest to God* was dismissed by conservatives like J.I. Packer, whose vitriol tallied with a popular appeal for a more traditional and familiar kind of Christianity. A similar argument could be made with reference to changing moral norms, the perceived laxity of which urged some to rally to the conservative camp. This was exemplified by Mary Whitehouse and her attack on the popular media and by the Nationwide Festival of Light, which gained momentum by appealing to widespread worries about the dangers of a permissive society. While such concerns were unfashionable, they nevertheless found sympathy among a significant population of moral traditionalists, both within and outside of the churches. Within this context, as David Bebbington puts it, 'Conservatives gained credit for standing up for received Christian convictions.'[47]

At the same time, evangelicals did not simply adopt an attitude of resistance, and there are signs of a significant accommodation to broader cultural and intellectual trends. For example, studies of clergy during this time suggest a liberalisation of values, with dominant perspectives moving towards an emphasis upon the immanent over the supernatural, and an inclusive, humanitarian perspective over an exclusivist, dogmatic one.[48] Comparative studies of the American evangelical movement have also charted a broadening of values and a relaxation of received doctrinal and moral

---

[45] Ellwood, *Sixties Spiritual Awakening*, p. 335.

[46] Bebbington, *Evangelicalism in Modern Britain*, pp. 181-228; See McLeod, *Religious Crisis*, p. 111.

[47] Bebbington, *Evangelicalism in Modern Britain*, p. 255.

[48] Robert Towler and Anthony Coxon, *The Fate of the Anglican Clergy. A Sociological Study* (London: Macmillan, 1979), pp. 196-7.

norms since the 1960s.⁴⁹ In the UK, this process was complex and multi-faceted. A useful framework might take note of a gradual blurring and challenging of traditional boundaries, as evangelicals increasingly engaged with parties and movements outside of their traditional remit. In this vein, I focus on three separate developments, all of which represent a relaxation of traditional norms and conventions: the rise of the ecumenical movement, the reconception of evangelism to include social welfare, and the embrace of popular culture and the arts. Previous studies have focused on the practical reconfiguration of worship and social action, and this has led some to assume processes of accommodation and change were cosmetic, reflecting the common assumption that while evangelicals are adept at donning the clothes of the age, they have remained committed to a doctrinal core that has been largely unadulterated. However, this is to misunderstand the nature and extent of cultural accommodation, and my argument here is that both dimensions are inextricably intertwined, so that changes in forms of expression inevitably impact upon the content of shared evangelical values.

Ecumenism

It is perhaps a sociological inevitability that it is those who seek to preserve a purity of Christian faith who will view shifting institutional boundaries with the most suspicion. This was especially so earlier in the twentieth century, when ecclesiastical institutions carried more theological significance in the eyes of the British populace than they appear to now. During the 1960s, such suspicion was directed at the ecumenical movement, and some evangelicals began to see the ecumenical initiatives of the British Council of Churches and World Council of Churches as a capitulation to theological liberalism. In 1966, Martyn Lloyd-Jones, minister of Westminster Chapel and an influential figure in the evangelical movement, called for all evangelicals to sever their links with denominations affiliated to the WCC.⁵⁰ John Stott, the respected rector of All Soul's, Langham Place, publicly rejected this separatist approach. In doing this, he affirmed the place of evangelicals *within* their respective denominations. It had sometimes been thought that the non-conformist, voluntarist spirit of evangelical piety was at odds with the requirements of established churchmanship. Indeed, this was a common conviction within the American movement. Stott quashed this notion by emphasising the ecclesiological aspects of evangelical responsibility, affirming the corporate elements of Christian duty alongside personal piety.

Stott, arguably the most influential figure within British evangelicalism since the 1960s, reaffirmed his position on behalf of British evangelicals at the International

---

⁴⁹ E.g., see James Davison Hunter, *Evangelicalism. The Coming Generation* (Chicago, IL, and London: University of Chicago Press, 1987); and Quebedeaux, *Worldly Evangelicals*.

⁵⁰ David L. Edwards, *The Futures of Christianity. An Analysis of Historical, Contemporary and Future Trends within the Worldwide Church* (London, Sydney, Auckland and Toronto: Hodder and Stoughton, 1987), p. 426.

Congress on World Evangelization at Lausanne in 1974. Breaking with the more sectarian, exclusivist sentiments of Billy Graham and the other American representatives, Stott emphasised the collective responsibility of the church over individual and non-denominational mission. Stott was an influential figure at the conference, the elder statesman of the British movement, and effectively represented the more moderate evangelicalism that was emerging within the English churches.

Enveloped in this was a positive drive towards ecumenism. Denominational identity was no longer viewed as a barrier to dialogue, and evangelicals increasingly affirmed the value of church unity. Indeed, as charismatic renewal and the house church movement gained pace, more and more evangelicals came to see denominational structures as either incidental to Christian identity or, in some quarters, as an impediment to its full expression. More common, however, were cautious steps towards finding common ground. The National Evangelical Anglican Congress (NEAC) at Keele in 1967 marked the beginnings of significant dialogue with Roman Catholics. By 1977, at the NEAC meeting in Nottingham, the Revd David Watson was able to make the controversial claim that 'In many ways, the Reformation was one of the greatest tragedies that ever happened to the Church...',[51] on account of its ultimately divisive consequences. Inspired by the unifying power of charismatic renewal, Watson called for Christians of all denominations to put aside their differences and recognise their shared status as sinners saved by Jesus Christ. While discussions about evangelical relations with Roman Catholics at the 1977 meeting reflected some persistent areas of discomfort – e.g., Marian dogma, universal primacy and mixed marriage – the official NEAC statement was still able to commit evangelical Anglicans to 'work towards full communion between our two churches', seeking 'the visible unity of all professing Christians'.[52] Such sentiments of inter-denominational unity were fostered most visibly by the charismatic movement, which taught a faith based on a common experience of the Holy Spirit, rather than on doctrinal correctness.

The consequences of these developments for the construction of the evangelical worldview were twofold. First, in affirming the importance of inclusion within institutions defined by denomination rather than dogma, evangelicals have expressed a new openness to other Christian traditions, including Roman Catholicism. Second – and more crucially – the fact that evangelicals accepted that there was something to be learnt from ecumenical dialogue was 'an admission that they did not possess a monopoly of truth'.[53]

---

[51] David Watson, cited in Teddy Saunders and Hugh Sansom, *David Watson. A Biography* (Sevenoaks: Hodder and Stoughton, 1992), p. 186.

[52] Cited in John Capon, *Evangelicals Tomorrow. A Popular Report of Nottingham '77, the National Evangelical Anglican Congress* (Glasgow: Fount Paperbacks, 1977), p. 94.

[53] Bebbington, *Evangelicalism in Modern Britain*, p. 249.

Social Action as Evangelism

During the nineteenth century, evangelicals were distinguished by their welfare projects, focused on relief for the poor and social reform. Indeed, during the Victorian age, social improvement was defended on Christian grounds as both part of the task of bringing in the kingdom of God on earth and as a means to achieving the spiritual and moral betterment of the impoverished. By the mid-twentieth century, however, theological controversies had forced a turn inward, and on to matters of religious truth over social welfare. This 'great reversal', which precipitated change on both sides of the Atlantic, was triggered by a number of factors. A sense of moral and spiritual crisis following the First World War led to pessimism about social reform and a belief that the necessary changes were only possible through divine intervention. This fed enthusiasm for millennialist doctrine and the conviction that only Christ's second coming would see the resolution of these apocalyptic times, with the kingdom of God dramatically established by Christ himself, not by men on earth, as advocates of the social gospel would have it.[54] The popularity of the Keswick sanctification doctrine[55] among evangelicals across the denominations fostered a watchfulness about personal behaviour, rather than an engagement in the wider social sphere. In addition to this, the growing influence of Darwinism and higher biblical criticism threatened traditional evangelical convictions about biblical authority and the status of Jesus' miracles.[56] Such trends generated accusations of cultural accommodation. The absorption of such fashionable intellectual, political and social currents, so advocates of this new conservatism claimed, polluted the true gospel and distracted the attention of Christians away from a proper life of faith. In sociological terms, this was expressed in a turn away from social engagement and towards matters of personal religiosity as the defining element of Christian identity. If there was a duty to go out into the world, then it was to save souls by converting non-believers, rather than to reform the social and political landscape.

By the 1960s, things had changed again, as themes of social responsibility and humanitarian outreach were again brought to the fore, and were taken up as new priorities by evangelical Christians. The Evangelical Alliance Relief (TEAR) Fund was established in 1968, committing itself to addressing issues of poverty in the Third World, and the Shaftesbury Project was established just a year later, with the support of the IVF, to promote thought and action in all spheres of evangelical

---

[54] An evangelical critique of the kingdom theology of the social gospel movement, within the context of the 'great reversal' debate, is offered by John Stott in his *Issues Facing Christians Today* (Basingstoke: Marshall Morgan and Scott, 1984), pp. 6-10.

[55] The belief, rooted in the proto-charismatic tradition of the Keswick Convention, that a process of inner renewal by the Holy Spirit may descend upon the faithful individual as a gift from God. For a theological discussion, see J.I. Packer, 'Keswick and the Reformed Doctrine of Sanctification', *Evangelical Quarterly* 27 (1955), pp. 153-67.

[56] For a detailed account of these developments, including a consideration of other germane factors, see David Bebbington, 'The Decline and Resurgence of Evangelical Social Concern: 1918-1980', in John Wolffe (ed.), *Evangelical Faith and Public Zeal. Evangelicals and Society in Britain 1780-1980* (London: SPCK, 1995), pp. 175-97.

social involvement. Again, the reasons for the change were complex, although one important factor was the weakening of adventist theological currents, at least on the UK side of the Atlantic, which in turn softened any enthusiasm for premillennialism and tempered the associated withdrawal of evangelicals from public affairs. In addition to this, ecumenical and international links exposed British evangelicals to similar efforts at social reform elsewhere, and the sense of moral urgency within a libertarian 1960s triggered a call among many to adopt a more interventionist approach to social problems. This culminated in the congress at Lausanne in 1974, which expressed a fresh sense of social responsibility among evangelicals the world over, the Lausanne Covenant, declaring that 'evangelism and socio-political involvement are both part of our Christian duty'.[57] Evangelicals had again found their civic voice.

Embodied most visibly in TEAR Fund, this new vision blurred the distinction between evangelism and social outreach, emphasising aid to the needy alongside the need to convert non-Christians to the faith. In this sense it reflected the highly influential *Rich Christians in an Age of Hunger*, written by Ronald Sider in 1977.[58] Understandings of evangelism were effectively broadened, with missions of social outreach focused on remedying injustice and inequality. By the 1980s, there were clear signs of a widespread organised return to social activism, through organisations such as the Evangelical Coalition for Urban Missions, which addressed inner-city poverty and violence and Evangelical Christians for Racial Justice, which addressed racial problems.

During the 1980s, evangelical social concern was publicly personified in David Sheppard, Bishop of Liverpool, who championed the needs of the socially excluded in his groundbreaking volume *Bias to the Poor*[59] and in his work on the *Faith in the City* report, which identified Urban Priority Areas where the need for remedial intervention was most urgent. Of recognised evangelical integrity but advancing a progressive vision for urban regeneration, Sheppard represented a 'growing minority amongst evangelicals for whom politically radical positions' could 'coexist with orthodox theology'.[60] Whereas evangelicalism had been previously associated politically with a Conservative perspective, Sheppard addressed issues of urban poverty and deprivation in a tone that was often critical of the Thatcher government of the time. Sheppard's work and example offered a point of convergence for churchmen of different theologies, and thus opened the way for new opportunities for ecumenism, as demonstrated in his collaborative work with the Roman Catholic Archbishop of Liverpool, Derek Worlock.

Left-wing evangelical voices could also be heard in the magazine *Sojourners* and through the American radical Jim Wallis, who has criticised right wing evangelicals

---

[57] Cited by Stott, *Issues*, pp. 9-10.

[58] Ronald Sider, *Rich Christians in an Age of Hunger* (London: Hodder and Stoughton, 1997 [orig. 1977]).

[59] David Sheppard, *Bias to the Poor* (London: Hodder and Stoughton, 1983).

[60] Kenneth Medhurst and George Moyser, *Church and Politics in a Secular Age* (Oxford: Clarendon Press, 1988), p. 138.

for their complicity in the social inequalities of western culture.[61] For Wallis, countering common criticisms of liberal Christianity, it is the new religious right who are excessively worldly, as they conflate capitalist and consumerist values with the message of the gospel. Wallis and his associates represent a widespread tendency across the US movement, which James Davison Hunter identifies as the 'radical' or 'young' evangelicals, whose voices have been heard in journals such as *Radix*, *Seeds* and *Inside*. They are social action oriented and distinguishable by their tendency to advocate social ministry as an end in itself, i.e., independent of conversion-based evangelism.[62] Richard Quebedeaux associates this faction with an appreciation of the arts, the abandonment of traditional moral taboos and a generally more positive engagement with the secular sphere.[63]

Evangelical social action has rarely strayed into British politics, and evangelicals maintain a sensitivity towards matters 'worldly' that is often expressed as a rejection of left-wing concerns. For example, *Third Way*, an evangelical journal offering social and political comment, became independent from its evangelical publishers in 1987 following accusations that it had 'left-wing' leanings.[64] Even so, it had attained a circulation of over 3,000, its readers representing a liberal-minded wing amongst the evangelical populace, and one that may be reasonably described as the political-theological equivalent of the US contingent described by Hunter and Quebedeaux. Here also, they are scattered and not organised, but they draw from similar inspirations to their US counterparts. Many regulars at the Greenbelt festival – similar in orientation to *Third Way* – explain their allegiance with reference to the more conventional theology and apolitical mood of Spring Harvest. A significant left-wing minority appears to persist among British evangelicals, supporting open spiritual dialogue and political engagement. A notable spokesperson for this outlook is Graham Cray, one time vicar of St Michael-le-Belfrey and currently Bishop of Maidstone. In the Restorationist journal *Tomorrow Today!*, Cray has argued that the demands of the kingdom of God extend beyond those within the church, and requires 'both the challenging of dominant political ideologies and the announcement of good news to the economically poor and the socially powerless'.[65]

Cray's teachings are shared by many, but evangelicals rarely express such convictions in open public protest or political challenge. The current climate is better exemplified by CARE and Jubilee, organisations affiliated to the Evangelical Alliance which quietly lobby the government on a variety of issues, while not adopting a partisan political perspective. At the other end of the spectrum, the campaign group Christian Voice has recently attracted the media spotlight by virtue of its conservative evangelical critique of contemporary culture, its attacks on gay rights and on *Jerry Springer the Opera*, all presented as a concern for the moral and

---

[61] Jim Wallis, *The New Radical* (Nashville, TN: Abingdon Press, 1983).
[62] Hunter, *Evangelicalism*, p. 42.
[63] Quebedeaux, *Worldly Evangelicals*, pp. 81-142.
[64] Hall, 'The Current Evangelical Resurgence', p. 276.
[65] Cited in Smith, *Transforming the World?*, p. 111.

spiritual health of the nation. However, its perspective represents that of a small minority and it is unclear exactly how much influence the organisation enjoys.

It is worth noting that if evangelical social action has penetrated both fields of pastoral concern and political lobbying, it has also found a voice on environmental issues. While perhaps less audible and less pervasive, the sense of urgency surrounding the need for a Christian voice on the environmental crisis has been sufficiently keen to provoke the 'Whose Earth?' initiative, led by Youth for Christ and TEAR fund. This in turn led, in 1994, to the Evangelical Alliance publishing *Creation Care*, a booklet aimed at encouraging evangelicals to live a more environmentally friendly lifestyle.[66]

The above trends represent a broadening conception of evangelical social action, as evangelicals have sought to engage with a larger cross section of concerns as legitimate fields of Christian practice. This has arguably softened a pre-existing commitment to person-centred conversion, especially as projects in social action and in evangelism have become in many cases combined, thus blurring any distinction between mission priorities. But this change has gone further, with a subtle but potentially profound shift in understandings of evangelism itself. In recent decades, evangelicals have had to acknowledge that their traditional proselytising strategies can often have the opposite effect to that intended. Within a culture sceptical of religion, impassioned attempts to persuade others to one's own point of view – especially when the consequences are conceived in ultimate terms – can be viewed as oppressive, coercive, intrusive and obnoxious. Our culture is increasingly intolerant of worldviews that claim exclusive access to truth and, as such, people are wary of those who affiliate themselves to such ideologies and press them on to others. In recognition of this by-product of secularisation, evangelicals have developed new ways of sharing their faith, so that the notion of 'friendship evangelism' has entered into the evangelical vocabulary. 'Friendship evangelism' cannot be traced to a single definition, author or school of thought, and has been conceived differently in different contexts. What it always appears to represent, however, is an effort to be sensitive to the suspicions of non-Christians and respectful of them as people, within an evangelism that takes place not *via* confrontational encounters, but through longer-term relationships. For example, Floyd Schneider's model of friendship evangelism advocates winning others for Christ by first getting to know non-Christians and befriending them out of interest in them as people. They may eventually be challenged to make a faith-decision by being among those who visibly live their lives according to God's word, and who nurture their new friend's spiritual questions through conversation and shared Bible reading.[67] Arthur McPhee warns against an approach that is confrontational and which treats non-converts as potential trophies, in favour of a friendship evangelism that arises out of community, hospitality and a willingness to disciple the new convert within their own cultural context, among

---

[66] Clive Calver, 'Afterword: Hope for the Future', in Wolffe (ed.) *Evangelical Faith and Public Zeal*, p. 208.

[67] Floyd Schneider, *Friendship Evangelism* (Eastbourne: Monarch, 1989).

their own friends and relatives, rather than in the potentially alienating environment of an unfamiliar church.[68] Roger Forster, leader in the 'new church' Ichthus fellowship, has explicitly followed the recommendations of the 1974 Lausanne Covenant in combining good works with preaching the gospel, claiming the two evangelical priorities need to be treated as one. Ichthus implements what Forster calls 'presence evangelism' by demonstrating, as well as preaching, God's love through community-based projects concerned with employment and education.[69]

Such strategies encourage new methods for facilitating evangelism, without diverging from the desired end result – the conversion of the non-Christian to a radically new understanding of the world, grounded in their acceptance of Jesus as their Lord and Saviour, and founded on the truth of scripture. However, they do advocate toning down this message so as to be less confrontational and less strident in its expression of the conditions of inclusion, and this in practice may transform the process altogether. Other understandings openly accept this transformation, and justify it on theological grounds. For example, Pete Ward, one time advisor for youth work to the Archbishop of Canterbury and leader of Oxford Youth Works, has argued that youth ministers should continue to engage with young people regardless of whether they convert or not, as a 'sign of "grace", that is the free gift of God's love in Christ'. Rather than conversion, the main goal of Christian relational care should be 'To move towards the good', involving 'an appreciation of corporate, community-based issues and a desire for justice'.[70]

The consequences of these changes for the relationship of evangelicalism to its surrounding culture are profound. In so far as mission is conducted along ethical or pastoral, rather than purely conversionist lines, evangelicals are all the more exposed to discourses external to the movement itself, both religious and secular. But more importantly, the more that conversion (understood as decisive identity change) is treated as optional or secondary, the less likely it is that explicit assent to predetermined core values of the faith will be treated as obligatory and necessary for all. Binding and timeless truth is transmuted into optional choice. The boundaries of the Christian faith are blurred, and what were once treated as non-negotiable teachings are opened up for reconfiguration at the popular level.[71]

---

[68] Arthur McPhee, *Friendship Evangelism. The Caring Way to Share Your Faith* (Eastbourne: Kingsway, 1978).

[69] David Hilborn, *Picking Up the Pieces. Can Evangelicals Adapt to Contemporary Culture?* (London: Hodder and Stoughton, 1997), pp. 188-9. Also influential in the emergence of 'friendship evangelism' was the work of Rebecca Manley Pippert, especially her book *Out of the Saltshaker: Evangelism as a Way of Life* (Leicester: Intervarsity Press, 1980).

[70] Pete Ward, 'Christian Relational Care', in Pete Ward (ed.), *Relational Youthwork. Perspectives on Relationships in Youth Ministry* (Oxford: Lynx, 1995), pp. 29, 36.

[71] The widespread discomfort that churchgoers feel about evangelising is also evident in the results of the recent English Church Census. Clergy responses suggested their congregations valued evangelism far less than they did, and when asked about mission priorities, respondents' aspirations focused on the need for mission to be 'Spirit led',

The Embrace of Popular Culture and the Arts

The 1960s also saw the beginnings of an exchange between evangelicalism and popular culture, including the arts. This was partly driven by the charismatic movement, which ushered in a new age of creativity in worship. But it was also a consequence of the fact that pop culture itself – including music, cinema, television and fashion – had become inextricably bound up in the identities of young people, including evangelical Christians. Church leaders became increasingly sensitive to the fact that, if churches were to appeal to young outsiders, and retain young converts, they would have to adopt the stylistic media of popular culture. The slogan of the evangelical organisation 'Youth for Christ' was 'Geared to the Times but anchored to the Rock'. This conviction, carried forward by enthusiastic young leaders, gave birth to a wealth of artistic creativity, mostly expressed in new worship forms, but also in creative evangelism that used drama and dance alongside rhetorical proclamations of the gospel message. The 'cultural austerity' of British evangelicalism was to give way to an increasingly colourful and artistically abundant subculture.

The inroads that evangelicals made into popular music were advanced at various age levels. *Buzz* magazine catered to the teenage market for Christian pop. Launched in 1964, it had attained a circulation of more than 30,000 by 1981.[72] 1974 saw the beginnings of the Greenbelt festival, which soon established an appeal to older teenagers and young adults, promoting Christianity through the arts and popular music as well as offering forums for the debate of topical ethical and theological issues. In 1979 it drew an attendance of 2,700; by the mid 1980s, this had grown to nearly 30,000. Evangelicals were beginning to use popular cultural media in the expression of their faith, whether for worship – as with the publication of *Youth Praise* in the late 1960s, and the light folk pop worship of the 'Fisher Folk' in the 1970s – or for evangelism, through festivals and crusades. The 1980s saw the beginnings of Contemporary Christian Music (CCM) and the emergence of Christian artists onto the secular pop scene, though they achieved far more credibility in the US than in the UK.

This blurring of boundaries between evangelicalism and popular culture has been a two-way process. While churches baptised pop media for their own ends, representatives of pop culture made inroads into evangelicalism. Cliff Richard converted whilst attempting to retain popularity as an artist, as did Rick Wakeman of the progressive rock band 'Yes'. Even the acerbic Bob Dylan, who was born a Jew, was 'born again', famously voicing his new-found faith on such tracks as 'Gotta Serve Somebody' and 'When He Returns'.[73] Evangelicalism has been thrust into the public spotlight, open to comment and criticism, but also to emulation by those who find a new credibility in the associations of popular culture.

'Transforming' and 'Empowering people', rather than 'Evangelistic'. See Brierley, *Pulling Out of the Nosedive*, p. 241.

[72] Bebbington, *Evangelicalism in Modern Britain*, p. 263.

[73] See the albums *Slow Train Coming* (1979) and *Saved* (1980), which cover Dylan's 'born again' period.

The most radical embrace of pop culture from within the evangelical camp was undoubtedly triggered by the infamous Nine O'Clock Service (NOS), which was established in Sheffield in the mid-1980s. Established by a group of young evangelicals, NOS was founded on the belief that the church had lost touch with Britain's youth and had become politically and morally apathetic. Their response was to start a new Sunday service in connection with their home church, St Thomas's, Crookes. Worship was charismatic and multi-media, employing advanced visual and audio technology, and the favoured music was house and techno, in reflection of the popular 'rave' culture of the time. Soon, hundreds of young people were attending services each week, drawn to both the 'cutting edge' worship as well as to the NOS message of ecological responsibility, social justice and radical Christian commitment. Those most committed to the project lived communally in local houses, pooling their financial resources and mobilising support for the evangelistic initiatives of the church. Organisational structures were hierarchical, with an expectation that members submit to the authority of a series of elders, a system not unlike the discipling common among house church groups. Theology was radical and strict, emphasising the exacting demands of scripture within the practical lives of members.[74] Its sense of being tuned into the subcultural 'cutting edge' was original and unequalled within the church. Church leaders championed NOS as successful evangelism – an exciting sign of the vibrancy of Christian youth within an otherwise moribund church.

But the dream did not last. The Nine O'Clock Service collapsed in 1995 amidst accusations of sexual abuse and abuse of power directed at the Revd Chris Brain, its self-styled leader and spiritual guru. Many members suffered psychological trauma as a result of their involvement. However, before the service fell into disrepute, it acted as the inspiration for a whole host of other new services that were to imitate the NOS vision. The 'alternative' worship (or 'alt.worship') movement embraced the multi-media worship pioneered at NOS, but rejected the strict authority structures that had been instrumental in its downfall.[75] By the mid-1990s, a growing number of small service groups had established themselves in connection with evangelical churches all over the country. These groups tended to give themselves aphoristic names, chosen to convey a sense of both mystery and vitality, whilst deliberately and implicitly questioning the boundaries between religion and pop culture. London spawned *Abundant, Grace* and *Vaux, Joy* arose in Oxford, *Be Real* in Nottingham, and *Visions* in York.

---

[74] In yet another example of how St Michael-le-Belfrey appears as the hub of so much evangelical innovation, the Nairn St Community, which gave birth to NOS, was originally inspired by the model of simple Christian living described in David Watson's influential book *Discipleship* (London: Hodder and Stoughton, 1981). This in turn was born out of Watson's experience of the 'households' of St Michael's during the late 1970s (see chapter 3).

[75] Paul Roberts, *Alternative Worship in the Church of England* (Cambridge: Grove, 1999), p. 12.

Groups remained unconnected institutionally, each usually attached to a more mainstream local church (usually Anglican or Methodist), but participants operated within a defined network, swapping worship resources and engaging in dialogue *via* web discussion lists or at the Greenbelt festival. Alternative worship spread from the UK to the USA and to Australasia, although there remain significant differences in emphases and popularity. Not least, the American groups have tended to be more entrepreneurial in their approach to community and outreach, but have been less radical theologically, while the denominational context of evangelicalism in the Antipodes has meant that the Baptist churches have been natural homes for many groups there. In the UK, alt.worship has been shaped by an effort to create environments in which culturally authentic experiences of God and worship are possible, a quest driven by the subcultural identities of members but also distinguished by a ritual and ecclesiological experimentation inspired by pre-modern church tradition as much as by ideas associated with post-modernity. The movement has persisted in small, often close-knit groups, which stress the importance of in-group support and of fostering a 'safe' space for the open exploration of spirituality. Public visibility, while seldom expressed in large and vibrant congregations, has been achieved at Anglican youth events for progressive worship, such as the millennial celebration 'Time of Our Lives' and always at Greenbelt.

The *avant garde* style of alternative worship has attracted some suspicion from mainstream evangelicals, who have associated it with the deplored 'New Age Movement'.[76] To be sure, while these creative worship groups have embraced ritual experimentation and been eclectic in their choice of spiritual resources, they have not openly embraced or oriented themselves within the New Age Movement in the way that more liberal churches like St James's, Piccadilly, have.[77] However, the location of alt.worship groups within evangelicalism has exposed them to criticism from Christians more wary of theological syncretism. From this perspective, alt.worship has absorbed popular culture to a degree that has left it unrecognisable as an evangelical initiative to many within the wider movement.

In many respects, developments since the turn of the millennium have fostered a more tolerant perspective. The Church of England's *Mission-Shaped Church* report, published in 2004, acknowledged that there are many forms the 'church' may take, and that changes in the wider culture render certain expressions of church more or less meaningful than others. In taking account of the diverse 'fresh expressions' of church already emerging in the UK context, the report places 'alternative worship

---

[76] When a new evangelical festival – Junction 1 – was proposed in 2000 and arranged to take place on the same weekend as Greenbelt, conflicting theological undercurrents emerged in open debate, reported by the church press. Debate focused on whether the exposure of young evangelicals to traditions outside of mainstream Christianity, a central distinguishing feature of Greenbelt, is good for Christian development and responsible debate, or a threat to the fragile faith of the vulnerable (see Simon Mayo and Martin Wroe, 'Put Young People at Risk, Please', *Church Times* 18 February 2000, p. 8).

[77] See Daren Kemp, 'The Christaquarians? A Sociology of Christians in the New Age' (PhD thesis, King's College, London, 1999).

communities' at the top of the list, thus affirming the legitimacy and value of this now well-established network.[78] Furthermore, a debate has emerged on both sides of the Atlantic, which is in part driven by the same impetus as alt.worship, i.e., a frustration with the rigidity of mainstream evangelical churches and their reluctance to engage with significant cultural change. The subsequent 'emerging church' movement, which within the collective evangelical consciousness has very much absorbed alt.worship, continues to rethink the nature of church in a postmodern world, while emerging church participants and leaders use their online blogs as a new site for the exploration and promotion of their innovative ideas. The resulting expansion of the evangelical mainstream has created a sense that alt.worship groups are not as marginal as was previously thought, their appeal to resources from Christian history highlighting a *participation with*, rather than a challenge to, the Christian tradition. The alt.worship passion for liturgy, holistic worship and the sacramental also resonates with those evangelicals who are dissatisfied with their conventional diet of contemporary worship, signalling a widespread shift away from the abstract and the cerebral towards the sensate and the theatrical.[79] In this respect, the engagement with the postmodern has extended well beyond the radical margins of the evangelical movement.

In addition to a general broadening of boundaries, specific movements stand out as particularly noteworthy because of their novelty and wider influence. Two movements addressed here are the Alpha course and post-evangelicalism, selected because they represent different – perhaps divergent – routes whereby evangelicals have self-consciously engaged with the surrounding culture as a means of expressing their Christian identity, with very different consequences.

Alpha

While the 1990s is now widely viewed as an ineffective 'decade of evangelism', the Alpha course has to be noted as an exception. Initially launched in 1979 as a modest refresher course for lapsed Christians, it has, over the past few years, exploded into a successful tool for global evangelism. In 1991, there were four churches running Alpha courses; by 1999, the number quoted by its organisers was 11,430, based all over the world in prisons and universities as well as in local churches. According to Peter Brierley, 'By the end of 2005, 2 million people in the UK and 8 million worldwide had attended an Alpha course.'[80] Alpha has produced a Christian industry of its own, including accompanying books, video and audio cassettes, as well as promotional material like sweatshirts and car-stickers. Nicky Gumbel's *Questions of Life*,[81] on which the course is based, has now been translated into twenty-eight

---

[78] *Mission Shaped Church. Church Planting and Fresh Expressions of Church in a Changing Context* (London: Church House Publishing, 2004), p. 44.
[79] David Hilborn, *Picking Up the Pieces*, p. 133.
[80] Brierley, *Pulling Out of the Nosedive*, p. 229.
[81] Nicky Gumbel, *Questions of Life* (London: Kingsway, 2001).

languages and has sold 500,000 copies.[82] The course has also received significant media attention, with substantial revenues securing bill-board evangelism and television interest resulting in a much hyped, if lukewarmly received, documentary series in 2001. Meanwhile, newspaper reportage has focused upon celebrity Alpha converts, including former page three model Samantha Fox and disgraced Tory politician Jonathan Aitken.

Alpha's birth-place and administrative centre is Holy Trinity Church in Brompton (HTB), a hub of charismatic evangelical innovation throughout the 1980s. Alpha has also helped to make it the richest single church in Britain, with an annual income in 1999 of £5.1 million.[83] The Alpha course is the brain-child of Nicky Gumbel, vicar of HTB and perennial front-man for Alpha. Working from the assumption that successful evangelism depends upon minimising the cultural boundaries between the church and its target audience, Gumbel has devised a fifteen-week course which plays down proclamation and confrontation and instead attempts to nurture potential converts in a 'safe' and comfortable environment. In practice, this means sharing a meal, listening to an informal lecture and discussing arising issues in small groups. Each week is devoted to a set topic – e.g., prayer, Jesus, resisting evil – which is addressed in accordance with the guidelines set out in the Alpha literature. Towards the end of the course, participants are invited to a weekend or day away, and spend their time considering the Holy Spirit. Talks and discussion proceed as usual, but there is also a session during which the leader will call upon the Spirit to fill those present. Glossolalia and emotional responses are not uncommon, and this is often a point of decision for the cynical or newly committed. In this way, according to its organisers, Alpha responds to certain basic needs in today's society, by offering: 1. straightforward answers to existential questions (what is the meaning of life? what will happen when I die?), and 2. an encounter with the spiritual.

While official in-house statistics are impressive, it is unclear how many of those who complete Alpha were formerly non-churchgoers and how many make a lasting commitment to any church. In his recent survey of Alpha participants in England and Wales, sociologist Stephen Hunt found that only 8% were non-believers with no church experience, 16.3% were agnostics with some experience of church life, while 74.4% had some connection with the church running the course.[84] Hunt also found that only one in six participants actually convert to Christianity.[85] Cynics would claim that the style of the course translates into a certain attenuated Christian commitment – non-threatening, gentle and easily slotted into one's established lifestyle. Aside from this, Alpha is undoubtedly a channel for a particular kind of charismatic evangelicalism: theologically conservative yet expressed in simple narratives and dichotomies; charismatic but not vociferously so; affirming the

---

[82] Stephen Hunt, *The Alpha Enterprise. Evangelism in a Post-Christian Era* (Aldershot: Ashgate, 2004), pp. 14-15.

[83] Jon Ronson, 'Catch Me If You Can', *The Guardian Weekend*, 21 October 2000, p. 19.

[84] Hunt, *Alpha Enterprise*, p. 171.

[85] Hunt, *Alpha Enterprise*, p. 186.

importance of in-group support and affective relationships; encouraging moral reform in the light of spiritual warfare; and stressing uncompromising boundaries between Christianity and other religious movements. These themes are gently but consistently affirmed and are clearly expressed in the course resources, now subject to copyright law as a guard against unsound local deviations.

Alpha has not been without its critics. Liberals object to its inherent suggestion that the charismatic evangelical way is the only route into Christian faith, and point to the lack of space given to doctrine, the church or Christian history within the Alpha programme. Others point to its distinctively middle class appeal: the sit-down meal, lecture and discussion groups may resonate with the university set; they hold little familiarity for many working-class people. Widespread reservations about Alpha have prompted the emergence of alternative courses, some developed locally, others on a more ambitious scale, such as Emmaus, which, established in the late 1990s, offers an introduction to the Christian faith markedly distinct from the Alpha agenda. Not least, Emmaus endorses a more gradualist approach to conversion, conceiving faith as a journey, and emphasises growth and discipleship over dramatic transformation. On the practical side, its authors allow churches to adapt the course to their own needs, and make course materials available at a low cost, in pdf and photocopiable form,[86] in contrast to the glossy products of Alpha, which are sold to churches and in Christian book shops on a mass scale.

In an erudite critique of Alpha, Pete Ward has drawn from George Ritzer's 'McDonaldization' thesis,[87] arguing that Alpha courses are designed and executed according to the values of efficiency, calculability, predictability and control. Ward is concerned that Alpha may promote religious uniformity and stifle creativity among new converts. In reducing evangelism to a predictable and comfortable process, Alpha risks trivialising Christian commitment in deference to consumerist values.[88] However, it would be simplistic merely to dismiss Alpha as a straightforward capitulation to contemporary culture. Not least, in embracing the need for a clear and propositional presentation of Christian truth alongside fostering an embodied experience of the Holy Spirit, it taps into both modern and postmodern models of reality, appealing to rationalists and New Agers alike. It is arguably its capacity to successfully manage the tension between the two that accounts for its success as a tool for evangelism.

Post-Evangelicalism

In 1995, Dave Tomlinson, a former House Church leader, wrote *The Post-Evangelical*. Tomlinson's book is both a description of and comment upon changes

---

[86] See http://www.e-mmaus.org.uk/emm_index.asp, accessed 24 January 2007.

[87] George Ritzer, *The McDonaldization of Society. An Investigation into the Changing Character of Contemporary Social Life* (Thousand Oaks: Pine Forge Press, 1996)

[88] Pete Ward, 'Alpha: The McDonaldization of Religion?', *Anvil* 15:4 (1998), pp. 279-86.

already in motion, and a positive call for their understanding and development. He proceeds from the premise that present-day evangelicalism has been shaped by the culture of modernity, but that many individuals – 'post-evangelicals' – relate more to a culture of post-modernity. This dissonance leads to mutual misunderstanding and to some individuals abandoning spiritual homes that no longer have meaning for them. Tomlinson embraces liberal scholarship in claiming that faith and culture are inextricably entwined. Therefore, he argues that the faith of post-evangelicals should be evaluated within the context of an understanding and appreciation of post-modern culture, including its critique of truth, tradition and authority.[89]

The post-modern frame of reference, according to Tomlinson, calls for a radical rethinking of how the gospel is perceived. In the face of notions of cultural chaos which pose a threat to religion, he favours a positive engagement rather than a retreat into the old certainties of modernity. This involves a move away from the 'parental' authority which characterises the relationship between evangelicals and their church leaders. Tomlinson describes this as a child-like mode of compliance to an unquestioned and dominant authority and connects this trend to the urge to insulate the 'faithful' from outside forces that may have a corrupting influence.[90] By contrast, Tomlinson highlights the need to allow individuals the freedom and space to think through their faith-lives in dialogue with their experience, to voice their doubts, and to encourage thought which is open-minded, creative, reflective and holistic.[91] He extends this into a critique of the nature of evangelical language, typically rational, propositional and absolute, arguing that ambiguity, intuition and symbolism carry more resonance in a post-modern world, and have the advantage of provoking rich, open-ended debate about truth and meaning.[92] Running throughout Tomlinson's book is a passion for the autonomous, but sincere and responsible search for truth, replacing doctrinal or textual conformity as the essence of Christian faith.

Warmly received by kindred spirits who identified with his call for open and exploratory dialogue, Tomlinson's book received harsh criticism from many within mainstream evangelicalism, who viewed his radical rethinking as either theologically superficial or an abandonment of evangelicalism altogether. While not known as an evangelical himself, Martyn Percy has voiced a common concern: 'How can "core" doctrines be rescued in a cultural scheme that contents itself with surface meanings? ... who decides which are the core doctrines?'[93] And yet Tomlinson insists that his intention is to '*take as given many of the assumptions of evangelical faith,* while at the same time moving beyond its perceived limitations'.[94] While he advocates a kind of spiritual *bricolage*, Tomlinson's perspective is not without limits, advocating 'plurality without a necessary collapse into pluralism and relativity, without sinking

---

[89] Dave Tomlinson, *The Post-Evangelical* (London: SPCK, 1995), p. 9.
[90] Tomlinson, *The Post-Evangelical*, p. 53.
[91] Tomlinson, *The Post-Evangelical*, p. 59.
[92] Tomlinson, *The Post-Evangelical*, p. 90.
[93] Martyn Percy, 'Review Article: The Post-Evangelical', *Journal of Contemporary Religion* 11:3 (1996), p. 359.
[94] Tomlinson, *The Post-Evangelical*, p. 7 (my emphasis).

into the "anything goes" of relativism'.[95] But what are these limits? Tomlinson is notably vague, preferring to encourage a spirit of questioning rather than prescribe a set of firm guidelines. He distances himself from the discursive reductionism of Don Cupitt, the Enlightenment project of modern liberalism, and from the apparently limitless experimentalism of the New Age. But his rootedness in evangelicalism is manifest in inversions rather than consistencies. The Christ-event, and its portrayal in scripture, forms the zenith of revelation, but is given to us in symbolism and metaphor, the cultural distance between ourselves and the biblical writers calling for continued reinterpretation.[96] And while Tomlinson clearly advocates the provision of 'safe' contexts in which spirituality may be explored communally, he prescribes no formal ecclesiology and appears to be happy conceiving Christianity as a non-structured, individualistic network. He appreciates Donald Miller's concern that liberal Christianity may, in engaging with culture, actually end up mirroring it.[97] His guard against this – amounting to a call for communal reflection, allowing scripture to 'fund our deliberations' and maintaining an uncompromising integrity – is characteristically vague and radically open-ended for one claiming an evangelical (or at least quasi-evangelical) position.[98]

Having said this, it is important to bear in mind Tomlinson's intention that his book first and foremost serves a pastoral, rather than theological, purpose, i.e., to reassure those with doubts about their faith and the church that they are not alone, and to suggest possible ways forward. An interview conducted in 2001, some six years after his book was published, also suggests Tomlinson's rather open-ended ecclesiology has given way to a more 'catholic' understanding following his ordination into the Church of England. It is in engaging with Christian history and tradition, rather than in loosely organised discursive networks, that Tomlinson finds the rich resources necessary to fund his faith and enrich his spiritual development.[99]

Tomlinson's vision of post-evangelicalism is a theological legitimation of James Beckford's sociological portrayal of religion in the contemporary West. Where Beckford argues that religion functions as a 'potent cultural resource',[100] Tomlinson points to the capacity of Christianity to fund the postmodern imagination.[101] Both imply detraditionalisation and the relocation of the locus of spiritual authority within the experience of the individual seeker. Truth is to be found in a series of resources and traditions which are not restricted to Christian convention or ecclesiastical

---

[95] Tomlinson, *The Post-Evangelical*, p. 83.

[96] Tomlinson, *The Post-Evangelical*, p. 115.

[97] Donald E. Miller, *The Case for Liberal Christianity* (London: SCM Press, 1981).

[98] Tomlinson, *The Post-Evangelical*, pp. 136-7.

[99] Heather Webb, 'Continuing the Journey: A Conversation with Dave Tomlinson', *Mars Hill Review* 18 (2001), pp. 64-77.

[100] James A. Beckford, *Religion and Advanced Industrial Society* (London: Unwin Hyman, 1989), pp. 170-2.

[101] Tomlinson, *The Post-Evangelical*, p. 142.

dictate. Moreover, and most importantly, truth needs to be 'grasped in ways that are personally authentic'.[102]

Tomlinson's book is significant in marking a change across the evangelical world at large. His reflections have been prompted by conversations with disenchanted evangelicals, not least through *Holy Joes*, the 'alternative church' which Tomlinson founded as a low-key discussion group in a London pub. There are signs that many more have found a kindred spirit in Tomlinson, including the 24% of the readership of *Third Way* magazine, who claimed they identified with the label 'post-evangelical' shortly after the book was published. While the results of the 2005 English Church Census suggest very few clergy would claim this label for their church,[103] the hundreds of letters Tomlinson has received in response to his book suggest a widespread population of sympathisers, located within mainstream evangelicalism as well as at its margins. Tomlinson even cites contact with sympathisers from other traditions – post-catholics and post-liberals – who have similar questions to post-evangelicals, forged out of critical reflection on the place of Christian faith within a postmodern culture.[104] Some post-evangelicals have gathered together to form new communities of faith, stressing mutual support and spiritual exploration over correct doctrine and religious authority. Many of the alternative worship and emerging church groups fall into this category, typically forming enclaves of individuals dissatisfied with conventional evangelicalism and seeking a more open approach to meaning and Christian identity.

Comment: Accommodation and Resistance

Discussing the American evangelical movement, James Davison Hunter describes the twentieth century in terms of rapid change, characterised by a broadening of shared conceptions and a corresponding weakening in the plausibility of old assumptions. He cites Mary Douglas, noting that change, ambiguity and compromise 'have always been the enemies of purity'.[105] As evangelicals have increasingly engaged with institutions and ideas outside of their traditional remit, so they have capitulated to various facets of late modern culture. While in the UK, evangelicals have not enjoyed the wealth, power or position of religious hegemony that applies to their counterparts in the USA, a comparable process has clearly occurred. Evangelical tradition has become embroiled in wider changes, and has absorbed media, norms and standards external to its subculture. These inevitably have a bearing on shared attitudes on the ground. But how can we characterise these changes, and what do they reveal about shifting priorities or trends in belief?

---

[102] Gordon Lynch, *After Religion. Generation X and the Search for Meaning* (London: Darton, Longman and Todd, 2002), p. 40.

[103] Brierley, *Religious Trends 6*, p. 5.12.

[104] Dave Tomlinson, *The Post-Evangelical* (revised North American edition) (Grand Rapids, MI: Zondervan, 2003), p. 19.

[105] Hunter, *Evangelicalism*, p. 186.

David Smith suggests that evangelicals endorsed what was actually a *liberal agenda* at the National Evangelical Anglican Congress at Keele in April 1967. The resulting 'Keele Statement' committed Anglican evangelicals to 'social concern, ecumenical activity as loyal members of the Church of England, and a determination to relate the Gospel meaningfully to the modern world'.[106] It is testimony to the pivotal role of the 1960s that these have remained priorities for Anglican evangelicals ever since. To be fair, social concern has fluctuated over time, achieving prominence in the 1980s but arguably flagging under the more individualistic emphases of the 1990s. Paradoxically, ecumenism appears to have faded as a project precisely because of the perceived meaninglessness of denominational boundaries. In that sense, evangelicals have achieved the dialogue originally intended, but have lost much of the ecclesiological diversity that once characterised differences between Anglicans, Baptists and Methodists. This has of course been helped along by normalising movements like charismatic renewal, the Alpha course and perhaps 'fresh expressions', which have arguably refocused evangelical culture into a fresh perspective, with no obvious or formalised reference to ecclesiology or churchmanship.

Engagement has also brought with it an accommodation in moral norms. Notable is a decline in the maintenance of taboos relating to alcohol or the cinema, due to a weakening fear of the contamination of 'the world'.[107] In this sense, moral behavioural standards have been relaxed. An openness to intellectual and scholarly dialogue also encourages a more complex and nuanced understanding of faith, especially among middle- and upper-middle class evangelicals who possess the cultural capital to engage in these resources without betraying their social identities. We may also note the tendency to absorb social norms of tolerance and extend them into religious and moral issues, a trend that Hunter sees as a response to pluralism.[108] Ian Hall perceives this among UK evangelicals in terms of an avoidance of extremes and a moral diplomacy. Taking the issue of abortion, he comments that, although some evangelicals may be incensed by this, most prefer to

> ... register their opposition through the ballot box, or simply ignore the whole issue until it becomes 'their problem'. Extreme positions on any issue are less acceptable among evangelicals today. Moderation in belief and expression characterises both modern society and Evangelicalism as part of that society.[109]

Indeed, such moderation was detected by theologian J.I. Packer in the late 1970s, who argued that the 'rumbling hiccups and fumbling pickups' evident at the 1977

---

[106] Smith, *Transforming the World?*, pp. 89-90.
[107] Bebbington, 'Evangelicalism in its Settings', p. 368.
[108] Hunter, *Evangelicalism*, p. 152.
[109] Hall, 'The Current Evangelical Resurgence', p. 301.

NEAC conference in Nottingham were symptomatic of how evangelical clergy had become less determined in their defence of correct doctrine.[110]

According to one interpretation, therefore, attitudes have become liberalised and beliefs more profoundly defined by the wider cultural climate. While the take up of more culturally accommodating perspectives will inevitably be conditioned by factors of social class, differences between leaders and parishioners, and to some extent denominational identity, its underlying shifts have certainly opened up a wider remit in which all evangelicals may make sense of their faith. Engagement with external institutions, some of them previously anathema, has opened up opportunities for evangelism and for the re-conception of core ideas. Alpha has harnessed methods drawn from management culture while keeping fundamental charismatic evangelical standards intact. Post-evangelicals embrace an ethic of questioning, given meaning and legitimacy by postmodern philosophy and which, almost by definition, resists the closure necessary for a sustainable project of reform. Meanwhile, the charismatic movement has intensified the evangelical focus upon subjective experience and mobilised new opportunities for empowerment and authority. A softer, 'affective' strand in its development has secured a place for healing and the sharing of problems in small groups, as will be explored further in chapter 7. The contemporary movement is strongly characterised by an affective individualism alongside expectations of practical commitment.

However, while a general structural – and to some extent attitudinal – broadening has taken place, this exists as a steady, often unacknowledged process beneath a public oscillation between liberal progression and conservative backlash. A striking example of the latter would be Reform, an Anglican pressure group established in 1993 by a group of clergy based in large conservative evangelical parishes. Endorsing the authority of scripture, the uniqueness and finality of Christ and the complementarity of the sexes, Reform has criticised the Church of England, including centre-ground evangelicals, for being morally and theologically adrift. They have focused particularly on opposing the ordination of women, and on criticising the Church for not taking an unequivocally condemnatory stance on homosexuality.[111] The Evangelical Alliance's publication of its report on the nature of hell in spring 2000 may be treated as a similarly conservative move but within the evangelical centre ground. The report contradicts the official Church of England position that hell consists in the absence of God, associated with a human state of

---

[110] J.I. Packer, *The Evangelical Anglican Identity Problem. An Analysis* (Oxford: Latimer House, 1978), p. 13.

[111] Roger Steer, *Church on Fire. The Story of Anglican Evangelicals* (London, Sydney and Auckland: Hodder and Stoughton), p. 331.

non-being,[112] instead arguing that hell constitutes a place of eternal damnation and punishment and should be taught as such to school children.[113]

Therefore, while UK evangelicalism makes its way along what would seem to be an inevitable and irreversible inroad amongst the forces of modern cultural change, its various constituents react in different ways to this process. Though rarely named as such because of its negative connotations, 'liberalisation' as a self-consciously implemented project is evident, but only among relatively marginalised or diffuse factions. Evangelical academics and post-evangelical alt.worshippers have less of a public voice than the Evangelical Alliance or Holy Trinity, Brompton. These relatively conservative agencies continue to react against what they see as corrupting, worldly powers, though their tone is markedly gentler than many of their predecessors, focusing upon the moral anomie of modernity rather than the evils of Roman Catholicism, for example. While content to exist in a state of hybridity, absorbing some modern trends but not others, evangelicals are nonetheless still concerned with policing their own boundaries. As Christian Smith has observed with reference to North American evangelicalism, *there has to be a project of resistance* even if it is sporadic and even though inconsistent with changes within the broader movement. For it is the visibility of resistance that sustains a sense of the set apart nature of evangelicalism, set apart, that is, from non-evangelical churches and from the culture which it has so extensively absorbed into its remit.

---

[112] See *The Mystery of Salvation. The Story of God's Gift. A Report by the Doctrine Commission of the Church of England* (London: Church House Publishing, 1997).

[113] See The Evangelical Alliance, *The Nature of Hell* (Carlisle: Acute, 2000); and Stephen Bates, 'Children should be 'told of Hell': Liberals twitch as Evangelicals turn to Fire and Brimstone', *The Guardian* 15 April 2000, p. 9.

Chapter 3

St Michael-le-Belfrey: Blazing the Trail

Now that I have offered a portrait of the evangelical movement as it exists in the UK, it is necessary to examine the church community that forms the heart of this book. St Michael-le-Belfrey is an Anglican church that has enjoyed a reputation as a vanguard of charismatic evangelicalism since the 1960s. Its imposing Gothic structure was constructed in the sixteenth century and it joins many other churches in the area in attracting significant historical interest, but it is for its most recent history that St Michael's is most famous, having established itself as a 'showcase' for evangelical revival. It has been the site not only of church growth, but of innovation in evangelism, creative worship and charismatic renewal, often capturing and prefiguring the evangelical climate of the time, while inspiring evangelicals nationwide. In this sense it stands as a fascinating case study as it embraces all of the major currents of change in the contemporary evangelical world, including small group fellowship, the Alpha course, charismatic spirituality and 'alternative' worship. In this sense, St Michael's exemplifies broader trends while also often acting as a chief initiator of these innovations.

Chapters 4, 5, 6 and 7 will address specific issues in the life of St Michael's which reveal how the beliefs of members and the collective identity of the congregation interrelate. For now, I will present an account of the church's recent history and current status, placing the national trends identified in chapter 2 within a local context. Telling the local story is also an important aspect of my method. One cannot understand congregational cultures simply by applying abstract sociological theories to institutional case studies. Rather, it is necessary to show how processes of local historical change have absorbed wider developments in order to unravel the narrative strands of the current situation. Following Stephen Warner's approach in his own exemplary congregational study, I intend to use history as a way into sociological discussion: to trace the process, in order to explain social and religious change.[1]

---

[1] R. Stephen Warner, *New Wine in Old Wine Skins. Evangelicals and Liberals in a Small-Town Church* (Berkeley, Los Angeles, CA, and London: University of California Press, 1988).

Local Context

York is one of the major historical centres of the north of England. While its population is relatively small for a major city (around 181,000 in 2001),[2] its importance as a site of English history and ecclesiastical government is secure. Surrounded by residential areas, the city centre is largely populated with shops and small businesses (only 1.9% of the population actually live within the Roman city walls). Although the town is situated in the north of England, it has experienced significant gentrification in recent years, with some newcomers even commuting to London during the week. This has raised house prices and accentuated the middle class character of the city and its surrounding areas.

Although not significantly industrialised, the area is home to several successful confectionery and transport businesses. However, the chief industry of the city is tourism, with over four million people per year visiting York from all over the world, so that local residents are used to interacting with strangers to the city. This long-standing trend has also brought many a visitor to St Michael's over the years and has certainly helped to spread its reputation as a thriving church among wandering evangelicals. Equally important has been the local university, which was established in 1963 and currently has over 11,000 students. Situated just outside of the city, it provides a constant influx of young people. Its Christian Union describes itself as an 'evangelical organisation', adopts the UCCF doctrinal statement and maintains strong links with several local evangelical churches. The most popular with students is St Michael-le-Belfrey.

Ever since Pope Gregory sent Augustine to bring order to the English Church, York has been the chief Christian centre of the north. It serves as the administrative base of the northern province of the Church of England, with the Archbishop of York lodged in nearby Bishopthorpe. A key source of interest to tourists as well as Christian pilgrims is the Minster, the largest Gothic cathedral in Northern Europe. St Michael's is situated directly adjacent to it, officially remaining the Minster's parish church.

Robin Gill conducted a case study analysis of churchgoing in York in his influential book, *The Myth of the Empty Church*, published in 1993. He counted twenty-three Anglican churches (excluding the Minster), seven Roman Catholic churches and twenty-three Free Church chapels: twelve Methodist, two Baptist, two United Reformed, one Pentecostal church and six further independent chapels or house churches.[3] York has also been a historical centre for Quakerism: Gill finds two meeting houses situated in the city and a third on the edge of York.[4] He counts eleven Anglican churches in the city itself and, according to diocesan records, this

---

[2] This is well under half the population of several other major cities in the North of England, including Leeds, Manchester, Sheffield and Liverpool. (Source: National UK Census 2001 – see http://www.statistics.gov.uk/census/).

[3] Robin Gill, *The Myth of the Empty Church* (London: SPCK, 1993), pp. 248, 256-7, 259, 265.

[4] Gill, *Myth*, p. 256.

number has not changed since, although two churches have become amalgamated with other parishes. York has more church buildings than active parishes, and several redundant churches are now used as markets and cafés, including the Spurriergate Centre (formerly St Michael's, Spurriergate), which is partially staffed by St Michael's members.

While it boasts a thriving university and café culture, York does not have a very significant 'New Age' presence. A few 'alternative' shops are scattered around the city centre, but the general culture of the city is more traditionalist. Predominantly white, middle class and British (apart from the tourists), non-Christian religions also enjoy only a limited presence. While York does have two mosques, the nearest Hindu Mandir, Jewish Synagogue and Sikh Gurdwara are all twenty-five miles away in Leeds.

As noted earlier, the St Michael's parish is situated at the very centre of the city, and includes the Minster itself. At the time of the 1991 census, there were 482 people living in the parish. It is a relatively expensive area, largely dominated by the white middle classes, retail entrepreneurs and Minster clerics. According to the census, only 1.9% of its population were from ethnic minorities, a pattern that was actually replicated at the diocesan level. There was an even smaller proportion of single parent families: 3.93% in the diocese but only 0.4% within the parish. The location of the church also means that many of its regular attenders live at a significant distance from the church building.

Past and Present, Growth and Change

The life of St Michael's is expressed by its long term members as a narrative – a story of revival and growth. It is a story that is usually traced back to 1965, when the Revd David Watson and his wife Anne arrived at St Cuthbert's, a church a short distance from St Michael's, whose membership was so depleted that it was being considered for redundancy by the diocesan authorities. Watson was appointed curate in charge of St Cuthbert's under the parochial oversight of a vicar in nearby Heworth, who felt Watson's reputation as an evangelist might be useful in attracting students from the new university. Watson was a Cambridge graduate who had been converted whilst a student by the Revd John Collins and mentored by the famous David Sheppard. He had served his first curacy under Collins at St Mark's, Gillingham, where charismatic renewal had broken out in the early sixties. Upon arriving in York, Watson introduced his vision of living faith into St Cuthbert's, laying the foundations of 'regular, believing prayer' and 'faithful preaching of the gospel'.[5] Being a charismatic, Watson also emphasised the importance of being regularly filled with the Holy Spirit. Although accounts of Watson's impact are coloured with hyperbole, they are largely borne out by the available statistics. In 1963, the service register of St Cuthbert's recorded a weekly average of just seven communicants. By 1969, a local newspaper reported an evening attendance of 350 (a

---

[5] R. Gledhill, 'Blessed by the Spirit', *The Times*, 24 February 1996.

fifty-fold increase), filling St Cuthbert's and the annexe in St Anthony's Hall next door.[6] Watson had turned a dying church into a thriving evangelical stronghold, and all within four years.

This period was marked not only by exponential growth but also by an increase in community involvement. Watson initiated several innovations in church organisation and practice that were designed to include as many of the congregation as possible. Prayer meetings, missions, guest services, creative worship using drama and the arts, banner making and the publication of a church magazine, not only provided legitimating roles for many of the St Cuthbert's congregation, but also served as channels through which the gospel message could be actively lived out and seen to be alive in socially visible forms.

Furthermore, Watson's ministry at St Cuthbert's included a strong social ethic of community, expressed in mutual support – financial, material and pastoral – amongst the congregation. Financial giving, before negligible, became substantial and consistent and David Watson established the October harvest festival as a special time for Christian giving. Before his arrival, in 1963, the average contribution per communicant at the festival was eleven shillings. By 1966, just a year after his arrival, this had risen to seven pounds, eighteen shillings and five pence, a tenfold increase. Levels of giving continued to rise. In between 1966 and 1970, the Easter collection increased fivefold, from just over £26 to £130. David Watson's ministry led people to make greater financial sacrifices in the name of Christian faith, reflecting high levels of commitment to the church and its mission-focused priorities. Cohesion was also fostered through the Thursday evening prayer group, an informal weekly Bible study held in the rectory, which strengthened in-group bonds and attracted further participants from other local churches.[7]

In 1973, the congregation moved wholesale to St Michael-le-Belfrey, another church set for redundancy which had a capacity of 700. Situated in the centre of York city, adjacent to York Minster, Watson perceived the evangelistic potential of the church and eagerly took up his curacy there, taking the existing St Cuthbert's congregation with him. In their first week, the number of communicants increased by 243 and the previous week's collection was multiplied seventy-five times over. Attendances also continued to increase. In 1974, the number of Easter communicants stood at 395, compared with a national average of 98.[8] By 1976, Easter communicants were at 806, and the collection reached £1,225. The church was moving from strength to strength, expanding numerically and establishing itself as a centre of innovation in worship, Christian drama and evangelism.

The various developments that distinguished St Michael's throughout the 1970s have now become the stuff of evangelical folklore, innovations whose influence was far flung and which became instilled in models which inspired many other centres of

---

[6] Gill, *Myth*, p. 243.

[7] Teddy Saunders and Hugh Sansom, *David Watson. A Biography* (London, Sydney, Auckland: Hodder and Stoughton, 1992), pp. 102-6.

[8] Peter Brierley and Heather Wraight (eds), *UK Christian Handbook, 1996/7 Edition* (Bromley: Christian Research, 1995), p. 244.

evangelical revival. Detailed accounts of these innovations can be found in David Watson's books and elsewhere, but it is still worth noting those which have an enduring significance for the ongoing life of the St Michael's congregation. On the one hand, there were efforts to build on the sense of Christian family and interdependence established in St Cuthbert's during the late 1960s. A system of pastoral elders was established in 1970; these, then exclusively male, leaders shared in the spiritual leadership of the church as Watson's missionary work took him increasingly away from the parish. Home groups became more important, and a model of simple community living was practised in a series of 'households' in each of which several members would live together and pool their incomes in order to release others for lay ministry, particularly in drama and music. On the other hand, there was a centrifugal movement, as the church reached out to a wider population and in doing so extended its influence. On his worldwide missions, David Watson was often accompanied by teams from St Michael's, and 'renewal weeks' were run by the church for the benefit of visiting Christian leaders – clergy and lay – who would learn from the example of St Michael's before taking lessons back to their own congregations. The drama teams who accompanied David Watson on his missions eventually formed the Riding Lights Theatre Company, now a leading institution in religious drama. A notable but ill-fated example where the two trends were combined was the Mustard Seed, a Christian café intended to affirm a Christian presence within York city centre, run by a team living together as a St Michael's 'household'.[9] These developments are worth noting not just because they form part of the St Michael's story, but because they form the narrative context within which the endeavours of many long-standing members continue to take place.

In 1982, David Watson left York to focus full-time on his thriving global ministry. He had become an international campaigner for renewal through his numerous publications and highly popular university missions. While responsible for turning St Cuthbert's and St Michael's from flagging into thriving churches, Watson had also set St Michael's within the branches of evangelical legend. Boasting connections with St Mark's, Gillingham, and the origins of charismatic renewal, with John Collins, David Sheppard and later John Wimber, David Watson had moved among the movement's elite. His influence was far-flung and his reputation as an evangelist preceded him. Moreover, his church had achieved a status comparable to his own, and many are still prompted to join St Michael's after being inspired by his writing or reputation. In 1984, he tragically died of cancer. Thousands mourned within York and around the world, lamenting the loss of one of the great leaders within twentieth-century evangelicalism.

---

[9] The Mustard Seed was closed in 1979 after a breakdown in relationships, not unconnected to a disagreement between the elders and those in charge of the project about women's leadership. See Saunders and Sansom, *David Watson*, pp. 151-60, for a more detailed account.

In 1978, Watson had handed over the role of vicar to the Revd Graham Cray.[10] Cray had been northern co-ordinator for the Church Pastoral Aid Society, a St Michael's congregant since 1975 and had subsequently become an established elder in the church with a special interest in relating the gospel to contemporary culture. Whereas both claimed to be charismatic evangelicals, while Watson was an evangelist, Cray was an intellectual. His sermons were academic and involved, intellectually stimulating for some, but bewildering for others. They also adopted different models of leadership. Watson was seen as a spiritual father, a beloved and respected figure who was relied upon for firm theological direction. Cray was a more consensual leader, willing to act as the guiding force behind a myriad of differing viewpoints. He expanded the church eldership and established fixed three-year terms of service, on the understanding that extended regimes of leadership can stifle creativity and make the congregation dependent upon the elders. Revolving responsibilities encouraged a flow of fresh ideas and perspectives and more interdependency,[11] both of which cohered theologically with the church's emerging understanding of charismatic renewal – a way of life that is dynamic and ever seeking out new ways of affirming the gospel.[12] In anticipation of Roger Simpson's approach twenty years later, Cray sought to stimulate creativity by releasing the laity for ministry, and delegated different areas of church life – from youth work to evangelism, pastoral counselling to social responsibility – to individual department heads. The emerging spiritual diversity is recalled by members using the image of a cord of many strands, including the charismatic, the evangelistic, social justice, and the contemplative. Diversity of focus was also matched with a more extensive engagement with cultural developments outside of the church, including the incorporation of insights from psychology and psychotherapy into ministries of healing and pastoral care.[13]

Cray's incumbency also saw an emphasis on the social action of the church within the wider community, and on creative evangelism. He re-established links with other city churches and initiated missionary projects aimed at the reinvigoration of struggling rural parishes in the broader diocese. St Michael's continued to grow during this time, reaching its peak around 1980, when Easter communicants hovered

---

[10] Between 1978 and 1982, Watson held the title of rector, with overall accountability for St Michael's, while Cray served as vicar, responsible for the day to day running of the church. This arrangement was established in response to the increasing demands of David Watson's worldwide ministry, and followed the model pioneered by John Stott and Michael Baughen at All Souls, Langham Place.

[11] An approach described in Graham Cray, 'A Renewed Community as a Sign of the Kingdom: Lessons from St Michael-le-Belfrey, York, England', in Bill Burnett (ed.), *By My Spirit. Renewal in the Worldwide Anglican Church* (London, Sydney, Auckland, Toronto: Hodder and Stoughton, 1988), p. 133.

[12] A vision articulated by Patricia Beall in her 1980 article 'A Place to Grow', in Jeane Hinton (ed.), *Renewal. An Emerging Pattern* (Poole: Celebration Publishing, 1980), pp. 142-7.

[13] Cray, 'A Renewed Community', p. 139.

around the 850-900 mark. Throughout the 1980s, these figures would show a steady but fluctuating decline, reaching 553 in 1989. However, church attendance levels consistently remained well above the national average (see Figure 3).

It was during this time, in the late 1980s, that the 'Warehouse Community' – later to become *Visions* – first emerged. They were heavily inspired by theories of cultural change and were keen to explore how ideas of the 'post-modern' might apply to church. In this respect it was Graham Cray who was their key influence, as it was he who incorporated ideas of postmodernity into sermons and home group teaching. Cray was instrumental in encouraging the group to initiate its worship project and allowed members to relinquish their commitments to St Michael's in order that their vision be fully realised. They established themselves as an 'alternative' service – officially the 'fourth service' of St Michael-le-Belfrey – although they remained a separate initiative in many respects. (See chapter 6 for a full account of the origins and development of the *Visions* group.)

Following Graham Cray's eventual departure to become Principal of Ridley Hall, Cambridge, the Revd David White was appointed vicar of St Michael-le-Belfrey in September 1993. White had trained at the strongly evangelical Oak Hill Theological College in London, and had taken curacies in the South East and London, before working as a team vicar in the Salisbury diocese. His approach to ministry was of a very different style to his predecessor, and some members welcomed a new sense of focus after the diversity of the 1980s. White emphasised a directive authority as church leader and favoured a strict evangelical theology, issued in clear convictions and expressed in a confrontational style of preaching. He introduced the Alpha course to St Michael's and strongly encouraged all members of the congregation to attend a full course. Indeed, he realigned the church home group structure and incorporated Alpha as a new starting point for each group. Soon into his incumbency, David White welcomed the experience of the Toronto Blessing into St Michael's services. Influenced by John Wimber, he expressed a faith in visionary experiences and was keen to express his supernaturalist theology from the pulpit. The congregation were divided in their reactions to this, some embracing the 'Blessing' as a continuation of charismatic renewal, others remaining suspicious of a phenomenon they saw as contrived or hysterical.

This proved to be a difficult time for many people in the St Michael's community. According to current members, the new vicar tended to concentrate his efforts on very specific areas of church life, predominantly charismatic worship and Bible teaching, and his gift for profound theological exposition is recalled fondly by the congregation. Some parishioners felt alienated by the Toronto manifestations. Others took exception to the vicar's views on women's leadership or homosexuality, views that he made quite public, occasionally delivering sermons which some say left the congregation divided. (Both David Watson and Graham Cray, by contrast, had revised their traditional view of women's leadership in the late 1970s, Cray appointing several female curates and lay readers, in addition to elders, during his incumbency.)

On the whole, this period is viewed by church members with significant ambivalence. Some, who shared David White's theological vision, rally to the support of a preacher who, they feel, had passion and conviction; others look back to what they see as a time of division and decline. Although some congregants claimed that many left the church during this time, a mass departure is difficult to detect in the available figures. The electoral roll shows a depletion of sixty-nine names over two years from 1994, but Easter figures suggest an increase of sixty-four communicants for the same period. It is possible that visiting worshippers increased in number while committed members declined. According to some insider accounts, many of those who left were or had been centrally involved in the church leadership structure, suggesting that conflicts between vicar and congregation were at least in part to do with issues of authority. Some were uncomfortable with David White's directive style after Graham Cray's more consensual approach, which was valued partly because it was seen as supporting and continuing the various elements of ministry fostered in David Watson's heyday. Undoubtedly, White's reception was shaped by the fact that he was, effectively, the first entirely new vicar appointed to St Michael's in twenty years and was especially constrained by the expectations of the congregation, who measured his 'fit' with reference to the very different models of leadership established and embedded in the life of the church by his two influential predecessors.

David White left St Michael's in 1999. He was replaced some months later by the Revd Roger Simpson. Converted by John Stott as a young student, Simpson received his clerical training at St John's College, Nottingham, and served his curacy with Stott at All Soul's, Langham Place. Simpson met David Watson on one of his mission events, and asked his advice about what to do next. Encouraged by Watson to 'find an empty church', he did just that, overseeing the rapid expansion of St Paul and St George's, Edinburgh, from around twenty to 800 congregants in ten years. In 1995, Simpson and his family moved to Vancouver, where he served as a parish vicar with the additional responsibility of overseeing the introduction of the Alpha course to Canada.

The appointment of Roger Simpson can be interpreted as an attempt to re-establish St Michael's on a trajectory, combining elements of its ministry under David Watson and Graham Cray twenty years earlier. Simpson embodies the inclusive ecclesiology of Cray – celebrating diversity in worship and devotional practice – together with a thirst for evangelism and outreach. On those issues that have forced division in the past – notably charismatic gifts and women's leadership – he is significantly inclusive, supporting a diversity in charisma and the sharing of authority. Indeed, if there is one value that characterised Roger Simpson's ministry at St Michael's at the turn of the millennium, it was his emphasis on the unity of the church. Immediate innovations were the introduction of a mid-week service and of a monthly prayer meeting which the whole church was strongly encouraged to attend. In 2002, a new female curate was appointed to the church staff.

Although sensitive to the intellectual and cultural complexities of Christian life, Simpson nonetheless preaches an evangelical message characterised by simplicity and passion. He is first and foremost an evangelist, and accordingly his sermons are shot through with the themes of repentance and the need for all to turn to Christ. His teaching draws heavily from biblical texts, but is also illustrated with anecdotal evidence, for the most part based on his own Christian life. Such an approach gives a sense of humanity to his sermons, and his affable demeanour and keen sense of humour follows him to the pulpit.

Reactions to Roger Simpson by the congregation during my research were generally positive. Many commented on his affable personality and his concern to foster unity in the congregation and he is seen by some as a remedy for past divisions. As one long-term parishioner put it, 'Roger is seen as, and is, working to pull things back together again.'

St Michael's has been a centre of charismatic evangelical renewal for the past thirty years. Embracing an evangelical theology and expressive worship, it has enjoyed exponential growth – peaking around the early 1980s – which has kept attendance figures consistently over six times the national average. As a congregation, it has embraced a commitment to fostering community, expressed in home and prayer groups, and a strong sense of mutual support. It has also affirmed its commitment to social action through substantial financial giving. St Michael's has experienced a varied series of leaders: a classical charismatic evangelicalism with Watson, a more liberal, social agenda with Cray, a more doctrinally conservative, supernaturalist theology with White, and a return to diversity and evangelism with Roger Simpson. All four considered themselves to be charismatic evangelicals, and yet adopted very different approaches to leadership.

Growth and Decline

The changing fortunes of the St Michael's congregation are represented in Figure 3. Levels of participation can be gauged using two main sources: the church electoral roll and the service register. The electoral roll lists 'members' of the church, defined as those either living within the parish or who have been attending for six months or more. As it is incumbent upon individuals to sign up to the electoral roll, and as so few attendees actually live within the parish, this is a potentially reliable record of committed members. The service register is the record of communicants at the eucharist, noted down by the presiding clergyman at each service. For this study, I have noted the highest attended service from October of each year.[14] The church address list is also included here, recording all of those who are on church records and who also fill in and return 'welcome cards' at services. This understandably records higher numbers than the other sources as it does not count attendance or rely on any ongoing commitment to the church. Due to the limited availability of records, only recent address list figures are available for comparison.

---

[14] October was chosen for several reasons, not least it is a month without a major festival which might distort the figures and it is within the university academic year, important as students form a significant portion of the congregation.

St Michael-le-Belfry: Blazing the Trail

Figure 3 reveals the extent to which levels of church involvement at St Michael's have consistently outpaced national trends (provided here as the average number of Easter communicants across the Church of England).

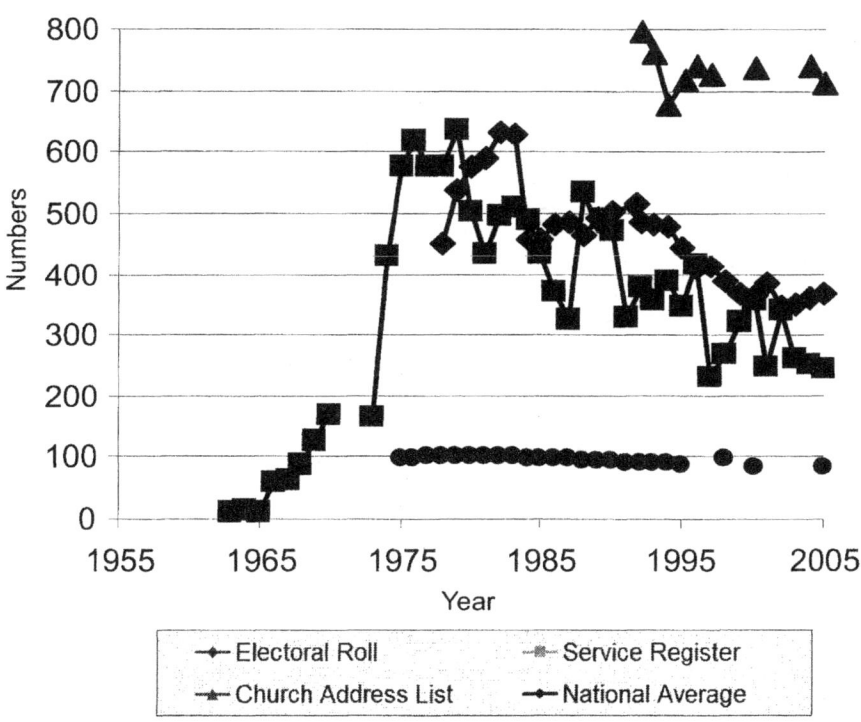

Figure 3: Levels of Involvement at St Michael-le-Belfrey, by Multiple Sources, 1963-2005

If I were to take the St Michael's Easter figures, the gaps are equally striking: four times the national average in 1975; over eight times the national average by 1980. While St Michael's attendances have showed a steady drop since the early 1990s, the gap is still very wide: in 1995, for example, the national average stood at eighty-nine; St Michael's, by stark contrast, drew in 752 worshippers across its three Easter services and had an address list of members running to 712 names.

St Michael's has also consistently outpaced its immediate neighbours. Peter Brierley claims that Yorkshire/Humberside contained one of the lowest proportions of growing churches in the late 1980s (21%)[15] and that during the 1990s there was almost as much decline among evangelicals as non-evangelicals, 'the only region for which this is so'.[16] In 1989, of the eleven Anglican churches in the city, the second most well attended was still less than half as populous as St Michael's and there is little reason to suggest that the situation has changed drastically since. In 1993, Robin Gill noted the mean attendance at Anglican churches in York as 142; meanwhile St Michael's is listed as drawing in as many as 357.[17]

However, while attendance at St Michael's has towered above national and local averages, there has also been significant fluctuation during the period in question. The figures suggest, for example, that the exponential growth of St Cuthbert's during the late 1960s had plateaued by 1970, shifting to massive growth again only after the congregation moved to the St Michael's building in 1973, and there is some evidence of a levelling in attendance soon after that. This lends weight to the argument that growth is limited by the material conditions of the church building, which militates against further expansion once the congregation begins to exceed its resources.[18] The 1970s were certainly a highpoint in attendances for the church, peaking in 1979 with 637 attending the October evening service, but St Michael's has experienced a gradual and uneven decline since then. Taking attendance at its evening service (by far the most popular), levels fell by 6% in the 1980s and by 31% in the 1990s. Brierley's figures suggest that, during the 1980s, St Michael's declined less than the average for Anglican churches in its region (Yorks/Humberside; -26%), less than Anglican churches in England as a whole (-24%), less than levels of decline among all churches in its region (-16%) and less than the measure of national church decline (-13%). During the 1990s, St Michael's attendances declined more than almost all of these comparable variables: by 31% compared to 22% (Anglicans in the region), 23% (Anglicans in England), 33% (churchgoers in the region), 22% (English churchgoers). Decline also exceeded levels of attrition among evangelicals in the region (-29%) and among evangelicals in England (-3%).[19]

While there has been an overall decline in between David Watson's departure in 1982 and 2001 – 39% according to the electoral roll – this has not followed a steady, linear trajectory. The electoral roll figures suggest the 1990s were a period of steady decline (of 24%) but the service register figures suggest a much more uneven pattern. Recent decline has not been a gradual process of attrition, but more of an ebb and

---

[15] Peter Brierley, *Christian England. What the 1989 English Church Census Reveals* (London: MARC Europe, 1991), p. 153.

[16] Peter Brierley, The *Tide is Running Out. What the English Church Attendance Survey Reveals* (London: Christian Research, 2000), p. 65.

[17] Gill, *Myth*, p. 263.

[18] An argument offered by Canon John Poulton, who led the Archbishop's Council on Evangelism's investigation into St Michael-le-Belfrey in 1977. See John Poulton, 'St Michael-le-Belfrey', in Edward England (ed.), *David Watson. A Portrait by his Friends* (Crowborough: Highland Books, 1985), pp. 119-36.

[19] Brierley, *Tide*, pp. 56, 62, 65.

flow shaped by changes in the life of the congregation. Moreover, the fact that decline in the 1990s outpaced average rates of decline among evangelical and non-evangelical Anglican churches in the area, suggests that it is decline attributable to factors specific to St Michael's, and not its environment.

While proportionate decline is unquestionable, St Michael's had achieved such high levels of participation by the mid-1970s that in numerical terms it has continued to outshine its ecclesiastical neighbours by a significant margin. Working from 1998 figures, Peter Brierley claims that only 11% of English churches have a regular congregation of over 301.[20] Although Brierley also claims that evangelical churches have, on average, the largest congregations, this average amounts to a weekly attendance of only ninety-seven.[21] Therefore, St Michael's is not only thriving by national standards, but also by the standards of the evangelical community at large.

Internal explanations of the meteoric rise of St Michael's inevitably focus on the charisma and magnanimous Christianity of David Watson and subsequent success has undoubtedly built on his innovations in worship, evangelism and small group fellowship. His biographers make an important point in highlighting factors of accessibility, informality and relational care. Watson's key early innovation was the family service, including a short, simple sermon using visual aids, intended to be relevant for all ages.[22] Until very recently, St Michael did not have anything resembling a Sunday school, on the understanding that children are not merely part of tomorrow's church, they are also an important part of today's, and should therefore be included in Sunday services as much as possible. Instead, a series of age-related mid-week groups met for teaching, fellowship and shared ministry. This policy seems to have worked: a 1998 survey of evangelical churches revealed that Sunday schools had, on average, thirty children;[23] by contrast, around the same time, St Michael's had no less than 225 individuals on its youth and children's prayer list.[24]

Of course, this is not the same thing as claiming that St Michael's has contributed to church growth as a whole. Anecdotal evidence suggests that much early growth was through transfer, drawing criticisms of 'poaching' from church leaders and in the local press.[25] Robin Gill considers the alternative possibility that it has been high attendances at St Michael's which have ensured that 'the overall Anglican churchgoing rate in York declined so little between 1969 and 1989'. Figures show a slight decline in churchgoing from 3.5% to 3.4% of the population,

---

[20] Brierley, *Tide*, p. 47.
[21] Brierley, *Tide*, p. 53.
[22] Saunders and Sansom, *David Watson*, p. 102-6.
[23] Brierley, *Tide*, p. 169.
[24] St Michael's has since adopted a different model, with Sunday teaching aimed specifically at young people taking place in classes held in parallel to, but partially separate from Sunday services. However, these are held in addition to, rather than in replace of, the evening youth meetings held for specific age groups during the week.
[25] Gill, *Myth*, p. 243.

contrasting with a national slide of 3.5% to 2.4%. However, this assumes that the entire St Michael's congregation resides within the city boundaries, whereas many members actually travel from further a field. It also assumes that members would not have otherwise gone to church.[26] The picture is inconclusive, and recent trends such as cross-attendance, mid-week rather than Sunday attendance and the high mobility of middle-class attendees further complicate the issue. A consideration of why St Michael's has grown and declined in the way it has will be offered in chapter 8, in light of the subsequent analysis of congregational culture.

Who Goes to St Michael's?

After spending some time with the St Michael's congregation, I attempted to piece together a picture of its demographic make-up. Running through the current address list with, first, the church administrator, and then two further long-standing members of the congregation, helped me to match names with categories of age and occupation. This information is here supplemented with data gathered *via* a questionnaire survey of the congregation which was administered just after Easter, 2000.

Working with this data, the gender divide in St Michael's worked out at 60% female, 40% male. This reflects national trends, recent figures suggesting that women make up in between 61 and 65% of the English churches.[27] According to the year 2000 church address list, 19% of these women were above retirement age and 26% were students. Of those women of a working age who were not in education, only 16% were housewives. 6% were unemployed, with the remainder (78%) working in various white collar jobs and service occupations, with a few professionals. 13% were teachers. The majority of women in St Michael's did not appear to conform to the traditional evangelical model of the domestic homemaker.

National figures suggest that many churches have an ageing population, with the elderly often outnumbering the young. In 1998, 25% of all churchgoers were over sixty-five while 9% were in their twenties. The figures were 21% and 10% for the evangelical churches.[28] This trend is turned on its head at St Michael's: in 2000, around 38% of its members were in their twenties and 16% were over sixty. The distribution across the middle age brackets was fairly even: 16% in their thirties, 16% in their forties, and 13% in their fifties. The majority of the congregation were young and active, with only 16% retired from work.

Because of its high percentage of students, only 52% of the congregation were employed. 5% were professionals, mainly doctors, accountants and university lecturers. 8% were employed in manual work, chiefly skilled occupations such as

---

[26] Gill, *Myth*, p. 244.

[27] Churches Information for Mission, *Faith in Life. A Snapshot of Church Life at the Beginning of the 21st Century* (London: Churches Information for Mission, 2001), p. 9, and Heather Wraight, *Eve's Glue. The Role Women Play in Holding the Church Together* (Carlisle: Paternoster Press, 2001) p. 21.

[28] Brierley, *Tide*, p. 93.

plumbing or farming. The remaining 39% virtually all worked in the service professions, either as managers, administrators or in the public sector. Many were nurses, teachers, civil servants or worked in computing. 3% of the congregation in 2000 were unemployed.

In terms of its ethnic make-up, St Michael's is a predominantly white church. This was so overwhelmingly apparent from my fieldwork that I did not enquire about ethnicity in the questionnaire or through the address list analysis. There were a handful of students from the Far East in the congregation, as well as probably two or three of African origin, but the majority – perhaps as much as 99% – were white and British.[29]

By far the largest occupational grouping is that of student, with 29% of the congregation active in higher education. In addition to this, many older members have also passed through the university system. According to the questionnaire survey, in 2000 40% of the congregation *already* held a university degree, compared with around 15% of the UK's white population.[30] 9% of the congregation also held postgraduate degrees. If these figures are added to address list data, then assuming the two data sets are compatible and equally representative of the congregation, we arrive at the striking conclusion that almost 70% of the congregation had either passed through or were currently engaged in higher education. This adds weight to the argument that this is an overwhelmingly middle-class church, and has been for some time. It also tells us something about the social networks in which many congregants have moved.

Also noteworthy are the 24% who had received post-school religious education. This ranged from diplomas at Bible college, Christian counselling courses to several who had taken a Church of England reader's certificate. The crucial point is that most of these are not taken for professional reasons, but as further channels for the strengthening of one's faith life. Parishioners seek spiritual enhancement and faith development through scholarly reading and taught classes, a trend that reflects their class status and in turn, the way in which they make sense of their Christian identity.

While recognised as a charismatic evangelical church and for the most part attended with this in mind, St Michael's attracts a fairly broad selection of Christians. Only two in the survey sample claimed to have never attended church regularly before attending St Michael's. Of the remainder, 33% had an exclusively Anglican background, while the majority – 63% – had attended churches of various denominations during their lifetime. 79% had attended church during their childhood, and 42% claimed this was an evangelical church. 97% had been baptised – 66% as

---

[29] This picture has changed somewhat since my original research, following the establishment in 2004 of a service specifically aimed at the local Chinese population. However, by the following year, attendance levels at this service were still only around the twenty-five mark, well under 5% of those on the address list.

[30] Jill Matheson and Carol Summerfield (eds), *Social Trends, no. 31* (London: The Stationery Office, 2001), p. 69.

infants, 21% as adults. 9% had been baptised as both. 64% had been confirmed as members of the Church of England.

Asked how they would describe their Christian identity, 18% said 'Anglican', 27% 'evangelical' and 37% 'charismatic evangelical'. The remainder gave other responses, or just preferred 'Christian'. A similar diversity presents itself in relation to conversion experiences: 40% claimed they had always been a Christian, 21% reported a gradual development into a life of faith, and 39% converted to Christianity after a 'born again' experience which marked a radical turning point.

As a consequence of its location and of the mobility of its members, very few St Michael's members actually live near to the church building. Its fame and evangelical identity also predispose St Michael's to function as what some have called a 'gathered congregation', typically recruiting people who align themselves with its professed values and theology, rather than those who reside within the immediate vicinity of the church building.[31] In the year 2000, there were 365 people on the church electoral roll, but only six of them lived within the parish boundaries. The questionnaire data suggests that in 2000 only 21% of the congregation lived in the city centre, with nearly 18% living more than five miles away.[32] One of the clergy claimed that congregants travel from within a twenty mile radius of the church building, and the address list reflects this, listing residents of Malton, Selby and Harrogate. The global reputation of St Michael's also regularly attracts a high number of visitors to its services, some from overseas, who are either passing through York as tourists or living temporarily in the city.

Geographical dispersion is matched by a high turnover. In 2000, over 10% of the congregation had been regularly attending for less than twelve months, and another 24% had attended for less than five years. A partially overlapping 24% had lived locally for less than five years. These features are in part a consequence of the geographical and class mobility of the congregation.[33] Many are newcomers to the

---

[31] See Mathew Guest, 'Reconceiving the Congregation as a Source of Authenticity', in J Garnet *et al* (eds.), *Redefining Christian Britain. Post-1945 Perspectives* (London: SCM Press, 2007), pp. 64-5.

[32] Surveys of the congregation conducted by the St Michael's leadership suggest that, in the years subsequent to my fieldwork, the church has begun to attract even more attendees from within a wider geographical radius. For example, in 2005, based on a sample of 592 questionnaire returns, gathered from across all six of its Sunday services, it was found that 37% of the congregation lived more than five miles from the church building.

[33] The report on St Michael's issued by the Archbishops' Council on Evangelism contains evidence that high mobility was a feature of a significant portion of the congregation at least as early as 1977. For example, they found that nearly 60% of the congregation had been in their present place of residence for less than four years, and many had moved house several times in recent years. However, it is not clear whether the evidence points to an early elective parochialism, as many of those who had recently moved had done so within the immediate neighbourhood, rather than from elsewhere in the UK. The report does reveal a different connection between domestic mobility and congregational culture, though, in that a high proportion of the leadership claimed to

area, whose jobs may also take them on to new locations in the not so distant future. The high proportion of undergraduates carries the same implications and attendance levels fluctuate with the university terms. In 1998, attendance levels at the evening service dropped by 32% for August but picked up again by mid-September.

St Michael's appears to incorporate a high proportion (perhaps 40 or 50% if one includes students) of what some sociologists have called 'elective parochials'.[34] According to a common description of late modern culture, one of the consequences of social mobility and perpetual uprootedness is the lack of an enduring place in any community. Elective parochials attempt to re-create the connections and relationships of community life by forging temporary allegiances with local institutions, one option being the church. The most significant consequence of this is the attenuated nature of commitment that such allegiances foster, not least because they are recognised as temporary. For example, many individuals may be unable or unwilling to engage in church involvement which makes demands on time outside of Sunday worship. This is a visible feature of congregational life in St Michael's and a problem noted by church leaders. While the fostering of Christian community is a shared priority, it is a project that is subject to the limitations that elective parochialism brings. As one member of the St Michael's leadership put it,

> St Michael's is a great place. There is a lot going for it. But, it isn't what you might call a real ... church ... because we have an eclectic congregation. It comes in, it listens to what it wants to listen [to], it puts into practice what it wants to put into practice, and the rest is thrown out. Because, we don't see one another from week to week. We meet on a Sunday, have a great time, and then we go into our worlds, and we meet again on Sunday. Don't we have community?

St Michael's has a distinctive demographic profile. Turnover of younger parishioners is quite high because of the significant student population, but the church also retains a large number of long-standing members. The gender divide reflects the national profile and the church boasts a disproportionately high number of young people in their twenties, in contrast to the ageing population of the church in general. The majority of the congregation are of a middle class background, mostly working in non-manual, and often service-oriented, careers. The vast majority have enjoyed a university education. The social mobility of the congregation is reflected in the high turnover of members and in the distances which many travel to attend church. The elective parochialism that this generates inevitably limits the

---

have moved house to be closer to the church and 'in response to divine guidance'. See 'Report from The Archbishops' Council on Evangelism Team which had Studied the Life of the Congregation of St Michael-le-Belfrey Church, York in November 1977', p. 2.

[34] See Steven M. Tipton, *Getting Saved from the Sixties. Moral Meaning in Conversion and Cultural Change* (Berkeley and Los Angeles, CA: University of California Press, 1982), and Warner, *New Wine in Old Wine Skins*.

fostering of community relationships among congregational members,[35] so what does this mean for a church that has for so long emphasised the importance of a strong community and of evangelical activism? Within the general context of congregational life, what does it mean to be a committed member of St Michael-le-Belfrey?

Community and Commitment

Given the discrepancies between address list and attendance figures, it is fair to say that St Michael's has a large active body of over 700 people, but a regular Sunday attendance of around 300. One interpretation might refer to the elective parochials who show less commitment to church life, though the evidence is inconclusive. The church may be viewed in terms of two overlapping populations: those who are connected to the church in a general sense, including committed members and occasional attendees (altogether and henceforth referred to as *the congregation*), and those who are committed members, attend regularly, are involved in church government and administration and whose membership extends well beyond attendance at Sunday services. Such a distinction between core and periphery is discernible within congregational life, and the variety of church activities at St Michael's allows different kinds of commitment to flourish and be recognised. In addition to Sunday and mid-week services, St Michael's organises home groups, Alpha courses, prayer meetings and other social gatherings all on a regular basis. 'Members' of the church measure their Christian devotion and community participation within a broader frame of reference than that offered by the Sunday service.

As far as Sunday services are concerned, in 1999 St Michael's held four. Traditional morning worship was at 9.15am; the family service, including all-age teaching and light-hearted sermons for children was at 11am; and at 7pm was the evening service, a more charismatic celebration which has consistently proved the most popular of the three. *Visions* held evening services three Sundays a month in the nearby St Cuthbert's centre. At the time of fieldwork they took three forms: a multi-media communion service on the first Sunday of each month; the prayer installation of the labyrinth on the second;[36] and an upbeat dance service on the third. Communion was held at one of the four services each week, on a rotational basis. Attendance levels for 1999 are given below.

---

[35] An issue negotiated to some degree through the church's network of small group meetings, explored in chapter 7.

[36] Modelled on the medieval labyrinth in Chartres Cathedral, the labyrinth has been used by *Visions*, as with many other alt.worship groups, as an aid to prayer and meditation. Slowly and silently, participants traverse the complex floor pattern at their own pace, pausing at the centre in a symbolic meeting with God. See Mathew Guest, "'Alternative Worship': Challenging the Boundaries of the Christian Faith', in E. Arweck and M. Stringer (eds.), *Theorising Faith. The Insider/Outsider Problem in the Study of Ritual* (Birmingham: University of Birmingham Press, 2002), pp. 46-7.

Service	Average weekly attendance, 1999
9:15am	110
Family	180
Evening	275
Visions	20 (estimate)

Table 1: Average Attendance at each of the services at St Michael-le-Belfrey, 1999. (source: service register)[37]

In addition to the Sunday events, a Wednesday lunchtime service was introduced in October 1999. According to Peter Brierley, 42% of English churches now hold a mid-week service, average attendance being just twenty-one people in 1998 (actually increasing to twenty-nine by 2005).[38] The attendance at the St Michael's mid-week service started at around forty, but saw a subsequent steady increase, reaching fifty-eight by February 2000. The description of an evening service in the prologue illustrates the many opportunities afforded within services for lay leadership; the various roles – from leading worship and giving Bible readings to running the crèche or manning the bookstall – are shared and different parishioners occupy different roles each week. Prayers are not only read but also composed by a different person at every service, thereby offering a channel of empowerment and opportunity for a public expression of personal values. In 2000, 51% of the congregation said they had given a reading in church at some point. In the years since then, lay empowerment has become an even greater priority for the church, and the minutes of the Annual Parochial Church Council Meeting report that, by 2005, almost 200 people were in leadership roles across the St Michael's community (nearly 30% of those on the address list).

In keeping with evangelical tradition, the members of St Michael's believe that the Christian life carries practical demands which extend well beyond Sunday services. According to the pastoral co-ordinator, in 2000, around 63% of the congregation were involved in a home group. As mentioned earlier on, these have a long history, originating in an initiative in the 1960s to foster Bible study, prayer and fellowship apart from Sunday worship. A by-product has been a strong

---

[37] The problem of multiple attendance is difficult to gauge. Estimates from the church leadership suggest that around 20% of the congregation regularly attend more than one service; my own questionnaire survey suggested that over 50% do. Observation of service attendance during fieldwork gave me the impression that at least 20% attended more than one service, possibly many more, although I would be surprised if the actual figure was as high as 50%. In this case, the small size of my survey sample may have distorted the emerging figures.

[38] Brierley, *Tide*, p. 157; *Pulling Out of the Nosedive. A Contemporary Picture of Churchgoing* (London: Christian Research, 2006), p. 215.

community ethic and sense of practical moral responsibility among members of the congregation. At the time of my research, the network of St Michael's home groups functioned according to a variety of different arrangements: some were based around an area, drawing in parishioners living locally; other regular meetings were based on interest or gender. There was a men's group, a women's group, numerous general prayer meetings, and each of the worship bands met as a home group to rehearse and pray together. Each home group had around fifteen members, although regular attendance could average out at much lower than this. All centred on weekly Bible study and prayer, although some also incorporated sung worship and charismatic gifts. Questionnaire returns suggest that 67% of the congregation had led a home group meeting at some point; 45% prayed in groups on a weekly basis. Although anecdotal evidence suggests that home groups were not as popular or as active as they were during the 1970s, participation was still a majority pursuit. The fact that a clear majority claimed to have led meetings in the past suggests a strong ethic of shared lay leadership and of commitment to home groups across the congregation.[39]

The Alpha course offers further opportunities for involvement. By 2000, three courses were being held each year and a new daytime course was established for those unable to attend during the evenings. According to my questionnaire survey, 73% of the congregation had completed the course. More importantly, 16% had been a leader on an Alpha course at some point; 19% had functioned as a Christian helper, assuming a supportive role in discussion groups. Significantly, Alpha appeared to be less a means of successful evangelism and more a focus of strong commitment and cohesion among existing members, reflecting what Stephen Hunt has discovered about Alpha on a national scale.[40] Although total attendance on St Michael's courses had seen a steady rise over five years (from fifty-four in 1995/6 to 113 in 1999/2000), helpers and existing Christians made up a large proportion of these numbers. According to internal church reports, only around 60% of participants usually complete Alpha, while conversations in the field suggested that a great number of St Michael's members had actually participated in the course several times. While outsiders are seeping through, there appears to be no shortage of lay evangelists, ready to take up the course for a second or third time.

Practical commitment extends beyond the confines of church events and informs the behaviour of individuals within 'secular' contexts. In particular, individual members often feel it their duty to speak about their faith to outsiders with a mind to bringing them to Christ. Evangelism is practised on an everyday basis, and a gently interrogative style of informal conversation before and after Sunday services was encountered repeatedly by the author. When asked in 2000, 82% of the congregation claimed to have invited a friend to a St Michael's service at some point. 34% claimed they had been responsible for someone new joining the church. However, it is important to note that not all members appear equally comfortable with pressing

---

[39] The incorporation of cell church principles into St Michael's has transformed its home group structure post-2000, this being described in more detail in the Epilogue.

[40] See the discussion of Alpha in chapter 2, and Stephen Hunt, *The Alpha Enterprise. Evangelism in a Post-Christian Era* (Aldershot: Ashgate, 2004), p. 171.

an evangelical message onto their non-churchgoing friends and associates. While many still invite colleagues and co-students, they often attempt to maintain a 'no pressure' approach, minimising conversionism while highlighting the less confrontational aspects of services such as sung worship. A gentility is evident in shared attitudes, especially among the young, who, wary of popular stereotypes of the zealous Christian, are conscious that in issuing invitations to services they may be judged by non-Christians as well-meaning, but also as oppressive and sanctimonious. As a consequence, the friendship evangelism described in chapter 2 is very much in evidence, reflected in an urge to convey warmth and hospitality over ideological difference, and to spread Christian values *via* relationships, rather than by seeking radical changes in the lives of one's peers. However, the urge to build up the fellowship remains, even if the methods employed to achieve this have become somewhat tempered. Indeed, the 'culture of invitation' consciously fostered by St Michael's in more recent years is premised on creating a welcome space for those outside of the church, even if made sense of internally as a form of evangelism.

Commitment to St Michael's is also expressed financially. I was told by the leadership in 2000 that around 100 members of the congregation regularly 'covenant', giving a large proportion – perhaps 10% – of their income. By 2002, this applied to 170 members. According to the questionnaire survey, in 2000, 42% of the congregation donated 9% or more of their gross income each month. The accuracy of this figure is of course subject to the honesty of congregants although, during fieldwork, there were other clear signs that financial giving was high. According to the Annual Finance Report, in 1999-2000 the total unrestricted income of the church was £404,000. £368,949 of this was listed as 'voluntary income'. £80,000 alone was raised at the annual 'Gift Day', a sum earmarked for the church hall renovations. Taking the 2000 address list as an index of membership, these figures amounted to an average annual donation of almost £500 per member. Anecdotal evidence strongly suggests that the distribution of donations is skewed: some parishioners – especially those registered with the 'covenanting' system – donate a lot more than others. However, these exceptionally high figures alone are sufficient enough to demonstrate the generally high degree of financial commitment within the church. The report by the Archbishops' Council on Evangelism (ACE) in 1977 claimed that, when corrected to take into account inflation, levels of giving in St Michael's were actually falling.[41] The available figures for more recent years are inconclusive, but a comparison of average levels of giving per parishioner in the early 1970s with levels in the late 1990s suggests that, in real terms, financial giving has significantly declined.

The members of St Michael's express their commitment to its mission and evangelical identity through high attendances, consistent and time-consuming practical effort, and substantial financial sacrifice. By its own standards, in 2000 there were certainly signs of depression: fewer home groups, generally lower

---

[41] Teddy Saunders and Hugh Sansom, *David Watson. A Biography* (London, Sydney, Auckland: Hodder and Stoughton, 1992), pp. 143-4.

attendances, levels of financial giving lower in real terms, possibly fewer outreach projects. And yet this remains a church that elicits significantly high degrees of commitment from its members, on a level that is unheard of in most Anglican circles. However, as a community it also functions in a peculiar way, shaped not least by the demography of its membership, its established reputation as a centre of evangelical revival and its diverse network of meetings, which extends the range of channels through which the commitment of members is expressed. All of these factors foster a congregation which is characterised by a desire for and perception of unity, cohesion and direction, while at the same time appearing somewhat fragmented, and this arrangement has a profound impact on how the beliefs and values of the congregation are expressed and maintained, as will be explored in later chapters.

We have seen how the members of St Michael's invest a great deal in their Christian identities, expressed in various ways but manifest in a strong sense of community. The *Visions* group appeared in some respects as a microcosm of this larger collective, but in other ways they have developed a different experience of community among their members, focused more on the aesthetic demands of worship, mutual member support and wider reaching ethical projects (see chapter 6). However, these are all Christians who embrace a religious identity that appears to absorb a large portion of their time, and to create channels of practical activity in the name of the gospel. This inevitably helps to forge strong bonds of friendship and effective support networks among the congregation. Members tended to meet with other parishioners outside of church, and some saw St Michael's as the centre of their social as well as religious life. Indeed, the ACE report's comment that for some, being a member of St Michael's appeared to be a 'full time occupation' was arguably as accurate in 2000 as it was in the late 1970s.[42] However, the scale of St Michael's can militate against the maintenance of a strong sense of cohesion, thus, while levels of commitment appear to be high, St Michael's fails to maintain hard social boundaries around its membership, and its strong activist ethic must be viewed alongside an evident differentiation of participation by core and periphery.

The history and demographic make-up of St Michael-le-Belfrey reflect wider trends in the evangelical movement. As it has grown it has absorbed the movements that often engender liberalisation – including creative evangelism and worship – and has embraced charismatic renewal, which has fostered both a diversity of spirituality and a more directive, theatrical spiritual style, depending on changing trends. It attracts a predominantly middle class, educated congregation, characterised by some authors as the 'knowledge class'[43] who are conceived as a major vehicle for modern values, such as individualism, tolerance and an openness to new ideas and to intellectual enquiry. These are qualities that have not always sat comfortably within the evangelical fold but which, according to studies such as Hunter's, have increasingly penetrated the

---

[42] See 'Report from The Archbishops' Council on Evangelism', p. 8.

[43] Robert Wuthnow *et al*, *Cultural Analysis. The Work of Peter L. Berger, Mary Douglas, Michel Foucault and Jurgen Habermas* (London, Boston, MA, Melbourne and Henley: Routledge and Kegan Paul, 1984), p. 69.

evangelical subculture since the mid-twentieth century, bringing about a liberalisation of evangelical Christianity. This inevitably prompts the question: to what extent has a liberalisation of tradition taken place within St Michael's, and how has this affected the cohesion of the church and the beliefs of the congregation? These questions will be addressed in detail in the following two chapters.

CHAPTER 4

Holding the Many Strands Together: Community and Diversity

'St Mike's is a bit liberal for me...'

When I first interviewed him early in 2000, James had been attending St Michael's for several years. Initially only attending to accompany his wife, he had since been employed by the church in a pastoral role, his primary responsibility being the extensive home group network. James was twenty-five at the time, has a university degree in sports science and is trained as a school teacher. He comes from what he describes as a 'conservative evangelical' background. As a Christian, he places most emphasis upon the authority of the Bible and measures all other things against this. Correspondingly, he objects to Christians who reject aspects of scripture that do not match cultural convention. He does not believe in infant baptism and is unconcerned with denominational identity, affirming a strong belief in salvation by faith alone as expressed in a mature and considered confession of Christian commitment. James believes that women should not occupy positions of headship in the church or in the household as they are 'designed emotionally [and] physically for different roles' and, more importantly, because this is what the scriptures teach. He also claims that evil has its origins in the Garden of Eden, and believes in the devil as a fallen angel who functions as a force of evil in today's world. He is personally uncomfortable with the use of charismatic gifts in church, but puts this down to a matter of individual spiritual style. As he stresses, 'I see God through understanding His word.'

James expresses a classically evangelical set of values, a moral and religious conservatism that we might expect to find in an evangelical church. He leans towards a conservative evangelical rather than charismatic evangelical stance, but does not perceive any serious theological divergence between the two. However, I was surprised to discover that James actually considered St Michael's to be excessively liberal. He saw a significant diversity of values expressed by the congregation and viewed this as a problem, commenting that he would rather see the church commit to a more narrowly defined theological agenda. He had also been surprised and disappointed with how liberal many of the home group leaders were. In his opinion, they followed their 'feelings' rather than the scriptures. He had encouraged the leadership to compose a 'mission statement' that church members would be asked to sign up to, but implies that he is fighting a losing battle. He saw himself as a radical on the periphery of the church – not alone, but certainly in the minority. James also saw Roger Simpson's style of leadership as far too consensual, claiming that he is trying to please everybody. He would prefer a far more uncompromising and directional headship. He even went as far as to question the evangelical identity of the church. 'What I see is not evangelical', he said, referring to what he sees as an insufficiently biblical approach to Christian faith, instead describing St Michael's as 'liberal charismatic', adding, with some humour, that he would 'probably get shot for that!'

James's comments alerted me to a number of important features of congregational life. In spite of the claims of the new vicar, spiritual diversity was not affirmed as a positive feature by everyone in St Michael's and for a significant number it signalled a loss of direction. There was a discernible, though not destructive, tension between parishioners who embraced a broad vision of evangelical spirituality – including a celebration of the many routes into faith and many ways of expressing it – and those who favoured a more narrowly defined approach. This very much reflects differences of opinion about the styles of former leaders, summarised in the previous chapter. Those favouring a more narrowly defined faith, uncompromising and moving in a single and clear direction lamented the loss of David White, while others welcomed the more inclusive embrace of diversity advocated by Graham Cray and currently by Roger Simpson. Interestingly, the memory of David Watson's ministry was drawn from by members at all points on the theological spectrum. Some preferred to focus on his passion to find ever more novel ways of expressing the gospel and his willingness to change his mind when faced with fresh experiences and new theological arguments; others emphasised a clear theological purpose and simple affirmation of the gospel that was invoked in order to distinguish Watson from more exploratory or intellectual styles of ministry.

The adjective 'evangelical' was clearly understood in different ways by different members of the congregation. The perspectives that James viewed as overly liberal, and insufficiently Biblical to be counted as 'evangelical', were embraced by others as signs of an authentically evangelical faith, especially in so far as 'evangelical' was taken to mean 'alive' and therefore 'culturally engaged'. From an objective viewpoint, the very diversity signalled by such patterns of usage suggests that the congregation has indeed become 'liberalised' to a considerable degree. In other words, this lack of agreement on matters of belief and doctrine implies either erosion in the number of congregants prepared to conform to a single, authoritative body of ideas, or else the general absence of an authoritative body of ideas altogether. Either way, James's comments point to the broadening, 'softening' and diversifying of the evangelical belief system that James Davison Hunter associates with a general accommodation to the norms of secular modernity. This chapter attempts to map this process more precisely by gauging patterns of belief and degrees of diversity within the St Michael's congregation. The picture presented will primarily be based on the situation at the turn of the millennium, when my field research was first carried out, although it is impossible to understand contemporary trends without looking also to past developments. Later on, we will also examine how St Michael's has evolved since the year 2000, and hence will be able to see whether dominant trends identified then have persisted to the present day.

What it Means to be Liberal

'Liberal' is a difficult concept, conveying numerous meanings. It has always carried notions of freedom, developed positively as generosity and negatively as lack of restraint. The political sense emerged in the early nineteenth century, focusing upon the freedoms of individuals, and in the USA it continues to carry overtones of the progressive or radical, serving as the foil for political and religious conservatives.[1] Within evangelical rhetoric, it has long been a dirty word, carrying connotations of compromise and capitulation to secular values. In theology, it stands for a positive engagement with the norms of modern knowledge.[2] Amongst sociologists, uses have been similar, though less obviously value-laden, suggesting an effort to engage with and adapt to an often-changing culture.[3] As this inevitably involves a broadening in orientation, liberalisation might be defined as a move from a narrow to a more open position. In Hunter's terms, it is to re-draw the boundaries of a social group in a way that leaves them less narrowly circumscribed.[4]

In his book on the changing values of American evangelicals, *Evangelicalism. The Coming Generation*, James Davison Hunter uncovers a relaxation of the boundaries of evangelical religion. He argues that there has been a move away from an understanding of the Bible and evangelical tradition as external, non-negotiable authorities. Instead, evangelicals are becoming more tolerant of non-Christians, less rigid in their readings of the scriptures and more open to possibilities of change within the evangelical worldview.

Hunter's argument is that the boundaries of evangelical tradition are suffering from a gradual erosion in the face of modernity. Moreover, he claims that evangelicalism is incapable of reinforcing these boundaries, for three reasons. First, an 'ethic of civility' has pervaded the evangelical subculture. Originating in the political sphere, there has, over the course of the twentieth century, emerged a code of civility that, while acknowledging radical differences of opinion, also encourages the acceptance of the right of others to hold opinions that diverge from one's own. This has passed into the religious sphere, so that evangelicals are compelled to be not only tolerant of others' beliefs, but also *tolerable to* others. 'Anything that hints of moral or religious absolutism and intolerance is underplayed.'[5] In this sense, the open public affirmation of firm boundaries of belief is implicitly discouraged.

Second, a decreasing number of evangelicals actually believe in the sanctity of these boundaries. This is especially the case with respect to scripture, no longer perceived as issuing demands that are objective and binding, but rather as offering guidelines, the meaning of which is generally apprehended as symbolic and

---

[1] Raymond Williams, *Keywords. A Vocabulary of Culture and Society* (London: Fontana, 1976), pp. 179-81.

[2] Stanley J. Grenz and Roger E. Olson, *20th Century Theology. God and the World in a Transitional Age* (Carlisle: Paternoster Press, 1992), pp. 51-62.

[3] Steve Bruce, *Firm in the Faith* (Aldershot: Gower, 1984), p. 90.

[4] James Davison Hunter, *Evangelicalism. The Coming Generation* (Chicago, IL, and London: University of Chicago Press, 1987), pp. 19-20.

[5] Hunter, *Evangelicalism*, p. 183.

subjective. Third, there is no longer any binding consensus on what these boundaries actually are. As Hunter puts it,

> From all indications the pluralism of opinion over theological, moral, familial, and political issues in Evangelicalism (already wide-ranging) is expanding and not coalescing into a new consensus.[6]

While the arguments in Hunter's book have since been challenged by subsequent empirical evidence,[7] his theoretical framework remains useful, particularly within the UK context, where the cultural forces of pluralism and 'civility' are arguably more pervasive than they are in the USA. In many respects, Hunter's case echoes H. Richard Niebuhr's famous argument that, as religious groups grow, they experience a transition from sect into denomination, the latter characterised by a greater accommodation to external forces. Niebuhr isolates three main pressures which drive this process: younger generations become less committed as they inherit rather than choose religious identity; increasing wealth and status makes worldly accommodation more likely; and the necessary development of a more formal leadership and organisational structure 'subverts the initial radical impetus'.[8] These pressures may, with some qualification, be mapped onto the development of St Michael-le-Belfrey, charted in the preceding chapter. A moribund church was revitalised by a charismatic leader who attracted many new members. He introduced a charismatic evangelical model of faith and encouraged strong community ties which in some ways may be characterised as sectarian. Teaching was conservative and stressed the boundaries between saved and unsaved. Participation was regular and extended outside Sunday worship and the congregation was close-knit and interdependent. Subsequent years have seen a greater influx of middle class members, a high turnover of members and several changes in leadership. St Michael's has increasingly engaged in dialogue with external agencies: ecumenical dialogue, university links, local social aid projects and creative evangelism. The 1980s marked a peak in what members refer to as a great spiritual diversity, a 'cord made of many strands': charismatic spirituality, the contemplative tradition, evangelical biblicism and social justice. The deep-seated entrenchment of this broad agenda was made apparent through the more conservative reforms of the early 1990s, which provoked significant dissonance among the congregation. Within the present life of St Michael's, correlations can be made with developments across the British evangelical movement, discussed in chapter 2 in terms of a broadening of horizons and charted in local detail in the preceding chapter.

But a further comment must be made about the way that the people of St Michael's feel their church deals with the outside world, relating to the notion of

---

[6] Hunter, *Evangelicalism*, p. 185.

[7] See James M. Penning and Corwin E. Smidt, *Evangelicalism. The Next Generation* (Grand Rapids, MI: Baker Academic, 2002).

[8] Steve Bruce, *God is Dead. Secularization in the West* (Oxford: Blackwell, 2002), p. 24.

cultural relevance. Returns from the questionnaire survey I administered around Easter 2000 suggest that being 'culturally relevant' is a priority among congregants. 73% of the sample felt that 'thinking through the Gospel message in order to relate it to your own culture and personal situation' is 'very important'. This scored higher than 'caring for the homeless' (42%), 'providing a moral example' (67%) and even 'telling others about Jesus' (69%). The only task ranked more important was reading the Bible (82%).

However, despite its reputation for remaining at the cutting edge of the evangelical movement in terms of innovation and creativity, many members felt that St Michael's was falling short of its ideals. During interviews, I asked parishioners whether they thought the church as a whole related well to culture. Every one of them responded in the negative, claiming that the church could, and should, do a whole lot more in its efforts to be 'culturally relevant'. Only 37% of the questionnaire sample felt that sermons in St Michael's adequately dealt with contemporary culture. There was a widespread view that, in order to be a successful church and grow, St Michael's would need to change itself in order to meet the needs of the unchurched. As one parishioner put it,

> ... there's a hunger for spirituality out there but the church is not meeting it ... and there are more and more people out there, and they're not going to fit into church. We must get to the point where, you know, church has to fit them.

Clearly, Dave Tomlinson's argument that the church must adapt to its postmodern context would carry some weight among the St Michael's congregation. To be fair, this does not tend to generate a radical theology as 'cultural relevance' is often embraced only in so far as it serves the more fundamental aims of evangelism and growth. The value of cultural dialogue is measured by the degree to which it attracts the unchurched, rather than the degree to which it offers meaning to those already within the faith, or indeed, those at its margins.

Most St Michael's parishioners would not go as far as the post-evangelicals, but they generally recognised a need to adopt an orientation to contemporary culture characterised by tempered accommodation and acclimatisation. The medium should change but not the essential message – in theological terms, being 'in the world, but not of the world'. However, as argued in chapter 2, the relationship between medium and message is far more complex, and changes in expression inevitably filter into the formulation and maintenance of shared beliefs and values. We might assume from this that, not only is St Michael's demographically predisposed to a liberal evangelical outlook (middle class, highly educated, upwardly and geographically mobile), it also *embraces* a perspective that encourages a degree of capitulation to the cultural forces that surround it.

St Michael's presents itself as an exemplar – and in some senses an initiator – of major shifts in the wider evangelical movement and these shifts have generally been characterised by an ever greater engagement with the wider culture, resulting in part in the internal diversification of congregational life. But what bearing do these developments have upon the religious values expressed by individual members of the congregation? What vision of Christianity is shaped and negotiated within it? Hunter's analysis draws attention to the ways in which a sense of spiritual diversity might be extended into a liberalisation of attitudes, characterised by tolerance, an openness to change and the weakening plausibility of old beliefs. The following section addresses the extent to which this description may be fairly applied to the St Michael's congregation. It does this by examining the expression of beliefs that fall within two of the key axes of evangelical identity identified by Bebbington: biblicism and crucicentrism, i.e., how does the spiritual diversity of the congregation manifest itself in expressions of belief about scriptural authority and about personal salvation?

Scriptural Authority

One trend that emerged very clearly in my interviews was a firm conviction in the authority of the Bible. According to the evangelicals of St Michael's, the scriptures are placed above the church, its leaders and above charismatic experience as the foundation of Christian truth and as the sole guide to Christian living. Alan expressed a commonly held perspective,

> ... I do believe that it is the living word of God. I do believe it is God's revelation to men through men, and I think all other forms of revelation, you know, prophetic or whatever, have to be measured up to what the Bible says ...

Correspondingly, the common benchmark for a valuable piece of advice or for a good sermon was: is it biblical? Parishioners often explained their movement between different churches in terms of how 'biblical' the teaching had been. Some interspersed biblical stories and references into conversations to demonstrate the validity of a viewpoint or the significance of a recent incident (see chapters 5 and 7 for further discussion of this trend).

A willingness to submit to the scriptures was also reflected in everyday practice. The Christian life was conceived as a perpetual learning process and its sourcebook, the Bible. Individuals therefore absorbed themselves in the texts in order to both achieve an understanding of moral and religious duty, but also to make sense of the world around them. Many parishioners brought along their own Bibles to Sunday services, especially the evening service, and some keenly made notes in the margins during the sermon. Home group meetings were based around Bible study, undertaken as a means of developing one's personal faith in fellowship with others. Sunday sermons were conceived as resourcing this process, delivered as expositional analyses of specific biblical texts. Teaching was always applied to the contemporary everyday life of Christians, but was also frequently grounded in a point-by-point discussion of a chosen passage.

Regular private Bible reading was also viewed as an important aspect of daily life. When interviewing individuals in their homes, I became accustomed to seeing a copy of a well-used Bible – usually the New International Version – dog-eared and book-marked, placed ready on the living room coffee table. In Spring 1999, the St

Michael's leadership administered an internal survey on Bible reading, which exposed the widespread popularity of this practice. Attendees at all services were surveyed, including the *Visions* group, and 504 individuals completed a questionnaire on a single Sunday. 39% claimed that they read their Bible daily and a *further* 38% said they read the Bible a few times a week. Only 6% claimed that they only read their Bible in church, and 5% less frequently. The results also suggested that those who read their Bibles most frequently were evenly distributed across differences of age and preference of Sunday service. It is worth contrasting the results of the 2005 Church Census, the closest comparable data set, which revealed that only 27% of churchgoers read the Bible at least once a week outside of church, a third of the proportion of the St Michael's congregation claiming at least this level of regular engagement. The national census also revealed the surprising finding that frequent Bible reading does not distinguish evangelicals generally – the proportion of weekly readers was only 29% for evangelicals, trailing behind liberals (32%) and those of a 'broad church' (42%).[9] Hence while one more ambitious leader commented that the results of the St Michael's survey were 'disappointing', by national and English evangelical standards, the St Michael's congregation exhibits a significant zeal for the scriptures. Indeed, the fact that the leadership conducted this study implies a desire to measure signals of personal piety among the congregation, and an assumption that regular Bible study is a legitimate measure of this.

While the Bible was comprehensively affirmed as the primary authority and foundation of the Christian life, congregants were less united in their views about the precise truth status of its texts. This is a complex issue; as the scriptures were read and invoked in a myriad of contexts, there was room for a diverse set of approaches to appropriating the text as a spiritual resource. For an initial impression, one can appeal to questionnaire returns, which reveal a clear diversity of opinion. Respondents were asked which of the following statements best reflected their view of the scriptures.

The Bible is the inspired Word of God, not mistaken in its statements and teachings, and is to be taken literally, word for word.

The Bible is the inspired Word of God, not mistaken in its teachings, but is not always to be taken literally in its statements concerning matters of science, historical reporting, etc.

The Bible becomes the Word of God for a person when he/she reads it in faith.

The Bible is an ancient book of legends, history, and moral precepts recorded by men.

---

[9] Peter Brierley, *Pulling Out of the Nosedive* (London: Christian Research, 2006), p. 231-2.

Responses are presented in tabular form below, compared with responses to the 1998 British Social Attitudes Survey.

	St Michael's	Britain
Bible as literally true	24%	4%
Bible true but not always to be taken literally	51%	34%
Bible true when read in faith	18%	–
Bible as ancient book of legends	0%	44%
This does not apply to me	–	8%
No answer	5%	2%

Table 2: Attitudes towards the truth of the Bible in the St Michael's congregation (2000), and in Britain as a whole[10] (a dash symbol indicates where an option was not offered within that particular survey).

Biblical literalism has never sustained a level of support in the UK comparable to the American evangelical movement, and since the 1960s evangelicalism has steered decidedly away from a stance with 'fundamentalist' overtones. However, among churchgoers, there are signals of significant minority support. Citing the British Household Panel Survey, Robin Gill claims that in 1994, 28% of weekly adult churchgoers 'strongly agreed' with a literalist statement.[11] Given that this figure does not discriminate by churchmanship, we might expect levels within evangelical churches to be higher than this. Therefore the figure of 24% for St Michael's is especially telling, and signals an overwhelming majority discomfort with the literalist position and a majority assent to the more qualified, second response which is closer to the norm among the general population.

So what kind of approach to the scriptures did those uncomfortable with a literalist model favour as an alternative? As the majority support for the second option implies, it was acknowledged by many that the Bible is not always to be taken literally on matters of history and science, suggesting a capitulation to a rational scientific worldview on certain issues. However, those holding to this position did not see a problem with this, as they did not see the legitimacy of the scriptures as resting solely in any status they might have as historical or scientific texts. Rather, they were viewed as taking multiple forms and literary genres, in

---

[10] Figures taken from Roger Jowell *et al, British Social Attitudes, the 16th Report. Who Shares New Labour Values?* (Aldershot: Ashgate, 1999), p. 363.

[11] Robin Gill, *Churchgoing and Christian Ethics* (Cambridge: CUP, 1999), p. 101.

which are embedded 'essential' religious truths. Moreover, these 'truths' were not seen as grounded in factual statements. As Alan put it, 'I don't have hang ups as to whether, you know, did Jonah, or Job really exist ... they may have done, or they may not have done but I think the deep truth[s] revealed by the accounts of their lives are truly valid ...' In other words, truth is embedded in the biblical narratives, but was not seen as always straightforwardly present in propositional statements.

I discussed with one of the St Michael's clergy his views on the truth of the scriptures. His response was highly instructive and very much reflected many of the other views I encountered amongst the congregation.

MG: Is the whole of the Bible to be taken as absolutely true?

CLERGYMAN : Yes. Of course, but what is truth? If you want to ask me whether we should take it literally, I think ... that would be impossible, because the Bible is not one book, it's a library. You've got history, you've got poetry, you've got, you know, songs, you've got narratives ... you've got letters, you've got accounts of ... what people have done and so on ... I think to actually say that it's got to be taken literally ... could you imagine the Psalms – talking about the sun, you know, rising and running the race? You know, he's talking poetically, that's what he is saying. He's not giving you facts, he's only giving you things as he sees them.

Not only is there here an acknowledgement of literary diversity within the Bible, there is also recognition that the content of the scriptures is conditioned by the perspective of the author. Stories and teachings are to be interpreted in light of the historical and cultural context in which the author was writing. In an effort to retain a sense of divine authority, one parishioner claimed that the Bible is 'God-breathed' but was also written by various authors in different cultural contexts. The 'meaning' of the scriptures is, therefore, something to be generated from an act of interpretation, something to be unpicked from the complexities of the texts. Given that the scriptures were taken to be permeated with symbolism and are subject to the contingencies of authorship, we might ask how its so-called 'essential' truths are accessed.

In interviews, parishioners expressed two approaches to this problem, two kinds of appeal to two different sources of authority. They were not affirmed as mutually exclusive nor in consistent terms, but were discernible as methods of interpretation embraced by members of the congregation. The first was often implied rather than openly developed, and referred to rational, scholarly argument as an authority by which to unpack and elucidate the biblical narratives.

To take one example, Hannah felt that the scriptures are a resource, to be used according to personal need. She was aware of how history and culture complicate our attempts to find truth in them, but did not see this as an irresolvable issue. As she commented, '... I think you can apply a bit of common sense to that and see how things tie up with independent historical records.' In her estimation, the 'factual authority' of historical records serve as a means of validating certain claims made in the scriptures themselves. An appeal to scientific and scholarly arguments was also apparent in sermons and public teaching. The 'authority' of the scriptures was sometimes spoken of as a matter of historicity, and the authenticity of the texts seen to be strengthened by referring to literary or archaeological evidence. In this sense, the evangelicals of St Michael's affirmed what might be called *historical foundationalism*, i.e., the belief that the Bible can be demonstrated as more or less reliable by advancing arguments for the historical authenticity of different passages. This may be seen as discontinuous with the stress on symbolism discussed above, but no sense of tension was acknowledged by parishioners. Rather, the scriptures were interpreted according to the specific needs of the immediate context in which they were being read. According to parishioners, this approach did not equate to inconsistency, but allows a 'full' appreciation of the richness of the biblical texts.

In relying upon secular canons of authority, parishioners imply a qualified sense of the Bible's own. The scriptures are no longer simply taken as an authority before all others, but as subject to the limitations imposed upon them by the findings of science and the norms of rational thought. Doubtless this has a lot to do with the demography of the congregation, the majority of whom have had their perspectives shaped by higher education and their faith-lives continually nurtured by an educated church community. Some were even conversant with the issues of biblical criticism after short courses in Bible college and extensive theological reading.

While some appeared to defer the claims of scripture to science, others divided the two, thus avoiding problems of conflict. For one minister, science provided the answers to questions the Bible does not attempt to answer. While science concerns itself with questions of fact, the scriptures are preoccupied with questions of meaning, with 'why [things] happened'. Factual claims in the texts were thereby regarded as of secondary importance to questions of salvation, which were seen as couched in a different, theological idiom. The 'essential' truths for this minister were about having a loving relationship with God, and this is invoked as overriding the minutiae of belief or doctrine.

> ... if the world wasn't created in seven days...in a way, well, it's neither here nor there. When I get to heaven, God is not going to tell me, and did you believe my creation or not? He is going to say, welcome home son, it's good to see you. Ultimately, that is what is important.

To defer the 'how' questions to science marks a clear capitulation to secular modernity, evoking Peter Berger's notion of an ongoing 'bargaining process with secular thought'.[12] As the norms of scientific rationality are increasingly embraced, so the truth status of *the scriptures alone* is eroded, and their function shaped by cultural forces that have effectively superseded them in importance. However, it is also important to note that parishioners did not see this as a threat to their evangelical faith. Rather, notions of symbolic truth and uncompromising biblical

---

[12] Peter Berger, *The Heretical Imperative. Contemporary Possibilities of Religious Affirmation* (London: Collins, 1980), pp. 158-9.

authority were apparently held concurrently, invoked according to the demands of particular discursive contexts.

Martin Stringer found a similar tension among statements of belief made by Anglican, Roman Catholic and Independent churchgoers in Manchester. Stringer found that members of a church could make regular use of disconnected belief statements while also affirming the existence of a system of beliefs, in which they are embedded.[13] The latter reflects a need for authority, while the former is a consequence of how individual statements are shaped by the needs of different situations and interactive contexts. Within St Michael's, the authority of the Bible was affirmed while popular invocations of its meaning and significance shifted according to the rational convictions of individuals and the pastoral needs of the situation. My argument here is that this freedom of application is made possible by a general process of liberalisation that both broadens the possibilities of biblical meaning and increases the degree of tolerance extended to readings viewed as divergent or deviant. While there was no top-down attempt to rein in the inevitable hermeneutical diversity that this produced, there persisted an unwavering affirmation of scriptural authority, which in turn conveyed an impression of shared purpose and mutual understanding.

The other source of enlightenment that was invoked with respect to understanding scripture was the Holy Spirit. According to one long-term parishioner,

> ... I think that the whole of the Bible has a relevance in terms of laying down principles ... and giving us information and insights of God's relationship with man ... for me it is a very important guide, [an] inspiration for daily living ... beyond the ... printed page, there is the Holy Spirit of God that opens one's mind, one's intellect to the reality of it. It's not just an intellectual analysis of what it's saying. There is a spiritual assistance, if you like, behind the mind.

There is a sense in which the Holy Spirit is invoked as a guiding force through which individuals are able to perceive the meaning of scripture. This is a non-rational resource, felt within oneself and often conflated with ideas of conscience or intuition. Parishioners often told stories of how they had been 'led' to a particularly apposite verse that guided them through a difficult time or provided them with well-needed advice. As one put it, '... on certain occasions, when I haven't been looking for it, verses have jumped out and hit me, so I think God does speak to you through it [i.e. the Bible]'.

Rational thought and the Holy Spirit are sometimes conceived as radically conflicting, relying as they do upon reason on the one hand, and subjective experience on the other. But their co-existence is unsurprising in St Michael's given the educational background of the congregation and the charismatic history of the church. They were invoked as authorities to be drawn from in a way that did not

---

[13] Martin D. Stringer, *On the Perception of Worship. The Ethnography of Worship in Four Christian Congregations in Manchester* (Birmingham: University of Birmingham Press, 1999), pp. 179-80.

generally provoke disagreement or conflict. What is significant here is that they both go hand in hand with a liberalising approach to biblical interpretation. Rationality and intellectualism usurps the place of the biblical in generating scientific or factual truth. Invoking the Holy Spirit relocates the act of interpretation within the subjectivities of the individual devotee. The meaning of the text is negotiated in terms of the subjective needs of the person, rather than as objective and non-negotiable truth, a phenomenon explored in greater detail in chapters 5 and 7.

This is the essence of what Hunter presents as the neo-orthodox position, that the Bible becomes the word of God when read in faith, which is ultimately traced back to the theology of thinkers like Karl Barth and Emil Brunner.[14] History is secondary to the subjective experience of reading the texts, which is more determinative in the emergence of religious knowledge. The low score of 18% for this option in the survey precludes the need for any extended discussion. However, it does highlight an important trend among the congregation, to prioritise the subjective experience of reading the texts over a more collectively shared and externally authorised understanding of scriptural truth. This pattern attaches significant value to independent reading and reflects the perception that issues of Christian knowledge may be pursued on an autonomous, individual level.

This is more vividly apparent in statistics on devotional reading. According to my own survey data, 82% of the congregation had read C.S. Lewis at some point in their lives. The figures were 79% for the works of David Watson, 58% for John Stott and 58% for John Wimber. At the same time, more radical or innovative Christian writers were less popular: 21% had read Norman Vincent Peale, 6% Scott Peck and 4% Dave Tomlinson. It became clear to me during fieldwork that parishioners were engaged in a *pro-active* search for meaning, but within the confines of acceptability defined by the tradition of their church. At the same time they embraced these authors in so far as they shed light on their own spiritual lives. In other words, Christian devotional literature – as with the scriptures – was selected according to evangelical convention, but appropriated in so far as it funded subjective Christian identities.

Salvation

If there was one theological motif which appeared to remain uncompromised and intact throughout the St Michael's congregation, it was that of a penal substitutionary atonement. The model of salvation through confession of faith in Jesus as the exclusive means of deliverance from inevitable sin was apparently embraced by all. It pervaded sermons and was affirmed without question by individual parishioners. Indeed, it was frequently expressed in a highly articulate and intellectual form, members often providing a detailed and theologically sophisticated account of the salvation process, a reflection of their middle class, educated status. This exposition by Peter, of what 'evangelical' means, was not untypical:

---

[14] Hunter, *Evangelicalism*, pp. 26-27.

The word itself obviously is from 'evangel', the Gospel – the Gospel of Jesus Christ, that he is the saviour of mankind, he's the world saviour, and therefore sent by God, as God incarnate, who identified himself with man, took man's sin on him, on the cross, to be punished on behalf of man. That sacrifice was accepted, demonstrated by the resurrection of Christ, and then eventually his ascension into heaven ... and that salvation is on the basis of confession of sin, acceptance of Christ's sacrifice for oneself, and then a testifying of the reality of that, by one's words.

This conception of salvation embodies several other key ideas for the evangelical: the radical sinfulness of man, the importance of an open confession of faith, the urgency behind a personal decision to follow God. That these ideas were consistently affirmed by the St Michael's congregation is not surprising. They form the theological cornerstone of evangelicalism, conveying crucicentrism and conversionism while implying biblical authority. They were relentlessly taught by David Watson, whose books have been enthusiastically read by those parishioners too young to remember his sermons.

James Davison Hunter has called evangelical soteriology the most 'socially offensive' aspect of Christian theology.[15] All other models of salvation are viewed as patently false and the result of delusion or Satanic machinations. All those who do not profess faith in Jesus are seen as destined for eternal torment and damnation. There is a sense in which boundaries are strongest at this point in the tradition, and the differences between those inside and those outside of the faith are often conceived in dichotomous terms. Although the British movement has generally softened this exclusivism, the spirit of separatism that it sustains – accompanied by a vociferous defence of moral purity – remains a resilient and potent identity marker within evangelical churches. As the vicar of St Michael's pointed out to me, and not without a degree of evangelistic urgency, 'we're either for Jesus, or we're against him'.

During interviews, I asked members of St Michael's about the salvation process as they understood it. Using evangelical language, I asked them, 'how are we saved?' The responses they gave were fairly consistent, invoking the model of substitutionary atonement described above: we are saved by faith in Jesus as our Lord and saviour. This idea was not invoked naively, and many individuals jokingly reminded me that they knew this was the 'standard' answer. But the model of substitutionary atonement was not questioned or challenged in any significant way. However, when I turned to the question, 'What will happen to those people who are not Christians?', people were far less certain. There was a discernible hesitancy and awkwardness in their responses that suggested they were not entirely comfortable with the issue. None were willing to commit to a definitive or uncompromising answer.

One might expect evangelicals to be comfortable with the notion that non-believers are destined for eternal punishment. Indeed, this belief may be seen as a

---

[15] Hunter, *Evangelicalism*, p. 34.

potential source of strength and cohesion, reinforcing evangelical exclusivity. However, I found many interviewees consciously avoiding any degree of commitment to this position. Rather, they appeared keener to embrace the possibility that outsiders might somehow be included in the destiny of the faithful. Some even turned the issue around, adopting a critical perspective on the narrow conceptions of evangelicals. As Alan expressed it,

> I would have to say that I think the term 'Christian' is wider than some evangelicals think it is, and I think the evangelical wing of the church has a very narrow idea of who is acceptable to God. I mean, God alone is judge and it's not for us to decide whether only those who go through a ... particular set of actions get saved, or whether even just a ... simple, almost sub-conscious acknowledgement on someone's part that actually God does exist is good enough. I don't know and it's not for me to make any judgement.

Alan's comments were not untypical of the congregation as a whole. There was an implicit willingness to entertain, though not openly or fully to embrace, a more liberal, inclusive outlook on the fate of those who fall outside of the traditional evangelical boundaries of the faith. More clearly, there was a definite resistance towards unquestioningly accepting the view that non-believers are destined for punishment and damnation.

This is reflected in questionnaire results. 67% of the congregation claimed that those who are not saved will exist in hell, but as a state of *separation* from God. Only 10% opted for the traditional view of hell as a place of punishment, a figure matched by the proportion of respondents who said that we cannot know for sure. A further 9% claimed that the unsaved will have a chance to confess their sins after death. Taken together, we arrive at a striking 86% of the congregation preferring to reject the understanding of hell as a place of punishment in favour of a less 'offensive' or less clear-cut perspective.

Interview responses suggest similar sentiments. One parishioner said that he believed in hell as a place, but did not see God actively punishing people in it. Others openly endorsed the alternative notion of a place where God is absent, conceiving the individual's choice as between 'eternity with God or eternity without God'. A discomfort with eternal punishment was driven for some by a deep-felt concern for unconverted family members, while other parishioners felt that eternal punishment was simply inconsistent with the image of a loving God. As Hannah put it, 'I struggle with the idea that God can love us so much that ... He'd be prepared to just let people trip off down into eternal misery ...' In general, the views of parishioners tended to reflect the Church of England's 'official' position on hell rather than the more conservative report issued by the Evangelical Alliance (see chapter 2).

Given this tendency to stress mercy and love over judgement and damnation, it is unsurprising that views about the fate of the unevangelised also followed a fairly liberal line. A perpetual problem for evangelicals is how they reconcile the need for faith in Jesus alone with the fact that some people are untouched by missionary endeavour. How are these people to be judged, and what is their destiny? This was not an issue addressed often in St Michael's, either in informal discourse or church teaching. But when it did arise, for example, in small group discussion, a consistent perspective was adopted by many. That is the view, derived from Paul's letter to the Romans (2.6), that those untouched by the faith will be judged according to the light they have received, i.e., by factors other than an open confession of faith in Jesus. This was most frequently glossed in terms of whether people have the right 'heart', or as one minister put it, 'they [the unevangelised] will be judged with their conscience'. This is a common method of reconciling classical Christian soteriology with the notion of a just God. Its presence here implies a softening of boundaries that was also reflected in views on the fate of the unsaved.

Just as parishioners appeared accepting of unbelievers generally, so they also tended to shy away from an openly condemnatory view of other religious faiths. The questionnaire asked parishioners about their views of a series of other religions, including world faiths such as Islam and Hinduism, and non-mainstream Christian groups, such as the Jehovah's Witnesses and the Mormons. Although the majority of respondents felt that most of these traditions were wrong and misguided, for most traditions a significant minority did not endorse the view that they should be converted to the true faith or denounced. That is, a sizeable portion of the congregation, while recognising these traditions as 'untrue', remained unwilling to advocate an actively negative response to them. For example, 54% felt that Islam is misguided and that Muslims should be brought to the true faith. Another 9% felt that Islam is the work of the devil. But 22%, while recognising that this tradition does not lead to God, felt that people should respect this tradition. Similar results emerged with respect to Buddhism and Hinduism, and 18% even viewed Judaism as an alternative path to the true God. Respondents were more condemnatory of marginal Christian groups such as Jehovah's Witnesses and Mormons, reflecting Mary Douglas' argument that it is phenomena which threaten group boundaries rather than phenomena which fall outside of them which are most problematic for religious groups.[16]

Interview responses, while not exclusively positive, exhibited a discernible effort to find positive qualities in other religions. Alan felt that other religions inevitably contain an element of truth, because of the universal breadth of God's creation and activity. Because God created the world, and lives in the world, surely many of the world's religions 'to a greater or lesser extent reflect something of the true myth'. June went further than this, suggesting that, although she feels that other religions are 'on the wrong track', Christians could learn a lot from some of them. When I asked her to expand on this, she referred to the greater degree of moral discipline in other religions, which leads to less sexual immorality and abuse of the body. Hannah expressed a view that exceeded even this, veering closer to a kind of religious

---

[16] Mary Douglas, *Purity and Danger. An Analysis of the Concepts of Pollution and Taboo* (London: Routledge, 1966).

universalism. Responding to my question about how she views other religions, she said,

> ... if it is an attempt of whatever society to fill that God-shaped hole, I don't see any reason why it shouldn't be a search for the same God ... I'm quite aware of the way that Christianity has become part and parcel of British culture and so I can see that just because I've taken this stance, it doesn't necessarily mean that I wouldn't have been a completely devoted Hindu if I had been brought up somewhere else ... I think when it comes to the crunch, it's God's decision, and I think that's what's important.

These are isolated views, but their presence within an evangelical community is highly significant. They represent a discomfort with an exclusivist and antagonistic stance, in favour of an outlook that underplays difference and even, in some cases, affirms a partially favourable perspective on non-Christian religions. To be fair, although they often expressed a meandering viewpoint, most respondents maintained that other religions are deficient in some way. But even then, they did not see this as sufficient grounds for condemning them. As one parishioner put it, 'I can't condemn people for their religious convictions if they don't happen to align with mine.' This attitude is commonplace within the tolerant, inclusivist discourses of multi-cultural Britain. But it is strikingly incongruent within a Christian community traditionally seen as conservative and 'firm in the faith'. If nothing else, the presence of these views in St Michael's demonstrates the pervasion of the modern gentility and civility that Hunter found in the changing tradition of American evangelicalism in the 1980s. It is no longer seen as acceptable to openly affirm views that are socially offensive or which emphasise the radical difference between those inside and those outside of the faith. An implicit accommodation to modern trends has made this so, consequently triggering a reconfiguration of evangelical values in a thoroughly liberal direction.

The Role and Status of Women

I have focused upon scripture and salvation as key topics which highlight patterns in the expression of belief among the St Michael's congregation. Restrictions of space prevent a more extended discussion of shared values, although other areas of interest could be mentioned. Most clearly, both questionnaire and ethnographic data suggest a widespread conservatism on moral issues, especially sexual morality. 81% of questionnaire respondents claimed that homosexual relations between consenting adults are always wrong, with 90% and 73% saying the same for extra-marital sex and pre-marital sex respectively. The contemporary figures are 39%, 52% and 8% for Britain as a whole,[17] a comparison that draws out the severe way in which these issues are viewed among evangelical Christians.

---

[17] Jowell *et al*, *British Social Attitudes*, p. 348.

This is to be expected among evangelical churches, the value structure of which is very much based on the integrity of traditional family roles. That which challenges or undermines the nuclear family – divorce, abortion, homosexuality – is frequently condemned in the strongest terms. It is quite surprising, therefore, to find within St Michael's a fairly liberal attitude towards the role and status of women. Questionnaire respondents were given the following statement: 'The primary role of the Christian woman is to support her husband as provider by caring for the children and tending to the household duties.' The following table compares the extent to which members of the St Michael's congregation agreed with this, with responses drawn from the British Social Attitudes Survey.

	Agree	Neither agree nor disagree	Disagree	Can't choose/don't know
St Michael's	30%	–	57%	8%
Britain	18%	23%	57%	0.5%

Table 3: Attitudes towards traditional gender roles within St Michael's and Britain.[18]

Although the national sample was offered a larger series of options, answers are grouped together here so that certain patterns can be discerned. Notably, the proportion of respondents answering negatively is exactly the same for both St Michael's and Britain as a whole (57%). While a greater proportion of St Michael's congregants supported this statement than those among the British population (30% versus 18%), supporters are still in the minority. Indications are that evangelical and wider cultural understandings of gender roles are closer than might be anticipated.

It is important not to overstate this point. While there were clear indications of a majority unease with traditionalist understandings of gender roles, St Michael's retained a deep concern for what might be called 'family values'. It fostered a shared culture which placed marriage and the nuclear family unit at the centre of church life and as the end point of personal fulfilment. Homosexuality and co-habitation were regarded with a marked discomfort and occasionally provoked open condemnation. There was also arguably an insidious pressure upon younger members to marry early, a trend which reflects church sponsored ideas of a shared lay ministry. Common expectations of members and their contributions to church life were framed by the institution of the nuclear family, a persistent symbol of moral integrity and wholesome living.

However, the statistics invoked above do suggest that, if this model is persistent, it is not impervious to modification, particularly with respect to understandings of authority. There were signs throughout the congregation that, while retaining the

---

[18] Figures taken from Jowell *et al*, *British Social Attitudes*, p. 361.

family as sovereign, roles within the nuclear family are open to reconfiguration and rearrangement. For example, during fieldwork, I encountered several married men who were taking time out of their careers to look after their children. The congregation featured a number of respected female professionals, including doctors, university lecturers, school teachers and social workers, who appeared to provoke no significant disapproval from more traditionalist members. Analysis of the church address list from 2000 reveals that, of the 210 adult female members of the congregation fit for work, under retirement age and not in education, only 35 (16%) were full-time housewives. Of those working, 62% worked part-time and 38% full-time. The ideal model of the nuclear family has been at least partially accommodated to modern standards of equal gender opportunities and the acceptance of women in the workplace.

A shift away from an acceptance of male dominance was also evident in advice offered by church leaders. At an Alpha course session, one preacher claimed that Paul's teachings on marriage do not imply total submission by a wife to her husband. Rather, the essence of his message is really about having the right relationship – a sentiment notable for its ambiguity as well as its liberal slant. When pressed on particularly conservative teachings from the Old Testament, he reverted to a relativist position, and spoke of the importance of putting these passages in their historical context. There was a discernible tendency to avoid any advocacy of a traditionalist, patriarchal position, or to give it biblical endorsement.

An egalitarian spirit was most evident in attitudes towards authority roles which, it appears, were only minimally associated with gender difference. A mere 6% of the congregation agreed that the Bible teaches that women are subordinate to men, and only 24% agreed that women should always obey their husbands, a figure that actually surprised the church co-ordinator when I discussed the survey results with him. Liberal views were extended into issues of leadership in the church, with 78% *disagreeing* with the statement that all members of the clergy should be male. Faced with the statement, 'Women should never occupy positions of leadership in a church', 88% disagreed. And 73% *supported* the notion that women should be given equal opportunities to men to serve the church *in every respect.*

It is true that, at the time of fieldwork, the majority of the church leadership were men: all three of the clergy, all five of the lay readers and three out of the four churchwardens. However, women often took on leadership roles in church services, and James informed me that there were actually more women than men among home group leaders. The vicar also commented that he would like more women to be involved in the leadership, and there are no discernible signs that he will be met with significant opposition from the congregation. (Indeed, this trend has persisted since my original research – see the Epilogue for further details.)

In sum, while entrenched leadership norms prevent the onset of radical institutional change – the arrival of a female vicar would, I was told, have provoked significant opposition – the congregation of St Michael's appeared to accept gender equality in most areas of Christian practice. Questionnaire responses, in particular, suggest an emphatic rejection of traditionalist ideas of femininity, which centre on domesticity, the nurture of children and a submission to male authority in one's spiritual life. Thus, while family values remained axiomatic, ideas about the distribution of authority have been accommodated to wider cultural norms.

Capitulating to Modernity?

Employing Hunter's understanding of contemporary social change, these patterns of value can be explained as accommodations to specific dominant forces that are enshrined in processes of modernisation. Most strikingly, cultural pluralism promotes an 'ethic of civility' – a pressure to adopt a tolerant view of outsiders, in this case, non-believers and people of other faiths. Cultural norms of gender equality have also been embraced alongside, rather than in spite of, the continuing centrality of the nuclear family as the cornerstone of sound Christian living. In both cases, wider secular norms have been absorbed into the evangelical subculture, causing an erosion of traditional standards and a blurring of the boundaries that mark out evangelicals as distinct from the culture that surrounds them. Shared values have become more liberal and less offensive to outsiders, and the integrity of internal barriers has given way to a less fixed, almost exploratory approach to dealing with ultimate reality.

We could invoke the dominance of scientific rationalism as the force which has undermined literalist readings of the Bible and ushered intellectual argument into evangelical discourse. But treatments of the scriptures also invoked the Holy Spirit as a guiding light and source of meaning. Tempered intellectual scepticism co-existed with a belief in the reality of supernatural powers and their role in human affairs. In this sense St Michael's exhibits aspects of the 'post-modern primitivism' that Miller finds in 'new paradigm' churches.[19] While Biblical literalism is generally rejected, a more subjective source of knowledge is invoked that effectively undermines the rationalism of the modern project. Unlike 'new paradigm' Christians, however, St Michael's members appeared to embrace these two authorities – rational thought and subjective experience – concurrently. One was not seen as undermining the other, and neither did they appear to generate a tension within the shared discourses of the community. In this respect St Michael's retains both rationality and experience as resources to be drawn from according to personal need and shifting context.

On another level, the key issue here is not modernisation as a macro social process, but the construction of a model of 'modernity' by the congregation, with reference to which they may then define their own value structure. In addition to expressing a religiosity that reflects their social status, thus to some extent embodying the values of modernity, parishioners also colluded in a collective construction of secular modernity which is wholly negative. Unlike many fundamentalist groups, the congregation did not tend to associate modernity with

---

[19] Donald Miller, *Reinventing American Protestantism. Christianity in the New Millennium* (Berkeley and Los Angeles, CA: University of California Press, 1997), p. 125.

science or secular learning, and embraced these positively alongside biblical inspiration and charismatic healing. Rather, understandings of secular modernity centred on moral depravity and licentiousness, a breakdown in community and traditional bonds of mutual commitment, and an impression that non-Christians caught up in this are spiritually homeless. Indeed, this conception appears to lie behind Roger Simpson's description of 'a world of alienation and pain', cited in the prologue.

Therefore, simultaneously, congregants are bound up in modern change while also rallying against it. This is important to note, as it captures Christian Smith's insight that, essential to the social integrity of evangelicalism is *its sense of distinctiveness from secular culture*.[20] While many of the St Michael's congregants appeared to embrace a set of beliefs which were significantly 'liberalised', in one sense the boundaries of the community depend upon this *not* being seen as a capitulation but as a continuation of evangelical tradition. By way of this process, understandings of the evangelical worldview are reflexively developed and reconstructed, along increasingly broad parameters.

In spite of its current belief structure – which is undeniably liberalised in the ways described above – St Michael's has continued to attract, and sustain, a strongly conservative element (exemplified by James, above). These congregants are aware of this liberal trend and identify it as a problem. Indeed, both perspectives – broad and more narrowly defined – are clearly accommodated by the subculture of this church. This is highlighted by the survey responses to issues such as the authority of scripture, the nature of humanity, life after death, baptism and the status of other religions, all of which split the congregation into significant divisions, though analysis of the figures does not suggest factionalism. The following section addresses the ways in which the tensions that this highlights are managed within St Michael's as an internally complex evangelical community.

Negotiating the Boundaries of the Faith

The above discussion demonstrates that the St Michael's congregation is 'liberalised' in two related respects. First, a large proportion of its members appear to embrace 'liberal' views on key issues such as the truth status of scripture and the place of women. This indicates a re-drawing of the boundaries of the evangelical worldview along broad lines, centring on tolerance, universalism and an openness to spiritual exploration. Second, as this outlook tends to exist hand in hand with a sense that one possesses the freedom to rethink Christian tradition, it also tends to engender more individualistic understandings of faith. In other words, liberalisation often also generates diversification, and both trends are evident among this congregation.

However, the existence of critical figures such as James suggests that such trends are not embraced positively throughout the community. Indeed, my research revealed

---

[20] Christian Smith, *American Evangelicalism: Embattled and Thriving* (Chicago, IL, and London: University of Chicago Press, 1998).

a significant contingent of members who appeared far more conservative – emphasising exclusivism, moral discipline and traditionalist gender roles – than the aggregated questionnaire results suggest. There is clearly no overall consensus among the congregation on what the essentials of Christianity actually mean when translated into norms of belief and practice.

The majority of scholars in the sociology of religion associate liberalisation and diversification with the fragmentation and decline of religious groups.[21] The perceived lack of a common core of belief is thought to undermine the possibility of group cohesion. Moreover, according to scholars like Peter Berger and Steve Bruce, liberalisation compromises conservative religious groups by eroding their sense of difference from the outside world. In undermining these boundaries, it also undermines the reasons individuals have for remaining members.[22] As the boundaries of evangelical identity become ever more blurred and subject to popular contestation, it is reasonable to expect members to drift away as fragmentation and individualisation occur among the congregation's ranks. However, as demonstrated in chapter 3, St Michael's is a thriving church by national comparison, achieving high attendance levels and eliciting a significant degree of practical commitment from its members. While it has experienced some decline in attendances since the late 1980s, this has not offset its comparative success. Moreover, periods of decline in recent times appear to have coincided with a turn to a more conservative, rather than liberal, theology. If attrition has occurred, there is no evidence that this has simply proceeded in parallel with the expansion of more liberal convictions among the congregation.

This apparent paradox provokes the obvious question: how are the tensions generated by liberalisation dealt with in St Michael's in such a way that processes of attrition and fragmentation are allayed? Put another way, how is a sense of unity and inclusion fostered in a congregation whose members are characterised by an apparently diverse and liberalised culture of belief? Part of the answer, I would argue, lies in the way the church organises its public discourse, that is, how it communicates its identity discursively to its members. For it is by way of this process that sufficient boundaries are set in place to hold the divergent positions within the congregation together.

In describing the complex processes which achieve this, it will be useful to draw insights from 'Ben' Pink Dandelion's *A Sociological Analysis of the Theology of Quakers*. According to Dandelion, contemporary Quaker belief is characterised by a pervasive liberalism. This is typified by a significant acceptance of internal diversity, grounded in the perceived need to affirm the diverse religious experiences of individuals. However, this is framed by what he calls a credalisation of form and practice; while a diversity of belief is accepted, the spiritual practices of the group are

---

[21] E.g., See Steve Bruce, *A House Divided. Protestantism, Schism and Secularization* (London: Routledge, 1989); Bryan Wilson, *Religion in Secular Society. A Sociological Comment* (Harmondsworth: Penguin, 1966).

[22] Peter Berger, *A Rumour of Angels. Modern Society and the Rediscovery of the Supernatural* (London: Penguin, 1969); Bruce, *A House Divided*, pp. 152-3.

generally defended in a way which leaves them relatively non-negotiable.[23] Practice becomes 'credalised'. While it is possible for an individual to disagree with other members on matters of Quaker belief, and still remain within the group, disagreements on norms of Quaker practice are more likely to cause fracture and be accepted as in sufficient contravention of group order to warrant disinvolvement. In this case, it is practice which forms the focus of group identity and shared boundaries.

Similarly, St Michael's exists as a liberalised group, at least by standards internal to its (evangelical) tradition. This liberalisation was acknowledged by some members, opposed by others, and was embraced as an indication of positive diversity by most of the leadership. As Roger Simpson put it, '... diversity is something that strikes me and thrills me because I am aware that different people find different entry points into the church'.[24] However, a sizeable conservative element and the negative associations of liberalism within the evangelical world prevents this from becoming the 'dominant discourse'.[25] In other words, the notion of a liberalised worldview is prevented from entering 'official' expressions of collective identity, such as a doctrinal statement (St Michael's has none),[26] because of the tensions which associated notions of compromise, worldliness and a lack of direction generate. An inevitable and apparently irresolvable clash of viewpoints persists. However, like the Quakers of Dandelion's study, the St Michael's congregation appeared to be held together by a mechanism that ensured a sense of unity and which consolidated a set of boundaries around the community. While contemporary Quaker groups are held together by norms of practice, St Michael's was held together by a public discourse which accommodated its various schools of belief while also controlling public utterance so that conflict was avoided. While this discourse was discernible in prayer, prophecy and other forms of public address, I shall take Sunday sermons as an illustrative example.

---

[23] 'Ben' Pink Dandelion, *A Sociological Analysis of the Theology of Quakers. The Silent Revolution* (Lewiston, Queenston, Lampeter: Edwin Mellen Press, 1996), p. 101.

[24] This self-understanding has arguably become more dominant in recent years. In their return questionnaire response to the English Church Attendance Survey in 1998, the St Michael's leadership described their church as 'evangelical' and 'charismatic'. For the 2005 survey, they chose to describe themselves as a 'broad' church as well.

[25] This builds on Gerd Baumann's distinction between 'dominant' and 'demotic' discourses, which he develops in his analysis of how social identities are negotiated in contexts characterized by ethnic difference. See Gerd Baumann, *Contesting Culture. Discourses of Identity in Multi-Ethnic London* (Cambridge, New York and Melbourne: CUP, 1996).

[26] The leadership has resisted calls for the church to affirm a definitive statement of belief, partly because of its potentially divisive consequences. However, developments since 2000 have included the articulation and passionate promotion of mission targets, which have effectively become the ministerial focus of the life of the church (see the Epilogue).

Sermons: Trends in Public Teaching

During my field research, I listened to forty-nine sermons at St Michael's, delivered by various preachers at the morning, family and evening services each Sunday. I took detailed notes on each of them, either during or after the event, and some were also made available to me as cassette recordings. Although they purported to focus on numerous topics – sometimes following the readings suggested in the Church of England's *Common Lectionary* – subsequent analysis revealed a tendency to focus on certain issues on a regular basis, and with the same key emphases. Central to the majority of sermons were three main areas of concern, which can be summarised as universal sin, conversionism and the ongoing Christian life. I take these in turn.

First, there was a continual emphasis upon a vision of humankind that was both uniformist and thoroughly negative. As Roger Simpson preached on one occasion, humans are basically all the same and are typified by misery and a tendency to fail. Attending Sunday services, I was repeatedly struck by the emphasis upon the inevitability of sin and wretchedness, which was stressed in in-house versions of the liturgical confession as well as by preachers and in prayer. This stress on the negativity of humankind is perhaps an obvious corollary to a belief in substitutionary atonement, which is its theological resolution. But the stress on sin and confession extended beyond the logic of shared theologies, and fostered what Stephen Warner has called a 'culture of public humbling', a readiness to express a mutual neediness which opens the way for religious exchange and mutual support within the fellowship.[27] This sense of humility was repeatedly stressed by Roger Simpson, whose claims to being a normal 'sinner' were an effective levelling device, his parishioners often remarking to me on how reassured they felt that their vicar was as imperfect as they were.

Second, sermons were ridden with a repeated call to faith and to repentance, emphasising the need for parishioners to base their lives 'entirely on Jesus' and to accept and embrace the Holy Spirit. In Bebbington's terms, there was an overwhelming focus upon conversionism. This was rather curious in one respect, as key evangelical themes were constantly repeated and rarely developed, sermons often evoking the style of a revivalist altar call rather than an ongoing body of teaching, steered towards the nurturing of an established parish community. It is possible that 'elective parochials' and visitors were kept firmly in mind, so that preaching retained an evangelistic urgency and I actually heard of no complaints from the congregation that their sermons were insufficiently didactic. Congregants appeared perfectly happy to hear the same message of faith and repentance each week, possibly focusing upon the emotive draw of sung worship and charismatic gifts as their source of fulfilment.

Invoking a call to convert and turn to Christ, it would only be logical for sermons to also address the practical consequences of this radical change of identity, which takes us to our third area of concern: the Christian life. This formed a large

---

[27] R. Stephen Warner, *New Wine in Old Wineskins. Evangelicals and Liberals in a Small-Town Church* (Berkeley, Los Angeles, CA, and London: University of California Press, 1988), pp. 293-4.

part of public teaching, and preachers always found room to emphasise the importance of prayer, financial giving, reaching out to the needy, embracing charismatic gifts and developing the God-given gifts of individual members. What was striking about their presentation was the relatively undefined or non-committal way in which they were dealt with. For example, one morning sermon was concluded with a call for us all to embrace the Holy Spirit in our lives. The preacher then went on to say that he was not going to define what this meant, but that we should put this idea into practice ourselves and find out that way. The common teaching on financial giving was that, although important, it was not a 'gospel issue' and should be left up to the conscience of the individual. In sum, while congregants were implored to follow a devoted, Spirit-filled life of prayer, sacrifice and neighbourly love, preachers left these ideas in such a vague and malleable form that they could easily be moulded to fit the existing everyday lives of the average member. A radical challenge becomes a mild accommodation. These common trends and the values embodied in them are summarised in the following diagram.

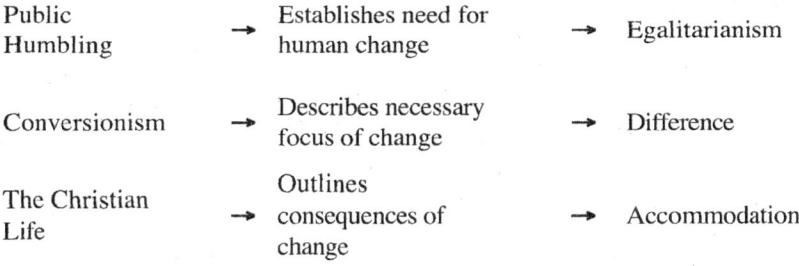

Figure 4: Key themes in public teaching

Sermons are interesting not only for what they cover but also for what they avoid or rarely comment on. One notable omission from sermons – and from most public discourse in fact – was moral teaching. This was especially striking, considering the usual emphasis that evangelical churches place upon correct Christian living and resisting the temptations of the world. Of all forty-nine sermons analysed, I found only three clear references to moral issues that also offered a clear judgement on them. Other references were largely embedded in narratives aimed at communicating a different message, so that on occasion, issues such as abortion were mentioned but left without moral comment. On other occasions, a sense of moral prescription was implied, but not concretised, as in one preacher's comment that the Bible is a good source of reproof and correction, as well as guidance. What he failed to point out was what it was the Bible actually says is worthy of reproof. More emphasis was placed throughout on positive qualities like love, care and responsibility, usually invoked in a fairly non-specific sense. On the rare occasions when a preacher isolated particular qualities as morally wrong, the solution suggested was not behavioural reform as such, but openness to the Holy Spirit in the same non-specific, undeveloped vein discussed earlier. A typical example is provided in this account of a midweek sermon given by the vicar on living a moral life before God.

> So how can we deal with these problems of hypocrisy, greed and faithlessness, which the vicar says are 'common sins in the West'? Roger says the best way to put them right is to be filled with the Holy Spirit. To eradicate hypocrisy in our lives, we need to ask God to fill us with the Holy Spirit of Truth. To combat greed, we need to ask God to fill us with the Holy Spirit of love, which will inspire us to give, rather than receive. And to deal with faithlessness, we need to ask God to fill us with the Holy Spirit of holiness. And we need to be filled with the Spirit everyday – we cannot live off yesterday ... (From field-notes, 16 February 2000.)

In short, sermons were characterised by both an evasion of moral issues and by a tendency to avoid offering specific moral prescriptions and sanctions. As with teachings on the 'Christian life', advice was more often than not affirmative rather than judgemental, generalist rather than directive, and as such was often malleable and open to interpretation.

The lack of clear moral instruction within the public discourse of St Michael's is especially curious as, in response to the questionnaire survey, individual members expressed highly conservative views on personal moral conduct. While we may not be surprised by the 81% who claimed that homosexual relations between consenting adults are 'always wrong', perhaps more striking are the 67% who said this about drinking to excess or the 64% who said it about using profane language.

Moreover, the overwhelming majority of respondents also said the church *should* speak out on such moral issues: 81% claimed this for abortion, 90% for extra marital affairs, 87% for homosexuality, 91% for the Third World, 72% for unemployment, 78% for euthanasia. What we are faced with is a separation of public and private discourses, the first characterised by a general tolerance and the second by a rather strict moral economy. Furthermore, the fact that 76% also claimed that St Michael's Sunday sermons adequately covered moral teaching suggests that parishioners were, on the whole, satisfied with this arrangement. One explanation of this would be that such moral teaching is so well-entrenched among the congregation that preachers feel there is no need for it to be taught. However, the fact that preachers clearly cater to 'elective parochials' – most clearly in the essentialist conversionist message outlined above – suggests that there is a felt need to repeatedly address core aspects of the Christian life explicitly.

I would rather argue that the reason moral judgement and directive advice are avoided relates to the need to accommodate the liberal diversity of belief within the congregation. There is a collective requirement for a shared public discourse which underplays issues likely to provoke conflict or divide the community. Field observations suggested that an individual freedom of spirituality is valued by many members, to a point where they view firm instruction on how to conduct their moral or spiritual life to be an affront to personal autonomy. Indeed, styles of leadership reflect this, leaders remaining firm and convicted but at the same time gentle and encouraging rather than authoritarian or prescriptive. In this sense there is a strong sense of the privatisation of religious identity – the Christian life is, to a degree, something forged around personal circumstances rather than group goals. So, rather than risk alienating members, the church has developed a public discourse which leaves specific issues vague and consequently open to individual interpretation, reflecting a *selective privatisation*.

I say 'selective' because public discourse appeared to retain a conservative, 'hard' stance on certain issues. Contrary to Hunter's comments on the liberalisation of evangelicalism, anything that hinted at moral or religious absolutism or intolerance *was not underplayed*.[28] Rather, public teaching presented itself as a curious mixture of hard, directive doctrine and inclusive, ambiguous or non-judgemental commentary suggestive of a more tolerant outlook. While it avoided moral issues, affirmed a generalised, undefined picture of the faith-life, and an overall emphasis on accommodating to diversity within the group, public discourse also stressed sin, the moral depravity of secular modernity, and the consequent radical difference between those inside and those outside of the faith. Conversely, privately expressed convictions downplayed notions of hell and punishment for the unsaved, and veered away from affirming strong boundaries between the saved and unsaved. At the same time, they reflected a thoroughly conservative take on moral issues, especially on sexual matters (see above). This complex pattern is summarised in Figure 5.

SCRIPTURE AS FOUNDATIONAL AUTHORITY (Drawn from according to context)	
Private Discourses	**Public Discourses**
Ambivalent Anthropology	Conservative Anthropology
Conservative Morality	Inclusive, affirmative morality

Figure 5: Selective Privatisation among the St Michael's congregation.

In summary, while aspects of the shared evangelical worldview held within St Michael's have clearly been liberalised, this process has become subject to a notable selectivity, by topic as well as by context. Divergent emphases can be found in public and in private discourses. Of course, expressions of belief are inevitably shaped by contextual factors, and changing contextual needs generate significant variations in the kind of claims individuals make.[29] But these variations are not

---

[28] See Hunter, *Evangelicalism*, p. 183.
[29] See Martin D. Stringer, 'Towards a Situational Theory of Belief', *Journal of the Anthropological Society of Oxford* 27:2 (1996), pp. 217-34.

random, and the patterns described above suggest a discernible religio-moral order, whereby certain issues are privatised and others dominate public exchange. Moreover, I would argue that this arrangement is instrumental to the avoidance of in-group conflict. Dandelion speaks of disputes over norms of Quaker practice as provoking conflict and disinvolvement. The equivalent trigger for St Michael's would be the mobilisation of ideas which challenge the framework described above, characterised as a selective balance of liberal and conservative convictions.

Public Tensions and the Avoidance of Conflict

Simply put, the boundaries of the group have come to coalesce around a set of ideas which encompasses both liberal (open, broad and tolerant) and conservative (narrow, exclusivist) camps, while attempting to compromise neither. Indeed, the public discourse – exemplified in sermons, public prayers, prophecy and any other spoken address open to the congregation as a whole – appeared to function as a unifying force by keeping these two 'narratives' in tension. It did this by avoiding the open endorsement of extreme positions and evading issues likely to provoke disagreement. Effectively, liberalisation and re-traditionalisation appeared as co-existent forces working within the same community, but without any kind of resolution that could be construed as compromise. While Dandelion's Quakers are bound together by a credalisation of form, the congregants of St Michael's achieved a sense of inclusion by selectively identifying with aspects of an available public discourse. Fracture occurs, not when members disagree with this discourse as such, but when they *openly* endorse one pole of the tension at the expense of the other, and in so doing risk dissolving the delicate separation of public and private discourses. Hence it is tension – but also its propensity to hold conflict at bay – that generates unity, and which consolidates the boundaries of congregational identity.

A glance at the history of St Michael's suggests that this pattern may have been entrenched within congregational culture for some time, as key moments of fracture have occurred when it has been challenged. In the early 1980s, under the influence of American Restorationists, a splinter group broke away from the church because of disagreements over women's leadership and the authority of charismatic prophecy. In the mid-1990s, similar innovations were introduced alongside the Toronto Blessing, with strong efforts to re-assert a more narrowly defined theology. On both occasions, emerging theologies were rejected or questioned by a significant proportion of the congregation, protest being expressed in open disgruntlement and some disinvolvement. The reaffirmation of a 'spirituality of diversity' can also be read into the appointment of Roger Simpson who, in many ways, personifies the identity of St Michael's as internally perceived: middle class, with a large family, of sound evangelical pedigree and, unlike his predecessors, an extrovert. Most importantly, he is a priest with an eclectic vision.

Extremes of the liberal kind are unsurprisingly less common, although the *Visions* group may be seen as an example. *Visions* embody a form of worship which many in St Michael's appeared to struggle with as it embraces an experimentalism that they found objectionable or unsettling. In this sense, they endorse an openness to change and diversity that is seen by some parishioners as excessively liberal. While they were not openly denounced and have not been ejected from the fellowship, they were certainly distanced and treated with some caution (see chapter 6). It is developments such as these, which challenge the dominant tension of conservative and liberal convictions, that render the boundaries of the congregation most clearly visible.

The process of liberalisation is subject to local filters that shape which aspects of a shared worldview are most susceptible to change and which are most resilient. Additionally, changes in the structure of shared values bring with them problems for the maintenance of a shared sense of unity and belonging. As the above analysis demonstrates, within the St Michael's congregation, understandings of what an 'evangelical' identity entails exhibited significant diversity. And yet conflict was avoided and a sense of dissonance effectively minimised. The church was able to sustain a sense of unity in part because of its scale. While networks among the congregation appear close-knit, no single person can know everyone, and many parishioners only knew one another by sight. Some long-term members rarely saw one another as they attended different services each week, and the high number of visitors and elective parochials meant that there was always a certain absence of intimacy at Sunday services. St Michael's has no formal doctrinal statement as such and many newcomers arrive with the simple expectation that this is a 'successful' charismatic evangelical church. Consequently, members rely on the public discourse for their impressions of what the congregation believes and represents.

Research into sermons 'suggests that there is typically quite a large gap between what the preacher intends and what members of a congregation perceive'.[30] In conversation, Roger Simpson said that his main aim in sermons is to interpret the Bible, so that people understand it better, and his main hope that they have encountered Jesus in it. Conversations with individual parishioners revealed a vast diversity of responses to sermons, from boredom to incredulity, enthusiasm, emotion, deep reflection and an experience of being inspired to make life-changing decisions. But a clear latent function of sermons was the fostering of a sense of inclusion in a common purpose, and of membership and unity against the common enemy – variously glossed as western culture, moral decadence or Satan. But as noted above, unity was secured by avoiding issues likely to provoke conflict, thus revealing how public teaching responds to, as well as shapes, perceived congregational needs.

The fact that the leadership should wish to adjust public teaching so as not to provoke dissonance is not surprising given the make-up of the congregation. The high number of visitors means that there is constant pressure to couch teaching in congenial rather than challenging terms, so as to retain rather than alienate potential new members. Moreover, according to sociological research into the nature of suburban culture, the tendency to suppress and avoid conflict is a characteristic of

---

[30] Gill, *Churchgoing*, p. 221.

middle class communities.[31] Penny Becker, drawing from the work of Lewis Coser, takes this idea further in her analysis of conflict in North American congregations:

> Coser ... suggests that, more generally, groups where members have a close and family-like attachment suppress disagreement and avoid debate on political or social issues. One of the consequences of thinking of the congregation as a family, at least in this predominantly middle-class community, is the avoidance of issues and persons who seem overtly controversial, political, or ideological.[32]

While the scale of St Michael's precludes a wholly family-like attachment among all members, this model of relationality was taught and supported by the leadership and was embraced among networks of close-knit members, as well as being fostered in small groups. Becker's argument is that such attachments are often incongruent with open debate or any presentation of issues likely to provoke disagreement. This notion will be taken up again in chapter 7. It is enough to note here that an avoidance of conflict appears to be driven by the cultural identity of the congregation as much as by the tensions produced by liberalisation and the socio-political history of this particular church.

---

[31] M.P. Baumgartner, *The Moral Order of a Suburb* (New York: OUP, 1988).
[32] Penny Edgell Becker, *Congregations in Conflict. Cultural Models of Local Religious Life* (Cambridge: CUP, 1999), pp. 86-7.

CHAPTER 5

Taming the Spirit:
Charismatic Experience after the Third Wave

In their influential book *The Spiritual Revolution. Why Religion is Giving Way to Spirituality*, Paul Heelas and Linda Woodhead chart the rise of 'spirituality' in the West, and make sense of this as part of a 'subjective turn' in late modern culture. They argue that 'life-as' religion – characterised by a conformity to external authorities, duties and roles – is gradually giving way to religion as 'subjective life', 'life lived in deep connection with unique experiences of my self-in-relation'.[1] While the latter form of religious identity is most often associated with alternative religions or the 'New Age Movement', Heelas and Woodhead do not make clear-cut distinctions between 'spirituality' and 'traditional religion'. Indeed, they recognise significant elements of 'subjective life' spirituality within the congregational realm, not least within charismatic evangelicalism, which celebrates personal experience as a site of spiritual significance. However, this celebration of the subjective has undergone significant changes of emphasis in recent decades, raising questions of the extent to which charismatic churches retain a distinctive Christian spirituality, and whether their appeal to experience fosters spiritual diversity or religious individualism. Moreover, has this appeal to experience, now so popular in the wider religious and cultural landscape, eroded boundaries between Christian churches and the social forces that surround them?

As an initial way into exploring these questions, I sent St Michael's parishioners questionnaires, presenting them with the notion that 'life is basically spiritual' and asking for their response to this idea. One respondent, a retired woman in her sixties, answered in depth, filling the back sheet of the questionnaire. This is what she had to say:

> The more I mature in the Christian faith, the more aware I become of the Spirit of God. I am usually aware of God's presence. Sometimes He is nearer than breathing, and at other times He is more distant. If I go through a period where I forego my quiet times, His presence recedes. At these times I suddenly realise that I am giving first priority to other things, rather than to God. There have been some occasions (a few) in my life when I have been very afraid and could not pray, but it was at these times that the Holy Spirit seemed to take over, causing me to say whatever needed

---

[1] Paul Heelas and Linda Woodhead (with Benjamin Seel, Bronislaw Szerszynski and Karin Tusting), *The Spiritual Revolution. Why Religion is Giving Way to Spirituality* (Malden, MA, Oxford and Carlton, Victoria: Blackwell, 2005), p. 3.

to be said to God. On these occasions my fear was completely removed and replaced by a deep peace. At other times I have been guided in such mysterious ways that in my view this guidance could only have come from God. Because of these experiences, I would agree that life is basically spiritual. In my case, it's all about choices. The more time I choose to spend with God, the more I am aware of His presence as I go about my daily life.

This parishioner affirmed with some eloquence a series of themes that I began to discern among the St Michael's congregation during my research. She stresses the radical immanence of God and the close, guiding influence of the Holy Spirit. For her, life is basically spiritual because the presence of God pervades her daily experience. His presence is not unconditional, but requires that she prioritise her devotion to God over worldly matters. Above all, this is a presence and a closeness that implies an ongoing personal relationship between God and the individual believer. In theoretical terms, this indicates what Heelas and Woodhead, among others, have called a *turn to the subjective* in that (1) the sacred is somehow present within the self or enveloped within personal experience, and (2) this experience is described drawing from the subjective resources of the individual.

The account quoted above could be seen as fairly conventional discourse for a member of a charismatic evangelical church. Other questionnaire responses were more intriguing, and challenged my perceptions of the congregation and its understanding of spirituality. Some parishioners discerned in the word 'spiritual' a lack of substance or a basic imbalance, calling for a more grounded understanding of the Christian life. For example:

In my opinion life is not basically spiritual – it is very real.

As Christians we should at all times be aware of how God's Spirit is leading us/working. God recognises we have physical and intellectual needs too. It is little use being over spiritual when it prevents us being relevant to non-Christians.

We are spiritual beings but live in a material world. It has to be both.

Other respondents went the other way, affirming an understanding of the Christian life that was thoroughly bound up in the internal complexities of the spiritual self. For some, this was extended into a universalist notion of the spiritual.

I believe that there is a spiritual element in everyone, which some acknowledge more than others. All of our activities affect us on a spiritual level even if we do not reason it out in that way.

This would seem to conflict with the exclusivism often associated with evangelicalism and also implies a conception of human nature that is basically benign, rather than sinful. Another respondent endorsed an almost trinitarian understanding of human nature, emphasising the role of the Holy Spirit in fostering an inner unity:

> Man is a 'plurality in unity'. Spiritual, emotional, physical, mental, aspirational etc are all equal parts of a whole human being. Through new birth into union with Christ, the potential exists for God's Holy Spirit to fill every part of this whole human being, giving life in all its fullness.

This is less unorthodox, and suggests deep theological reflection. But the 'plurality in unity' notion hints at language traditionally used with reference to God, rather than man. It is a far cry from the Augustinian fallenness traditional to the evangelical worldview, which gels so well with ideas of substitutionary atonement and radical conversion.

The most unorthodox response came from a female parishioner whose conception of 'our innate oneness with spirit' veers close to understandings of selfhood most commonly associated with the 'New Age' Movement.

> We become less spiritual as we become more sophisticated and materialistic. We are spiritual beings and much is lost between childhood and adulthood as we 'learn' to do things in a 'socially acceptable' way and suppress our 'innate oneness' with spirit. Under pressure to do what is 'right' in the eyes of others it is easy to ignore what we know instinctively to be right (and wrong).

This woman was not alone in adopting 'New Age' language in speaking of the 'spiritual' in life. Evoking language often used in the 'New Age' publishing world, one male parishioner claimed,

> Life consists of the body, the mind and the spirit. We should develop all three of them.

In asking parishioners what they thought about the notion that life is basically spiritual, I was expecting to receive a collective endorsement of traditional charismatic theology: that life is only truly 'spiritual' for those who accept the Holy Spirit into their lives and turn to Jesus. I got hints of this, as with the parishioner who claimed that 'everyone has a spiritual need, [but] this can only be fulfilled in Jesus' and who added the caveat, 'not alternative religions'. But the majority of responses were varied, inconsistent and unorthodox. They exhibited little reference to doctrine or scripture, a striking tendency towards idiosyncrasy and an occasional evocation of the 'New Age'. They expressed a search for the spiritual dimensions of the self, but sometimes without the apparent guidance of any obvious ordering paradigm. In this sense they signify reliance upon subjectivity, but also a tendency towards significant diversity. This reflects James Davison Hunter's comments about the nature of modernity, which, as institutions multiply and pluralism gains pace, is characterised by a process whereby 'stable and well-defined patterns of individual conduct, social relationship, and thought lose their taken for granted plausibility'.[2] As institutions, including churches, cease to provide clear answers to important

---

[2] James Davison Hunter, 'Subjectivization and the New Evangelical Theodicy', *Journal for the Scientific Study of Religion* 20:1 (1982), p. 39.

existential questions, individuals increasingly turn inwards to the resources of the self.

Robert Bellah has developed this idea in terms of two different orientations, which he says are common throughout contemporary western culture. Utilitarian individualism refers to the approach to life that seeks fulfilment through the satisfaction of self-interest; expressive individualism focuses upon feelings and intuitions associated with authenticity.[3] It is the latter that has featured most in discussions of religious innovation after the 1960s and notions of authenticity associated with selfhood and personal experience are used to explain the popularity of such varied movements as Zen Buddhism, the International Society for Krishna Consciousness, the Rajneesh movement and the Jesus Army. Expressive individualism engenders a preoccupation with the internal character of the self and of the relation of the self to other selves (subjectivity). In terms of the structure of religious forms, expressive individualism – while exhibiting a significant synergy with wider cultural trends – is thought to be precarious and unstable. As individuals turn away from external tradition for a sense of meaning, instead appealing to the resources of their subjective selves, religious identities become increasingly diverse and disconnected.

Such might be said of the examples from the St Michael's congregation given above. Conceptions of the 'spiritual' are not necessarily nor predominantly shaped by the external authorities of scripture, doctrine or church tradition. Rather, they appear to be constructed with more reference to the internal resources of the self, namely memory, introspective reflection and personal experience. The diversity of the responses suggests that individual parishioners are not participating in a single, unified tradition, but are drawing from internally felt notions of significance, a pattern that suggests either the absence of a binding authority or its lack of plausibility in the eyes of these parishioners.

Some commentators have argued that a stress on 'experience' tends to lead to a 'deregulated' spirituality,[4] characterised by a propensity for spiritual *bricolage*, i.e., the selection of material from a variety of sources, chosen in response to personal preference or need, rather than in accordance with the norms of established tradition. The diversity of responses above suggests that there is some substance to this argument, and that St Michael's parishioners are, to some extent, building their own spiritual identities out of the multitude of resources at their disposal. However, within St Michael's, the invocation of the subjective as spiritually significant is not entirely without a sense of structure and order, and neither can it be understood as a simple unfiltered response to wider trends within late modernity. A focus upon the personal, subjective life of faith has been a central characteristic of the evangelical

---

[3] Robert Bellah *et al*, Habits of the Heart. Individualism and Commitment in American Life (Berkeley, Los Angeles, CA, and London: University of California Press, 1985).

[4] Mark J. Cartledge, 'The Future of Glossolalia: Fundamentalist or Experientialist?', *Religion* 28 (1998), pp. 233-44, building on an analysis in Harvey Cox, *Fire from Heaven. The Rise of Pentecostal Spirituality and the Reshaping of Religion in the Twenty-First Century* (London: Cassell, 1996).

tradition for centuries, and this was intensified by the charismatic renewal movement, in which St Michael-le-Belfrey has been a keen and influential participant. Charismatic activity – glossolalia, 'words of knowledge' and emotional, impassioned sung worship – feature heavily in St Michael's services, prayer meetings and in some home groups. As such, parishioners embrace a spirituality built around the infusion of divine reality and power into everyday experience. In order to account for patterns of expression in the subjective faith-lives of St Michael's members, it is necessary to examine how the church has participated in recent developments within the charismatic movement. For it is in dialogue with shared experiences and interpretations of charismata that the subjective identities of these parishioners take on their present form.

The Charismatic Movement: The Story So Far

According to Ian Hall, the first recorded case of charismatic renewal within the Church of England occurred in 1963, at St Mark's, Gillingham, the church led by the Revd John Collins.[5] A year later, The Fountain Trust was established by Michael Harper as an agency for the promotion of renewal within the mainstream denominations, through conferences and a bi-monthly journal, *Renewal*, which was also edited by Harper. While the charismatic movement had sectarian dimensions, e.g., in the House Churches, charismatic renewal has largely been contained within existing denominations. By 1989, there were almost as many charismatics in the Church of England as in the rest of the Restorationist churches put together.[6] And while many evangelicals were hostile to these developments, charismatic renewal had a radical effect upon a large proportion of those within the English movement – over 40% attending 'charismatic evangelical' churches by the mid-1980s.[7]

Charismatic renewal has always been phenomenologically similar to traditional Pentecostalism, embracing the manifestation of the charismatic gifts described in Acts 2 and 1 Corinthians 12, most notably speaking in tongues, prophecy and healing. A shared experience of being inspired by the Spirit also fostered a Pentecostal style of worship: emotional, loud, exuberant and celebratory. However, the renewal movement was distinct in several respects. Firstly, it was predominantly a middle class phenomenon whereas the Pentecostal churches were for the most part comprised of working-class Christians. More significantly, it had what Andrew

---

[5] Ian Rodney Hall, 'The Current Evangelical Resurgence: An Analysis and Evaluation of the Growth of Contemporary Evangelicalism in Britain and the USA' (PhD thesis, University of Leeds, 1994), pp. 106-7.

[6] David Bebbington, 'Evangelicalism in its Settings: The British and American Movements since 1940', in M.A. Noll, D.W. Bebbington and G.A. Rawlyk (eds.), *Evangelicalism. Comparative Studies of Popular Protestantism in North America, the British Isles, and Beyond, 1700-1990* (New York and Oxford: OUP, 1994), p. 371; Peter Brierley, *Prospects for the Nineties* (London: MARC Europe, 1991), p. 52.

[7] Peter Brierley, *Christian England. What the 1989 English Church Census Reveals* (London: MARC Europe, 1991), p. 161.

Walker calls a different 'tone', suggestive of a more genteel set of revisions rather than a radical overhaul of existing tradition. Worship was less emotionally extreme, music more reflective of modern trends than old style hymnody. Transformation was through inner as well as physical healing. Effectively, charismatic renewal was Pentecostalism 'redefined by class, taste and the late modern preoccupation with therapy and self-fulfilment'.[8]

Andrew Walker places the heyday of the charismatic movement in the 1970s, a period of charismatic resurgence among congregations and clergy. The 1980s and 90s, while seeing additional growth, were also times of radical change. One strand embodies a move towards unification and an ironing out of sectarian and phenomenological differences. By the early 1990s, the Evangelical Alliance had persuaded most of the Restorationist groups to join them and Spring Harvest – under the influence of Clive Calver – had become a generic charismatic celebration, a 'catch-all charismatic supermarket', as Walker puts it.[9] This is symptomatic of a levelling process, whereby Pentecostals, renewalists and independent charismatics have become indistinguishable in terms of their practices, songs, myths and favoured gurus. Dave Tomlinson has associated this process with what he calls 'charismaticisation', i.e., the movement whereby charismatic values and conventions have become so normative as to become infused into the culture of the majority of evangelical churches.[10] Even churches which do not claim the charismatic label are happy to worship without robes or much ceremony, include significant lay participation and sing Vineyard and Graham Kendrick choruses. In this respect, the charismatic has become broadened and diversified almost beyond recognition, so that it is much more difficult to draw clear boundaries between charismatic and non-charismatic churches. Furthermore, the charismatic has come to function less like an unchanging tradition and more like a repertoire of spiritual resources that one may dip into according to changing practical and devotional needs. Part of this repertoire has been healing services, variously interpreted as inner emotional healing or physical remedy and practised by the laying on of hands, counselling or through more meditative methods. Charismatic churches have adapted strategies from psychology and psychotherapy as legitimate tools for pastoral ministry within a broader understanding of renewal, and chapter 3 described how this occurred within St Michael's during the 1980s. Healing, and renewal as its theological context, has taken on a broader meaning, appealing to a larger range of churches, and by 1998 over 70% of English charismatic churches were holding healing services.[11]

---

[8] Andrew Walker, 'Thoroughly Modern: Sociological Reflections on the Charismatic Movement from the End of the Twentieth Century', in S. Hunt, M. Hamilton and T. Walter (eds.), *Charismatic Christianity. Sociological Perspectives* (Basingstoke and London: Macmillan, 1997), p. 30.

[9] Walker, 'Thoroughly Modern', p. 33.

[10] Dave Tomlinson, *The Post-Evangelical* (London: SPCK, 1995), pp. 15-7.

[11] Peter Brierley, *The Tide is Running Out. What the English Church Attendance Survey Reveals* (London: Christian Research, 2000), p. 178.

At the same time, a series of upheavals intensified and dramatised charismatic experience, prompting significant backlash from mainstream churchgoers as well as from within the charismatic movement itself. In 1981, John Wimber brought his 'signs and wonders' ministry to the UK, subsequently exerting a significant influence over British evangelicalism throughout the 1980s. Wimber had been centrally involved in the American Vineyard movement since the early 1970s, and taught a charismatic theology that went beyond both classical Pentecostalism and the charismatic renewal movement. According to Wimber, our secular rational worldview prevents us from recognising the present day reality of supernatural forces, and part of the mission of all those who are born again is to demonstrate the power of the Holy Spirit through healing, casting out demons, and 'power evangelism', just as Jesus did.[12] Such 'gifts' were not confined to the New Testament period, as the cessationists believe, nor are they restricted to singular experiences of 'second blessing', as some Pentecostalists would have it, but are available to all who have faith within the context of an ongoing and practical ministry. This was dubbed the 'third wave' of charismatic renewal, and prepared the way for the Toronto Blessing in 1994. The 'blessing' emerged from the Toronto Airport Church, at which possession by the gifts of the Spirit had become manifest in hysterical laughter, uncontrollable weeping, bodily jerking, shaking and animal noises. It quickly spread all over the charismatic world, following the many thousands of visitors who encountered the Toronto phenomenon,[13] though its intensity meant that it burnt itself out within the space of a few years.

Unsurprisingly, the Toronto Blessing prompted widespread accusations of hysteria and generated fracture and disillusionment among charismatics, although only after exerting considerable influence on the charismatic evangelical subculture across the English churches.[14] John Wimber's Vineyard fellowship severed links with the Airport Church in 1995 and criticisms focused upon an unchecked abandon (some manifestations had semi-erotic overtones) and theological vacuity.[15] The autocratic

---

12 See John Wimber, *Power Evangelism. Signs and Wonders Today* (London, Sydney, Auckland, Toronto: Hodder & Stoughton, 1985).

13 Jonathan Ruthven cites a figure from 2002 of 300,000 visitors, while Martyn Percy, writing in 2005, claims that 'around 2 million visitors or 'pilgrims' have journeyed to Toronto to experience the blessing for themselves'. See Jonathan Ruthven, 'Back to the Future for Pentecostal/Charismatic Evangelicals in North America and World Wide: Radicalizing Evangelical Theology and Practice', in Craig Bartholomew *et al* (eds.), *The Futures of Evangelicalism. Issues and Prospects* (Leicester: Inter-Varsity Press, 2003), p. 305, and Martyn Percy, 'Adventure and Atrophy in a Charismatic Movement: Returning to the Toronto Blessing', *Journal of Contemporary Religion* 20.1 (2005), p. 72.

14 Nigel Scotland claims that, at one point, 'it was reckoned that as many as 3,000 UK churches were experiencing the Toronto Blessing'. See Nigel Scotland, 'Evangelicalism and the Charismatic Movement (UK)', in Bartholomew *et al* (eds), *The Futures of Evangelicalism*, p. 287.

15 Martyn Percy, *Words, Wonders and Power. Understanding Contemporary Fundamentalism and Revivalism* (London: SPCK, 1996), p. 153.

structures of the 'third wave' have also contributed to a growing cynicism both among charismatics and across the wider church. Its tendency to invest great authority in the hands of individuals has been open to abuse, to the misuse of power by dominant leaders and the consequent domination and maltreatment of the marginalised. Observers recall a classic and sobering case in the Nine O'Clock Service, which was originally inspired by Wimber's preaching during a 1985 visit to Sheffield.

There is a sense in which the performative, supernaturalist facets of evangelicalism are now treated with an added caution and with an air of suspicion. Given this, it is perhaps unsurprising that the number of charismatics among evangelicals declined by 16% during the 1990s while 'mainstream' evangelicals increased by 68%.[16] This can be contrasted with the 1980s, when growth among evangelicals could almost entirely be accounted for with reference to its charismatic wing.[17] The charismatic growth of the 1980s gave way to the subtleties of a centrist position, as a large number of clergy, while not disowning their charismatic heritage, felt sufficiently uncomfortable with what had become of the charismatic movement to distance themselves from the label. Moreover, while the charismatic wing of the movement is now declining at a slower rate, suggesting any disillusionment was particular to the experience of the 1990s, it is the black Pentecostal churches which are showing most signs of vitality.[18] Indeed, among white middle-class English evangelicals, the loudest and most vociferous voices of recent years have come from a more Reformed, rather than charismatic, tradition.

The Charismatic Identity of St Michael-le-Belfrey

As a church very much in the vanguard of charismatic renewal, St Michael's has been caught up in all of these developments. David Watson had 'received the gift of the Holy Spirit' when he was a curate in Cambridge during the early 1960s and he brought his vision of charismatic renewal to St Cuthbert's in 1965. Since then, St Cuthbert's, and then St Michael-le-Belfrey, have been associated with the charismatic tradition, as their growing congregations have been attracted to Spirit-filled worship and fellowship, and as its successive incumbents – all of them self-consciously and unapologetically charismatic in their theology – have justified and advanced the church's various innovations with reference to the Holy Spirit. This pervasive thread in the church's development has not been immune to changes in the wider movement, as the language of renewal has focused on lay empowerment, new forms of community and spiritual diversity, giving way occasionally to more divisive developments, as charismatic theology has been used to justify the exclusion of women from positions of leadership, or when prophecy has been used to challenge the authority of appointed leaders.

---

[16] Brierley, *Tide*, p. 146.

[17] Brierley, *Christian England*, pp. 164-5.

[18] Peter Brierley, *Pulling Out of the Nosedive. A Contemporary Picture of Churchgoing* (London: Christian Research, 2006), p. 98.

Many parishioners first attended St Michael's because of its reputation as a charismatic evangelical stronghold, and this informs their expectations of it. These individuals arrive with what might be called a 'charismatic ethos', a moral and aesthetic style or mood that has divinely touched subjective experience at its centre.[19] They measure the vitality of the church by the extent to which this ethos is fostered and given channels of expression. Many are happiest in the evening service, support charismatic gifts in prayer meetings and prefer an emotional style of worship.

For some, this ethos is grounded in what might be called a 'charismatic worldview', a comprehensive perspective on reality, ordered according to the designs and powers of supernatural beings. This worldview often conflates human struggle with spiritual warfare between the forces of good and evil. Some parishioners feel that humans are inevitably caught up in this struggle, and are often preyed on by Satan. June explained the occurrence of sin in this way:

... there is a battle – sometimes you can feel that within yourself, sometimes you're pulled two ways. So I think people are tempted by Satan, and they give in, and that's how evil happens.

This supernaturalist model of reality was not embraced by the entire congregation, but evidence suggested that it was a significant aspect of Christian identity for the majority. According to my questionnaire survey, in 2000, 79% believed in the devil as a 'personal being who causes evil in the world', that is, rather than an 'impersonal force' or something less clear. Belief in spiritual warfare was widespread and shaped how the congregation dealt with everyday life on a personal level.

I found that charismatic discourse – as aesthetically or ontologically significant – pervaded the interactive culture of the congregation. Some explained their continued attendance with reference to the influence of the Holy Spirit: 'it's where the Spirit has led me'; 'I have left a few times but God kept dragging me back!' Some described the church as 'Spirit-filled' and many claimed that they 'felt the presence of the Lord' when they entered St Michael's for the first time.

St Michael's has also played its part in affirming and maintaining the two different charismatic trends described above, and these shape the culture of the church. It has exemplified the notion of a unified charismatic tradition beyond denominational or ecclesiastical difference, allowing the emerging emotive, experience-centred, expressive style to be channelled through its worship, in particular. It has also been instrumental in the UK's embrace of John Wimber, the Vineyard tradition and 'signs and wonders' theology, thus endorsing the hyper-dramatic innovations of the third wave. Wimber became a close friend of David Watson following a visit to Fuller Theological Seminary in the early 1980s, and it was at Watson's invitation that Wimber made his first visit to England in 1981. He

---

[19] This use of 'ethos', and of 'worldview' later on, builds on a conceptual discussion by anthropologist Clifford Geertz, found in Clifford Geertz, 'Ethos, World View, and the Analysis of Sacred Symbols', in *The Interpretation of Cultures* (New York: Basic Books, 1973), pp. 126-41.

would return to St Michael's several times during the 1980s, including after Watson's death, so that the Vineyard teachings on healing and power evangelism became infused within the life of the congregation. Those most receptive would also welcome the Toronto Blessing, which David White embraced with such enthusiasm during the mid 1990s, although Wimber's version of renewal was a step further than some would have liked.

It is difficult to paint an accurate picture of perspectives held within the congregation at the turn of the millennium, but conversations with long-standing members revealed a discernible set of tensions. While charismatic renewal in itself was embraced by most as desirable and essential to the vitality of the church, it was interpreted by some as best channelled as a constrained, organic, broadly experiential phenomenon, a force through which the church's most creative innovations had been made possible, but which was not inconsistent with a reflective, sober faith-life. Others yearned for a more overtly emotional spirituality, associating the charismatic with the intuitive, the dynamic and the supernatural, often generating wider benefits for the church, but usually manifest in experiences which are immediate and dramatic. Those in the former category tended to view the latter as emotionally excessive and insufficiently reflective; those in the latter group tended to see the former view as indicative of a reluctance to wholly embrace the life of the Spirit. Both positions informed a revision of both charismatic ethos and worldview by individuals in light of their own experience, effectively fostering a whole host of perspectives held concurrently within the same community.

In this respect, charismatic gifts have become a spiritual resource from which to draw according to personal need rather than a prescribed set of defined practices. At the same time, a series of dramatised and emotionally intense 'revivals' have provoked widespread disillusionment so that some have turned away from charismatic experience altogether. Arguably, the former trend has been urged on by the latter, a sense of suspicion towards hyper-emotional episodes leading individuals to switch to an outlook which stresses gifts as optional, occasional and altogether toned down. The dominant mood in St Michael's could be characterised in this way, and during my research I witnessed no occasions of intense or extreme activity – no falling down, no being 'slain in the Spirit' and no hysterical laughter. If inspiration by the Spirit had taken on a diversity of forms, those forms were often staid and discursive, rather than dramatic, more story than possession, at least in public. Indeed, narrative expressions were particularly important, as they provided parishioners a channel through which the subjective experience of God working in and through one's life could be communicated and affirmed among fellow members.

Personal Narratives

In recent years, it has become fashionable among anthropologists to emphasise narrative as constitutive of identity. According to a common argument, it is through our capacity as storytellers that we construct our identities and the identities of the people around us, including those individuals who are the subjects of academic enquiry.[20] James Hopewell adopts the idea of narrative in his attempts to understand Christian congregations, arguing that congregations construct their identities out of the stories or narratives they tell about themselves. Interestingly, he associates charismatic Christians with a romantic kind of tale in so far as they stress the loving and dramatic heroism of God as He comes to save us on earth. God intervenes in history, thus suspending the normal laws of nature, in order to offer salvation to the individual. In accepting Him, the individual receives God's indwelling love and power.[21]

Although Hopewell's description of the charismatic narrative is idealised and perhaps far-fetched, it is not without substance, and certainly reflects many of the stories that I heard the charismatics of St Michael's tell about themselves. Many of these had a dramatic, romantic tone, and all stressed the loving intervention of God within the human realm. Such tales abound among parishioners, and in speaking to them informally I was immediately struck by the extent to which their everyday discourse was punctuated with references to God's influence, guidance or presence, often in very concrete terms. Telling these stories is a way of infusing daily experience with order and meaning. By re-interpreting what might be described as the mundane into something that has been touched by the divine, congregants are imposing a theological framework which bestows plausibility onto their lives and grants them spiritual significance.

It will be useful to examine some examples. The following are derived from two main sources. Many are drawn from observations and conversations from the field – my encounters with charismatic ideas were predominantly through informal conversations with parishioners. I also draw from extended questionnaire responses. Respondents were asked to describe one experience that had been most significant to them in their life as a Christian. Together, examples may be grouped into three overlapping categories: testimony, explanation and guidance.

The most structured and ritualised presentations of God 'working in one's life' were in *testimony*. These personal accounts of coming to faith or of crises within one's faith-life were often delivered by individuals in church, warmly encouraged by the vicar and generally followed by applause from the congregation. The following example was delivered at an evening service, following a Bible reading of the parable of the prodigal son.

> The vicar invites Tom and his wife to come up to the front of the church. Apparently Tom has a story to tell us that is very much like that of the 'lost son'. Tom, a tall, stocky man is his early forties, approaches the lectern and begins to tell the congregation the story of his conversion. In 1980, he was 22

---

[20] For examples of influential discussions of this approach to identity and the writing process, see Clifford Geertz, *Works and Lives: The Anthropologist as Author* (Cambridge: Polity Press, 1988), and John van Maanen, *Tales of the Field. On Writing Ethnography* (Chicago, IL: University of Chicago Press, 1988).

[21] James F. Hopewell, *Congregation. Stories and Structures* (London: SCM Press, 1988), pp. 61-2.

and had an experience which left him converted to Christianity; as he says, I 'invited Jesus into my life'. Tom was so passionate about his Christianity that he told all his friends about Jesus and managed to convert several of them within one week. He was reading his Bible and praying all of the time. He even took his Bible into the shower with him, wrapped in a plastic sheet! His devotion was rewarded. He had been earning £8 thousand a year; within twelve months, he was bringing in £70 thousand a year. Soon afterwards, he says 'God allowed me to buy a bungalow' for £50 thousand, which was soon worth £250 thousand. He assures us that he is not boasting, but wants to talk about the extent to which God had blessed him. However, in the early 1990s things started to go wrong. He went bankrupt and 'hit rock bottom'. He started taking soft drugs and drank heavily. His wife left and divorced him and his son abandoned his education with a drug problem. He describes himself as a very bad person, he had turned to sin. He was 'in the pig swill', just like the lost son. On the point of suicide, Tom sold everything he owned and went to Texas to stay with a friend. He describes himself as 'an embarrassment' at this point – he couldn't go anywhere, constantly breaking down in tears in public. Eventually, his friend persuaded him to go to church with him and, during the service, while the preacher was still speaking, Tom ran to the front and begged for forgiveness. He said he'd do anything, just live a simple life, just be a simple Christian, and begged God to forgive him. After this moment of crisis he was able to rebuild his life. It was too late for his first marriage – his wife had already remarried. But now he has a new wonderful wife, and talks about how wonderful things are now that he is 'back with God'.

(Adapted from fieldnotes, 17 October 1999.)

Tom's story is in many ways typical of the testimonies associated with contemporary charismatic revivalism. He stresses the temptations and evils of modern life, conversion as radical existential transformation and a tendency to become a zealous Christian and evangelist immediately afterwards. Unlike many testimonies though, Tom's lapse into moral decadence occurred after his conversion, and as a consequence of relying too heavily upon 'worldly' gratification. His account implicitly warns against the dangers of lapsing into complacency, of the ever-present danger of 'the world', and perhaps even of confusing worldly and divine favour. His experience has taught him this, and he described his past in terms of God guiding him into a life of Christian integrity and moral decency. He talked to me about his life, saying he 'does alright' now, but works alone and prefers to live a simple life, his aim simply being to 'love God, love my wife and try to show love to all those around me'.

Tom's story echoes the testimonies given by numerous other St Michael's members, both in church and in ordinary conversation. I noticed that it was clearly important to be able to draw readily from a defined narrative, and questions about conversion invariably prompted colourful and detailed stories of personal journey and identity transformation. Many stressed conversion as a passage from chaos into a new order, as the door into a new freedom, a freedom *from* corruption and decadence. Indeed, such oppositional pairs – chaos/order, slavery/freedom, uncertainty/certainty – help to endorse and sustain the association of western modernity and secular culture with moral and spiritual bankruptcy. One parishioner captured this quite simply: 'My faith is what keeps me sane.'

Testimonies provide individuals with a narrative form through which to construct their spiritual biographies and make sense of their experience in terms of divine order. They allow individuals to capitalise on their subjective resources and present their evangelical identities in terms of a participation in a larger narrative of revival, spiritual betterment and the ongoing struggle between godly and ungodly forces.

A second kind of appeal to subjective experience focuses upon the explanation of especially fortuitous or unfortunate events. One member reported a time when he had been experiencing problems with his eyesight because of a computer monitor at work. When he was provided with a new computer, his explanation was that it was God who had provided for him. Another young female parishioner shared a story during an Alpha discussion session, about her quest to find a place to live in London, after applying for a job there. Her preference was for a nice flat that was cheap, in the centre of London, where she could live with fellow Christians who were also female. Not only was she offered the job (which she claimed she was unqualified for), but a clergyman who was an acquaintance had managed to find her a flat fitting all of her criteria within four hours of her enquiry. Such fortuitous events are seen as divine blessings, as God caring for His flock through the human agencies of the everyday world.

For a congregation that exhibits some belief in spiritual warfare, it is not surprising to find also negative experiences attributed to Satanic influence, especially when they can be viewed as attempts to thwart the faithful. Referring to an agnostic work-mate who had rejected his invitations to attend St Michael's, one parishioner said that he had felt 'the enemy' at work. An Alpha discussion group leader once reported how, due to circumstances such as illness and family problems, certain leaders had been uncertain whether they would be able to attend the all-important Alpha 'Away Day'. As it happened, the day trip proceeded as planned, although she still explained these issues in terms of Satan, threatening the success of God's plan. The assumption is that Satan has a great deal at stake in disrupting God's work.

Writing about the charismatic movement among Roman Catholics in the USA, Thomas J. Csordas argues that the ways in which charismatics find meaning in everyday life events may be compared with the mode of reasoning that the famous anthropologist E. E. Evans-Pritchard identified among the witchcraft practices of the African Azande.[22] That is, witchcraft – as with superstition – serves to explain the coincidence of several factors which result in an incident that is especially fortuitous or unfortunate for those parties involved. This is especially important when the

---

22 E.E. Evans-Pritchard, *Witchcraft, Oracles and Magic Among the Azande* (Oxford: Clarendon Press, 1976).

incident markedly enhances or threatens the goals of the group.[23] The distinction lies in how individuals respond to such affairs: witchcraft demands an inter-personal resolution which often engages social conflict; by contrast, Satanic interference or 'demonic harrassment' is 'an affair for the self'.[24] It does not provoke social conflict but refers to the *individual's* struggle with supernatural powers. By focusing upon the subjective experience of individuals in isolation, this process actually enhances internal social cohesion. Individuals attribute good or bad fortune to agencies outside of the human remit while forging a shared discourse through which to discuss these encounters among their peers in the church. While negative incidents are interpreted as an intentional threat to the activities of the group, they actually affirm group order by allowing an explanation of this threat in supernaturalist terms. In this vein, an appeal to subjectivity facilitates a cognitive function, as individuals together seek meaningful explanations of events in the light of a shared worldview. Moreover, while this worldview was not wholeheartedly shared by the entire St Michael's congregation, it was never openly challenged either, and dissidents were notable for their subtlety and diplomacy. Order and harmony are powerful, if not always explicit, priorities, as demonstrated in the previous chapter.

A third form of subjective narrative has as its focus divine guidance – the perceived experience of divine intervention through advice, new knowledge or reassurance. Such accounts often arise in connection with prayer, but are also associated with dreams or 'words from God', i.e., messages which offer insight at moments of crisis or radical change. For example, one parishioner spoke about how a friend had received a 'word from God' affirming the health of her unborn child. The woman took this as 'a promise that this baby would be OK, that we were important enough for God to choose a godmother for my baby'.

Here, God's blessing is received second hand, through a message delivered to a fellow Christian, although the message carries consequences for both the direct recipient and the person who is the subject of the message. God is treated as the source of future knowledge, but also *of comfort and as the guiding force behind a life decision* – choosing a godmother for one's child. Such instances which operate on an interpersonal level demonstrate the extent to which the common experience of divine immanence is entrenched within the culture of St Michael's. It is shared among members, a process that allows for the reinforcement of this belief and which fosters greater cohesion among congregants who share the same convictions.

It is the experiential element in charismatic evangelicalism that helps members to find solace and comfort through their inner lives. The culture of St Michael's stresses the intimacy and warmth of divine immanence, encouraging members to

---

[23] Thomas J. Csordas, *Language, Charisma and Creativity. The Ritual Life of a Religious Movement* (Berkeley, CA: University of California Press, 1997), p. 62. For the parallels with western ideas of superstition, see Nicholas Abercrombie *et al*, 'Superstition and Religion: The God of the Gaps', in David Martin and Michael Hill (eds.), *A Sociological Yearbook of Religion in Britain* (London: SCM Press, 1970), p. 122.

[24] Csordas, *Language, Charisma and Creativity*, p. 62.

seek out Jesus as an ever-present guide and friend. Narrative accounts of such guidance can be specific and isolated, as in the example given above, but can also take the form of a general sense of reassurance, as in the retired woman who claimed that '... Jesus spoke to me through his word, telling me not to worry about my life, but to seek his kingdom and everything would fall into place'. Other experiences of divine guidance amount to a radical turnabout in a life-changing decision, or the final urge to make a long-standing one. One elderly woman said she had received 'very direct guidance from God' in obtaining her divorce.

Generally speaking, parishioners were encouraged to find meaning and direction in their ongoing experience of life, and responded by forging narratives that were shared among co-members. In this sense reality is seen as essentially orderly and pregnant with spiritual significance. Individuals were encouraged to engage in an 'extended dialogue with the entirety of [their] experience, processing it for its latent spiritual implications'.[25] In this way, even negative encounters, although often treated as Satanic in origin, were also often perceived retrospectively as having positive consequences by developing self-understanding and knowledge of God.

These examples demonstrate how narrative serves as a discursive method for achieving meaning; particularly because it is shared. As Peter Berger sagely comments, 'the subjective reality of the world hangs on the thin thread of conversation'.[26] Narrative tales are a basis of plausibility, both for those who hear them and, more importantly, for those who construct and tell them. These stories both situate the individual within a living discursive community, and within a divine plan, thus generating a sense of purpose, of 'chosenness', and of being cared for within the context of a network of divine *and* human relationships.

To be sure, if these narrative examples share an implicit theological framework, it is very broad, often conveying no more than the goodness, closeness and power of God. In this way it is more similar to a kind of 'folk religion' than to church doctrine. But it is this malleability that allows for such narratives to achieve such a universal appeal among the congregation. As they are largely shaped by the subjective experiences of the individual, rather than by external authorities, they allow for all aspects of social reality to be potentially infused with religious significance. This makes for a radically inclusive medium, as it does not discriminate according to biblical knowledge or position in the church. Rather, all congregants are offered the opportunity to construct their own narratives shaped around their own lives, thus affirming spiritual significance for their own social identities.

It is also worth noting that this use of subjectivity has a prophylactic function. If all of social reality is potentially touched by the supernatural, as these stories claim, then the distinction between the sacred and the secular becomes meaningless. The world outside of the church is effectively integrated into a single meaning system, so that competing paradigms lose some of their secularising force. The secular

---

[25] Stephen J. Briers, 'Negotiating with Babylon: Responses to Modernity within a Restorationist Community' (PhD thesis, University of Cambridge, 1993), p. 42.

[26] Peter Berger, *The Sacred Canopy. Elements of a Sociological Theory of Religion* (Garden City, NY: Doubleday, 1967), p. 26.

arguments of an atheist colleague become the insidious machinations of the devil, and are thereby undermined as inevitably false and misguided. In this way secular and sacred are integrated into a single meaning system. The differentiation and pluralism of contemporary culture only has a propensity to fragment in so far as it is perceived to signal genuine difference. If this difference is undermined by a meaning system that incorporates all of reality into a divinely structured order, then for those who embrace this system, this difference may cease to be a threat. Stephen Briers finds the same phenomenon among Restorationist Christians:

> This devolution of responsibility to individuals is actually a strategy that safeguards the long-term interests of the group. Because a person carries his spiritual awareness around with him, the nomos of the group is not undermined by the competing environments through which he moves.[27]

The appeal to subjectivity through narrative serves three main functions. It bestows meaning, it offers inclusion in a community of experience and it acts as a counter-force against secular influence. However, like the processes of liberalisation charted in the preceding chapter, it also fosters diversity and broadens conceptions of evangelical identity.

Subjectivity in Ritual Forms

Most of the narrative examples given above relate to the personal lives of individuals rather than their experiences within the context of congregational life. This may, in part, be attributable to the high turnover in St Michael's – many parishioners have spent significant periods of time elsewhere. But it could also be due to the tendency towards privatisation and idiosyncrasy engendered by the particular embrace of the subjective fostered in this church. As individuals seek significance in the non-institutional, so they are less likely to associate authentic spiritual experience exclusively with activities that are connected to congregational life. And yet trends in the embrace of subjectivity are also discernible in forms of public ritual that are shared across the congregation. In this sense, subjectivisation has become institutionalised in the ongoing life of St Michael's.

For example, prayer was used alongside personal narrative as a discursive device for the negotiation and expression of spiritually-infused subjectivity. It is a channel of communication between the divine and the human, the validity and efficacy of which is presented in narrative accounts. In this way the two media feed off one another in providing the ritual basis and discursive expression of divine–human dialogue. The content of prayer and conception of its divine response appeared to be so broad that prayer served an inclusivising function, just as narrative did. It was a marker of inclusion in a complex ongoing relationship, participation in which was seen as a sign of one's place among the faithful. It also had an empowering function,

---

[27] Briers, *Negotiating with Babylon*, p. 44.

allowing individuals the means to actively engage in the furtherance of their life goals with a sense of guidance and divine endorsement.

At the time of my research, charismatic gifts were not practised by the entire congregation of St Michael's and yet their centrality in public worship meant they influenced its collective identity and shaped the styles of expression that were viewed as legitimate. Expression of charismata took on various forms. While prophecy was accepted as authentic, and certain individuals were known for their 'prophetic gifts', phenomena clearly identifiable as 'prophecies' were rare in regular public meetings. More common were 'words of knowledge', a term used to refer to messages delivered to individuals from God, and then delivered in public for the benefit of the congregation. Similarly, while healing by the Holy Spirit – both physical and emotional – was accepted as a reality, it was not a regular occurrence. During my research, a time of 'ministry' was offered at the conclusion of each Sunday service, at which individuals could be prayed over, and these experiences could be conceived as healing, whether physical or emotional. The other key manifestation of charismatic gifts was glossolalia, or tongue-speaking, which was practised both in services and in other contexts. I will take both glossolalia and words of knowledge in turn, paying particular attention to the way in which subjective experience is invoked as religiously significant.

The phenomenon of speaking in tongues appeared, for many members, to be an experience that could arise in a variety of social contexts. The vicar of St Michael's, Roger Simpson, even claimed to speak in tongues whilst riding on his bicycle around York. Another, long-standing, parishioner spoke of having conversations with 'the Lord' whilst working in her kitchen, suggesting an intimacy of relationship that was akin to an ever-present companion or friend. For most members, glossolalia appeared to be primarily confined to the private sphere. Indeed, my questionnaire survey suggested that the use of glossolalia in private was generally viewed more positively than its expression in the public arena of the church service. 24% of respondents claimed that they often spoke in tongues in church, while 40% said they often did this privately. This solitary practice was seen by many as an aid to prayer and was conceived in terms of a direct process of communication between the devotee and God. Moreover, private glossolalia was frequently described as a source of personal liberation, its semantically reduced nature apparently generating a momentary emancipation from the constraints of normal verbal discourse. Several parishioners claimed to take solace in speaking in tongues when they did not know what else to say to God. As one parishioner put it, '[it's an] outpouring of your spirit but without knowing what words to use...'

Glossolalia was also a major element of worship, particularly within the popular evening service, where it was predominantly enveloped into the extended 'blocks' of sung worship. The tone of worship was relaxed, but exuberant, and the congregation threw themselves into the experience with an almost tangible enthusiasm. Indeed, this experience of worship – noted by many for its informality, intensity and abandon – elicited responses from many parishioners that were deeply emotional. Some could be seen to be weeping, others swayed with the rhythm of the music, many held their hands aloft in praise and others spoke or sung in tongues. This set of responses was sometimes consciously encouraged by the worship band, who would slow down the beat to a song and continue to play through the chords at a subdued volume while the worship leader prompted the congregation with whispers of 'thank you Jesus' or of sung glossolalia. As the music intensified in volume so the congregation would respond with even more emotional intensity and a dulled murmur would grow into an emotional rapture of numerous voices, until it reached a crescendo in a repeat chorus of the original song.

What is most interesting about this kind of glossolalia is that whilst clearly public, it is also strangely private. Those parishioners who practised it within church services appeared to be absorbed into the anonymity of the congregation. In fact, glossolalia was so enveloped into the experience of sung worship that at first, I failed to notice it. It was only after hearing reports to the contrary and then discovering over time what it was that I should look for, that I realised that speaking in tongues was actually taking place.

I would suggest that the corporate expression of sung worship was used by many as a favoured context for speaking in tongues partly *because* of the anonymity that this experience allows. Public performance of glossolalia as a solitary act before others was extremely rare in any context, and spontaneous expressions which were 'Spirit-led' were notable for their performance *during* sung worship, rather than at any other points in the service. Furthermore, when questioned on the nature of glossolalia, members were more likely to treat it as a medium for worship than as a source of divine knowledge or wisdom, and as primarily voluntary rather than involuntary. Like private prayer, it was treated as a form of communication with God, whether as praise or petition, rather than as a message from God through the individual for the benefit of others. In the charismatic tradition, substantive messages have traditionally been extracted from episodes of tongues through the medium of interpretation. However, this was not often practised within the worship meetings of St Michael's. Glossolalia remained for the most part a personal act, engaged in without expectation of human response and without any necessary substantive meaning attached to it.

Some social scientists, following the classic work of Emile Durkheim, have interpreted charismatic gifts as phenomena that are generated out of the power of the assembled group.[28] Csordas describes 'loud praise' – i.e., impassioned sung worship – as having a 'life of its own', 'in which the reality of the collectivity becomes more vivid than the reality of individual members'.[29] Within St Michael's it was both the power but also the anonymity of the group that appeared to provoke individuals to engage in tongue-speaking during sung worship. There was certainly a sense of being caught up in the collective experience, but also a notable lack of performance – individuals threw themselves into worship, but without the kind of dramatic

---

[28] E.g., see Meredith McGuire, *Pentecostal Catholics. Power, Charisma and Order in a Religious Movement* (Philadelphia, PA: Temple University Press, 1982).

[29] Csordas, *Language, Charisma and Creativity*, p. 110.

behaviour which might set them apart from their peers. In this sense glossolalia is not so much 'privatised' as immersed in anonymity, collective rather than performed with an audience, and is expressed as worship rather than inter-personal politics. Explanations for this trend must refer to the recent history of the church, and to an increasing discomfort with charismatic performance, addressed later on in this chapter.

In contrast to glossolalia, words of knowledge were performed exclusively before an audience, as their value rests on their significance for an external party. Words of knowledge were a common feature at the St Michael's evening service during my time with the community. Usually towards the end of the evening, the service leader would approach the lectern and ask the congregation if anyone 'feels that God is saying anything to them' that they would like to share with the rest of the congregation. This would usually elicit responses from three or four parishioners. Each would walk to the front of the church and address the congregation at the lectern, before returning to their seat, and then another parishioner would rise to take their turn.

These speeches varied in length, content and style of delivery. All were confided to the service leader before being delivered to the congregation, as a means of checking their suitability and, presumably, their theological soundness. When I asked Roger Simpson about this process, he supported the need for authority on these occasions, saying that it was always useful to know a person's character, and to be sure they are not living in sin. This process functioned as a subtle form of policing and ensured that no radical or 'heretical' messages were delivered before the congregation. As such, it could be conceived as a means of social control, and as a way for leaders to exert their authority over the performance of gifts and over the communal worship process in general.[30] As argued in chapter 4, the public discourse of the congregation, while apparently relaxed and informal, is actually tightly ordered.

It is possible to classify the various words of knowledge that I heard during my research according to factors of source, audience and purpose of message. Some speeches were clearly composed with reference to the imaginative resources of the individual speaker, some of which were based on a central image which was then interpreted in terms of a specific message for the congregation. Others had a more discursive basis and were either based on, or were entirely composed of, a reading from a written work deemed to be of some spiritual value. In these cases, although speakers would not claim that the text itself was given to them by God, a common interpretation would be that God had guided them to that particular reading.

The intended audience of words of knowledge varied between the congregation as a whole – the message was valid for everyone present – and 'words' that were aimed at particular individuals. In a case of the latter, individuals were never named, but aspects of their person or station in life might be cited, so that recognition was at

---

[30] Martyn Percy, *Power and the Church. Ecclesiology in an Age of Transition* (London: Cassell, 1998), pp. 24-5.

least potentially possible by the person in question, or by those closest to them. Words of knowledge appeared to be employed for five main purposes: as a call to action by parishioners, as a solution to a proposed problem, as a report of God's miraculous work, as a means of reassurance, and for predictions about future events. Parishioners deployed this charismatic medium as a way of affirming their own concerns and spiritual identities, but also as a channel through which to deal with inter-personal issues.

I have analysed a sample of sixteen different words of knowledge, all of which were witnessed by me personally. All took place towards the end of a St Michael's evening service, and all but two were spoken by the recipients of the message.[31] As I witnessed these incidents, it struck me that a great variety of people would offer words of knowledge. They were often delivered in a solemn tone, and although often with enthusiasm, rarely with an open display of emotion. The congregation would quietly listen as these speeches took place, and the service leader would often respond by encouraging us all to 'weigh these words carefully', i.e., reflect on their significance for our own lives.

Out of respect for those present, I did not make notes on words of knowledge in church but wrote down whatever I could as soon as possible after the service. This means that my descriptions are not always thorough, although most are fairly detailed, and I was able to classify them according to the following framework. The majority of speeches were discursively improvised, focused on the general congregation, and had the ostensive purpose of providing reassurance or comfort for the parishioners present. This classification is expressed in tabular form below.

SOURCE	AUDIENCE	PURPOSE OF MESSAGE
Image-based (2)	General (13)	Call to action (3)
Discursively improvised (11)	Specific (individual or group) (3)	Advice concerning a specific problem (2)
Drawn from external text (3)		Report of God's miraculous work (1)
		Means of reassurance/ comfort (7)
		Prediction (3)

Table 5: The classification of words of knowledge occurring at evening services at St Michael-le-Belfrey, 1999-2000.

---

[31] The remaining two were read out in church by the service leader, who had previously been confided the 'word' personally by the individual receiving it, or who was communicated the details on a piece of paper.

The other major feature which unites most of these examples is that they dealt with life issues, i.e., with the everyday experiences of individual members of the congregation. They were focused, either directly or indirectly, on the personal activities of parishioners. Consideration of three examples in detail will shed light on how the medium of the word of knowledge was used as a way of working through personal issues in this sense. Three very different examples have been chosen, in order that the diversity of this medium may be properly explored.

Example #1
A middle aged woman approaches the lectern. She says that the Lord gave her a 'burden', and that she used to suffer from depression. However, He wonderfully healed her, so she wants to 'shout to the Lord', just like in the song we have just sung. He is a 'loving, gracious God, who understands exactly where you are and is able to seat you in heavenly places.' She says that she had six electric shock treatments, but nothing seemed to cure her. Then God healed her. Someone in the congregation shouts 'Hallelujah!' and a round of applause breaks out.

This is a typical example of an individual bringing a set of experiences to the context of the worship event, and then setting them within a theological framework before the congregation. The woman speaking emphasises how God's power cured where human science failed, thus offering evidential proof of His active power in the contemporary world. The account is also expressed in semi-poetic form – God is 'able to seat you in heavenly places'. This conveys a sense of legitimacy and authority by way of a stylistic similarity with biblical language. In this way, the speaker may experience a sense of empowerment on two levels: both from the opportunity to speak authoritatively to the congregation, and from invoking scriptural language which invests her message with additional status. The public platform achieved in the delivery of words of knowledge makes this empowerment possible, and as the speaker achieves authority in the eyes of the congregation, so the congregation itself is offered renewed evidence of God's work.

Example #2
A woman in her forties addresses the congregation, and reads out her message, which is based around an image God has given to her. She describes a sea, onto which a carafe of oil is poured. She interprets this as God telling us about the way the church is to be transformed, from something that is difficult to get inside – like the carafe – to something that is flexible and which develops with the context in which it is situated. Just as the oil blends and moves with the sea, so we must adapt to our own material circumstances in order that the church perform its function in bringing in more believers.

This speaker was known throughout the congregation as a prophetess, due to the vivid and poignant messages she often delivered in church services, home group gatherings and prayer meetings. She read out the message, suggesting that this was an image she had received in a different context. The written medium also allowed her speech a certain eloquence of expression and it was indeed visually striking. As with the above example, her message has no specific intended audience, but is assumed to be relevant for all. By contrast with the first speech, however, this one has a normative message: there appears to be a call to action on the part of the church as a whole. The visual imagery carries with it a certain vagueness of intention; she could be urging for cultural adaptation, for increased missionary activity, or for radical changes in worship, although she does explicitly affirm the priority of evangelism. One reading of the image could be an endorsement of the tempered enculturation described in chapter 2. That is, the church is called to adapt to its cultural surroundings, not in order to have more meaning but as a means of attracting the unchurched.

Words of knowledge were often couched in terms that could suggest at best equivocal and sometimes even multivalent messages. The consequence of this, of course, is that a broader range of people may then perceive some personal meaning in the message. Moreover, the more vague the message, the more difficult it is to contest or challenge its content. Never, during my research, did I hear words of knowledge that were so specific in detail as to be amenable to falsification. A vagueness of language is thereby used to protect the integrity of the tradition, and also to affirm a sense of divine mystery.

Example #3
Towards the end of the service, the service leader, a man in his seventies, approaches the lectern. He tells us of two instances of God speaking to people in St Michael's. He does not give names, but reports what they have said to him, and responds with advice. The first is about someone who does not like making decisions; his advice is that we all have to make difficult decisions in life, and that this person must also do so. The second is about someone who is worried that on becoming a member of St Michael's, they will be swamped by its huge body. He responds to this by saying that this huge body is made up of lots of little bodies, and that they all have a part to play.

This is a rare example of a message being delivered through the service leader, rather than by the recipient. It was unclear on this occasion whether the advice offered was that of the service leader or that it was meant to stand as part of the original message. However, the first is more likely, for two reasons. First, the service leader in question is a well-known charismatic and often delivers his own messages in the first person – i.e., invoking God's voice through his own. Second, his advice is clearly improvised – his delivery, in an attempt to use poetic language, was often stumbled, suggesting that he was composing the speech there and then.

This example differs from the earlier two in that specific individuals form the focus of the message. The issues dealt with are of a practical, inter-personal nature and are easily met with advice and proposed solutions. The fact that these solutions are delivered through the medium of a 'word of knowledge' gives them an added credence by virtue of them being divinely ordained. Moreover, these problems are thereby introduced into the public realm, and are announced as issues for the church as a whole to consider. They are sufficiently general to apply to many of those present in the church, and the leader's advice serves as a means of reassurance whilst avoiding the discomfort of personal confrontations. In this way inter-personal problems are dealt with on a public, but non-confrontational level; all are audience to the discourse, yet no public response is demanded of any parishioner.

The 'Turn to Life'

While often viewed as spontaneous and emerging from an immediacy of religious experience, words of knowledge here reveal how the charismatic proceeds according to specific rules of conduct. Explicitly imposed by the vicar through a system of vetting contributions (see above), regularities may also be observed in terms of the topics chosen by individuals for presentation to the congregation. In my field notes, after observing several weeks' worth of words of knowledge at the evening service, I wrote down my impressions:

> ... the language used is often poetic, using specific formulae, and following certain themes rather than others, e.g. they nearly always involve some sense of reassurance of God's presence/action/blessing/etc, aimed at those who may feel lost or alienated, or who are suffering. It is as though a problem is assumed, and an answer is called for, is required. The difficulties of life and of the Christian path, perhaps, are the starting point for most, if not all, of these speeches. (Field-notes, 13 February 2000.)

This pattern is presented in Table 5: speeches tended to focus on offering reassurance and comfort to the marginalised and celebrating God's work within the lives of individuals, rather than on prediction or a call to revival. In other words, they were oriented inwards, to the life of the congregation, and to the personal and inter-personal lives of its members. Using Heelas and Woodhead's language, the 'word of knowledge' becomes a site for the expression of the congregational self in relation to others on the Christian path, and it is their immediate and familiar concerns that are dealt with and which are thereby endowed with spiritual significance. In this way, religion experiences a 'turn to life', as the subjective everyday lives of individuals become the public focus of the congregation. What is most noteworthy is that individuals were not named, nor called to the front – indeed, exposure of any kind was avoided, a by-product of which is the vague, inclusive language deployed in these speeches. As a consequence of this, specific concerns were aired as general subjective experiences – feeling lost, a sense of being without purpose, being scared of commitment – which may then apply to the congregation as a whole. In this way, words of knowledge channel the expression and resolution of existential problems associated with the difficulties of sustaining a life of faith.

One may reflect here on the extent to which charismatic ritual generates actual social consequences for those taking part, in this case, for example, whether existential or intersubjective problems were effectively resolved or addressed. This relates to what Csordas has called the question of the creativity of ritual language, something that must be measured by looking at the social relationships of ritual participants following episodes of charismatic ritual.[32] A detailed examination of the social consequences of taking part in such rituals would require more in depth ethnographic investigation, including further interviews and observation, and my own fieldwork does not allow such a profound analysis. However, two observations can be made, and which may steer future research. First, part of the significance of words of knowledge lies in the fact that they communicate an idealized set of relationships. The interchanges embodied in the speeches analysed above imply the legitimate public expression of personal struggle and the collective support of the congregation. The relationships between speaker and audience, and between speakers and leaders, are characterised by warmth, affection and constructive, affective support, and such sentiments are projected as a public reality before the congregation, whether or not they feature in subsequent relationships between members. As such, a model of human relationships is set before the community as desirable and real, a model congregants are invited to emulate in their everyday lives.

Second, there was a less frequent, though not insignificant, invocation of vivid metaphors, exemplified above in the second example, but which found echoes in other exchanges to which I was privy during my research. Members occasionally spoke of images sent to them by God in prayer, meditation, or during a service, and then discussed with their peers what the image could mean. Significantly, several of these images, such as the carafe of oil mentioned above, or of a glass ornament of coloured sand, mentioned in another context, were taken to represent the church, and, moreover, a church characterised by diversity, fluidity, adaptability and movement. A positive model was communicated which celebrated the complexity and diversity of St Michael's, a pattern which raises interesting questions about the relationship between visual prophecy and charismatic innovation, and about how power functions within charismatic churches.

The preoccupation with internal, subjective issues very much reflects the tendency across contemporary charismatic Christianity to focus on that which is life-affirming, stressing vitality, the interpersonal and the immediate. In St Michael's, this was expressed through its preference for exuberant, Vineyard-style sung worship. Favourite choruses – *I Will Be Yours*, John Wimber's *Isn't He Wonderful* and *You're Beautiful Beyond Description* – all have romantic overtones and celebrate a personal intimacy with God. The majority of the congregation claimed to believe in the kingdom of God as something that is 'here and now in the life of the church', rather than associated with a future, spectacular event. Most strikingly, there was virtually no attention in church teaching given to death or the afterlife, an omission

---

[32] Thomas J. Csordas, 'Genre, Motive, and Metaphor: Conditions for Creativity in Ritual Language', *Cultural Anthropology* 2:4 (1987), pp. 445-69.

reflected in diverse questionnaire responses to these subjects. Rather than focus on issues of a lofty, doctrinal or theological kind, the congregation appeared more concerned with issues of a this-worldly nature. Words of knowledge acted as a ritual means of drawing in subjective concerns, fostering a pastoral negotiation of existential problems for the benefit of the congregation.

I have examined the invocation of and appeal to subjectivity through four media: personal narratives, prayer, glossolalia and words of knowledge. While diverse in the discursive forms they take, they embody similar themes in their expression within the culture of St Michael's. All imply a this-worldly presence of God, and all (apart from glossolalia) are preoccupied with mundane, everyday or inter-personal issues rather than with an other-worldly dimension. There was little reference to abstract or scriptural truth, or to prophetic messages which carry a global significance. Their focus chiefly fell upon issues of a personal or inter-personal relevance to the congregation. Public charismatic rituals also followed particular patterns. Many authors have noted the ways in which charismatic gifts have been used to impose power over others within religious groups. Within St Michael's, rather than offer opportunities for the obvious invocation and imposition of power, public rituals appeared to actually circumvent episodes of confrontation. Glossolalia was largely privatised and rarely interpreted into an authoritative message. Words of knowledge did not tend to adopt an imperative voice, and messages were generally affirming and supportive rather than instructive or judgmental. However, expression of charismatic experience was clearly ordered, not least *via* the control of public utterance by the service leader. In this way, while charismata are not used to impose power over individuals as such, the public discourse exerted power by controlling how the 'Spirit speaks'.

But how are these ritual and non-ritual phenomena related? In order to answer this question it is necessary to examine what theories of ritual practice have to say about the relationship between ritual and everyday conduct.

The Ritualisation of Life

In his classic sociological volume *The Invisible Religion*, Thomas Luckmann makes the following comment about religious rituals:

> Their purpose refers directly to the sacred cosmos. Sacrifices, rites of passage, burial rites, and such like represent ultimate significance without what we may term intermediate levels of translation into the profane context of everyday routine.[33]

Luckmann clearly separates rituals from the everyday routines of social life and may be read as implying that their validity derives from this radical separation. What I discovered within St Michael's was something quite different. Rather, there appeared to be a cross fertilisation between ritualised actions such as prayer and words of

---

[33] Thomas Luckmann, *The Invisible Religion. The Problem of Religion in Modern Society* (New York: Macmillan, 1967), p. 59.

knowledge, and the everyday world, through subjectively constructed narratives. I would argue that the media discussed above – personal narratives, prayer, glossolalia, words of knowledge – fed upon one another as they were variously drawn upon in the ongoing faith-lives of individual parishioners. Ritual was not radically separated from everyday life; rather, the two were mutually constitutive and, as such, embodied common themes.

This phenomenon can be better understood with reference to the work of Thomas J. Csordas on the rituals of Roman Catholic charismatics in the USA. Csordas noticed how embodied techniques learnt through ritual are not simply shut off once the believer leaves the ritual context. Rather, ritualised actions seep into the structures of everyday conduct. In making sense of this process, Csordas refers to the 'ritualization of life', the process whereby the boundaries between sacred and everyday activity are effectively dissolved.[34] Within charismatic churches, this process is made possible largely because of a pervasive emphasis upon subjectivity, upon the construction of subjective narratives in response to experiences of the divine. Just as the words of knowledge and personal narratives described above are believed to have the same source, so they are also constructed in a similar fashion, and serve as complementary resources in the ongoing development of individual identities.

A key mediating factor in this process is language. Whether through well-used exclamations of praise ('hallelujah', 'thank you Jesus'), episodes of glossolalia, or the use of accepted charismatic argot, language serves as a vehicle for the dissemination of ritual experiences into the everyday realm, and back again.[35] Congregants prayed or spoke in tongues whilst walking through town. Parishioners shared stories of how God had answered their prayers over coffee in the church hall. Words of knowledge were delivered in church before being discussed in the pub by inspired attendees. Language serves as the medium through which subjective experience is expressed, shared and infused into the interactive culture of the congregation.

Within St Michael's, the 'ritualisation of life' was made easier by the *domestication* of certain types of charismatic experience. In particular, within the context of congregational discourse, there was little phenomenological disparity between words of knowledge and regular conversation between members. As the church has de-emphasised the emotional, performative and dramatic in charismatic possession, so episodes of charismata have become more discursive and more focused on the everyday, subjective struggles of faith. They have become domesticated in shedding the spectacular, and domesticated in nurturing a concern with the subjective identities of members. As such they are concerned with the problems of individuals, but individuals caught up in the same set of problems: how to find meaning, hold onto security, make commitments and have the strength to live up to them. And

---

[34] Csordas, *Language, Charisma and Creativity*, pp. 100-1.

[35] See Simon Coleman and Peter Collins, 'The 'Plain' and the 'Positive': Ritual, Experience and Aesthetics in Quakerism and Charismatic Christianity', *Journal of Contemporary Religion* 15:3 (2000), p. 323.

while charismata do not elicit a general set of principles with which to resolve these issues, the ritualisation of life ensures that members are asking questions together, and sharing the resources of an interconnected experience.

In this respect, an embrace of the subjective as spiritually significant has not automatically generated a fragmentation of the congregation, a correlation some authors imply is inevitable. Rather, while in some respects encouraging a diversification of spiritual identities, the ritualisation of life also allows the emergence of *shared* priorities, substantively expressed as the affirmation of life, of sound relationships and of a healthy and unified community.

Cynicism Towards the Charismatic

Although a thoroughgoing charismatic spirituality appeared to be embraced by a great many of the St Michael's congregants, there were also hints of cynicism among a significant number. Particularly, the use of charismatic gifts in church was clearly not something altogether favoured by all. As part of my questionnaire survey, I asked parishioners how they felt about the use of charismatic gifts in church. While 37% felt they were an 'essential part of worship', the majority – 58% – felt that, while they were helpful for some, they were unhelpful for others.

Indeed, I met many individuals who did not appear to engage in charismatic worship at all. They did not speak in tongues, offer words of knowledge, or even engage in sung worship in a fashion consistent with the impassioned charismatic style. Questionnaire results suggested that, within St Michael's, these individuals constituted a significant minority. 49% had never spoken in tongues in church. 40% had never done so privately. 36% had never received a 'word of knowledge'. Most strikingly, when asked to align themselves with a particular Christian label, while the largest group preferred 'charismatic evangelical', they were still in an overall minority (37%).

Questionnaire data suggested that it was younger (nineteen to twenty-nine year old) members who were most likely to distance themselves from the charismatic label, and least likely to engage in public charismatic expression, particularly words of knowledge. One possible explanation for this is that those only old enough to have had adult experience of the charismatic movement in the 1990s were more disillusioned and less trusting of the spiritual practices associated with it. Additionally, they may have had less faith in the ideological associations of the more dramatic, intense aspects of the movement, including being 'born again' and the notion of spiritual warfare. One could additionally argue that they were more likely to see gifts as a resource rather than a necessity, in reflection of a recent 'levelling' of the charismatic, and of orientations towards religious phenomena in general. By contrast, parishioners who were in their thirties or older rooted their perceptions of gifts in experiences which preceded the heyday of John Wimber and the Toronto Blessing. As such, their convictions were less dependent upon these turbulent and disorientating developments, and were therefore less shaken by their passing.

My extensive interaction with St Michael's members suggested that any underlying suspicion of the charismatic was not allowed to disrupt the charismatic discourse discussed earlier. Individuals still spoke of God's work in their lives, of rewards and blessings and of the material answers to prayer, even while critical of the public exercise of gifts. It was not the supernaturalist worldview which was seen as problematic but its impassioned expression in public contexts. Individuals were tentative about the charismatic because of its emotional intensity and propensity to hysteria. Others saw a potential for power abuse – authority invested in the subjective resources of the individual removes lines of accountability and allows irresponsible discipling. Most clearly, it was the 'regulatedness' of human emotion which was the focus of most suspicion.

This last observation evokes the work of Croatian-American sociologist Stjepan Mestrovic, who argues that the process of rationalisation in modern societies has been extended to include expressions of emotion. Emotion is commodified, not least by the mass media, and emotional episodes are apprehended as 'bite-sized, pre-packed' and 'rationally manufactured'.[36] A consequence of this process is that emotion and emotional expression are often viewed with suspicion, as inauthentic and perhaps manipulative, which makes more cynical observers reluctant to trust their veracity. This observation resonates with wary comments made by St Michael's parishioners about the charismatic amounting to 'spirituality on tap'. One long-standing member remembered the influence of John Wimber: '... you're touched on the head, and bang! You receive the Holy Spirit and it's all happening'. This immediacy, along with a sense of the routinisation of revival, arguably inevitable in a long-standing charismatic church, has worn thin with some members, who have put aside what they see as 'emotional hype' for a more discursive, intellectual faith. One parishioner put it this way:

> I'm not particularly into experience because I don't trust it. I'm much more of a head person ... I know it's helpful to some people and I'm not gonna say it shouldn't happen but I don't find it very useful. I find it more useful to be able to sit down and talk about things ... and more credible to think that God works through our own minds and through our own decision making processes and our own trains of thought ...

Given that charismatic Christianity has at its heart a dynamic focused on the renewal – or recycling – of past emotions and experiences, it is worth asking whether the cynicism cited above is linked to the third wave in particular, or is simply grounded in a growing weariness with revivalism in general. Some parishioners were certainly of the view that, after hearing about the latest revival for the umpteenth time, it was difficult to respond to such things with the same excitement and expectation that they once did. But while the reasons offered for such cynicism may vary, the form that such cynicism took followed patterns discernible across the congregation. In

---

[36] Stjepan G. Mestrovic, *Postemotional Society* (London, Thousand Oaks, New Delhi: Sage, 1997), xi.

short, while modernity is commonly associated with a suspicion towards institutions, in St Michael's it was *institutionalised emotional excess* which was viewed with suspicion and as a sign of inauthentic subjective expression. It is its supposed spontaneity and yet ultimately consistent forms, which undermines the credibility of charismatic possession. This 'post-emotional' response is not merely to do with broader processes of modernisation – indeed, it counts against Berger's claims about the under-institutionalised subjective sphere. Rather, this is also a further aspect of the backlash against the intensification of the charismatic in the early 1990s, and is therefore bound up in the details of evangelical history. However, the fact that disillusioned parishioners remain within St Michael's is a testimony to how the church has subsequently broadened its approach to spirituality.

We might further argue that a suspicion of potential power abuse and alienation has been pervasive enough to shape the way that charismatic gifts are practised. Recalling the descriptions offered above, glossolalia is largely privatised and words of knowledge affirm rather than challenge the congregation. Conceptions of prayer and experience of God are largely subject to personal acts of verification rather than the legitimisation of leaders. As a medium of power, the charismatic has been 'softened' – or perhaps blunted – so that the predominant appropriation of experience favours the enhancement of spiritual lives rather than the imposition of power over others.

CHAPTER 6

Innovations at the Margins:
The Post-Evangelical Pathway

> The vision is that we may in time become a genuine catalyst for the wider church to lose some of its archaic clutter and become more accessible to the larger part of the unchurched population who find church so dead.[1]

I have examined the ways in which the St Michael's congregation have dealt with some of the major evangelical traditions which they have inherited, namely an internal spiritual diversity and a persistent but not unchanging commitment to the charismatic. Since the 1960s, the boundaries of tradition have been broadened as internal diversity is increasingly accepted as the norm and personal differences are viewed as enriching rather than divisive. Roger Simpson's sermon, summarised in the prologue, urged Christians to be set apart from the world and resist the temptations of modern life. And yet there is evidence of a significant accommodation to secular modernity in attitudinal trends among parishioners. Science and rational thought are apparently placed before the scriptures in many respects. There are indications of a tolerance towards other religions that reflects wider social norms rather than evangelical history. Attitudes towards women are liberal rather than traditionalist. Understandings of the spiritual dimension of life often reflect the language of the New Age Movement rather than the Bible. While public rhetoric often endorses the 'culture war' – emphasising a clear distinction between the faithful and the world – views on the ground suggest a mingling of perspectives. Moreover, while St Michael's still represents a 'religious package' that is quite distinctive from the wider cultural norm, the boundaries between the two have clearly become more permeable.

The church has, for the most part, absorbed these trends unwittingly; parishioners would deny that any significant degree of compromise *in beliefs* has taken place. As David Bebbington has observed, evangelicals have always maintained that they embody an immovable, timeless tradition of truth even during periods of radical change.[2] And yet, St Michael's has also been motivated by a need, recognised and supported by its parishioners, to be culturally relevant. In this sense it has embraced change and accommodation, although participants have always insisted – *post hoc* –

---

[1] Taken from a *Visions* internal document from 1994.

[2] David Bebbington, *Evangelicalism in Modern Britain. A History from the 1730s to the 1980s* (London: Unwin Hyman, 1989), p. 271.

that such changes are either peripheral to the doctrinal heart of the Christian faith, or else are merely a matter of medium rather than message.

The developments represented by the *Visions* group are quite different. My account of the 'Leaps of Faith' service in the prologue depicts a radical reconfiguration of evangelical worship. Pews are replaced by bean bags, scripture appears in word loops rather than on the written page, in place of lengthy sermons are movie clips, meditations, readings and innovative rituals. Music is loud, partly instrumental and draws from the popular styles of the dance culture. The predominance of words in St Michael's – both spoken and written – is exchanged for a constellation of images in *Visions*, reflecting a radical engagement with contemporary culture, and – echoing Dave Tomlinson – an embrace of the ideas associated with postmodern change.

But what are the consequences of these changes for shared belief within the group? The deregulation which drives the aesthetics of worship – drawing from resources with a Christian, secular or alternative-spiritual flavour – is suggestive of a significant challenge to tradition. The group's orientation to outsiders also implies a significant re-ordering of boundaries characterised by a pastoral and possibly theological inclusivism. Just what counts as legitimate and who counts as included are issues that are simultaneously questioned and undermined by the culture of the group. The public worship of *Visions* is heavily resonant with post-modern notions of *bricolage*, experimentalism and detraditionalisation. But how do the attitudes and beliefs of members relate to these processes? Do they represent a reconfiguration of evangelicalism which is 'hyper-modern', taking the processes associated with cultural accommodation to a further extreme than their parent church?

It is the purpose of this chapter to address the ways in which the *Visions* group have engaged with contemporary culture and forged for themselves a new orientation to Christian tradition. As the culture of the group is best conceived in terms of a process – the *reconfiguration of charismatic evangelicalism* – I will adopt a dynamic approach, focusing on dimensions of change rather than on their value structure as a static phenomenon.

'Warehouse': A Project in Friendship Evangelism

One [year] a whole bunch of people came back from Greenbelt ... They came back fired up with this [idea] ... saying, *there ought to be more to church than this*. Now, [at this time] ... I think we must be talking about the mid 80s ... I think St Mike's had lost its direction ... I think there was a touch of disillusionment, and small group wasn't doing very much – certainly wasn't doing anything for us ... and we agreed that we wouldn't mind having a meeting that was more academically oriented, more liberal in its stance towards what could be discussed ... in the sense of less dictated ... by the church ... and we wanted to have an open board, and to discuss things working out from first principles ... So it became a little bit of a hot house of thinking, and we talked about all sorts of things, and we argued the nights away ...

This was how Daniel, one of the founder members of *Visions*, described the birth of the group, charting a sense of disillusionment with conventional church practice, a need to work things out again from first principles, a need to broaden one's conception of what was possible and what was legitimate. The Monday Night Group emerged as an alternative home group of St Michael-le-Belfrey. It was built on a need for change, but had no concrete objectives. Its only guiding principles consisted in the need for discussion – rigorous, intellectual discussion – and an embrace of the postmodern as a model of contemporary culture.[3]

In 1989, after years of discussion, and inspired by the Nine O'Clock Service in Sheffield, members of the group decided to establish a local event for evangelism – 'The Warehouse Project' – which was intended to bridge the cultural barrier between the church and youth culture. The event was based around the idea of a Christian nightclub, later emerging as a long-term ambition of those involved, and Daniel negotiated access to a disused warehouse which would serve as a venue. The event took place in July of that year, was staffed by over 100 organisers and attracted over 1,200 people over two weeks. Around fifteen local churches took part, and various activities were held both in the warehouse building and out on the streets of York. Music was provided by local Christian and non-Christian bands, theatre and sketches were performed, and discussion groups explored topical religious and moral issues.

'Warehouse' was driven by the philosophy of 'friendship evangelism' (see chapter 2), emphasising a need to minimise cultural distance between the church and non-Christians, and a need to express Christian values in action over and above verbal proclamation. In this way, the Christian life is embodied within actions and contexts that have meaning and value to one's 'evangelistic audience'. As Daniel explains,

> ... You get alongside people, you live where they're at, you earn the right by demonstration to speak in their lives ... But you also give them something, you give them something they need – a space to be, in this particular case. I think it's based on fundamentally Biblical principles. You look at Jesus ... feeding the 5,000. He didn't just preach at them, he gave them something they needed. I think the concept of holding a meeting in a building that people don't normally go into, in a style that they're not used to that is culturally alien, is somehow the wrong way to go about doing evangelism, as far as I'm concerned.

In reflection of their understanding of friendship evangelism, Daniel and his associates affirmed the value of listening to people over talking at them, questioning the model of evangelism that leads to conversion 'at all costs'. Understanding and practical support were offered irrespective of response, extended to those in need whether they accepted the Christian faith or not. According to this model, the

---

[3] The group's understanding of culture in terms of 'postmodernity', while informed by their own reading, was predominantly shaped by the teaching of Graham Cray, who was addressing the place of the church within postmodern culture both within his St Michael's sermons, in talks given at the Greenbelt festival and in his capacity as community advisor to NOS in Sheffield.

starting point for the evangelistic project is not an authoritative presentation of the gospel message. Rather, it is, as Daniel puts it, the culture and needs of those who are 'heading for the cliff edge'.

Following the success of the 'Warehouse' event, several of those who were involved in its organisation arranged to meet in order to discuss the possibilities of a long-term project, based on the same principles. After two years of further heated discussion, this group decided to establish itself as *Warehouse*, a separate 'alternative' service initiative attached to St Michael-le-Belfrey. Remaining a firm advocate of an 'incarnational' view of mission,[4] Graham Cray encouraged the group to immerse themselves in the culture of the night-clubbers. Recognising the spiritual resonances and utopian imagery evident in the dance culture, Cray felt that the clubbers were particularly winnable for Christ. The *Warehouse* group began to make regular visits to Leeds, in which the rave subculture was thriving. By attending night-clubs and conversing with night-clubbers, the group's aim was to 'cross the bridge' into this culture and thereby develop an orientation to mission that was culturally authentic in the eyes of their new evangelistic audience.

In emulation of NOS, which several members were still attending on an occasional basis, the group split into several small committees. A finance group was established and a group bank account opened, *Warehouse* being funded by voluntary contributions from its members. An 'images group' was set up to oversee the development of service resources: slides, video and material artwork. A social action group focused on helping with the local homeless and giving to the poor, and a steering group oversaw the general direction and organisation of *Warehouse* as a whole. Daniel acted as pastor and effective leader of the group. Commitment to the group, both in terms of practical assistance and in moral and intellectual support, was stressed as essential. Members were placed in one of the working groups according to their skills, and expected to regularly attend weekly meetings, practice services and the home group session. At this stage, the group was still small, but had a committed core membership of around twenty, all making significant sacrifices in terms of time, practical effort and creative energy.

After a long period of rigorous planning, the *Warehouse* group held its first service in May 1992. Although the service exploited a great deal of technology in comparison with the services of its parent church – video, slide projections, dimmed lighting, dance music – it still retained elements of a traditional charismatic evangelical worship event. Its basic structure was centred on a block of sung worship, teaching by way of a sermon, followed by a 'ministry time', during which participants prayed over each other, calling upon the power of the Holy Spirit.

From then on the services were held on a more regular basis, first each month, then twice monthly. *Warehouse* soon won a national reputation for itself as a centre of innovative worship. The group became known as one of the first established UK 'alternative' service groups, alongside NOS and the Late Late Service in Glasgow,

---

[4] See David Bosch, *Transforming Mission. Paradigm Shifts in Theology of Mission* (New York: Orbis, 1991), pp. 512-13.

and became respected both locally and nationally for its use of technology and art in worship events. *Warehouse* also achieved credibility on the northern secular nightclub circuit for the visual images they would provide at regular club nights. These 'gigs' were perceived as natural contexts for friendship evangelism, and although the group would subsequently look back with humour on how few people they actually 'converted' to Christianity, they came to pride themselves on the positive feedback they received from non-Christian clubbers, especially on the visuals which 'made them think'.

Warehouse played an integral part in the organisation of the alt.worship study day held in Lambeth Palace in 1995,[5] following the collapse of NOS. The downfall of the Sheffield group came as a shock to some members of *Warehouse*, who had friends in NOS who had suffered under the manipulation and oppression of its leadership. However, the group as a whole did not suffer. In fact, the extent to which NOS had effectively distanced them from its leadership structure forced the group to develop independently with ideas and resources of its own. However, *Warehouse* still experienced problems fending off prejudice from mainstream evangelicals (both within St Michael's and outside of it) who assumed the corruption of NOS was also rife in its many imitators.

Ever since NOS performed its infamous 'Passion in Global Chaos' set in 1992,[6] the Greenbelt festival has been a major context for the promotion and development of alternative worship. *Warehouse* performed there on several occasions, organising contemplative prayer, dance and sung worship. National prestige has also been achieved through appearances at major alternative worship conferences in London and

---

[5] The study day included an alt.worship communion service in the Lambeth Palace crypt jointly organised by representatives of *Visions*, *Third Sunday Service* (Bristol), *Be Real* (Nottingham), *Abundant* (London) and *Joy* (Oxford), and the presentation of theological papers written by alt.worship practitioners. The event was partly arranged for the benefit of the Church of England's House of Bishops and heads of church boards, and succeeded in demonstrating that alt.worship groups were theologically and liturgically creative and diverse. More importantly, it showed that the abuses of NOS had emerged from its leadership structure, rather than from its style of worship, which was responsibly and imaginatively replicated by other alt.worship groups. As Paul Roberts comments, '[the event] made a strong case that alternative worship was a creative movement that should be encouraged, albeit with the caution born of painful experience'. See Paul Roberts, *Alternative Worship in the Church of England* (Cambridge: Grove, 1999), p. 12.

[6] 'Passion in Global Chaos' was the name of the worship event which the NOS team organized as a main feature of the 1992 Greenbelt festival, performed before 15,000 people. Multimedia technology was used to produce a dramatic and visually stunning presentation of the Christian message within the context of contemporary life, evoking notions of environmental responsibility and apolocalyptic upheaval. While the power and vibrancy of the set meant that it apparently dominated the entire festival, eye brows were also raised about the NOS group's use of bikini clad dancers and the literature they distributed at the event, which likened these 'postmodern Christians' to Buddhists in so far as they were 'embracing the void'. See Roland Howard, *The Rise and Fall of the Nine O'Clock Service* (London: Mowbray, 1996), 88-89.

York, and at groundbreaking worship events such as *Rave in the Nave* and *Time of Our Lives*. These events have helped the group to forge connections with other alternative worship groups, and as the alt.worship network has expanded and consolidated its identity, both through communal gatherings and in virtual space on the internet and in email discussion, *Warehouse* have remained one of the pioneering voices of the movement.

I first encountered the group in December 1998, when they were in their seventh year of existence. They had changed their name to *Visions* two years earlier, in reflection of how far they had moved on from the original 'Warehouse' idea. No Christian nightclub had been established and the project of achieving a mission to the dance culture had since faded. The group organised itself as one collective, not several committees, and decisions were made in discussion with all participating members. Although still effectively financed by gifts from its members, *Visions* was now integrated into the 'covenanting' system of St Michael-le-Belfrey, which provided them with a budget each year. There were no more visits to nightclubs, and not enough time to perform the visuals at club nights. The group had matured, relaxed its structures, and developed an outlook somewhat removed from the evangelistic zeal characteristic of its early years.

These changes have affected the structure as well as the shared attitudes of the group. As an initial insight into the culture of *Visions*, it is useful to first examine the structure and composition of its membership.

Participants: Core and Periphery

At the turn of the millennium, in a curious, but significant reflection of its parent church, *Visions* embraced a collective of participants that may be divided into core and periphery. Those most committed to its services, who attended regularly, contributed to service planning and orchestration, and who attended weekly small group sessions, referred to themselves as the 'core group'. At the time of my fieldwork they numbered fourteen, although several of these 'members' were attending less frequently than they used to, because of other commitments.

The core group formed the creative driving force behind *Visions* events. When I first researched the group in 1999, they were split equally by gender, comprising seven males and seven females. The youngest member was sixteen, the oldest forty-four. The median age of the group was thirty, in reflection of those several long-standing members who together joined in the early 1990s following their university years. The majority of the group had been involved for at least several years, and many were original members. A great number enjoyed an advanced knowledge of computer technology and visual reproduction, some having professional experience in these fields. Members who did not work in computer technology occupied jobs in expressive or service-oriented careers such as writing or teaching.

The core group also boasted a high level of academic proficiency. Virtually all of the members who were old enough had been to university, and four of them had postgraduate training in computing. In the past, this proportion has been even greater – of the twenty members I managed to contact, both past and present, eight have postgraduate training, either in computing or in theology. Several have PhDs. This factor has had a crucial influence upon the shifting orientation of *Visions* over the years, many decisions being taken after exhaustive academic discussion. Indeed, the advanced technical and theological knowledge shared by the group had come to be a key influence on the construction of group discourse within and outside of services.

Eight of the core members were married couples, and in two of these cases one half of the couple entered the group after their partner had become an established member. All of the other members were single. Participation in the group has tended to carry high demands, incorporating changes of lifestyle as well as a considerable time commitment, so it is hardly surprising that married and attached individuals have been immediately or eventually joined by their partners.

Although members come from a variety of denominational backgrounds, most have an evangelical background and the majority have graduated to *Visions* after attending St Michael-le-Belfrey. Consequently, the inherited repertoire of Christian tradition is significantly influenced by an experience of charismatic evangelicalism as it has been manifest in the St Michael's congregation. It is also significant that, of those who used to attend St Michael's services, most have not attended again regularly since the early 1990s. At the time of my research, those who attended sporadically favoured the family service, and felt least comfortable with the charismatic evening service.

Unlike in the early days of *Warehouse*, core members did not hold 'official' group positions. They did, however, adopt certain roles within the context of service preparation and performance. Rebecca Wilson, as full-time arts co-ordinator for the group, paid as a St Michael's staff member, was responsible for designing and facilitating services, although the processes of planning and running services were shared by the whole group, according to the technical expertise and talents of members. Core members also took turns in initiating topics and activities for small group meetings, which were sometimes based around theological discussion or were often purely social occasions, such as a barbecue or candle making. Although the group were adopting a less formalised structure than in the past, there were still expectations that core members commit significant time and effort to *Visions* projects. Indeed, the practical and creative demands of alternative worship made this a necessity.

In order to provide a more detailed picture of the core group, it will be useful to offer some brief descriptions of key members at the time of my original research.

Adam was thirty, and worked as a postdoctoral researcher in computer science at York University. He first began attending St Michael's as a student when he was eighteen, although because of his Presbyterian background, he did not get on with the charismatic worship there. Keen to embrace a more ritualistic spirituality, he became interested in paganism, primarily through discussion groups on the internet. He had also attended NOS in Sheffield, and was attracted to the worship, commenting that '… they aimed to give an experience of wonder and mystery surrounding God, which I suppose … I felt was missing from St Michael's …

[which] very much focused on intimacy with God.' He had met Daniel on a student outreach project and was inspired by his idea for a Christian night-club, and so agreed to help out with the 'Warehouse Project'. Two years later, in 1991, he decided to commit to the group permanently. In 1999, he was acting as DJ at *Visions* services after being introduced to dance music and recording technology through the group. When I asked him what he liked best about being a part of *Visions*, he referred to the multi-sensory nature of worship, and the opportunities for personal input. 'When you have some input into your worship event it becomes much more satisfying 'cause you feel that you own it ...'

Emma was thirty-one and worked as a secondary school teacher. She attended St Michael's as a student and retained a connection with the church after she began working locally, especially through the close connections she had made with the surrogate 'church family' the leadership had provided during her university days.[7] She entered *Warehouse* through her boyfriend (now husband), Phil, who had been an original core member. In 1999, she was attending regularly, although was finding it hard due to other commitments. She preferred *Visions* to other kinds of church because she felt accepted for who she is. As she commented, '... it's OK to be me ... we have got quite a broad range of beliefs on different issues, and we can live with that, and we do accept that different people have different attitudes'.

Robert was forty-four and worked as a freelance lecturer in history and local tour guide. After being brought up in a variety of evangelical churches he moved to York, and was attracted to St Michael's because of the high proportion of others in his age group. However, during the mid-1990s he began to question his evangelical faith. He questioned the authority of the Bible and the integrity of those who taught it. Disillusioned with what he saw as hypocrisy and prejudice within St Michael's, he began to attend *Visions*. Asked why he still attends, he said, 'I like the acceptance, the flexibility, the relaxed atmosphere ... *Visions* allow you space to sort of explore your own view.'

In addition to the core group, *Visions* events were also attracting a periphery clientele numbering in between ten and fifteen individuals. These ranged from regulars at St Michael's, to visitors from other churches, to members of other alternative worship groups from around the region and beyond. Whereas core members typically attended virtually every meeting, peripheral participants tended to come along perhaps once every two months, or more sporadically. Peripheral participants also tended to prefer, and therefore often limit their attendance, to particular *Visions* services. Some preferred the solemnity of communion, others the upbeat celebration of the dance service. Peripheral participants occasionally took an active part in services, but for the most part assumed a more passive role, and also restricted their participation to the Sunday service itself, rather than service planning

---

[7] In 2006, St Michael's was still running a similar scheme, now called 'The Link', which connects students with existing church members. Fliers available in the church narthex promote 'The Link' as a 'great way for students to meet and get to know "normal" church members', who may then offer 'the occasional home-cooked meal, a sofa to sit on, shoulder to cry on, and welcome respite from essays!'

or 'set up'. This is partly because the core group are very close-knit, and share a common history. Peripheral members could – and in some cases did – often feel excluded because of the inevitable barriers generated by such intimacy.

Over time the evangelistic zeal of the *Visions* group has faded, and attempts to foster a wider community have achieved only limited success, attracting a very selective audience. The group appears to have turned inwards, to focus more upon servicing its own needs than those of a target audience. They have shifted from being a community concerned with expansion and evangelism, to one preoccupied with sustaining a sense of meaning for those already within its boundaries and creating a particular kind of atmosphere in public meetings, characterised by mystery and creativity. But what forces have driven this change? Moreover, how has this shift in focus paralleled the development of shared values among its members?

These questions are explored below *via* an examination of how the *Visions* group embody a particular reconfiguration of charismatic evangelicalism. This can be described in terms of three dimensions: a 'defusal' of authority reacts against perceived problems in the tradition; a mobilisation of the aesthetic equips the group with new tools in the construction of its identity; and a reconfiguration of shared attitudes emerges which shapes fresh perceptions of Christian legitimacy. I will take each of these dimensions in turn.

'Defusing' Authority

The evolution of the *Visions* group has been largely shaped by a growing sensitivity to the power trappings of what Max Weber called 'charismatic authority', i.e., authority based on the exceptional character or qualities of individuals.[8] This kind of authority is seen as characteristic of charismatic evangelical churches, and is a focus of serious criticism. The phenomenon that *Visions* members refer to is authority associated with charismatic experience and sometimes biblical knowledge, but what is opposed is not the bases of these claims, but the paternalistic and uncompromising way in which they tend to be applied. In *The Post-Evangelical*, Dave Tomlinson argues that paternalism, the parent-like authority that demands compliance without compromise, is rife in evangelicalism and is the cause of many young people leaving the church.[9] Such unquestioned forms of authority, so Tomlinson argues, have lost their credibility in a postmodern world characterised by a suspicion towards grand narratives. Absolute claims to truth are seldom perceived as anything but the veiled expressions of someone else's self-interest.

The members of the *Visions* group are in some sympathy with this, and have focused their efforts for some time on 'defusing' the authorities that cause such problems. By 'defusing' I mean to refer to a combined process of undermining, rendering ineffectual and marginalising within public contexts. I observed that this

---

[8] Max Weber, *From Max Weber. Essays in Sociology* (ed. H.H. Gerth and C. Wright-Mills; London: Routledge and Kegan Paul, 1967), pp. 245-8.

[9] Dave Tomlinson, *The Post-Evangelical* (London: SPCK, 1995), p. 54.

effort pervaded the way in which they arranged services, and also the way in which they interacted with one another. They did not openly engage with other church bodies, including that of their parent church, in critiquing this issue, but arranged their own events as a response to it. In effect, *Visions* offer an 'idioculture'[10] – a system of knowledge, beliefs and customs shared by members of the group – that consciously attempts to remedy the problems associated with an overly-paternalistic evangelicalism.

The characteristics of this response are focused in the public worship that *Visions* offers. The group attempt to create an environment in which individuals can feel comfortable, and not oppressed or pressurised. Members refer to the fact that services are held in semi-darkness, that no collection plate is handed round, that there are no altar calls, no lengthy sermon and that the Bible is left to 'speak for itself' through readings or word loops, rather than through the medium of a preacher. In effect, very few practical demands are made of someone participating in a *Visions* event, and newcomers often remarked on how passive they were allowed to be. The effort to avoid pressurising or patronising gestures was also extended to the group's approach to charismatic gifts. Having since moved away from the 'ministry in the Spirit', *Visions* still occasionally offered to pray over people. However, they reserved this practice until after the service and performed the prayer in the church office, thus avoiding any public spectacle and ensuring a private and secure environment for the recipient. Their general outlook stands in direct opposition to the perceived confrontational tone of mainstream evangelical churches, with their stress on public confession and on bringing outsiders to a 'point of decision'. *Visions* favour what might be called a 'softer' approach, offering rituals that do not highlight personal differences nor call for public confessions. In this, they unwittingly echo trends in the 'post-emotional' take on the charismatic affirmed within St Michael's (see chapter 5).

The group also sees itself as offering a place where difficult questions can be asked without fear of judgement, especially in small groups (see chapter 7) and in post-service conversation. *Visions* attempt to provide a haven for the 'safe' exploration of personal beliefs, opposing the evangelical tendency to judge or restrict dialogue in order to limit deviation from an established theological norm. In doing this, the group is advocating a positive embrace of radical diversity, allowing for disagreement and difference without the need for judgement.

This 'open' approach was justified by the group with reference to the shortcomings of the mainstream church as a whole. As Daniel put it,

> There are people for whom the church has, and I mean the church in its sort of broad sense, has actually rejected them, specifically and in words of one syllable – you in your present form as a person are not acceptable. And *Visions* has just said, no, there's no problem, we take you as you are.

---

10 The concept of 'idioculture' is drawn from the work of Gary Fine. See Gary Alan Fine, 'Small Groups and Culture Creation: The Idioculture of Little League Baseball Teams', *American Sociological Review* 44 (1979), pp. 733-45.

The needs of the individual are placed above issues of theological correctness, in reflection of the friendship evangelism that originally inspired the 'Warehouse Project'. The group prided themselves on this open attitude, and often justified its validity with reference to the many people who have felt ostracised by the church, but welcomed within *Visions*. These individuals have often fallen within the categories most treated with intolerance or disdain by mainstream evangelicals: homosexuals, women, the mentally ill. Members also mentioned those 'damaged' people who are, because of their background, especially sensitive to the confrontation and exposure that evangelical churches often demand: those who have been abused, or who suffer from depression. Most significantly, members of *Visions* saw this accommodating, inclusive approach as part and parcel of their Christian identity. They are not merely a compensatory service for the disenfranchised, nor are they providing respite as a gateway to evangelism. Rather, they are embodying what they see as the most Christian of values. Characteristically, they look to Jesus as the primary moral example. To quote Daniel again,

> *Visions* makes a special point of this, of accepting people for who they are, how they are, wherever they are – sexual orientation, even sexual practice, belief system, religious extremism in a way – whatever it is, we in a rather, and I was hoping to avoid this word, a rather post-modern, pic 'n' mix fashion, we just say, you're welcome here, as you are, who you are because that's what Jesus would say ...

This of course raises the question: what are the boundaries of acceptance? *Visions* would certainly not advocate a *laissez faire* morality or any theological liberalism that has no limitations. The significant point here is that although members did recognise some viewpoints as objectionable or un-Christian, they did not see this difference as legitimate grounds for exclusion from their community. Moreover, members saw negative or dismissive judgement on the basis of such differences as essentially un-Christian. Their effort to foster outsiders as welcome extended to a resistance towards imposing any form of 'evangelical' discourse upon them. Consequently, theology was couched in the subjunctive, and individuals left to grow according to their own individual experience. This extended into ritual, in which participants were encouraged to find their own meaning in the event, rather than have one imposed upon them. For example, in explaining to me the structure of the *Visions* sung creed (see appendix 2), Rebecca Wilson advocated an approach to worship that offers opportunities for participation on a number of levels. The driving principle was clearly focused on the need to accommodate a broad spectrum of people, from the most orthodox, to those only able to commit to certain values held by the group.

> It was much easier to write what we didn't believe [rather than] about ... what we believed. And concentrate on the most important things in the chorus. God, a passionate creator. Christ who died to save us, etc. Then if people didn't feel able to join in with the chorus they could sing heartily in the verses.

In offering opportunities for participation that demand little change or adjustment from the outsider, *Visions* advocated an understanding of spiritual growth that is non-intrusive. The belief underpinning this is that such freedom of growth, apart from paternalistic authority, engenders a more authentic expression of selfhood. As one member put it, 'people should be left to experience the service and find God there, and then theorise it afterwards ... then, if people ask about Christianity, we could tell them'.

In this sense the group advocate the nurturing of a place of welcome for the marginalised at all costs. But although members tended to justify this position with reference to an orientation to outsiders, they also embraced this ethos because of their own experience. Many explained their attraction to *Visions* with reference to how they are able to 'be themselves' without fear of being judged. Rebecca exemplifies this attitude,

> ... you don't feel the 'thought police' are out to get you, if you say things the wrong way or disagree with a certain part of evangelical Christian subculture, or if your lifestyle doesn't quite fit, or what you do for a hobby doesn't quite fit ... people feel safe, I think, which is nice ... particularly vulnerable people ... gay people, people with depression feel safe. They don't feel that somebody's out to put a hand on their hand and say 'be healed', and if they're not healed, they accuse them of not having enough faith...

Suspicion towards external authorities extended into the way the group dealt with authority within their own ranks. In principle, the group adopted an approach to leadership that accepts the input of all members as equal. On one telling occasion, a suggestion from the vicar that Daniel was the chairperson provoked some discomfort and a firm rejection. Adam corrected the vicar – Daniel was merely taking the notes, thus evoking sociologist Harold Garfinkel's claim that embedded assumptions are made conscious through behaviour that challenges them.[11] The group had no conception of being subject to a chairperson, or any kind of leader for that matter, and were uncomfortable with the suggestion. While certainly driven by dominant personalities, the group as a whole saw itself as a democratic collective, and there was a shared cynicism towards institutional or official, role-based power. Moreover, in Adam's comment there is a clear effort to play-down the roles taken on by group members, emphasising collaboration and co-operation within an egalitarian exchange of ideas.

Members displayed a great deal of reflexivity in their explanations of these attitudes, and often referred back to experiences of evangelicalism as the source of their concerns. Indeed, the rapport sustained between members is premised on a tacit understanding of evangelical stereotypes and a willingness to undermine them with humour and irony. Even some of the printed literature produced by the group expresses such irreverent playfulness, displaying a cheeky humour that some

---

[11] Harold Garfinkel, *Studies in Ethnomethodology* (Cambridge: Polity Press, 1984), pp. 47-9.

mainstream evangelicals might deem quite blasphemous. A striking example can be found in one of the early *Warehouse* fliers, which advertised a forthcoming service. Designed around the style of a crisp packet, the emblem reads 'XP Crisps' (inverting the popular brand into the Chi Rho symbol), 'Smoky Jesus Flavour'. The flier continues to list the 'ingredients' of the service as 'smoke, God, video screens, The Spirit, techno, and the Word Himself'.

Some authors, such as Roman Catholic theologian Tom Beaudoin, have argued that such irreverent play with religious symbols is symptomatic of the postmodern disillusionment with institutional religion.[12] It is suggestive of *bricolage*, a tendency to take elements from disparate sources and reassemble them in an attempt to convey new meaning. What is clear within the *Visions* context is that this attempt is also driven by a pervasive need to undermine and question the norms of authority represented by mainstream evangelicalism. In subjecting them to humorous comment, in de-centring their place in services, and in problematising their integrity through discourse, the group effectively undermine key aspects of the evangelical subculture.

It is tempting to view *Visions* as inclusive in the extreme. Its 'defusal' of external authorities appears to lead to an embrace, or at least acceptance, of every possible channel of diversity. This prompts the question: which perspective, if any, would not be welcome among the group? The clear answer to this is the standard perspective of charismatic evangelicalism. In a sense, the group excludes nothing apart from an exclusivist framework. In practice, members also rejected the subcultural baggage that they associated with this – vociferous preaching, autocratic hierarchy, 'power evangelism' – in a way that reflects Dave Tomlinson's insistence that the heart of evangelical identity be separated from the cultural conventions of those who have come to be associated with it. A sociological comment on this trend might cite Hebert Marcuse, who long ago noted that liberation does not imply absolute freedom or a *laissez faire* ethos, but requires a discriminating tolerance.[13] Tolerance is, from this perspective, inevitably repressive, and while *Visions* appeared tolerant of most viewpoints, they were intolerant of what they perceived as most offensively exclusivist, and this is the tradition against which they defined themselves.

It is the omission of a more critical analysis of tolerance that is the most serious limitation of Donald Miller's work. In his impressive study of 'new paradigm' churches, *Reinventing American Protestantism*, Miller simply takes practical inclusivity to be a logical extension of a Protestant 'democratisation of the sacred'. In 'new paradigm' churches like those in the Vineyard network, all are welcome

---

[12] Tom Beaudoin, *Virtual Faith. The Irreverent Spiritual Quest of Generation X* (San Francisco, CA: Jossey Bass, 1998).

[13] Herbert Marcuse, 'Repressive Tolerance', in R.P. Wolff, B. Moore and H. Marcuse (eds.), *A Critique of Pure Tolerance* (London: Jonathan Cape, 1969), pp. 95-137.

by aesthetic judgements about the comparative efforts of one's peers, a process characteristic of discourse on pop music.[16]

In addition to these, often light-hearted aesthetic judgements, *Visions* assess their worship according to the reactions of individuals within the group. In the context of meetings, members often referred to what 'works' as a vague, instinctive and pragmatic notion of success or failure. Clearly, the individual 'gut' response is as important a criterion as any for the efficacy of a worship event. It depends upon whether individuals feel the worship has been *personally authentic* for them. Such ideas suggest an ultimately vague and undefined orientation to aesthetic expression. However, observation of services together with interaction with the group revealed a key set of features, consistently affirmed as positive aspects of the worship experience.

One could be described as a move towards holism, i.e., an engagement with all of the senses through worship. This was endorsed by members through a contrast with the predominantly rhetorical style of mainstream evangelical worship. Adam explained his preference as making up for the 'wordy' Presbyterianism with which he grew up:

> ... we try to engage all the senses so you have hearing and touch, taste and smell, with incense and so on, which feels more holistic than my earlier Christian experience ... Words were of paramount importance – words of hymns, words of the sermon, words of prayer ... there's no visual imagery at all in the Presbyterian church ... but there's an awful lot more when you come to the Orthodox church or alt.worship ... [it] expands the realms into which spirituality has a significance.

The generation of a multi-sensory experience is dependent upon technology – the use of multiple TV screens, video projection and slide imagery alongside constant dance rhythms and ambient mixes and – in *Visions* – the use of incense. But it is also invoked in the rituals performed by the group. Each *Visions* service included some kind of prayer ritual, and each involved physical participation – writing letters to God before offering them up in a burning boat, meditating over a small stone before placing it in a water fountain. For members, these rituals represent an effort to communicate with God in a way that moves beyond the limitations of language. Indeed, simple, silent physical acts could achieve great significance in the eyes of the group when performed in services. Daniel once recounted his feeling that even if participants did not take communion at *Visions*, their act of passing on the communion cup to their neighbour was an expression of community in itself. There was a tendency to attach importance to simple acts that require no commentary, to see the symbolic meaning in what might otherwise be viewed as banal or routine. Most pervasively, there was a consistent effort to marginalise the status of spoken words (especially in the imperative voice) as components of the worship experience,

---

16 See Simon Frith, *Performing Rites. Evaluating Popular Music* (Oxford and New York: OUP, 1996).

because all may have access to a personal experience of God.[14] This reflects the theology of the Vineyard, but not its social structure, which clearly tolerates some perspectives more than others. Miller fails to explore the cultural dynamics of exclusion generated by this ethos of the 'new paradigm', and thus arrives at an incomplete presentation of group boundaries.

While *Visions* are wholeheartedly suspicious of charismatic power, this does not mean that the group operate on a level playing field. Power does exist within its confines, but as a more subtle pressure to conform to a particular framework. It is through such pressure that dissenting views are excluded. Thus, while affirming an inclusive ideology, *Visions* still operate within particular boundaries of acceptability. The social mechanisms that sustain this set of boundaries will be more fully explored in chapter 7.

Mobilising the Aesthetic

Visions, and the rest of the alternative worship network, stand in many ways as a continuation of the charismatic movement and its introduction of a new vibrancy into worship, funded by art and technology. Such creativity owes much to the innovations of St Michael-le-Belfrey under David Watson during the 1970s, although most influential on alt.worship were the radical innovations of NOS, whose use of audio-visual technology expanded the symbolic capital with which Christians could legitimately experiment. It is this technology that has generated a blurring of boundaries between Christianity, youth culture, political action and communitarianism, further opening up the boundaries within which Christianity can be conceived and practised.

One consequence of this has been a tendency to conceive of worship within a broad frame of reference, driven by aesthetic as well as theological principles. The most obvious signal of this within *Visions* revolves around the question – often entertained – of whether an event was genuine 'alt.worship'. Some group members were quite firm in their understanding of this category, although their comments tended to focus on what it is not. Alt.worship does not use live instruments or involve charismatic choruses, for example, and alt.worship does not use conventional or lengthy sermons. Services that are multi-media based but incorporate these elements were seen as 'youth' services, or as 'more evangelical' or 'mainstream', rather than *genuinely* 'alternative'. Patterns of discourse here display parallels with what some sociologists have argued about youth sub-cultures. Identity is not only constructed around notions of otherness, but is also based on understandings of authenticity that arise from this.[15] Furthermore, identity is shaped

---

[14] Donald E. Miller, *Reinventing American Protestantism. Christianity in the New Millennium* (Berkeley and Los Angeles, CA: University of California Press, 1997), pp. 80-107.

[15] E.g., see Sue Widdecombe and Robin Wooffitt, *The Language of Youth Subcultures. Social Identity in Action* (London: Harvester Wheatsheaf, 1995).

and the emphasis upon silent actions could be interpreted as a natural response to this.

While promoting a multi-sensory experience, *Visions* services stress the visual aspect above all else. At each service, a new collage of slide images are constructed and projected onto the east wall, multiple TV screens show a concatenation of moving pictures that is mixed live, and a video projector adds more depth and dynamism to the vividly adorned building (see chapter 1). These images offer no obvious single message and suggest no simple narrative. Their rapid progression promotes a kind of 'translocalism', i.e., it creates a sense that one is participating in a larger project.[17] Taken as a whole, *Visions* services reconfigure the sensory dimensions in which one stands, and in so doing allow novel conceptions of sacred space.

The aesthetics of *Visions* – the stress on the visual, on engaging all of the senses, on ambiguity – can be explained in terms of their reaction to mainstream evangelical subculture as they see it. In particular, they stand as an implicit critique of embodied authorities and of the power of rhetoric. The multi-referentiality afforded by the exploitation of technology tallies with the group's unease with monolithic tradition, and offers opportunities for an experimentation of thought and practice. The heavy use of technology – of vivid and ever-changing visual imagery – could be interpreted as a vicarious form of religion, the group presenting a complex and provocative multi-dimensional reality in which the participant is left space for solitary thought and meditation. The passivity characteristic of services allows for a variety of individual responses. Moreover, the appropriation of the aesthetic in *Visions* has been used to generate a context for reflexivity without closure, a tradition without fixed boundaries. Ritually speaking, *Visions* repaint Christianity as a hierophany of many voices, and the resultant lack of clarity is embraced by the group as a positive feature of their project. This is not to say that members welcome confusion. They embrace the multivalency inherent in services as a welcome tension, or a variety of stimuli. Participants appear to find meaning in services in spite of – or perhaps because – they rule out any consistent or straightforward message.

But worship also offers the core group a sense of empowerment. They redesign each worship event anew – offering new combinations of themes, visuals and rituals each time. Most, if not all, members contribute to the design and setting up of services, forming a democratically organised collective of 'ritual entrepreneurs'. Even I was allowed to contribute to service planning, and one week found myself distributing candles, contributing to what was effectively sacred space. When I asked how I should arrange them, I was only given loose guidelines – the arrangement of the room was very much left to the creative impulses of those present.

In effect, *Visions* have radicalised the popular charismatic understanding that worship must come from the heart of the individual. They see worship as an

---

[17] This term is drawn from the work of Stewart Hoover, particularly in his *Mass Media Religion. The Social Sources of the Electronic Church* (Newbury Park, CA: Sage, 1988).

expression of their individual Christian identities through their practical control of the performance process. As Adam put it,

> I think worship very much has to be something that's from you and when you're just participating in somebody else's thing, that can be OK, but it doesn't really connect completely ... when you have some input into your worship event it becomes much more satisfying ... it comes from within you instead of being imposed on you.

This sense of ownership is in part dependent upon technology. The use of visual and audio equipment transfers the balance of power from the liturgical tradition and the institutionalised priesthood to those who have the necessary skills to use it. *Visions* only depend upon external authority within the context of holy communion, when they enlist the assistance of a local celebrant, but their services remain under the group's control, and feature their own liturgical and ritual preferences. There are also economic factors at play. In an article about the dance culture of the 1980s and 90s, Smith and Maughan have argued that, as advancing technology made it increasingly cheap to make and distribute dance records, so the cultural axis of the dance subculture shifted from the major record labels to the small time DJs who were producing the music. In effect, they became the producers of the culture.[18] A similar claim can be made for alternative worship, and for *Visions*. The increasing availability and affordability of technical equipment has helped the group assemble an impressive stock of TVs, video mixers, projectors and audio equipment. This, together with their growing expertise in the use of this equipment, has enabled them to explore in increasingly innovative ways the complexities of Christian worship and tradition. *Visions have become the producers of their own Christian sub-culture.*

But this sub-culture is not merely ritualistic in its expression; it has ideological dimensions as well. Ritual innovation has given rise to, and emerges alongside, a generation of new meanings and values, and although worship may sometimes imply a rather chaotic outlook, expressed attitudes follow clear patterns.

The Reconfiguration of Shared Attitudes

Most members of *Visions* have an evangelical background and view what they do as alt.worshippers as a reaction to the problems they have come to recognise in the evangelical tradition. These problems may be summarised as an overly narrow view of faith, an autocratic and paternalistic system of authority and an insufficiently reflective orientation towards tradition and evangelism. According to the *Visions* group, together these promote an objectionably judgmental mindset which excludes many people for either misguided cultural or misplaced theological reasons. While their alternative worldview is revisionist, however, it is not equally dismissive of all

---

[18] Richard J. Smith and Tim Maughan, 'Youth Culture and the Making of the Post-Fordist Economy: Dance Music in Contemporary Britain', *Journal of Youth Studies* 1:2 (1998), pp. 211-28.

facets of traditional evangelical belief. In fact, *Visions* members appeared to retain certain values that are arguably quintessential to the tradition they see themselves as critiquing.

They held, for example, to a belief in the radical dependency of humanity upon God, interpreting their lives as a struggle with God rather than merely with the church. This was accompanied by an unswerving faith in God's reality and immanence in the affairs of everyday life, a feature also pervasive throughout the St Michael's congregation (see chapter 5). In relation to this, *Visions* members took experience of God to be the basis of the Christian life, seeing processes within their subjective faith lives as divinely guided. Faith in the supernatural was retained, as was a belief in miracles. Moreover, in a direct continuation of the traditions of their parent church, *Visions* adopted an understanding of the faith life of Christians as necessarily holistic. Indeed, this notion was a precondition for the original birth of the group, which has always carried expectations of radical commitment from its members. Finally, *Visions* adhered to a conception of Christian identity as an achieved rather than an ascribed status. In common with evangelicalism at large, they viewed denominational identity as secondary to a personal relationship with God. However, as will be outlined below, the group's understanding and expression of this relationship complicates the boundaries usually maintained by their mainstream peers.

Visions treated the bulk of traditional Christian attitudes as things to be questioned and critiqued. This was not seen as a negative process of debunking and selectively throwing out key doctrines, but was seen as a positive process of debate and reflection, necessary if one is to avoid holding uncritically to tradition. In this respect, public and private discourses were far closer together in *Visions* than they were in the main body of St Michael's, a consequence of its small scale and of the fact that the construction of worship events is communal and shared. Following this, the ambiguity and detraditionalisation expressed in services was mirrored in a detraditionalisation of attitudes. The inevitable diversity in personal perspectives that this produces was not seen as a problem. Internal differences were seen as a welcome protective device against monolithic tradition, the group preferring a healthy tension of attitudes over an uncritical reiteration of orthodoxy. Whereas diversity in St Michael's was only affirmed as overlaying an essential unity, diversity was wholly embraced in *Visions* as creative, constructive and healthy. It was celebrated as a basis of mutual learning. Unsurprisingly, therefore, there was something of a diversity of perspectives within the *Visions* group, at least insofar as theology is concerned. What united members was the general direction in which their reconfiguration of mainstream evangelical attitudes moved.

A key aspect of this process might be described as a movement towards perpetual de-differentiation, the process whereby previously established or traditional differences become de-regulated, commonly associated with 'postmodern' manifestations of religion. It is a process that is closely connected to *bricolage*, the reassembling of phenomena in fresh configurations of meaning. What is evident among the *Visions* group is an attempt to problematise clear-cut distinctions frequently maintained by mainstream evangelicals. Drawing from the arguments of liberal intellectual discourse, *Visions* members reject these distinctions, seeing them as simplistic dichotomies. Church/culture, truth/falsity, sacred/profane – all are undermined in favour of a more subtle, complex, and less clearly defined outlook. Rejecting the straightforward boundaries commonly assumed between Christianity and other faiths, one member preferred to see the entire world of spiritual tradition as a potential source of value:

> I think there's valuable wisdom in all spiritual traditions, and, there's a lot of dross as well ... in Christianity – a lot of dross in Christian history, which could do with being thrown away, but that's something we've got to join together as sort of participants in faith, and try to sort out what's ... valuable and what's not.

In this way, Christianity as a tradition is distinguished from the Christian faith as a lived, complex path, a path which, when walked, may lead one to reject aspects of this tradition in order to retain spiritual or moral integrity. Just as there is much good in other traditions, so there is much that needs to be thrown out of Christianity. The criterion for a valuable spiritual resource is not restricted by traditional boundaries of faith. Several members adopted a liberal, relativist view of other faiths, some even extending their tolerance into a position that comes close to the notion of universal salvation. One commented that she would never condemn Muslims, as they are finding God as best they can, and suggested the possibility that Jesus might appear to them offering salvation after death.

The tendency towards de-differentiation was most strikingly evident in responses to my questions about salvation. Using common evangelical parlance, I asked *Visions* members in interviews: 'how are we saved?' They were fully aware of the 'stock' answers that evangelicals frequently give to these questions, and regarded them with some humour. Their position seemed to be that these were empty words affirming a position that was often ill-thought out or theologically problematic. One core member even implied that he now had trouble finding meaning in these words:

> I always think of being saved as odd because it's a phrase I grew up with ... it calls for a need for salvation and now I just think, saved from what? Saved from what? So I'm not really sure what it means ...

The alternative answers offered were varied, some ultimately claiming that they could not say; what is more, they appeared to prefer not to know, rather than claim one of the stock evangelical answers. Mystery and ambiguity were not things that troubled the group, even when associated with such fundamental questions. Indeed, members would probably suggest that it is because such issues are of fundamental importance that they are shrouded in mystery, ultimate truth remaining outside of the grasp of human limitations. Parishioners within St Michael's are united in voicing a clear affirmation of substitutionary atonement; within *Visions*, salvation is reflected upon in far less straightforward terms.

However, an alternative understanding of faith was evident, and centred on the idea of a journey or pilgrimage. Emphasising process and change without any confirmed or pre-determined end, this understanding undermines notions of conversion as an instantaneous, transformative experience. Rather, being a Christian is seen as a journey that is both divinely and culturally inspired, thus undermining the simple distinctions often made between Christians and 'the world', Christians and culture, or Christians and other faiths. Following this understanding, members sometimes made sense of their project as a source of spiritual nurture for people moving along their own journey. *Visions* is conceived as a place of respite, from which postmodern pilgrims may take comfort and sustenance, before moving on. As one member put it,

> We're talking about a 21st century perspective of moving down the road from one point to another, and there are many people for whom *Visions* has been a deeply significant factor in moving on that road. And there are a number of people who've said to me that they are so grateful for *Visions* doing what it does because it's showed them that you can have a faith and not commit cultural suicide, showed them that actually God *is* real and *is* relevant, showed them that there is hope, there is life, you know.

In this way a process of de-differentiation has transformed the evangelistic fervour characteristic of the early years of the group's life. *Visions* no longer measure their 'success' in terms of how many people attend, or how many non-Christians they have 'converted'. Rather, they take pleasure in the number of non-Christians or 'lapsed' Christians who have left with a sense of hope and a positive outlook. Even if people move on with only a vague religiosity, or no faith whatsoever, the fact that someone has shared in the vision is, for the group, a legitimate outcome of Christian witness.

This is well illustrated through an account of a conversation I had with Daniel and Alison, two of the core members, about halfway through my original research. After a service, we began talking about my own experience of the group.

> 'So what do you reckon to this alt.worship stuff then?', Daniel asks me. I consider my answer: 'I think if I'd gotten involved in my teenaged years, then things would have probably developed differently, with regard to my view of the church.' They acknowledge this with thoughtful looks but without comment ... Daniel says that he suspects no one in the group has asked me whether I am a Christian. 'But Roger [the vicar] has', he abruptly and knowingly adds. (I'm not sure how he knows this, but Daniel appears to be making a point.) I am taken aback, and say that yes, I had noticed this. I also say that throughout St Michael's, almost everyone has asked me this same question. I say that this assumes this category means something to me, and that people will understand my position upon a yes or no answer. Daniel seems to empathise with my concern, and says that the [*Visions*] group now recognises that these categories no longer have any meaning. He instead

suggested seeing Christian identity in terms of helping people on a journey, although Alison does add, 'which will have a Christian direction, hopefully...!'
(Adapted from fieldnotes, 16 January 2000.)

Having rejected many of the boundaries associated with mainstream evangelicalism (including a simple distinction between Christian and non-Christian), *Visions* embrace a perspective that resists judgement of others and any kind of evangelical exclusivism. In practice, as discussed above, this amounts to the fostering of minority groups who often feel alienated from the mainstream church. Whereas many evangelicals oppose women's authority and homosexuality on the basis of Christian teaching, *Visions* saw this as a rejection of lifestyle and considered this rejection to be un-Christian. Echoing Dave Tomlinson, they traced these attitudes to middle-class prejudice and an unwillingness to question the authority of church leaders.[19] In contrast to this, *Visions* together adopted a liberal attitude towards women and homosexuality, one member even going so far as to say they are 'anti-homophobic', a sentiment also expressed in the group's sung creed (see appendix 2).

Such a position carries inevitable consequences for the group's understanding of biblical authority. Moreover, their shared academic proficiency means that members feel the need to hold to theological positions that are intellectually robust. Therefore, several of them reject parts of the Old Testament and of the Pauline letters, due to an unequivocal condemnation of homosexuality, a conservative teaching on women, and the apparent advocacy of mass violence. Members rather drew from the texts insofar as they found them 'useful' in their spiritual lives, several including books from the Apocrypha in their preferred choice of reading. Effectively, the authority of church, tradition and Bible were all treated as subject to critical reflecton in the light of personal experience and reason. In searching for some final authority, members tended to focus on the figure of Jesus above all else, as both practical example and teacher. One member was particularly frank in expressing his position:

> An awful lot in the Bible, to be honest, repels me, particularly in the Old Testament. An awful lot in Paul repels me, but, it's the person of Jesus Christ that's so attractive really – such an interesting person, such a...fascinating character. I suppose I believe he's God as well, though ... or God's son or whatever, something special.

Such an openly selective approach to the Bible reflects the group's attitude that the texts are not infallible, but products of specific times and cultures, testaments by humans about what they experienced as God. It also reveals what they most readily support and embrace: teaching that is affirmative of humanity as a whole. The group reject the exclusivism of evangelical Christianity in favour of an orientation that is based on the acceptance of others, regardless of lifestyle, and they see the exemplar of this in Jesus himself.

---

[19] Tomlinson, *The Post-Evangelical*, p. 32.

That this outlook extends into understandings of the status of humanity is reflected in the fact that some members have come to reject the doctrine of original sin. Indeed, several *Visions* members came closer to the notion of 'original blessing', famously argued by Matthew Fox, one time guru of the NOS community.[20] Fox argues against the traditional Christian doctrine commonly associated with Saint Augustine, and that is centralised within evangelical culture as the teaching that we are all in sin, a state only redeemed upon our personal commitment to Christ. Several *Visions* members clearly saw this notion as far too open to abuse, stressing a simplistic exclusivism that sits uncomfortably with the loving accommodation they saw as the epitome of Christ's teaching. One individual was brutally frank:

> The doctrine of original sin was an invention of a Saint Augustine and I would have his books burnt and his own influence expunged from church history if I got my way.

This core member went on to connect original sin to evangelical ideas of salvation, describing how original sin condemns most of humanity (i.e., those who have not heard of Christ or converted to Christianity) to damnation. He saw this as incredible, ridiculous and unfair, once again expressing the common tendency within *Visions* to advocate a form of humanitarian egalitarianism over what they see as the offensive teachings of the mainstream church. Christian truth is to be worked out in dialogue and according to one's own experience and thinking. While many in St Michael's affirm a reflective, critical perspective on the scriptures, it is unlikely they would go as far as to openly question the validity of central evangelical doctrines or critique individual books of the Bible. *Visions* represent a more openly selective approach, which often includes a critical perspective on certain writers, teachings and ideas, many of which are revered within the evangelical mainstream, but which they view as falling short of Christian ideals on the grounds of being unscriptural or inhumane.

The most clearly stated and most uniformly shared values in *Visions* related not to theological issues, but to moral topics. In particular, the group maintained a consistent focus upon social justice and environmental responsibility, incorporating these into their service and small group themes. There was also a discernible effort on the part of the group to apply the principles they endorsed in their daily lives. In this way, they mark a sharp contrast with the main body of St Michael's, which fostered a public discourse notable for its moral ambiguity (see chapter 4).

Social justice, for the *Visions* group, refers to fair-trading, to the maintenance of global economic relations on equal terms, to the striving for human equality and the eradication of oppression and manipulation for monetary gain. It is grounded in a conviction of the basic human right for quality of life, and the recognition that the forces of our western culture are often complicit in compromising this right. Moreover, the eradication of injustice was seen as grounded in Christian identity and

---

[20] Matthew Fox, *Original Blessing. A Primer in Creation Spirituality Presented in Four Paths, Twenty-six Themes, and Two Questions* (Santa Fe, NM: Bear, 1983).

prescribed by God. According to an early *Warehouse* document entitled *Justice in Lifestyle*,

> We are not expected by God to stand on the sidelines and observe injustice. We are expected to get our hands dirty and resolve the problems. If we do not then we are complicit with the source of the injustice and will stand before God, condemned for our inaction.

In this sense, the Christian life is seen as a radically political one, and carries with it responsibilities that may imply contravening the cultural norm. Indeed, the group often expressed the conviction that it is our culture that prevents us from doing the right thing. We are led by peer pressure, by the contingencies of fashion, or by the inertia of social normality, whereas the moral route often requires us to move against the cultural grain. In this way the common evangelical notion of 'the world' is reconceived in terms of an opposition to western consumerism and global capitalism. In contrast to its parent church, forces of evil were not primarily discerned in moral anomie, sexual decadence and the New Age Movement, but in the corporate interests of big business, seen as a far greater barrier to moral integrity.

In practical terms, the rhetoric of *Visions* was not matched by participation in movements of mass protest. They primarily expressed their views on social justice by promoting initiatives like the World Development Movement and the Jubilee 2000 campaign through their services. Every three months a 'cause of the quarter' was promoted, detailed in the printed leaflet which the group made freely available at each of their events. The second 'cause' for the year 2000 was the local Credit Union, based on the idea of a financial co-operative of individuals who issue loans to one another at a reasonable rate of interest. The aim of Credit Unions is to bypass the profiteering of the banking industry in order that individuals and families gain a greater control over their finances. An anti-capitalist ethic and pro-community ethos is implicit in this project, in reflection of the particular take on social justice adopted by *Visions* members.

In liberal religious circles, a concern for social justice has often been accompanied by a concern for the environment,[21] and this is certainly the case in *Visions*. They expand the holism of the evangelical faith life into the adoption of an environmentally responsible lifestyle. Whereas St Michael's parishioners tended to focus upon working out an ethical orientation lived out in acts of giving and in the embodiment of 'sound family values', the *Visions* group saw their Christian responsibilities as incorporating recycling, buying fair trade goods, and minimising car use.

In advocating a concern for social justice, *Visions* may be firmly situated among what Hunter has called the 'young' or 'radical' evangelicals.[22] They represent what

---

[21] See Peter Beyer, *Religion and Globalization* (London, Thousand Oaks, New Delhi: Sage Publications, 1994), p. 209.

[22] James Davison Hunter, *Evangelicalism. The Coming Generation* (Chicago, IL, and London: University of Chicago Press, 1987), p. 42.

are basically left-wing political values and stress social action as an end in itself, rather than purely as a means to converting others. Bearing in mind major social changes since the late 1980s, we might also associate this group with environmentalism, a major preoccupation of the UK alt.worship movement. *Visions* have embraced these ideas as a political agenda alongside their reconfiguration of worship.

Explanations for Change

The reconfiguration of shared values within the *Visions* group marks a significant transformation of their original project. The group were once driven by evangelism, maintained a strictly ordered and role-based organisational structure, and held multi-media, but fairly traditional charismatic services with sermons and ministry prayer. By the turn of the millennium, they were driven largely by a quest to achieve meaning for their internal membership and to offer a 'safe' space for those alienated by the mainstream church. They were organised in an egalitarian style and shunned any suggestion of official role positions, at least ones that imply any kind of hierarchy. And their services used multi-media techniques to challenge Christian tradition, provoke questions and generate ambiguities. Alongside these changes, members have developed a shared value system that is passionately liberal, radically inclusivist and deeply experimental. So why the radical change?

First, the group have become increasingly proficient at running services. Early projects were by definition experimental, the group had little conception of its aims and limited experience in the use of multi-media technology. Their response to this was to resort to heavily structured procedures, implemented through a bureaucratised system of meetings and committees. As the group began to develop skills and technical expertise, this naïve insecurity faded. Members got used to working with each other's strengths and talents, and to the technology deployed in services, removing the need for such heavily structured organisation. A less rigid structure has fostered a more relaxed mood and has created room for exploration and discussion.

Second, the group have had to deal with the changing domestic circumstances of core members, such as marriages, career changes and house moves which have put new pressures upon the group as a whole. Whereas once members had plenty of time to commit to group projects, these factors have made this less possible. In turn, the group has had to become more flexible in its expectations of members, relaxing its structures and abandoning some of its more demanding projects. The fervour of youth has given way to the realities of domestic life.

Third, the group has become more and more sensitive to the power trappings of person-based authority. It is significant that the *Warehouse* community structure was inspired by NOS, and when the Sheffield group collapsed in 1995, *Warehouse* became more aware of the potential problems associated with adopting fixed, non-negotiable group structures. The group had already been highly sensitive to the possibilities of power abuse inherent in religious authority, but the fall of NOS crystallised these worries in incidents which were close to home. *Visions* have consequently abandoned any internal role differentiation in favour of a more relaxed shared governance. Part of this shift has been a movement away from evangelical norms such as the conventional sermon; the group maintain a focus on the Bible as a source of truth and wisdom, but no longer foster an environment in which Christian beliefs are taught or advocated from the authority of a public platform. This has created room for a freer flow of ideas, but has also meant that the group has seriously tempered its mission strategy, now driven less by a movement of the gospel into new cultural contexts, and more by the adjustment of their own sacred space. Moreover, the turn away from didactic proclamation reflects the fact that the group has, to quote one member, 'lost its evangelical tongue'.

Visions have moved away from evangelistic fervour and have instead adopted a kind of post-evangelical support structure. As Rebecca Wilson commented to me, 'It's less about authority now and more about the community thing.' *Visions* have always had an anti-institutional dimension to their ethos. But previous projects have also been firmly situated within the inherited traditions of evangelicalism: the centrality of evangelism, fellowship through prayer and Bible study, the performance of charismatic gifts. These traditions have since been reconfigured or distanced in favour of a new set of ideas – particularly the group's aesthetic interests, concern for social justice and shared passion for community building. Services are no longer designed so as to appeal to clubbers, but are arranged to be culturally authentic to *Visions* members and those disenfranchised from the mainstream church. In effect, evangelism has taken a back seat to a kind of communitarian expressivism, focused on fostering a collective experience that facilitates the free expression and exploration of Christian identity as conceived by its members.

This process of reconfiguration has, for some, signalled a rejection of key Christian values and a fading definition of group aims. The resulting discontent has led to conflict and dispute over goals, methods and leadership, and several core members have left. At the time of my research, the group did not appear to be experiencing such problems, although it is unclear whether this was because the more vocal members had left, or because some kind of resolution had been achieved.

Cultural Distance: *Visions* within the Context of St Michael's

The above description of how *Visions* has reconfigured certain elements of evangelicalism through their shared culture and worship projects now allows some account of how the group's values compare to those affirmed by the main body of its parent church. Although it would be inaccurate to suggest a strictly oppositional relationship, certain key contrasts can be made. Bearing in mind the internal diversity of both the St Michael's congregation and the *Visions* group as part of it, an effort will be made to restrict comment to those aspects which may be reasonably attributed to the majority of the members of each. These are summarised in Table 6.

Some aspects suggest a stark contrast: approaches to worship, organisational structure, the degree to which political issues are integrated into shared theological values. Others, such as the place of charismatic gifts, suggest a more subtle difference of emphasis in practice. Selectivity in the use of biblical texts and reluctance to condemn non-Christians is a liberal trend in both camps. The distinction lies in how *Visions* members are more explicit, more vociferous and more unified in claiming this perspective. St Michael's members appeared to sense a need to veil their liberal ideas – one liberally-minded parishioner claimed that there were other people like her in St Michael's, but they were not as vocal as the conservatives, as they 'don't want to be branded a heretic'. *Visions* were unabashed by their views, although they were not evangelistic in promoting them and were most open within the safe confines of the core group. Attitudes towards women, politics and the figure of Jesus approximate to a conservative/liberal divide, traditionally defined. However, as detailed in chapter 4, on at least the first of these, St Michael's reflects a compromise position, with widespread acceptance of female authority.

	St Michael-le-Belfrey	*Visions*
Place of the Bible	Highest authority; Canon unquestioned; Stress on personal meaning found in texts.	Highest but not sole authority; one resource among many; More open understanding of canon and authority; Selective use prioritises Gospels over Paul and Old Testament
Place of Charismatic Gifts	Not essential but valuable; Diversity acknowledged; Public and private practice.	Public practice avoided; Private and secluded practice favoured.
Moral Values	Multi-focused; Most conservative on sexual ethics.	Focus on practical giving, social justice, environmental ethics.
Gender	Moderately liberal, but leadership male dominated.	Equality stressed; Sensitive to non-inclusive practice.
Invocation of Jesus	Focus on his death and substitutionary atonement.	Focus on his practical acts (especially fostering the marginalised)
Politics	No clear position/trend; No attention given publicly.	Anti-capitalist and Anti-consumerist themes; Environmentalist; Broadly left-wing.
Organisation	Pyramid accountability structure; Stress on lay leadership.	Stress on non-structure; Shared leadership.
Worship	Stress on words: explanation and exhortation.	Stress on images: provocation and exploration.

Table 6: St Michael-le-Belfrey and *Visions* – Contrasting Values

Despite the obvious differences, which mark the group as distinct from both its parent church and parent tradition, *Visions* embody a set of core values that may be argued are basic to a charismatic evangelical expression of Christianity, most notably the importance of personal experience as a locus of the divine and an understanding of the Christian life as practically demanding. That these have proved most resistant to change is probably due to their reluctance to be bound in discursive, propositional descriptions. Experience and holism – unlike Christology, politics and morality – are difficult to pin down in definitive concepts or authoritative teachings. As such they may be transformed, reconceived, revised and put into practice in new ways whilst still apparently affirming the same basic principle. A similar case may be made for the shared understanding of evangelism within *Visions*. Many members maintained the necessity of sharing the gospel with non-Christians. That the application of their evangelistic efforts has been transformed into something more practical and more subtle, something perhaps unrecognisable to their mainstream peers as evangelism, did not concern them. To the *Visions* group, evangelism takes many forms, the least effective being confrontation and proclamation.

Considering the major characteristics that distinguish *Visions* from its parent church, we may ask how the two interact. Do these differences provoke tension, criticism or even conflict? At the time of my original research, in purely practical terms, there were few regular points of contact between them. *Visions* organised its own initiatives independently and rarely liaised with the St Michael's leadership. Members of *Visions*, although officially also members of St Michael's, did not seem to feel wholly a part of the church and so generally stayed away from church gatherings. In terms of cross-attendance at services, *Visions* members did occasionally attend Sunday services in St Michael's, but these visits tended to reinforce their sense of alienation from the style of worship practised there. According to my questionnaire survey of St Michael's members, 43% of the congregation had attended a *Visions* service at some point, although for the majority, this had been an occasional, isolated event like an Easter service, rather than attendance over time at any of the regular services.

What impressions did members tend to have of one another's identity? This became a curious issue during my research. I questioned St Michael's members about *Visions*, and *Visions* members about St Michael's, and reports rarely tallied with my own experiences of either. In many ways the one side simply did not appear to appreciate what the other was doing. As *Visions* prides itself on being a haven for people who 'don't fit into normal church', an element of social tension is perhaps inevitable. To core *Visions* members, St Michael's was their home church, their chosen place within the Anglican Communion, and yet also represented much of what they found problematic in mainstream evangelicalism. To St Michael's congregants, *Visions* were a strange fringe group who, although attached in some way to St Michael's, were somehow 'different', a bit 'weird' and to some, represented something that they could not recognise as church. When asked to classify the group, St Michael's parishioners were tellingly undecided: 30% thought

Visions were 'Celtic Christian', 15% regarded them as 'New Age'. 18% provided some other answer such as 'dance culture worship' or 'postmodern'. 30% simply could not say. Some parishioners said they saw the value in what the group was doing, but felt that they just 'do not scratch where I itch'. Many made sense of the group as a mission to the dance culture, and saw this agenda as excluding them from its events.

I heard very few St Michael's congregants criticise *Visions* for its theology or services. Many saw it as 'just not their thing', dismissing *Visions* on stylistic, aesthetic grounds. Most were unaware that *Visions* sees itself as a collective that stands for a particular set of values divergent from their own. Some leaders had reservations, expressing a wish that *Visions* would become more integrated into the main structure of St Michael's, or else go their own way. Another criticism cited the group's tendency to emphasise visual symbols without explaining them, and without giving appropriate time to biblical teaching. According to this viewpoint, in downplaying rhetorical content, the group were failing to achieve the primary function of a church service, which is to communicate the gospel in clear and comprehensible terms. Of course, this assumes that the gospel may be effectively couched in rhetorical formulae, which is where *Visions* breaks away from its parent church. But these differences in approach also reflect different understandings of the purpose of the service. To many in St Michael's, *Visions* was seen as a valid enterprise because it is evangelism, and this is why it needs to offer a clearer explanation of the gospel message. In the eyes of its members, *Visions* has moved beyond their original evangelistic project, and in primarily catering for its internal membership, the requirement for 'explanation and exhortation' is even less appropriate.

In summary, there was very little conflict between *Visions* and the rest of the St Michael's congregation because there was very limited contact between them. And yet there was still a curious tension between the two parties, a sense of moving in different directions, of mutual and muted intolerance. This could be described as a 'cultural distance', rather than ideological disagreement. *Visions* members merely felt that they did not 'fit' within their parent church any more and this generally applied to a greater extent *vice versa*. What is more interesting is that this 'distance' was not generally based on an ongoing experience of the other faction. Rather, perceptions were grounded in shared vague impressions, more shaped by past experiences than anything else. Members of each party appeared to project feelings of discomfort and unease on to the other. Moreover, for *Visions*, it was clearly important continually to invoke the aspects of mainstream charismatic evangelicalism – particularly narrow conservatism and charismatic power abuse – which they saw themselves as remedying. This process occasionally drew in the main body of St Michael's as an object of criticism, which says more about the symbolic construction of identity among the *Visions* group than it does about the charismatic culture of its parent church. In short, their sense of identity appears to depend, at least in part, on a strong sense of what they oppose; in embodying the movement that is the focus of this criticism, St Michael's is an obvious local reference point for such opposition.

However, as is clear from the above discussion, it is an opposition that is symbolic rather than material, grounded in a need to maintain a distinctive identity, rather than in an effort to change the wider church.

The Wider Context

While at first the developments in *Visions* may appear somewhat peculiar – perhaps radical and idiosyncratic – they are not without antecedent or analogy. It is not surprising that they share much of what is essential to their outlook with other groups who count themselves within the alt.worship or 'emerging church' network, and in many cases material connections can be traced, *via* common literary inspirations, the swapping of resources on the web, or friendship networks forged at conferences and festivals. Such developments also sound echoes from a more distant historical context. In their emphasis upon relationship-based outreach and the importance of reflecting the contemporary age, *Visions* share key features with the Oxford Group Movement which was popular among university undergraduates in the 1930s. Here also like-minded, often intellectually-minded, peers were bound tightly together by a common urge to live out a Christian lifestyle, characterised in practice by informality and uninhibited self expression.[23] In their concern for contemporary social and political problems, experimental liturgies and emphasis upon mutual support, *Visions* evoke descriptions of the Roman Catholic 'base communities' of the 1960s and 70s. Indeed, they share with the base communities a sense of being on the margins of the church, a church viewed negatively on account of its detachment from the experiences of ordinary people and from the social crises of the day. Their evocation of the spirit of the 1960s is also evident in the theology of *Visions*, which shares many of the convictions expressed by radical theologians like John A.T. Robinson: that Christian theology ought to be open to new knowledge and experience, that the church is trapped within its own subculture and is consequently insulated from the secular, failing to communicate in the language of the contemporary world.[24] The passion and practical application that *Visions* members demonstrated in terms of environmental values resonates strongly with the present-day anti-globalisation movements, focused on ethical trading, social justice and environmental sustainability and the revision of their theological priorities has clearly been influenced by such developments in recent years. In these respects the *Visions* group embody what might be described as classically liberal values – an openness to the world, passion for dialogue over conflict, and an overriding concern for human freedom and dignity, over dogmatic truth – and yet a closer look at the socio-religious identity of *Visions* as a collective suggests that such a description would be far too simplistic.

It is simplistic in large part because the developments of *Visions* very much reflect changes in the wider world of charismatic evangelicalism. *Visions* has indeed

---

[23] See Bebbington, *Evangelicalism in Modern Britain*, pp. 235-40.
[24] John A.T. Robinson, *Honest to God* (London: SCM Press, 1963).

embraced wider cultural trends, but it has done so in so far as they have been filtered through and reconfigured by the accommodation to culture across the evangelical movement charted in chapter 2. To take the most pertinent thematic example, the attempt by the *Visions* group to engage with the culture of postmodernity reflects attempts across the western evangelical world, both within the mainstream and at its margins, to do the same thing. In one sense this is inevitable; evangelical groups exist within a culture, with which they must engage, especially if they are to grow, and in so far as that culture may be called 'postmodern', then evangelicalism will inevitably absorb aspects of postmodernity. Quite apart from strict sectarian enclaves, the boundaries between religion and culture are always more permeable than many adherents would like to acknowledge. But the matter goes further than this, on account of the fact that evangelicals – especially charismatic evangelicals – have, in recent years, *consciously engaged* with the wider culture in an attempt to be culturally relevant, a strategy aimed at improving their chances of conveying a message that is meaningful in the eyes of the unconverted. Postmodernity has become a new mission field, and the notions of innovation and adaptability associated with postmodernity have been harnessed by evangelicals in making sense of their evangelistic creativity. Indeed, David Hilborn has argued that evangelicals have, in recent times, been doing 'postmodern things in postmodern ways'[25] because of the deeply engrained missionary pragmatism which lies at the heart of evangelical identity. His comments echo David Bebbington's focus on 'activism' as a core aspect of evangelical tradition, and Grant Wacker's account of the history of Pentecostalism in the USA, which has, he claims, always been distinguished by two key impulses, primitivism and pragmatism.[26] In short, the practical entrepreneurialism that has characterised initiatives across the evangelical world in recent years – in mission, cell groups, leadership, worship – is rooted in a pragmatic tendency at the heart of evangelical tradition. Postmodernity lends a new nomenclature to these endeavours, but their inspiration was there well before the cultural accommodations of the 1960s.

And yet clearly attempts to be 'postmodern' have moved in different directions and evangelical communities and individuals have varied in the degree to which they have allowed their interpretation of the postmodern to radicalise their outlook. For some, it simply amounts to a diversification of mission strategies, a cosmetic change, one of method, not of substance; for others, it demands a fresh understanding of truth itself. This diversity becomes clear when one considers the variety of communities identifying themselves as alt.worship, emerging church or post-evangelical, a series of labels which has become infused into the evangelical subculture in a way that has broadened their reference considerably. Moreover, while patterns of belief and ecclesiology vary in different nations, the diversity across these movements remains so great that nationality is not a reliable predictor of difference. For example, the

---

[25] David Hilborn, *Picking up the Pieces. Can Evangelicals Adapt to Contemporary Culture?* (London: Hodder and Stoughton, 1997), p. 6.
[26] Grant Wacker, *Heaven Below. Early Pentecostals and American Culture* (Cambridge, MA, and London: Harvard University Press, 2001).

assumption for some time was that the radical rethinking of evangelical identity contained within Dave Tomlinson's book *The Post-Evangelical* was not applicable within the USA, because it retained an evangelical movement which, while exhibiting immense inventiveness in its models of church and mission, was essentially resistant to changing certain core doctrines. Hence the descriptions of both 'new paradigm' churches like those of the Vineyard or Calvary networks, and of the 'GenX churches' which cater to youth subcultures. Both treat the traditional structures of Christianity, including rituals and institutions, as optional, secondary to the needs of mission, while retaining a firm commitment to biblical inerrancy, a conversionist model of recruitment and a strict moral code, centred around 'family values'.[27] And yet churches like Mars Hill, in Michigan, which situates itself within the 'Emerging Church' network, represent a more radical innovation. Here, rethinking Christianity in light of cultural change means questioning what the gospel actually means, abandoning old certainties and embracing mystery, and discovering new ways of reading the Bible as a human product.[28] Such churches are influenced by radical theologians like Brian McLaren, whose reconception of 'orthodoxy' centres on an embodied orientation, characterised by generosity, openness and humility, rather than a concern to be correct in ways which are verbally articulated and easily recognised.[29] McLaren shares with Dave Tomlinson both an upbringing in the Brethren church and a self-conscious urge to react against the constraints of traditional evangelicalism. The resulting visions for the future of evangelical Christianity both stress the importance of dialogue, faith as journey and the importance of reflection over judgement; they have also had tremendous influence over emerging trends on both sides of the Atlantic.

The direction in which a community moves in its attempt to engage with postmodernity depends on a variety of factors, not least educational background, the stage at which one finds oneself in a spiritual career, degrees of dependency upon leaders, resources at one's disposal, and, perhaps most importantly, the norms of legitimacy dominant within the group of which one is a member.[30] What is also important to recognise is that, within these contexts, postmodernity does not merely represent a series of cultural conditions, but exists as a social construction forged by each group or community according to its own pre-existing ideas, values, beliefs and

---

[27] See Donald E. Miller, *Reinventing American Protestantism. Christianity in the New Millennium* (Berkeley and Los Angeles, CA: University of California Press, 1997), and Lori Jensen, 'When Two World's Collide: Generation X Culture and Conservative Evangelicalism', in Richard Flory and Donald E. Miller (eds.), *GenX Religion* (New York and London: Routledge, 2000), pp. 139-62.

[28] See Andy Crouch, 'The Emerging Mystique', *Christianity Today* 48:11 (2004), pp. 36-43.

[29] See Brian McLaren, *A Generous Orthodoxy* (Grand Rapids, MI: Zondervan, 2004).

[30] The varying ways in which alt.worship groups in the UK and in New Zealand attempt to embody postmodern values are explored in Mathew Guest and Steve Taylor, 'The Post-Evangelical Emerging Church: Innovations in New Zealand and the UK', *International Journal for the Study of the Christian Church* 6:1 (2006), pp. 49-64.

conventions. *Visions* is no exception here, and constructs its own understanding of postmodernity, in relation to which members make sense of their identities, just as the members of St Michael's construct their own understanding of contemporary culture. In many ways *Visions* have embraced an approach to spirituality that is reflective of common academic understandings of the 'postmodern'. Using James Beckford's sociological definition of postmodernity as a benchmark, one could point to their emphasis on the expansion of knowledge beyond rational, propositional language; an eclectic approach to symbols and their arrangement in novel combinations; a celebration of fragmentation, playfulness or irony; and an incredulity towards over-arching metanarratives or frameworks of knowledge.[31] And yet this only paints part of the picture; while making plain broad brush strokes, it does not untangle the various routes by which *Visions* appears to occupy trajectories of challenge to and within the wider evangelical movement, trajectories which are then made sense of as postmodern. Three key areas of change may be singled out for further comment, relating to tradition, culture and community.

First, *Visions* reflects a movement among progressive, post-evangelical parties whereby the treasures of Christian history and tradition are being rediscovered. Tomlinson himself confesses to moving in the same direction, finding in a liberal Anglicanism a new freedom to explore the resources of Christian history that he did not have as a house church leader.[32] *Visions* enjoy the same freedom, and the control they have over the structure and content of worship allows them to incorporate a variety of sources. The most striking are from popular culture (e.g., see the prologue), but alongside these are resources from Eastern orthodoxy, Native American poetry, and Celtic traditions.[33] Their use of incense and liturgy also evokes the Anglo-Catholic tradition, although this is incorporated into a model of worship that, while emphasising material engagement and practical ritual, steers clear of formal ceremony. This reflects their orientation to tradition: it is used as a spiritual resource, to be respected and practised, but only in so far as it serves the established priorities of the group, which are centred on creating a safe and meaningful space for participants. The attraction of tradition is its rich potential as a multifaceted resource,

---

[31] James Beckford, 'Religion, Modernity and Postmodernity', in Bryan R. Wilson (ed.), *Religion. Contemporary Issues, the All Souls Seminars in the Sociology of Religion* (London: Belew, 1992), pp. 11-23.

[32] Heather Webb, 'Continuing the Journey: A Conversation with Dave Tomlinson', *Mars Hill Review* 18 (2001), p. 73.

[33] While the eclecticism of *Visions* exceeds some other alt.worship groups, the group have been keen to avoid accusations of unbridled syncretism. In a 'Frequently Asked Questions' pamphlet produced by the group some years ago, the question of whether the group's activities are a 'bit New Age' is confronted. The pamphlet affirms the group's strong opposition to practices such as astrology, and experimenting with the occult, while defending the need to speak the language of the broader culture if the gospel is to be communicated effectively, adding that the 'openness to talk about spiritual things within the New Age culture makes it much easier to talk about Christ than within a secular humanist culture'.

rather than as a prescriptive model for Christian practice. In this, they reflect the approach, popular in 'emerging church' circles, of 'looking for ways ahead for the Christian faith by reaching back at the same time'.[34]

Visions also share with many evangelical groups a concern to be culturally relevant, and to respect the culture of those outside of the church. I have discussed above how an initial rationale of enculturation for the sake of evangelism has given way to enculturation for the sake of meaningful community. Communicating a culturally meaningful Christianity has simply become more important than keeping a conventional tally on how many souls have been saved. This resistance to quantifying evangelism extends to a cynicism towards the codification of culture that is common in mainstream evangelical churches who wish to apply and measure their cultural awareness in terms of quantifiable results. One *Visions* member articulated her concerns in terms of the Alpha course; commenting on the importance of cell groups in St Michael's, she said they had nothing against this, she just does not like 'McDonaldisation'. In this sense, *Visions* are committed to a more organic approach to enculturation, allowing for a flexible understanding of contemporary culture, and fostering a process of engagement based on negotiation, whereby some aspects are embraced and others resisted. However, to some degree this more open approach appears to have collapsed the aesthetic and social boundaries between church and culture, generating a whole new understanding of Christian identity.

To expand, during fieldwork, I had a revealing conversation with an ex-member of the group, who spoke of the times when *Warehouse* were attempting to 'cross the bridge' into the culture of the night-clubbers. Although they always came back, she suggests that many of the group may have been more comfortable 'on the other side' all along. This captures the extent to which *Visions* have adapted and accommodated to a culture outside of the evangelical mainstream. In their early years this amounted to the dance culture, along with the equipment, records, clothes and sub-cultural markers that go with it. More recently, the 'culture' which serves as the benchmark of authenticity for the group amounts to a complex image of the postmodern, post-Christian West, which brings new challenges and fresh resources to the church. In many ways they are still exploring Graham Cray's question of, 'to what extent can a tradition re-embody its core values in a new cultural world?' The difference in recent years is that an 'incarnational mission' has brought about a radical accommodation of values whereby traditional understandings of humanity, sin and the nature of salvation are being reconfigured. More profoundly, a hyper-sensitivity to the cultural identities of outsiders has fostered a view of culture as being ontologically prior in matters of identity, driven by what might be called a process of humanisation. That is, a radical broadening of boundaries has undermined the importance of religious differences, leading to a focus upon humanity as the remaining common element. It is the human in people which is celebrated, fostered and afforded most respect, and

---

[34] McLaren, *A Generous Orthodoxy*, p. 18, citing the thinking of Leonard Sweet and Robert Webber. See Leonard Sweet, *Postmodern Pilgrims* (Nashville, TN: Broadman and Holman, 2000), and Robert Webber, *Ancient-Future Faith* (Grand Rapids, MI: Baker, 1999).

The Post-Evangelical Pathway

which as such, acquires exceptional value. This does not equate to a New Age self-spirituality, or to an individualistic 'cult of man', but amounts to an affirmation of human value and its cultural context as components of a shared, complex belief system which has an omnipotent but immanent God at its centre. Most radically, it amounts to an appreciation of culture as essential to identity, and its sympathetic understanding as central to the Christian life.

In this respect, *Visions* embrace a radical subjectivisation in the way they prioritise the individual self in relation to others. Their entire ethos revolves around catering to outsiders by offering experiences which may be embraced as personally and culturally authentic. A sense of meaning is contingent on whether something 'works' for the individual. Within this framework, rejection, disinvolvement and criticism are accepted as unproblematic. Former members are not begrudged for leaving, as this was 'right for them at the time'. Subjective identity is accepted independent of one's commitment to the group, so that legitimacy does not depend upon membership or conformity to a set of standards. Indeed, the imposition of standards is seen as an affront to subjectivity and to the authentic identities of individuals. A logical consequence of this is that the group have a relativist understanding of their outlook and projects; while their services may have meaning for some, they are acknowledged as equally alienating for others. And yet they retain a central focus on the importance of community, which functions as a means of mutual support, and as the context through which the complex dimensions of postmodern detraditionalisation described above are channelled and maintained. In exhibiting a thirst for community, *Visions* express much of what is commonly associated with postmodernity, not least a paradoxical embrace of diversity and experiment, alongside a quest for collective identity and some sense of belonging. Perhaps ironically, they share much with their parent church in wrestling with this paradox, and the following chapter will address how they both attempt to square the circle.

CHAPTER 7

Small Group Fellowship: The Experience of Community

Early in 2000 I met June, an elderly parishioner who had joined the St Michael's fellowship with her husband and two children in 1968. Her husband had since died and her children grown up and moved away, but she still attended St Michael's regularly. After several meetings, she agreed to be interviewed and to share her thoughts about her time as a member of the church.

After recalling her memories of how St Michael's had changed over the years, especially in terms of its leaders and style of worship, she moved on to the subject of home groups. Home group fellowship has been central to the life of the church since the 1970s. The tradition of regularly meeting for prayer, Bible study, worship and ministry within one another's homes was rooted in the meetings David Watson had originally held in the rectory not long after his arrival in York. A system of home groups, each meeting weekly as a supplement to Sunday worship, was soon established and became a key context for pastoral support and lay leadership. June told me that she had led a large group with her husband in their own home for seven years. She recounted how the group system had changed over the years, and was nostalgic for the time when home groups were a great source of intimacy, friendship and mutual support. She recalled how parishioners would be able to call on one another to borrow money, to ask for a lift when they were in a rush or the car had broken down, to be taken meals when ill in bed. There was a deep sense of trust and a spirit of giving among members, fostered through the experience of being part of a common fellowship. At the time of our interview, she was still attending a home group, but was unsure about the charismatic style of its two leaders. 'They are lovely people', she said, 'but they are into falling on the floor and shaking.' She said she felt this is fine if the Holy Spirit moves people in that way, but it had never moved her in this fashion. She was also a little sceptical, as people might follow their example because of peer pressure rather than out of a genuine experience of the Spirit.

I asked her what the greatest value had been in being part of a home group. Her response: 'Being in a small group where you can share your life, share your problems, talk more intimately, make relationships and close friendships.' In this she echoed the views of many older parishioners, who appeared to yearn for a close-knit community and strength of commitment that some felt was sorely lacking amongst the current congregation, especially among the young. I asked June whether she felt this way and she did agree that there is less community these days, and less love in society. But she reassured me that there are still strong bonds within the St Michael's congregation. 'Why I stay now? I've been here so many years, it's part of my life; it's my family.'

Just before I moved away from York, around Easter 2000, I interviewed Emma. Emma had been a member of St Michael's during the late 1980s while a student, and joined *Warehouse* with her boyfriend in the early 90s. At the time of the interview, she was still attending *Visions* regularly and was regarded as one of the core group. After a nervous start to the interview she began to relax and eventually embarked on a passionate and detailed explanation of how the *Warehouse* group had developed as a distinct community.

She described how, although the group emerged from a charismatic evangelical background, it did not want the culture that came with this branch of the church. They wanted church to reflect their own identities and cultural experience, feeling a sense of disillusionment with mainstream evangelicalism. The group wanted change – to be a new kind of church – and this meant they had to be open-minded; in terms of their early meetings, it meant that they welcomed an open and honest discussion of possibilities. The 'home group' meeting was less a supplement to the Sunday service, more a think tank for reconfiguring the nature of church itself. However, fostering an open forum led to in-group clashes, and strong personalities found that they profoundly disagreed with one another. Debate was passionate and I recall stories of slamming doors and angry confrontations. As Emma said to me, '... at one point everything was up for discussion and it was a whole new group and that's why it caused problems ... everyone had their own opinions'.

I wondered how they ever arrived at the laid-back, sedate attitude that they subsequently managed to maintain, and which now shaped the ambience of their worship and fellowship. Emma explained this with reference to their strong sense of mutual commitment to one another and to a common project: '... I think that there is some very real commitment to each other as people, and you don't just blow each other out or have an argument if you're committed to someone, you sort it out, and I think that's what happened in the past ...' She suggested that the mutual commitment among members over-rides any disagreement there might be between them. There are strong bonds of friendship and a sense of common purpose, and these have secured an ongoing unity in spite of conflicts of attitude: '... there have been clashes, [but] it's been worked out and there is some ... very real love, and there is very real community, and that is what has got us through any difficult [times]'.

Community Beyond the Congregation

The evangelical tradition has always included a certain inventiveness when it comes to ecclesiology; indeed, a flexible approach to the notion of 'church' arises from the thoroughgoing pragmatism discussed in the previous chapter. For evangelicals, the organisational structures of the church have often been secondary to individual piety and the demands of mission, and forms of communal gathering have often been embraced according to whether they have served these higher priorities, or fostered the collective piety of the faithful. In recent decades, an insidious separatism in the English tradition has been curbed by calls to be 'salt and light' within existing denominations, and by John Stott's affirmation of the ecclesiological responsibilities of evangelical Christians. And yet at the same time, a thoroughly creative activism persists and nurtures a spirit of adaptability and innovation among evangelicals keen to explore ever-new forms of mission, social outreach and community itself.

Ever since David Watson's arrival in York, the experience of community among the St Cuthbert's and then St Michael's congregation has been distinctive and key to the church's appeal. From the Thursday evening fellowships held in the Watsons' rectory in the late 1960s, to the area home groups, and the radical community living of the households, St Michael's has maintained a strong emphasis on fostering a sense of family and intimacy among its members. These communal contexts, maintained alongside Sunday services, have created leadership roles and hence opportunities for lay empowerment, a warmth and intimacy of fellowship members have rarely experienced elsewhere, and the opportunity to build relationships based on personal connections and a common faith life. Most importantly, perhaps, such contexts foster interdependency between individual members, opening up an extended role for the church as a centre for the management of personal lives, concerned with social, emotional and psychological, as well as spiritual, well being. David Watson conveyed this well in describing the ideas behind the St Cuthbert's Thursday evening fellowship, stressing the importance of sharing:

> It should be a truly 'family affair' – a fellowship for all ages where we can learn more of God's plan for our lives and where we can share together our personal needs and problems. God intends that every Christian should belong to a living, caring fellowship like this, where we don't have to pretend we're all super-saints. Far from it, we are ordinary folk with ordinary needs that ought to be shared. And if we don't share them with other Christians, we shall no doubt have to put up with far heavier burdens than the Lord ever meant us to bear.[1]

In fostering such a strong sense of community, the congregation of St Michael's has both outshone its neighbours while also echoing, and in some cases inspiring, developments across the wider evangelical movement. The house church movement was based in large part on its break from denominational structures in favour of a more authentic Christian fellowship. Several church growth authors have inspired comparable reconfigurations of community on a local level, with 'small groups' often hailed as 'building blocks' for a healthy and growing Christian community.[2] In more recent times, the Alpha course has placed small groups at the centre of its global ministry to the unchurched, with the small group the basis for discussion of

---

[1] David Watson, quoted in Teddy Saunders and Hugh Sansom, *David Watson. A Biography* (London, Sydney, Auckland: Hodder and Stoughton, 1992), p. 112.

[2] E.g., in Christian Schwarz, *Natural Church Development* (Carol Stream, IL: Churchsmart Resources, 1996).

key facets of the Christian life and the vehicle for the subsequent journey of the newly converted into the church. Some have built on the tradition of a more intimate fellowship in rethinking the very nature of church itself. For example, Ralph Neighbour and Lawrence Singlehurst have reconceived church as 'cell', a model that emphasises church as close-knit and cohesive, but also united in a common focus on saving souls. Warmth and mutual sharing are at its heart, but relationships are temporary in so far as cells are eventually expected to multiply as part of a mission strategy. Such objectives are often organised around highly rationalised structures and a pyramid system of leadership.[3] In a different, more progressive development, small group has been re-imagined by those within the Emerging Church network as a context for mutual sharing, open dialogue and a style of worship that emphasises active participation and interaction.[4] The relatively autonomous status of many 'emerging' groups also means that they provide a safe place for the exploration of Christian spirituality beyond the judgements or expectations of the mainstream. Both of these developments owe much to the pragmatic impetus at the heart of evangelicalism, but have taken shape in response to the very particular conditions of the late modern period. One harnesses structure and entrepreneurialism in a business-like manner, aiming to maximise the evangelistic potential of an energised laity. The other builds on western traditions of open expression, personal integrity and the value of the therapeutic, viewing the crisis in the church as less one of faulty mechanics, more one of cultural detachment.

As the two anecdotes cited above demonstrate, belonging to St Michael's is associated with notions of family, of mutual support and of a common purpose. Membership is consistently made sense of in collective terms, and in explaining to me why they continue to attend St Michael's, members consistently invoked the sense of belonging and experience of community that they achieve there. As one individual put it, '... I have grown to love and appreciate the family of believers and I now feel a part of this family.' While *Visions* stands in the tradition of small group fellowship established by David Watson, effectively fostering a common identity and encouraging mutual support among members, it has particularly benefited from another aspect of this community structure, that is, autonomy. As recounted in chapter 6, the innovations of *Visions* emerged out of vigorous and extended discussions which took place in the Monday Night Group, a group of like-minded peers who enjoyed space to explore their new ideas openly because they met separately from the rest of the St Michael's congregation. Their autonomy as a group also empowered them to pursue their experiments in worship, community and evangelism, urged on by Graham Cray's enthusiasm for postmodern mission. This is important as it highlights the paradox at the heart of the small group structure as a basis for evangelical fellowship: it tends to foster internal cohesion at the same time as inviting autonomy, and perhaps dissent, from the main congregation or from the

---

[3] David Harvey, 'Cell Church: Its Situation in British Evangelical Culture', *Journal of Contemporary Religion* 18:1 (2003), pp. 95-109.

[4] See Eddie Gibbs and Ryan K. Bolger, *Emerging Churches. Creating Christian Community in Postmodern Cultures* (London: SPCK, 2006), pp. 109-13.

tradition that congregation purports to represent. How this takes place in St Michael-le-Belfrey will be discussed below; for the moment, it is worth emphasising how an analysis of small groups connects with our preceding discussions of belief and community.

Earlier on, I argued that St Michael's has maintained a collective sense of common identity through a subtle control of public discourse which tends to marginalise fragmenting forces and paper over perceived tensions. The management of the subjective has also involved the public expression of shared problems, mainly to do with the struggles of a life of faith (e.g., in words of knowledge). These mechanisms appear to depend upon a marked division of public and private discourses. In a sense, this is inevitable. St Michael's has had to cope with an abnormally large congregation for thirty-five years and has evolved ways of managing the challenges that this presents, not least maintaining a sense of unity and interconnectedness amongst a diverse and only partially integrated congregation. This has been emphasised earlier on in this book when I have pointed to the two-tier character of the congregation: the high address list figures compared to Sunday attendances, and compared to the core committed membership, which is much smaller. There is a close-knit network of committed members, but they do not comprise the entire congregation, as there is also a more loosely structured, less integrated periphery who engage in the church in a very different way. Within this situation, public discourse in particular has taken on a role in integrating the various voices and offering channels of inter-communication across the congregation and these were explored in the preceding two chapters.

Small groups present a different phenomenon altogether. While not performing a mediating role in relation to individuals and the larger congregation as such, they do present an intermediate-sized fellowship which performs functions not achievable in larger contexts. Not least, they offer a context in which face to face fellowship can make up for the anonymity of existing within a large and famous church, and are clearly valued as such by committed members. They have for many years served as the context in which the sense of family and interdependency, established as normative by the late 1960s, could be realised and experienced on a regular basis. It is also possible that small groups have been popular because they offer an experience of community that is particularly suited to 'elective parochials', i.e., those socially and geographically mobile individuals who, uprooted from their original homes, re-create community relationships *via* temporary allegiances and secondary institutions. We have already cited the evidence that suggests the St Michael's congregation does, and perhaps has for some time, contain a significant proportion of individuals falling into this category. One is reminded of Robert Wuthnow's comments about support groups in the USA which, he argues, cater for the socially and geographically mobile by encouraging alliances that are not expected to be permanent. They provide 'a kind of social interaction that busy, rootless people can grasp without making significant adjustment to their lifestyles. [They] allow ... bonding to remain temporary.'⁵ While St Michael's elicits significant practical commitment from many members, the congregation also includes many who are indeed 'passing through', and small groups function in a way that allows their participation to remain temporary and partial. There is much to be learned from Wuthnow's analysis, including important implications for church growth, as will be explored in the final chapter.

While not all congregants participate in home groups – 63% of the congregation in 1999 – small group gatherings also feature in youth meetings, staff prayer, the Alpha course and the monthly church prayer meeting. It is fair to say that the majority of St Michael's members take part in small groups on a regular basis, as a focus for spirituality and a context for forging close bonds among other parishioners, and that this convention is long-established. A good example would be '20s', a group established as a large regular gathering of young parishioners – including several future *Visions* members – which achieved a membership of forty-three in 1990. The group was disbanded when home groups were re-organised according to geographical area. However, as one former member told me, participants so valued their regular meetings that some continued to meet informally as a home group. The perceived value of the gathering was so great that it continued outside official church boundaries, a sure signal of strong mutual bonds and a need for continued fellowship with familiar friends. Small group fellowship emerges as a pervasive form of social gathering at the popular, as well as officially organised, level of congregational culture. In light of this, it is useful to examine small group fellowship in St Michael's as it forms the context in which the experience of community most important to members is fostered and maintained. Therefore, it is in examining the nature of interaction within small groups that we may come to understand better both the appeal of St Michael's and the construction of shared values among members. In addressing this second issue and its broader theoretical implications, it will be useful to consider Penny Becker's work on congregations in the USA.

Family and Community Congregations

In her book *Congregations in Conflict*, American sociologist Penny Edgell Becker breaks new ground by analysing conflict within congregations not in terms of underlying variables – such as size or liberal/conservative orientation – but with reference to members' shared understandings of authority and of the nature of their commitment. Conflict and its management are shaped by a public consensus on 'how we do things here'.⁶ On this basis, Becker formulates a typology that includes a distinction between 'family' and 'community' congregations. While both foster 'family-like' connections between people, and thus mobilise mutual support

---

⁵ Robert Wuthnow, *Sharing the Journey. Support Groups and America's New Quest for Community* (New York, London, Toronto, Sydney, Singapore: The Free Press, 1996), p. 25.

⁶ Penny Edgell Becker, *Congregations in Conflict. Cultural Models of Local Religious Life* (Cambridge: CUP, 1999), p. 43.

networks among members, there are also important differences.⁷ Family congregations stress doctrinal unity for the sake of cohesion and an experience of togetherness as a church 'family'.⁸ Community congregations, by contrast, emphasise the importance of providing a context in which members may express their individuality. They stress the need for the congregation as an institution to adjust to the needs of its members.⁹ The first plays down difference for the sake of unity and emphasises conformity to an established religious and moral order; the second de-emphasises sameness in favour of accommodating the different needs of individuals within the community.

This distinction bears some similarity to the different kinds of community offered within St Michael's, especially when considering the culture of the *Visions* group. Chapter 4 emphasised how a pervasive liberalisation among the St Michael's congregation is nevertheless veiled through the control of public discourse. Public teaching plays down those differences likely to provoke conflict in order to sustain a sense of essential doctrinal unity. By contrast, the radical individualisation positively embraced by the *Visions* group has developed hand in hand with an understanding of community as that which nurtures personal needs, in all their inevitable diversity. Here, community is conceived as a place where the cultural outcast is welcomed and their difference affirmed as legitimate. This is not merely a distinction between 'right belief' and 'right practice', but signals two alternative ways in which each is put in the service of the other. In St Michael's, an established model of values is sustained by a process of policing the boundaries of shared discourse and group practice. In *Visions*, group practice encourages an exploratory approach to values, while still retaining a sense of orthodoxy through belonging and subscribing to the wider church. Both rely upon controlling dominant norms of interaction, and both require a certain degree of shared value. But while St Michael's demands the public appearance of a (limited) uniformity of belief, *Visions* fosters (and also requires) a public discourse in which a variety of perspectives might have a legitimate place.

Becker's approach to community is to examine the ways in which the demands put on members reflect a common ideology or value system. In focusing upon the interaction between the functions of local community and group attitudes, she offers a corrective to Peter Berger's failure to take account of mediating structures. Berger, and often those influenced by his perspective, appear to assume that the relationship between dominant cultural forces and individually held values amounts to a straightforward relationship between social structure and belief. In so doing, they fail to account for '... the different empirical relationships between the contents of socialization and different social structural configurations ...'¹⁰ These relationships are complex and difficult to trace with empirical accuracy, but Becker's 'institutional'

---

⁷ Becker, *Congregations in* Conflict, p. 65.
⁸ Becker, *Congregations in Conflict*, pp. 86-7.
⁹ Becker, *Congregations in Conflict*, p. 109.
¹⁰ Robert Wuthnow *et al*, *Cultural Analysis. The Work of Peter L. Berger, Mary Douglas, Michel Foucault and Jurgen Habermas* (London, Boston, Melbourne and Henley: Routledge and Kegan Paul, 1984), p. 71.

model for analysing congregations offers a useful starting point. I will take up Becker's theoretical approach in an analysis of the small group, which has been essential to the development of a culture of values within both St Michael's and *Visions*. I offer a comparison between the use of small group in the main body of St Michael's on the one hand, and in *Visions* on the other, as I believe they represent two distinctive arrangements which are instructive in reflecting on wider patterns of change in the evangelical movement more generally, in addition to offering a window on to the nature of community among the broad membership of St Michael-le-Belfrey. My emphasis will be upon how patterns of value are legitimated or challenged within each, and on how the family and community models described above are sustained.

Small Groups in St Michael's

During my field research, I attended numerous meetings which may be described as 'small group' gatherings, including those in church contexts, public places and in members' homes. Particularly interesting were a series of meetings related to the Alpha course and its follow up series, Alphalink. Alphalink is a scheme designed by Holy Trinity, Brompton as a continuation course for Alpha 'graduates' and stepping stone to local church membership. It also follows a prescribed literature and was transposed in St Michael's into the general home group structure, as a kind of halfway house between Alpha attendance and a full commitment to the St Michael's fellowship. Within this context, small group meetings can be especially interesting as they serve as the key communal structures for the mediation of external influences into the life of the congregation. A similar function is exemplified in *Visions* small group meetings, although the sources appropriated there are far less codified and remain more in the control of group members. But meetings among all factions of the church present similar research opportunities, and there remains to be conducted a detailed examination of small group fellowship as a context for the negotiation of evangelical identity across the UK movement.

For now, let us take the Alphalink sessions as an illustrative example of how small groups generally function. Although the Alphalink sessions were far more structured than Alpha small group sessions, the majority of time was still spent in discussion. We would spend the first fifteen minutes or so chatting informally, pray together, read through the set biblical text (usually a passage of about ten verses, read aloud by a volunteer), and then engage in group discussion. The group leader would typically pose questions for the group – why is baptism not enough to make us confident before God?; should we show the same concern for non-Christians as we do to Christians? – and wait for our responses. Questions were supposed to relate to the set text, and to a key theme raised by it: responsibility, friendship or generosity, for example. From the outset, no one was questioned directly and discussion remained thoroughly non-confrontational. When contributions were slow in coming forward, one of the St Michael's members would attempt to launch the discussion by voicing their own convictions on the issue. In this way the 'leader' adopted a non-intrusive role, setting the agenda and overseeing proceedings, rather than teaching or claiming any religious authority. Participants engaged in sessions in a relaxed and informal manner, and demonstrated their commitment to learning by bringing along their own Bibles and making written notes during discussion.

The group included the newly converted and those on the margins of Christianity as well as St Michael's members, and this meant that questions were occasionally challenging, and discussions revealed a great deal about where members felt the boundaries of belief should lie, as well as revealing how diversity or conflict are sometimes dealt with. Sessions were both informal and friendly throughout, and participants grew to trust one another more as friends as time progressed. This meant that discussion was increasingly relaxed and eventually, earlier traces of reticence had gone, as members appeared to freely and honestly contribute to group debate.

Given their evangelistic subtext, sessions were generally focused upon Christian 'essentials', especially the necessity and meaning of salvation. However, the way in which these issues were addressed displayed some resemblance to the reticence and civility discussed in chapter 4. In this respect, group discourse was often notable for what it did not include, rather than what it did. Even in these contexts of evangelism – in which full conversion of non-Christians is openly promoted as an end goal – there was a curious gentle negotiation of the issues. The shared theological gentility discussed in chapter 4 appears to have infiltrated norms of interaction with outsiders, as well as between members of the church.

The evangelical tone of the Alpha literature very much shaped the discourse of Alpha and Alphalink sessions – both through its recommended 'questions for discussion' and in the subliminal way in which St Michael's advocates reiterated its substantive emphases and re-enacted its styles of expression. Indeed, Nicky Gumbel, vicar of Holy Trinity, Brompton, and author of much of the Alpha literature, was soon incorporated into discussion as an authority, and his writings and persona were invoked as signifying sound Christian wisdom.

Given the discussion in chapter 4, it is interesting to reflect on how internal diversity is dealt with in small group meetings. For example, given the mixed membership of Alpha groups – including evangelicals, non-evangelical Christians and non-Christians – one might expect a degree of disagreement among participants. However, any disagreement that arose in the groups in which I participated was quickly defused, either made sense of as a positive sign of Christian diversity or else evaded and glossed over quickly before any sense of dissonance could be openly registered. A sense of dissonance was clearly evident, but I soon began to see that it was largely suppressed, subject to a carefully placed diplomacy. Most striking was the reluctance on the part of participants to offer any kind of clear judgement that might have alienated anyone there. Tolerance, alongside gentle urges in the 'right' direction, emerged as the defining but unstated group ethic.

For example, at one home group meeting, pre-empting one source of disagreement, one participant stated that it is important to be obedient to one's calling. Some are called to be vegetarians, but he had not been, therefore it was acceptable for him to eat meat. In other words, God chooses different paths for different servants, and this diversity goes some way towards explaining differences of opinion within the Christian camp. Another participant shared her concerns about Christians she had met who would not listen to the radio for fear of being corrupted by the mention of sex. She saw this as ridiculous, and there was some agreement amongst the group. However, another participant openly affirmed the importance of tolerance in this case. These ideas may seem ridiculous to us, but we should not judge these people. They might see things differently in the Bible – and that's OK for them – but it is important not to judge others, despite our differences. She added the caveat that, as long as the 'fundamentals' are there, then that's OK. However, these 'fundamentals', though affirmed, were not defined, implying, if anything, an emphasis upon relationships and relational commitment rather than on doctrinal correctness.

On the rare occasions when I witnessed any kind of judgement voiced and directed at a particular member of a small group, this was notable for its subtlety and muted expression and, tellingly, such occasions only arose when fundamental boundaries of the evangelical understanding of Christian faith were being undermined. For example, during one Alpha discussion, a young woman (not a St Michael's member) expressed her conviction that there was no dissonance between her faith in God and her faith in astrology. Questionnaire data from the time suggests that there is passionate opposition to 'alternative' spiritual practices amongst St Michael's congregants, a tendency not untypical among evangelicals.[11] 75% viewed mediumship as 'evil', a figure that was 72% for tarot reading, 72% for paganism and 87% for witchcraft. However, this remark within a small group gathering prompted a relatively lukewarm suggestion that should this woman put her whole faith in God, then she would not need to rely on astrology. She quickly restated her position, claiming that she would not delve into it again, thus conforming to the position by then established as acceptable.

However, I discerned among participants outside of the context of the small group meeting a sense of feeling a discernible pressure to 'say the right thing', and toe the party line that astrology is simply wrong and misguided. Some, especially Alpha participants who were not St Michael's members, said they would rather have discussed matters further and in more depth, and thought that some of the other group members felt the same. These comments were telling, and suggested a simultaneous awareness of the complexity of the issues addressed and yet a conscious reluctance to shift the discussion to take these complexities into account. While the implicit ethic of this group emphasised affirmation and gentle guidance over judgement, it also achieved conformity *via* repressing certain kinds of criticism or debate. A 'repressive tolerance' was thus not only implied in conversational exchange, but was also felt by peripheral participants as a norm of interaction that was dominant and imposed by the St Michael's members. Indeed, it was by gently

---

11 John A. Saliba, *Christian Responses to the New Age Movement. A Critical Assessment* (London: Cassell, 1999), p. 40.

encouraging capitulation to a dominant discourse that the group collectively sustained a tolerance of the 'right kind'.

To expand, the shaping principle of group conduct appeared to favour the assertion of boundaries between Christian and non-Christian, but only if the anomaly raised could not be reasonably incorporated into a vision of Christian diversity. For example, groups could generally acknowledge Christians who did not profess second birth, or who favoured less mainstream styles of prayer or worship; they could not tolerate the 'New Age Movement'. As group members were from a fairly limited range of social backgrounds, and several shared the same worldview, no contributions were seriously outlandish. Moreover, as the vision of Christianity embraced was also fairly broad (see chapter 4), there were few occasions when a definition of something as entirely 'other' was necessary. Effectively, the small group achieved a sense of agreement and unity in spite of any apparent differences among participants, and in so doing fostered a non-threatening, affirming environment. While participants claimed that those who are 'born again' naturally 'gel together', they did not dwell too long on the substance of this linkage lest these ties unravel and threaten the sense of cohesion otherwise maintained.

While offering a tolerant and affirming environment to its members, small group gatherings also served as a context for the positive legitimation of member ideas and a shared sense of status. By bestowing leadership roles onto lay congregants, for example, meetings provided significant occasions for empowerment, as ordinary parishioners were given the opportunity to lead worship, prayers and discussion, and to define key questions; in other words – within accepted boundaries – to set the agenda. Open discussion also allowed individuals to affirm their spiritual status by providing a channel for stories of conversion, spiritual awakening and the movement of God within the fabric of one's daily life. Taking up the argument in chapter 5, small groups provide further opportunities for the 'ritualization of life', as heightened spiritual experiences migrate into everyday life *via* narratives voiced in group contexts. If the charismatic worldview allows for the generation of subjective moments of a spiritual significance, small groups facilitate their conversion into 'spiritual capital'[12] as co-members provide a polite and affirming audience. One woman in particular, after giving a moving testimony in church, was received with an enthusiastic respect within a home group meeting. Other participants quizzed her about her experiences and she responded with further developments of her own story. In this way she embodied what was interpreted as spiritual maturity. Her status was affirmed through the narrative tales she shared with the group, their merit substantiated by a dual connectedness with the biblical texts she invoked in interpreting them, and with life experiences shared by other members.

In addition to legitimising a sense of personal spiritual status, small group meetings served as a site for the legitimation of existing beliefs and values shared

---

[12] For a discussion of the theoretical underpinnings and contemporary utility of 'spiritual capital' as a tool in the analysis of religion, see Mathew Guest, 'In Search of Spiritual Capital: The Spiritual as a Cultural Resource', in K. Flanagan and P. Jupp (eds.), *The Sociology of Spirituality* (Aldershot: Ashgate, 2007), pp. 181-200.

among those present. Robert Wuthnow has argued that small groups can engender an insidious conservatism, especially when members originate from similar social or religious backgrounds, and thus embrace similar beliefs and values and observe a common set of social conventions. Existing prejudices tend to be re-affirmed rather than challenged, as the group rarely has to deal with elements that are alien to its social constituency.[13] Within small group sessions that I attended, the values affirmed were often bound up in norms of lifestyle or respectability associated with the middle-class identities of participants. For example, while by no means affirming a prosperity gospel in the 'name it and claim it' tradition, some members were keen to defend economic advancement as a positive achievement, endorsed by God. This is arguably reinforced by the Alpha literature, which addresses the propriety of ambition in relation to the New Testament verse 'Do nothing out of selfish ambition or vain conceit, but in humility consider others better than yourselves.' (Philippians 2.3) Nicky Gumbel's guidebook expands on this (as if anticipating the concerns of his middle class, Knightsbridge audience), arguing that there is nothing wrong with ambition in itself, so long as it is subordinated to the will of God. He substantiates this with a quotation, not from the Bible, but from a book by John Stott, the leading evangelical writer and preacher.[14] One is reminded of the criticism that Alpha conflates middle-class conventions with biblical teaching.

In a discussion of this passage in an Alpha session, St Michael's members were not unreflective about this teaching, but several tended to follow the Alpha line, and the notion of 'honouring God in your job' was affirmed as a positive principle. As one group leader claimed, 'God wants us to do well, and excel in our jobs.' There was some sense of ethical boundary – we ought to 'play by the rules' – but this was a vague and undefined notion, which thereby blurred distinctions between biblical and corporate standards of practice. There was even evidence of a conflation of corporate and theological language. One woman emphasised how it was important to 'know who your boss is'. She had done quite well as she 'works for the Lord'. She then went on to tell how the Lord had looked after her by giving her a new office at work. The idea that God rewards the faithful through occupational advancement was openly endorsed by several other group members.

One could argue that the underlying themes of the Alpha literature and the participants' own support for human ambition are driven by the same factor, i.e., the preservation of middle-class social values and a reluctance to challenge the *status quo*. It is not insignificant that many St Michael's members are financially comfortable and have lucrative careers. To take a rather cynical perspective, Christianity becomes appropriated in a way that avoids inconveniencing its members, or challenging their existing lifestyles. As David Lyon sardonically puts it, quoting from Henry Mair, 'Jesus comes dressed up in the clothes of our own

---

[13] Wuthnow, *Sharing the Journey*.
[14] Nicky Gumbel, *A Life Worth Living* (Eastborne: Kingsway Publications, 1994), p. 44, citing John Stott, *Issues Facing Christians Today* (Basingstoke: Marshalls, 1984), p. 67.

culture.'[15] While members did not appear to adopt such an orientation unreflectively, in St Michael's this trend is encouraged by the belief that personal experience is a sound spiritual resource, in relation to which one may legitimately discern the meaning or significance of a particular biblical passage (see chapter 4). In these cases, experience draws in social convention as a factor in the authenticating process.

Beyond affirming internal tolerance and providing a context for the legitimation of member identities, small group gatherings were also used as a context for the provision of more personal, emotional support. Indeed, even within a relatively young Alpha discussion group, previously unfamiliar individuals slipped relatively quickly into a mode of interaction that stressed the sharing of personal problems within relationships of clear mutual trust. Some members were young, single and new to the area, and small groups allowed them to forge close friendships with others of a like-mind, before they moved on to new jobs or university courses. The style of the group was well-suited to 'elective parochials', who were especially attracted to the sense of warmth and empathy offered within this 'family congregation'.

A sense of intimacy and support was conveyed in the general interactive style of small group meetings; their informal mood, punctuated with light humour, soon gave way to the sharing of personal problems and experiences. Members openly made requests for advice; others freely offered it, and conversations before, after and during meetings covered a variety of topics. There was an overall sense of relaxed informality, and this appeared to overrule any degree of structure that was lightly imposed by the group leaders. The comments participants made in relating why they enjoyed group meetings all stressed an experience of community associated with open discussion and a warm and nurturing environment. It was the very act of meeting and sharing that was of primary significance, rather than any experience of 'learning the faith' through doctrine, texts or moral instruction.

But it was in ritualised acts of group prayer that dynamics of mutual support were most directly and vividly mobilised, and this applies to numerous small group meetings I attended while at St Michael's. Each meeting framed by prayer started with an opening petition, spoken by the leader, asking God to open our hearts to His word. Closing prayers were often more lengthy and took the form of a group exercise, with petitioners taking turns to lead. For example, in one home group meeting, participants each voiced their prayer requests in turn, including for a woman who had not been well recently, for a church leader recently out of hospital, and for a bereaved friend, who was not sure whether his recently deceased relative had 'come to know the Lord'. All of these issues, and more, were prayed about over a period of continuous prayer lasting about ten minutes. Four members of this group of ten took turns to pray out loud (although no order had been agreed beforehand) while the rest of us sat in silence. The group leader both began and ended the prayer. Interestingly, although all of these issues were covered – from comfort in physical

---

[15] David Lyon, *Jesus in Disneyland. Religion in Postmodern Times* (Cambridge: Polity, 2000), p. 137.

recovery to solace in bereavement – all were addressed by participants other than the people who requested them. A symbolic display of altruism and common support was thus spontaneously affirmed.

This intercessory prayer emphasises the importance attached to taking account of personal concerns and of praying for them as a group. The themes prayed for are mundane, everyday worries, particular to the lives of the individuals present, and this heightens a sense of genuine personal concern and care extended within and by the group. Indeed, this was sometimes extended into a more emotionally charged episode of personal empowerment, with the laying on of hands, and those participants who were party to this could clearly depend upon the session as a source of support in difficult times. While people asked after one another's welfare, such prayers were often not deliberately followed up at later sessions; confirmation was not explicitly sought. Individuals would say when prayers had been answered, and if they had not, this was never thought to challenge the legitimacy of the exercise. The stress here was upon the communal support that performing such prayer provides. The sheer act of praying makes members aware of one another's problems and in so doing – as with the 'words of knowledge' discussed in chapter 5 – serves as an indirect channel for advice and mutual care.

The small groups of St Michael's are clearly a site for the extension of mutual support among the congregation: a discursive affirmation of social identities and an expressive affirmation amounting to emotional support. Shared expectations of 'fellowship' have clearly come to encompass what Steven Tipton has called a 'therapeutic understanding of spirituality', i.e., the congregation and its religious life is, at least in part, focused on meeting individual emotional and psychological needs.[16] Although not all participants use them in this way, this is an accepted function of the small group. As Wuthnow comments, small groups give spirituality a 'pragmatic flavour by focussing on specific needs and the resolution of those needs'. In so doing, they embed spirituality in the 'relational character of the group ... In the caring they experience from one another, members are convinced that their prayers have been heard.'[17]

Small Group in *Visions*

As detailed in the previous chapter, *Visions* developed out of a small group venture: the semi-academic discussions of the Monday Night Group. Since then they have articulated their vision of the 'small group' as an aspect of their shared mission and as a self-conscious alternative to 'mainstream' versions. Central to this is the creation of a context for the open sharing of ideas and for the building of relationships within the group. As an in-house document states,

> Small group meetings are times for us to be together regularly in order to deepen our relationships with each other in God. We expect to do this in praying and playing,

---

[16] Cited in Becker, *Congregations in Conflict*, p. 146.
[17] Wuthnow, *Sharing the Journey*, p. 242.

and by exploring different ways of expressing our corporate relationship with God. When we are together, we want to listen to each other with respect, to challenge each other through study and discussion, and to draw from each other's creative gifts and acquired skills.[18]

Reflecting Becker's 'community congregations', this vision has focused on the need to offer a safe and affirming context for the expression of spiritual identities, regardless of their deviation from the evangelical norm. While Alpha is ostensibly oriented towards the secular unconverted, *Visions* small group is oriented towards those disillusioned with mainstream evangelicalism.

The core group have always held weekly small group meetings, typically as a time for prayer, Bible study, discussion and service planning. At the time of my research, all meetings were held in members' houses except for service planning, which was frequently convened at a favourite local pub or café. 'Small group' (as it is commonly known) has always played a key part in the life of *Visions*, serving as a context for 'business planning meetings' (BPMs), and as a welcome regular gathering of like-minded friends. Some core members even regard small group, rather than Sunday services, as the centre of the group's life as a Christian collective. In part, this is because the intimacy afforded by small groups suits those who find larger church gatherings impersonal and alienating. But it also reflects their need for a place to talk, share concerns and build on a sense of community. Most core members go along to every weekly meeting, although peripheral participants rarely attend. In this way, the small group marks out the boundaries of the core group more clearly than any of their other projects, and effectively consolidates the close bonds shared between core members.

At the time of my research, the group had established a rotational system whereby each form of meeting was held roughly once a month. In practice, this meant that prayer meetings, service planning and social occasions, such as barbecues or wine tasting, occurred on a regular basis, but traditional forms of Bible study less so. No explanation was offered for this, apart from the immediate practical needs of the group and the fluctuating extent to which core members were able to prepare and lead sessions. In addition, the group held monthly sessions called 'Focus', which were facilitated by a friend of the group who is also a trained counsellor. Denise (not her real name) was approached by the *Warehouse* group in 1995 to act as a facilitator at a time when several members felt the group was losing its sense of direction. In the wake of the fall of Sheffield's Nine O'Clock Service, *Warehouse* was keen to introduce channels of accountability and was concerned to ensure that members were not feeling oppressed by the power dynamics of the group. Denise was approached as someone who, as a trusted and informed outsider, would be well placed to elicit open discussion and encourage the sharing of problems among members, and continued to do this in her 'Focus' sessions. Californian in origin, raised a Pentecostal and later having significant contact with the Roman Catholic Church, Denise joined St

---

[18] Taken from in-group document, *What is Warehouse Small Group?*, dated 1 November 1996.

Michael-le-Belfrey in 1978 and was subsequently appointed elder for counselling by Graham Cray. Positively embracing the 'diversity of gifts' she felt was central to the church at that time, she later left St Michael's after a more unilateral, charismatic approach had begun to dominate. *Visions* see Denise as a spiritual guide and mentor and, to some degree, defer to her advice. According to one member, she has helped the group overcome internal conflicts by encouraging them to 'listen to one another'.

The fact that Denise is viewed as a figure of significant spiritual maturity and authority is not surprising, given her outlook. She embraces a broad and affirmative understanding of Christian spirituality that gels well with the attitudes of the group. But she is also a figure on the fringes of evangelicalism: having once embraced a charismatic evangelical faith, she has since become marginalised from the mainstream, not least *via* her departure from St Michael's. In this, she shares with *Visions* a common 'chain of memory' and a sense of having been alienated from an earlier spiritual home. Having steered a more independent path since then, she shares with the group a significant discomfort with the more dogmatic aspects of the evangelical mainstream, and an empathy with their struggle to find meaning along alternative routes, especially those inspired by the Catholic tradition. Moreover, as reflected in Denise's perspective and professional credentials, it is with the language and relational tone of the counselling movement that the group feels most affinity. Stressing personal affirmation, non-judgement and the need to create 'safe' spaces for the disenfranchised, it suits their self-image and shared ethos perfectly.

During the period of my research, I attended numerous *Visions* small group meetings, focused on service planning, Bible study, group reflection and a series of social gatherings, including one at which we made candles and another where a local wine merchant gave a talk on port tasting. The variety of small group foci was matched by a curious functional differentiation between sessions. For example, while a brief prayer might be offered at a service planning session, this was not the rule and the primary purpose of the meeting was always to plan and prepare for services in a very practical sense. While principles drawn from Bible study and theological reflection clearly influenced group activity, these were largely implicit, rather than articulated in an explicit or formalized medium. This is in stark contrast to the small group sessions of St Michael's, which all maintained certain formal consistencies – conventions of prayer, worship, Bible study and a dialogical style of group learning, all often expressed in recognizably stylised forms. These marked each meeting as spiritually significant and conveyed a sense of shared purpose, not to mention common identity. The *Visions* group appeared to be organised along more rationalist principles, and while meetings rarely followed any fixed schedule, their sense of thematic focus was consistent and unwavering. Moreover, the infrequency of any conventional rituals, such as extemporary oral group prayer, did suggest a deliberate distancing from spiritual practices which the group associated with the inadequacies of the 'mainstream'.

It will be worth spending some time examining the group's style of interaction in these contexts, drawing from examples observed during my field research. *Visions* share with the rest of St Michael's an embrace of small groups as useful contexts for the nurturing of relationships, mutual learning and support, and the expression and extension of shared values. But the processes whereby these values are expressed are quite different, and thus foster a very different experience of community.

The title of Robert Wuthnow's book *Sharing the Journey* lends itself well to the *Visions* group. It reflects their conception of the faith-life and the prime function they accord to the small group meeting. At one such meeting, convened for reflection on future group projects, the St Michael's vicar, Roger Simpson, was invited to contribute his thoughts on how the group might best develop. He voiced his opinion that *Visions* should include more 'teaching' in their services. One core member's response was that they got most of their teaching from small group gatherings. Sunday services were about the group making a public statement: we are worshipping; this is what we do. 'Tearing your soul up', he maintained, 'which is what teaching amounts to', is best suited to a different context. And while many in St Michael's favour a more traditional model of teaching, *Visions* make a point of living by the ethic of 'mutual discipleship'.

By the end of my research, it was clear to me that this ethic amounted to several different things. Most clearly, members want to respect one another as individuals and are willing to learn from one another as co-sojourners in the faith. As one put it, in today's culture we should not be listening to one person teach the Bible, we should be getting together in groups and working out the truth in mutual dialogue – everyone should have a part to play. Spiritual growth, according to the ethos of the group, depends upon creating spaces for nurturing individual autonomy within a supportive community. An in-house document describing 'small group values' defines the desired agenda by listing positive and negative qualities. 'Life giving qualities' include 'honesty with each other', 'acceptance of each other' and 'laughter'. 'Qualities we seek to avoid' include 'fear, mistrust, and a lack of forgiveness', 'a rigid code of cultural bondage' and 'inappropriate confrontation, and a critical spirit'. Keeping the balance between open, constructive dialogue and a caring, mutual affirmation is at the heart of their purpose.

In principle, this has produced a shared group ethic that seeks to maximise opportunities for genuine and uninhibited self-expression and minimise the use of structures or resources experienced as oppressive. In practice, any trace of convention that evokes the evangelical sub-culture has been ostracised, and the group foster a moral style that Penny Becker has called 'personalism'. That is, public issues are frequently connected to private needs and experience is invoked as a basis of moral authority.[19] Within *Visions*, 'experience' is more about sober reflection upon glimpses of the divine within life's highways and byways, rather than the mapping of religious meaning and the divine 'numinous' onto one's working week. But it does retain the individualism inherent in this subjectivised strand of the evangelical worldview.

---

[19] Becker, *Congregations in Conflict*, p. 197.

The small group meeting appeared to be wholly driven by the apparent personal needs of its members and the needs members feel apply to the group. This carried only limited explicit reference to external authorities, such as those repeatedly invoked in St Michael's sessions (e.g., scripture, influential writers and preachers). And while I found that prayer and Bible readings did appear, they were not allowed to frame or define meetings, or dictate any kind of agenda, without first being subject to serious critical reflection by the group. In open discussion, as well as in more structured exercises, it was often personal views and impressions that took precedence and which dominated the substance of what was said. This was especially apparent during 'Focus' sessions, at which Denise would encourage participants to express themselves openly, emphasising affirmation, non-judgement and a celebration of the diversity of individual experience. Ever sensitive to the feelings of participants, her aim was to facilitate self-expression, but without any uncritical or overwhelming appeal to a defining framework, whether theological or otherwise.

But if *Visions* members were keen to share one another's spiritual journeys, they were equally passionate about sharing the power base that defines and drives the group itself. As emphasised in chapter 6, the group appeared to view themselves as an egalitarian and autonomous collective, shaped by the values of each and every one of its members. In practice, this means that the form and meaning of *Visions* projects, as well as the identity of the group itself, are frequently put under the scrutiny of its members. Such regular reflexive rethinking of identity and shared goals is facilitated in small group discussion. As another group document states, 'ownership for planning is shared by the group, which reflects our understanding of the process'. This understanding allows for the very principles upon which the group was founded to be called into question and debated by its members. And while, in practice, members tend not to undermine established procedures as a matter of course, it is clearly important to them that individuals are made to feel that their input could have a shaping influence over the life of the group. In so far as *Visions* is openly built on personal relationships, it is accepted that group goals may be revised according to the changing needs of its membership.

In spite of the spirit of openness and acceptance in which small group sessions were convened, it is worth noting that, often, group discourse was rather restrained and awkward. Denise confided the difficulty she had getting the group to express themselves openly, and I experienced significant problems in my attempts to talk to them about their faith and values. Part of the problem was a general reticence about expressing personal spirituality using words, exacerbated by introverted personalities. Members simply did not seem to want to talk about their feelings, ideas or values, or at least found it difficult to find the appropriate words to do so. This reluctance to articulate belief was also possibly influenced by a desire to avoid retaining any outward signs of a conventional evangelicalism. It was part of their response to evangelical culture and tradition that both be questioned, and this spirit extended into styles of discursive exchange. A resistance to convention has evolved into a resistance to formulaic expression and this undermines any impulse to integrate shared beliefs into a singular system.

This could be seen in small groups in the laboured discussion, the awkward moments of silence and the tentative responses offered. These are individuals who have known one another for years and who have, in the past, shared moments of crisis and personal trauma, as well as jubilation, but for complex reasons they have come to affirm their Christian beliefs predominantly through music, image and ritual action, rather than through informal verbal expression. Of all the inherited elements of its evangelical heritage, it is perhaps the confessional culture, above all else, that *Visions* have so obviously moved away from and it would be interesting to explore this as a key medium of change for post-evangelicals more generally. While they insist that they are more unified as a group than their parent church, they do not affirm any obvious sense of ideological unity in internal dialogue. Indeed, perhaps it is because they are united on secure foundations that they do not need to observe the exercises in public affirmation and legitimation so apparent within St Michael's.

While *Visions* members exhibited some reticence in speaking about their personal beliefs, I did find that group discussion could become somewhat freer and less inhibited when members addressed subjects in a particular style. Notably, they engaged in the *intellectual* discussion of theological issues with a marked enthusiasm, interest and proficiency. Moreover, while the educational backgrounds of members meant that they held the cultural capital to engage in an academic discussion of, say, the relationship between ritual, liturgy and social action, the unusual passion with which they did this implied that they both valued and thrived on such exchanges.

At one service planning meeting, I was asked if I would lead a small group session, based on my research. This was only after a month's regular contact with *Visions*, an indication of their openness to outsider contributions and of their confidence in their stability and robustness as a group. They had little idea of my findings or academic background, and no inkling of my own beliefs and values at that stage. After a conversation with Steven, who assured me that small group meetings had 'no set boundaries', and who was thoroughly unconcerned by my self-conscious worries about being a sympathetic agnostic, I agreed to lead the session.

I decided to address the relationship between religion and contemporary pop culture, making use of Tom Beaudoin's innovative volume, *Virtual Faith. The Irreverent Spiritual Quest of Generation X*. Beaudoin examines the theology of 'Xers', focusing upon how young people make sense of their lives using pop videos, music and aspects of youth subculture. Through this process, popular culture achieves a spiritual significance.[20] Given the group's past history and shared goals, I hoped that this topic would be received as both compelling and relevant. I planned to talk for ten or fifteen minutes, before suggesting some questions for group discussion.

On the day, I was very nervous and stumbled through the first ten minutes, hastily summarising my main points and rapidly exhausting my notes. The six

---

[20] Tom Beaudoin, *Virtual Faith. The Irreverent Spiritual Quest of Generation X* (San Francisco, CA: Jossey Bass, 1998).

Visions members present appeared interested but said nothing. My field journal describes the subsequent exchange:

> ... after running through the common characteristics of Generation X, Daniel interrupted with a question. The others looked on expectantly. As he slowly and pedantically formulated his point, I began to worry that I was to be faced with an uncomfortable mixture of negative criticism and stony silence. But no, as it happened, his comments provoked a discussion which lasted, unceasingly, for another hour and which drew in every individual who was present. This was clearly a discussion to which they were all keen to contribute. We covered religion and pop culture, generational differences, and more abstract or complex ideas like transcendence, spirituality and consumerism. Daniel argued that the spiritual requires something outside of the self for its focus, while Adam mused about religious experience requiring some kind of dialogue between subject and object. The discussion was often abstracted onto several different levels and was highly intellectual. I knew it would be, but the subtlety and precision with which some participants expressed their arguments surpassed my expectations. Moreover, participants clearly understood one another and embraced this style of discourse. It became increasingly clear throughout the evening that, although there are many highly intelligent people in St Michael's, they would be unlikely to intellectualise matters so close to their faith in the way that the *Visions* group did tonight.
> (Adapted from field journal, 19 January 2000.)

The group appreciated my session and apparently found it highly stimulating, Rebecca commenting that it must have been good because so many members got actively involved. Subsequent observation suggested that it was not merely the topic of discussion that had triggered this enthusiasm, but the style of debate that it had initiated. Members were happier and more comfortable speaking of 'faith' issues in abstract, intellectualised terms, perhaps because of the distance that this affords. The emotive and sentimentalist discourses of St Michael's were conspicuous for their complete absence.

Within small group discussion, members often drew in knowledge and literary references that firmly located them among the young intellectual classes. They were also familiar with ideas and literature associated with postmodernism and were adept at using notions such as de-centring, meta-narrative and *bricolage* as intellectual support for their group projects. Scholarship was appealed to in efforts to challenge overly narrow expressions of Christian tradition and evangelical convention, and to facilitate an engagement with a much wider Christian heritage. In one 'Focus' session on the figure of Mary, Denise introduced feminist arguments to draw attention to the gender politics bound up in the image of the pure and submissive female. During a Bible study, a verse from Paul's letter to the Ephesians – 'And in him you too are being built together to become a dwelling in which God lives by his Spirit' (2.22) – was debated extensively. Eventually, a consensus was reached that the verse was essentially about 'community' – 'including rather than excluding', naturally. But this was only agreed after two members argued that a use of 'you' was plural in the original Greek. Members were articulating the group's ethos through the text, stressing collective responsibility and mutual care as central to the Christian message. But their authority for this relied upon awareness of the academic literature, rather than simply the text as they found it in its English translation or, indeed, upon its practical demonstration in their daily lives. While personal experience was important, it was not used as a legitimating resource in the way it was in St Michael's.

Not that discussion secures a resolution of the issues. Indeed, due to the often abstract, intellectualised style of conversation, discussion was not treated as something that must lead to an agreed truth. Members saw little problem in disagreeing and holding to a diversity of positions concurrently. And unlike the examples given of St Michael's small group meetings, internal diversity was not normalised or absorbed into a public discourse, precisely because, I would argue, it was not considered a threat to group identity. Group identity, as stated earlier, centres on the *affirmation* of internal diversity and members are comfortable functioning within this environment because this was the route by which they achieved a sense of being affirmed as individuals. The equivalent of astrology here is mainstream charismatic evangelicalism itself, which is seen as a threat to this model of affirming community.

Intellectual discourse facilitates a kind of postmodern reconstruction of tradition, providing the group with tools with which to challenge the evangelical mainstream. The seclusion of the small group gathering from central church authorities also allows *Visions* the space to voice their criticisms, as well as their more unorthodox ideas, with relative impunity. But intellectualism also initiates a rethinking of shared perceptions of authority. While *Visions* embraced a broad theology, significant for its diversity as well as lack of ordering frameworks, they expressed a firm faith in certain things. Academic discourse was one. Whether scientific, social scientific or theological, scholarship was embraced as a reliable source of knowledge and a sound set of tools to use on one's quest for truth. It was judged as more sensible than most preachers and less precarious than charisma. Significantly, academic discourse also represents a form of cultural capital that most of the group possess and which they can comfortably deploy. In other words, it readily confirms their sense of autonomy and control in the negotiation of religious legitimacy.

Donald Miller argues that, among 'new paradigm' churches, a stress on individual experience has 'democratised' access to the sacred.[21] While *Visions* would adopt a cynical perspective on this, they embrace a similar idea, but place independent (though interactive) thought at the centre of their version of Protestant egalitarianism. Individuals have equal access to God, but not merely because of His ready accessibility within human experience. Rather, they have equal access by virtue

---

[21] Donald E. Miller, *Reinventing American Protestantism. Christianity in the New Millennium* (Berkeley and Los Angeles, CA: University of California Press, 1997).

of their reflective capacity to search and apprehend the complexities of the divine as they follow their own journey through life. This is a cerebral vision, grounded in the vulnerability of humanity and the determination of the postmodern pilgrim. Drawing from intellectualism and scholarship, it favours the abstract over the relational, experiment and innovation over stasis. In so doing it fosters an individualistic kind of faith, but this is a faith that paradoxically depends upon community for its affirmation. 'Small group' holds the freedoms together, and is instrumental in sustaining a balance of diversity and unity.

As implied earlier, the interaction at *Visions* small group meetings was less emotionally charged than exchanges within St Michael's. Personal feelings were only voiced tentatively, personal problems faced with difficulty and intimate prayer for individuals, if practised at all, was rarely by the laying on of hands. And yet small groups still serve as the focus for a strong mutual support extended between members, who relied upon group meetings as the basis of their Christian identities. On one level, small groups have become a haven for 'homeless minds'. Marginalised from the mainstream, yet feeling a yearning for Christian community, members have come to value *Visions* – especially the intimacy offered by small group meetings – as a place of nurture in which their identities are fostered. One core member told me that the best thing about being part of *Visions* was that 'It's OK to be me.'

But while heterodoxy is tolerated and room created for spiritual exploration, the 'community' offered by *Visions* extends beyond the benefits of an encounter group. Mutual support between members adopts a decidedly practical form. Members loan their cars to one another, fetch shopping for each other and agree to dip into the common purse on occasions when individuals are in need. One core member contrasted this with her experiences of mainstream church life: '... they say they're there for you but you're not quite sure if they are, whereas in *Visions* you can rely on people to be there for you'. There was a perception of genuine personal concern for one another as individuals, which is not dependent upon confessions of faith or doctrinal conformity. And though a similar magnanimity was evident among the St Michael's congregation, it was not extended along such obviously practical lines. Some older members, such as June, whom we met at the beginning of this chapter, recall times when things were different, and it is possible that as St Michael's has grown and the rate of member turnover has increased, commitment to home groups has become attenuated, in accordance with the sociological arguments about the consequences of elective parochialism described earlier. *Visions* have not been affected in the same way, as while many core members have moved on, an equal number have stayed and maintained their high level of commitment to what is a highly distinctive project. They remain a close-knit group, having forged common bonds over a number of years, and their understanding of belonging to the group includes this sense of practical commitment, not just to shared goals, but to one another as individuals. Moreover, this very practical kind of assistance – unlike that offered among common home group members within St Michael's in the 1970s – was rarely made sense of openly in Christian terms.

The small group also consolidates the collective identity of the group by offering the means by which to sustain and refine a relatively closed system of communication. Robert Wuthnow's concern, that small groups become entrenched in their own heterodoxy, may be extended to include the very language members use in engaging in dialogue with one another. The isolation of *Visions* has apparently generated a shared argot, a style of spoken discourse which members have developed over time and which they understand. They practice something close to what Douglas Coupland has dubbed 'obscurism', 'the practice of peppering daily life with obscure references' as a means of 'showcasing both one's education and one's wish to dissociate from the world of mass culture'.[22] As always, however, their object of dissociation is a little closer to home.

While parallel media in St Michael's centre around theological shorthand ('fellowship'; 'coming to know the Lord') or relational sentiment ('my brother in the Lord'; God as 'Dad'), *Visions* distance themselves from such charismatic *lingua franca*. Instead, technical and academic language has filled the vacuum left by its exclusion and flows of conversation, dotted as they are with esoteric references, allusions to shared experiences and the technical jargon of audio-visual technology, have come to deploy these discourses so that they function as a powerful excluding mechanism. Although by no means the intention of the group, outsiders are sometimes kept at a distance by the boundaries of its communicative discourse.

Small Groups and Collective Identity

In many ways small groups serve as sites for the expression and negotiation of the patterns of belief and value hinted at earlier. For St Michael's, these are an internal tolerance of diversity alongside an affirmation of theological boundaries; the 'ritualisation of life' and infusion of subjective experience with divinely ordained meaning; and a general expression of the importance of community, worked out as regular meetings, personal interaction and problem sharing. For *Visions*, these are a de-centring of religious knowledge by way of endorsing a model of learning and power that stresses mutuality – rather than hierarchy – as its centre; a critique of mainstream evangelicalism using the tools of intellectual discourse; and an affirmation of Christian community embodied in practical mutual support. In this sense, the small group is a microcosm of shared values that extend into a much wider remit.

An analysis of small groups also highlights the degree to which shared social values are legitimated and embedded in a Christian framework, a process made possible by the intimacy and autonomy afforded by small group meetings. Individuals have a platform from which to voice their convictions without being subject to the same restraints found in church. In some small group meetings, I found that this generated an endorsement of commonly held middle-class lifestyles,

---

[22] Douglas Coupland, *Generation X. Tales for An Accelerated Culture* (London: Abacus, 1991), p. 192.

an extension, in some cases perhaps, of bias in the Alpha course materials as well as of an impulse of reflexive self-legitimation. This act depends upon the rather malleable spiritual resource discussed in terms of subjectivity in chapter 5. Given the tools with which to search for, discern, name and claim the divine and spiritual in one's own life experience, individuals may then draw connections which only demand the stamp of inner conviction. Peers then form an assembly which may affirm or contest one's claims, and small groups provide both stage and audience for the performance. Given the importance of evading conflict, addressed in chapter 4, it is unsurprising that affirmation is the norm. Moreover, as most congregants share a similar combination of social experiences and cultural capital, they are unlikely to contest claims which amount to a religious celebration of their social identity. The 'turn to life' is extended into social convention in addition to inter-personal problem solving.

In this sense, order and meaning receive their impetus from concerns forged outside of church life: relating to families, jobs, money and economic stability. Careers become divinely guided while nuclear families become centres of moral order. In one sense, as far as middle-class lifestyles achieve legitimation, they become a dominant authority and shaping influence over shared Christian teaching. While I would not suggest an uncritical parallel with New Age 'self-spirituality',[23] there is a discernible turn away from the purely external, prescriptive authorities traditional to evangelicalism, and a greater reliance upon channels of significance defined by individuals. Values are still constructed and negotiated with reference to external sources, not least church leaders, devotional literature, and a set of shared preconceptions about moral order. But these external sources are dealt with in a particular way, demanding not unwavering assent but functioning as resources appropriated according to the subjective needs of individuals.

This may be described as a *parochialisation* of evangelical identity, as Christian tradition is conflated with the norms of middle-class subculture brought to church life by St Michael's members. As noted above, this has helped engender a stress upon non-judgement, affirmation, expressivism and individual autonomy. Given the extent to which *Visions* carry these classically modern themes further (see chapter 6), it is perhaps ironic that their small group sessions only partially capitalise on them. Indeed, while expressivist in the sense of remaining open to individual contributions, in practice *Visions* small groups do not appear to foster an open, person-centred expressivism in the style that comes so naturally to St Michael's members. While keen to welcome outsiders (indeed the fostering of the marginalized has become a passionately affirmed group principle), *Visions* lacks the behavioural conventions and convivial, social effervescence that makes St Michael's so immediately familiar to many middle class visitors. There is less sharing of personal problems and mutual support is practical rather than tactile and demonstrative. The reasons for this are

---

[23] See Paul Heelas, *The New Age Movement. The Celebration of the Self and the Sacralization of Modernity* (Oxford: Blackwell, 1996), p. 36.

complex, but can be connected to the debate outlined in chapter 1, about the tension between modernisation and community.

According to Peter Berger, modernity generates serious uncertainties for the individual, who faces alienation and 'homelessness' as a result of the dominance of technology, bureaucracy and pluralism throughout primary social institutions. Individuals are forced to rely, in their search for meaning, on the subjective resources of the self, an authority which is precarious as it lacks significant social support. In suggesting social resources which may be mobilised against this trend, Berger draws from Arnold Gehlen, proposing 'secondary institutions'. These secondary institutions are to be contrasted with primary institutions, which are experienced as rigid and constraining, in reflection of Weber's vision of the 'iron cage' of modernity. However, they are also sufficiently institutionalised to provide guidance and structure, hence offering some refuge for 'homeless minds'.[24] As such, secondary institutions may be experienced as liberating but also as effective carriers of meaning, carving a middle way through the identity problems that Berger and many others argue characterise the modern condition.

Rather than demanding a strict conformity and deferral to hierarchy, secondary institutions offer experiences which are life-affirming and life-expanding, are 'soft' rather than 'hard', and emphasise autonomy, democracy and intra-personal exchange.[25] A good empirical example would be small group meetings, and recent studies by Donald Miller and Robert Wuthnow have revealed how small groups can be harnessed as enclaves of community and providers of meaning for those who experience the outside world as characterised by moral chaos and existential uncertainty.[26] Arguing along similar lines, Tony Walter suggests that Christian home groups provide places where individuals can be 'known', i.e., recognised and affirmed by others as people with distinct needs and qualities, in a culture typified by privatisation and a sense of isolation.[27]

The first point to make is that, drawing from the above analysis, small groups in both St Michael's and *Visions* do not simply serve as hedges against 'modern anomie'. It would be more accurate to suggest that small groups provide a set of filters for the mediation of dominant processes of value change, including a broadening of evangelical norms of acceptability and a more profound appeal to the resources of human experience as both authority and site of spiritual significance. In particular, they offer contexts for the empowerment and expression of subjective identities, and for the socialisation of new members into the 'dominant discourse' of the group.

---

[24] Paul Heelas and Linda Woodhead, 'Homeless Minds Today?', in Linda Woodhead (ed.), *Peter Berger and the Study of Religion* (London and New York: Routledge, 2000), p. 46.

[25] Heelas and Woodhead, 'Homeless Minds Today?', p. 53.

[26] Miller, *Reinventing American Protestantism*; Wuthnow, *Sharing the Journey*, p. 79.

[27] Tony Walter, 'Being Known: Mutual Surveillance in the House Group', *Archives de Science Sociales des Religions* 89 (1995), pp. 113-26.

The St Michael's sessions revolve around what might be called a *structured expressivism*. Meaning is constructed and conveyed using media familiar within the broader evangelical subculture: ritualised methods of group prayer, sentimental styles of worship, non-confrontational discussion and familiar language. These are deployed consistently, so that new participants quickly learn the rules of engagement. Moreover, the stylistic overlap with behavioural norms conventional to middle-class culture is sufficiently obvious to allay any lack of familiarity on the part of peripheral participants. (We note that those who dropped out of the St Michael's Alpha course first were those individuals least likely to fall into this middle-class, professional category.) In this sense, small group meetings provide a context for the gentle socialisation of newcomers into the shared culture of St Michael's. This would be a banal point if not for its striking success. St Michael's appears attuned to outsiders – at least to its target audience – and deploys mechanisms to include them within a common discourse, while nurturing them into their own worldview. As with the patterns of public discourse discussed in chapter 4, St Michael's appears to maintain a shared culture *via* subtle processes of control and repeated patterns of conduct. And while it is through conforming to these processes that one is taken as an authentic member of the fellowship, undecided sojourners (including myself) are given ample space to be absorbed gradually, with minimal coercion.

That said, within St Michael's if one does not agree with the dominant discourse, there is little room for saying so. Within a given remit, boundaries are noticeably policed. The woman keen on astrology was subject to this process of control, and her sense of exclusion was evident when she dropped out of the course soon afterwards. Members remained within the group by toeing the line or keeping quiet; those that could not left.

Longstanding *Visions* member Daniel noted this feature as an aspect of St Michael's church life as a whole. To him, it contrasted negatively with the way things are done in *Visions*.

> If *Visions* didn't exist I'd have to invent it! ... the thing is that here is an expression of us to God. That is an underlying facet. I think that's possibly one of the ways in which *Visions* differs from the rest of St Mike's. The rest of St Mike's exists, and gets twisted to being an expression of God but people have to flex themselves to be part of it. We have the privilege of flexing *Visions*, of flexing what *we* do, to be *our* expression ...

Daniel is speaking of general tensions, between conformity and innovation, legitimacy versus authenticity, which characterise some of the main differences between these two collectives, but his comments carry particular weight if applied to the norms of conduct in small groups. I noted in chapter 6 how *Visions* has come to focus upon the needs of members, rather than the needs of potential recruits, and discussed earlier in this chapter how this has played a part in the generation of a shared argot, meaningful to insiders but often relatively closed to outsiders and peripheral participants. In addition to this, *Visions* has developed a set of practical norms which shape group conduct in small groups and other contexts. They also reflect, as Daniel observes, the values and priorities of the group. But unlike small groups in St Michael's, these practices assume a more idiosyncratic form. Members avoid conventional rituals associated with prayer or Bible study, and speak about their faith often using complex language. Taking these alongside the strained, often awkward dialogue and the group's reluctance to conform to a charismatic *habitus* of sentiment, emotion and expressive performance, a picture emerges of a community that refuses to offer the behavioural norms that facilitate the expressivism typical in St Michael's.

Some attendees, disillusioned with the evangelical mainstream, find this alternative liberating and thankfully unburdened by what they see as the cultural baggage of conventional church. In this respect, the profound sense of innovation embodied in the *Visions* worship experience is matched in the adoption of alternative behavioural conventions, and both symbolize departure from a culturally outmoded evangelicalism. The 'post' in post-evangelicalism here represents a progression that includes modes of communication *and* styles of conduct, a trend that is symptomatic of how such developments are far from cosmetic and incorporate some of the most subtle and deeply embodied aspects of Christian identity. However, this development can present problems for outsiders, as well as for peripheral or occasional participants, some of whom are evangelicals who are confounded by the lack of familiar behavioural landmarks that, for them, would secure a degree of meaning and sense of significance. I spoke to numerous individuals who, having attended *Visions*, found the experience a little baffling, for reasons related to the very elements that the core group maintain in order to offer an accepting environment. While relative quietude and non-contact is refreshingly liberating and respectful for some, it leaves a lacuna that is suggestive of abstraction and confusion for others. Core members see no problem, as they have come to find their own meanings over time, and have the added benefit of having been empowered by the planning process. So, while the group has indeed 'flexed' what they do into an expression of Christian commitment, this is a model of commitment and practice that does not resonate with everyone and appears to appeal most to those who are most comfortable extracting themselves from the subcultural trappings of the charismatic evangelical mainstream. For others, this departure is a step too far, as their sense of Christian identity has come to depend on the very elements that have been exiled.

This is perhaps ironic; *Visions* was established because its founder members experienced conventional, mainstream evangelical church life – especially small group meetings – as culturally alien, places where they could not be who they really were. In this they were echoing concerns some might argue are shared by a large cross-section of British society who no longer find church meaningful. And yet, in establishing an alternative context that is sufficiently different from the mainstream to accommodate their needs, *Visions* have forged a way of being Christian that is so innovative and unconventional as to be insufficiently recognizable as church to many of those who might fall within the post-evangelical or post-church category.

Working with Becker's typology of congregational forms, it is tempting to conclude that the 'community congregation' model can, it seems, be self-defeating, as it promotes a turn inward, to a set of needs that is idiosyncratic as it is defined by a group's membership, and thereby represents a consequent failure to cater to the needs of potential new recruits. However, an observation of the development of *Visions* in the years subsequent to my original research suggests a more complex picture. During this time *Visions*, while not achieving steady expansion, has experienced periods of growth. On the occasion of a return visit in 2003, for example, I discovered that the group had actually doubled in size, and conversations with core members revealed that this had occurred after numerous peripheral members – long-term associates of the group – had gravitated inwards and committed themselves more fully to the group and its projects. In addition to this, the group had begun to eat together more regularly, reinforcing and expanding a sense of cohesion and momentum through mutual service and hospitality. Perhaps the key to expansion for 'community congregations' like *Visions* lies in establishing long-term relationships through existing networks of friends and associates, through the power of affinity and familiarity, rather than the articulation of a clear agenda or maintenance of an accepted set of ritual or behavioural forms. Becker's categories are useful in helping us identify key group dynamics, but it would be a mistake to use them uncritically. The focus of 'community congregations' on individual member needs does not, it seems, necessitate the development of a group culture that is entirely closed to outsiders, and a closer analysis of the sub-cultural affinities fostered at the boundaries of such groups may reveal a more complex picture.

CHAPTER 8

The Bigger Picture

The preceding chapters have presented an analysis of a single church. Occasional cross references to cognate developments have furnished something of a broader context, but this book has, for the most part, been concerned with St Michael-le-Belfrey. I make no apologies for this; St Michael's is a complex and fascinating church with a rich history and as such deserves close attention. Its significant influence over the evangelical tradition as expressed in congregations across the UK and further a field is another strong justification for a book-length analysis. I have attempted to paint a detailed picture of congregational life in St Michael's around the turn of the millennium, grounding this in an analysis of its history as a centre of evangelical revival. My chief aim throughout has been to explore the ways in which this church has successfully negotiated the challenges of contemporary western culture, while maintaining a strong sense of Christian community. While in many ways this has produced a single snap-shot, I have nevertheless attempted to examine processes of longitudinal change, in so far as my research has permitted this, by looking at how St Michael's has evolved since the 1960s. Further reflections on how it has developed since the time of my original research may be found in the Epilogue immediately following this chapter, which assesses the state of St Michael-le-Belfrey in 2006.

My reasons for offering an extended analysis of a single church are also methodological, and reflect my preference for in depth ethnography, based on participant observation. As chapter 3 shows, while St Michael's has generally continued to claim the same evangelical priorities throughout its recent history, it has embodied these convictions in a variety of different ways. Evangelical community (or 'fellowship'), for example, has been a persistent emphasis, and yet when filtered through the community structures embodied in home groups, households, worship groups, Alpha, *Visions*, and a variety of congregational models, it becomes a multi-faceted entity, capable of absorbing a range of theological undercurrents, social conventions and implicit moral assumptions, all embedded in the narrative histories shared among the congregation.[1] Similar comments could be made about worship, evangelism, social outreach, leadership and the Holy Spirit. The process of interpreting evangelical Christianity's common body of symbols, to use the language employed in chapter 1, is rooted in an experience of

---

[1] In sociological terms, this is built on the assumption that evangelicals are social actors, rather than simply embodiments of a clearly defined tradition.

how these symbols are embodied within congregational contexts. A multi-perspectival approach rooted in participant observation allows a proper consideration of this and an extended account allows for the necessary detail. Moreover, as I have been persuaded that many other congregational studies have painted only partial pictures of church life on account of their brevity, over-theorization or heavy dependence on quantitative methods, I would be remiss not to at least attempt something detailed and ambitious here. I leave it to readers to assess the extent to which this has been a successful exercise.

My discussion of evangelical identity and contemporary culture would, however, be incomplete (not to say undeserving of its title) without some attempt to relate its chief findings to broader trends in the evangelical world and reflect on the questions they might raise for future research.

Evangelical Networks and Markets

The foregoing analysis finds common ground with what many scholars have previously noted about the ongoing accommodation of evangelicalism to contemporary western culture. The boundaries that were previously guarded with caution have since been challenged and evangelicals have allowed their beliefs and practices to be coloured by changing cultural norms and mores, from the absorption of pop subcultures and technologies into worship to the adaptation of popular Christian morality to an ethic of civility grounded in tolerance. Opinions differ on the consequences of this process for the strength of the evangelical movement, including the cohesion of evangelical congregations, but many paint a picture characterised by decline and eventual disintegration. The previous chapters illustrate how an understanding of discourses emerging from within, as well as impinging upon, individual congregations may foster a more subtle analysis. Indeed, a consideration of St Michael-le-Belfrey suggests that cultural accommodation – theorised in earlier chapters as liberalisation and subjectivisation – does not necessarily erode or fragment religious communities. Rather, these processes are filtered by mediating structures, shaped by demography, locality and the history of individual groups. They are also subject to processes of negotiation within the confines of local cultures, and thus to processes of social interaction. The omission of these factors is raised as a problem with Peter Berger's work in an essay originally drafted by James Davison Hunter, and published as part of a collaborative work along with Robert Wuthnow, Albert Bergesen and Edith Kurzweil.[2] The authors point to the way in which Berger assumes a relatively straightforward relationship between identity and social structure. Changes in primary institutions, such as education or the workplace, are assumed to affect changes in the consciousness of individuals. This is no doubt the case, but Berger implies that these changes amount to a direct,

---

[2] Robert Wuthnow, James Davison Hunter, Albert Bergesen and Edith Kurzweil, *Cultural Analysis. The Work of Peter L. Berger, Mary Douglas, Michel Foucault and Jürgen Habermas* (London: Routledge, 1984), pp. 21-76.

almost logical response to the nature of structural conditions. For example, technology induces a worldview that stresses the componentiality of reality, bureaucracy the sequential, predictability of life.[3] What Berger does not do is explore the mediating structures which channel these relationships and shape the effect of one factor upon the other.

> Berger's theory, it would seem, could profit greatly from a more systematic discussion of the different empirical relationships between the contents of socialization and different social structural configurations – the structural bases of personality.[4]

Chapters 4 and 5 present a clear vindication of this point. Why does liberalisation fail to fragment the St Michael's congregation? Because diversity is celebrated and differences likely to cause fracture are papered over in *public* discourse. Why does subjectivisation within St Michael's not lead to atomisation and the fragmentation of community? Because subjectivity generates narratives which require *communal* channels of expression in order to secure meaning. In other words, the consequences of these two processes for the convictions of members are shaped by the *communicative culture of the congregation*. Chapter 7 took this argument a step further in suggesting that small groups not only serve as contexts for the legitimation of shared beliefs, but occupy a key role in the socialisation of new members into the dominant discourse of the church. In performing this role, they largely re-affirm the patterns of liberalisation and subjectivisation expressed elsewhere, while also fostering intimacy and mutual support among members. *Visions* stands as a decidedly different case, its reliance upon sub-cultural markers and its reactionary stance against its parent tradition call attention to the way in which these mid-level factors shape movements of innovation. Its use of technology, for example, cannot be understood without reference to the artistic heritage of the charismatic tradition and the group's post-evangelical perspective on person-based authority. Given the increasing popularity of small groups, especially as organised around the cell church model (see the Epilogue), future research will need to explore the role these groups play in evangelical churches. How do small groups function as mediating structures for the values communicated within congregations, and what role might they play in the negotiation of tensions or the resolution of conflict? What kind of community *experience* do they foster, and where does it stand *vis-à-vis* the Sunday service?

A consideration of mediating structures uncovers the shortcomings of the Bergerian model in accounting for the socialization of congregants into group values. In highlighting the role that small group meetings play in this process, we draw attention to an obvious example, which can easily be seen to filter structural influences by virtue of their status as secondary institutions, neither fully

---

[3] Peter Berger, Brigitte Berger and Hansfried Kellner, *The Homeless Mind. Modernization and Consciousness* (New York: Vintage Books, 1974), pp. 29-61.
[4] Wuthnow *et al*, *Cultural Analysis*, p. 71.

institutionalised nor hierarchical, and yet organised, regular and communal. In this respect, small groups represent an intermediate layer of collective activity, subsumed within the organisational structures of the congregation, but also semi-autonomous in so far as emerging discourses are in part a product of member interaction. Peter Collins has examined a similar dimension to the culture of Quakerism, drawing a distinction between canonical, vernacular and individual narratives as axes in relation to which Quaker identity is continually negotiated. The canonical refers to officially sanctioned ideas enshrined in texts and traditions authorised by the Quaker movement, whereas individual narratives emerge from the specific experiences of particular members. Vernacular narratives are the stories and meanings shared among members of a local meeting; like the evangelical small group, they provide a site for the collective negotiation of common ideas and values in light of both individual experience and a body of authoritative religious tradition.[5] But mediating structures need not always be vernacular, local or subsumed within larger congregational structures. In our late modern culture, in which traditional understandings of identity and community are constantly challenged, it is unsurprising that the ideas and values that issue from conventional institutions are filtered through a range of social forces that are altogether less fixed, less predictable and less bounded than we might have expected in a previous time. In taking account of the processes whereby evangelical identities are constructed and maintained, we continually encounter not just congregations, small groups or other discrete gatherings, but also networks, markets, and other transcongregational phenomena which are less bound by geographical locality or traditional authorities. While the existence of evangelical Christianity at this meta level is nothing new, the conditions of late modernity have heightened the prevalence and power of translocal networks to shape social life and influence social values. Some would go as far as to argue that the strong correlation between religious beliefs and community, associated with the sociology of Bryan Wilson and Peter Berger, is actually an historical contingency. According to Rob Hirst, for example, in late modernity, 'overarching religious world views' are not necessarily dependent on strong, cohesive communities in the traditional sense, but 'may be held and maintained by members of *discrete networks* which need not be local'.[6]

While it is not possible to test Hirst's claim here, it raises an important question for future research and highlights the power of networks within the current cultural context. I would not go as far as to say that networks are supplanting local communities, but they certainly add a further significant dimension to the process whereby identities emerge from within religious institutions. Within late modernity, evangelical ideas are negotiated within a far more complex, intricate and international network than ever before and this network not only shapes the construction of

---

[5] Peter Collins, 'Congregations, Narratives and Identity: A Quaker Case Study', in Mathew Guest, Karin Tusting and Linda Woodhead (eds), *Congregational Studies in the UK: Christianity in a Post-Christian Context* (Aldershot: Ashgate, 2004), pp. 99-112.

[6] Rob Hirst, 'Social Networks and Personal Beliefs: An Example from Modern Britain', in G. Davie, P. Heelas and L. Woodhead (eds), *Predicting Religion. Christian, Secular and Alternative Futures* (Aldershot: Ashgate, 2003), p. 88 (original emphasis).

evangelicalism as a global phenomenon, but also infiltrates the construction of evangelical identity within local congregations. In this sense, mediating structures need to be reconceived and the maintenance of religious values addressed using a new set of theoretical tools.

There are good reasons for saying that the evangelical movement is more radically shaped by translocal networks than any other faction within contemporary Christianity. The UK's largest, most thriving churches are typically evangelical and highly active, boasting lay-empowered programmes of evangelism and social action. This is certainly the case with St Michael-le-Belfrey and its scale and ambition means that networks emerge from *within* the congregation as convenient organisational media for these activities. The prominence of elective parochials among the congregation, demonstrated in earlier chapters, also highlights the presence of numerous *nodes* that offer points of contact with related networks. Those individuals who attend occasionally serve as channels of communication with other churches and denominations; those who stay for short periods convey the social capital endowed by their previous church, just as they pass on that acquired in St Michael's to their next. Increased geographical movement among evangelical congregations – often propelled by the upward mobility of their membership – heightens the importance of dispersed personal networks as it generates channels of communication, support and the cross-fertilisation of ideas among those who share a common set of Christian convictions. Indeed, the alternative worship movement emerged in the late 1980s and early 1990s in this precise manner. Mobile, creative and impassioned young evangelicals scattered across the UK found themselves inspired by the Nine O'Clock Service in Sheffield, but had no access to its resources, and so built their own tradition of ritual, worship and Christian fellowship extemporaneously, through personal networks consolidated through mutual visits, festival gatherings, occasional conferences and, later on, web-based interaction. Its momentum as a grass-roots movement has partly depended upon the ability of its participants to sustain personal networks on a national and increasingly international level.

In a more formal sense, the Universities and Colleges Christian Fellowship (UCCF) continues to exert a highly significant influence over the life of evangelical students within UK universities, fostering a network of Christian Unions held together by their commitment to a shared doctrinal statement and mission-centred ethos. Networks emerge around the various evangelical festivals, built up informally through the regular gatherings of believers, but often also in a more intentional fashion, with a central hub facilitating a wide-ranging programme of events, resources and training available to local churches sympathetic to a given set of Christian values. A good example would be New Wine, which was established by David Pytches, one-time vicar of St Andrew's, Chorleywood, in the late 1980s. Pytches had been a bishop in Chile and longed for the church in the UK to experience the spontaneous expansion he had witnessed in South America. Inspired by John Wimber's signs and wonders theology, particularly his teaching that growth emerges when ordinary Christians are equipped with the gifts of the Holy Spirit,

Pytches sought to promote this outlook among UK churches through a series of conferences offering seminars, worship and Bible teaching for all ages. New Wine has subsequently expanded its activities to include Leaders' Retreats (run in many different countries), Soul Survivor (a separate initiative to cover its burgeoning youth work), and New Wine Networks (gathering together church leaders into local networks to share New Wine values). Numerous evangelical organisations have emerged in a similar fashion, including Christian Voice and Reform, which function as campaign-based groups. Parachurch organisations like the Evangelical Alliance and World Vision, while older and more complex, serve as rallying points within evangelical networks, looked to for benchmarks of legitimacy and for guidance on appropriate expressions of Christian charity. The World Wide Web expands the networking possibilities associated with these organisations immeasurably, adding email discussion, blogs, online forums and chat-rooms to the usual seminars and annual conferences.

In addition to formal and informal networks, there is another dimension to the transcongregational layer of evangelical communication which, to use an economic metaphor, primarily concerns processes of production rather than consumption. That is, it refers not to personal networks as media through which evangelical ideas flow and are shared, but to the powerful, transnational structures from which these ideas often nowadays emerge. One crucial factor here is the passage of influence that flows across the Atlantic and there is important future research to be done on the Anglo-American evangelical tradition and its hegemonic status within the global movement. This trend has long established roots: from the time of George Whitefield and John Wesley, evangelicalism has had a transatlantic flavour, with travelling preachers and influential authors maintaining a flow of influence and exchange across the subsequent centuries. One may find examples of how US evangelicalism has exerted significant influence over the British churches in the recent history of St Michael-le-Belfrey. The famous schism in 1980, which resulted in the establishment of the breakaway Acomb Christian Fellowship, was partly triggered by the importation of teachings on prophecy and authority, newly embraced by those who had been attending an independent evangelical church which submitted to the authority of leaders based in Florida. John Wimber, who subsequently had huge influence over the charismatic movement in Britain, embarked in 1981 on his first ministerial visit to this country partly at the invitation of David Watson, who had met him during a recent visit to Fuller Theological Seminary in Pasadena, California. This flow of ideas and influence is well established and played a particularly important role in the development of the theology of the House Church Movement during the 1970s.[7] The flow of influence has also worked in both directions, with numerous British evangelical authors successfully penetrating the US movement, key figures being C.S. Lewis, John Stott and David Watson, and

---

[7] Nigel Scotland, 'Evangelicalism and the Charismatic Movement (UK)', in Craig Bartholomew *et al* (eds), *The Futures of Evangelicalism. Issues and Prospects* (Leicester: Inter-Varsity Press, 2003), pp. 284-5.

perhaps more recently, Steve Chalke. What distinguishes the character of this phenomenon in recent years is the extent to which global politico-economic forces have become vehicles for this flow of evangelical capital, which has thereby achieved greater circulation and, in turn, greater social significance.

One of the most striking examples of this development is the evangelical publishing industry, which increasingly operates within a globalized environment, targeted at a niche market. The tools of marketing associated with the secular world of business are here deployed in the promotion of an evangelical worldview on an international stage. Well-known evangelical authors such as John Stott, Gerald Coates and Adrian Plass achieve celebrity status through their popular appeal, emerging as brand names within the Christian publishing industry, and while publishing houses like Inter-Varsity Press and Kingsway benefit from enhancing the appeal of their books to the Christian market, branded authors build their reputation and that of their church by gaining an international platform for their teaching.[8]

In terms of book sales, the major growth areas continue to be spirituality and devotionalism, but the globalisation of evangelical publishing has also flowed through less obvious genres, including the fictional thriller. For example, the phenomenally successful *Left Behind* novels, by minister Tim LaHaye and author Jerry B. Jenkins, intentionally tap into apocalyptic themes in the evangelical imagination and actively teach a premillennialist message through the compelling medium of an adventure story. The dazzling, glamorous methods of the popular media – now including three movie adaptations – are used to great effect in the promulgation of a clear evangelical message, structured around the rapture, tribulation, coming and then defeat of the anti-Christ, followed by eschatological judgement, all embedded within a story of ordinary citizens facing the calamities of these tumultuous end times. *Left Behind* is no exception in the use of mass media, including the internet, to promote products which carry an evangelical message. The evangelical publishing industry now extends well beyond the printed word, and a glance through UK Christian bookshops will reveal the abundance of evangelical software and audio-visual products, many of them of US origin, which serve as conveyors of an evangelicalism that circulates within a global market.

Closer to home, courses such as Alpha have provoked accusations of McDonaldization as Christian agencies have adopted the principles of calculability, efficiency, predictability and control that have become increasingly normative in other fields of culture.[9] Christianity is standardized, packaged and reconfigured into easily digestible bite sized portions; a convenience food for the late modern spiritual consumer. The dynamics of McDonaldization open up novel channels for the dissemination of Christian teaching, filtered through the material culture of the market: books, videos, DVDs, car stickers, sweatshirts, all emblazoned with the

---

[8] Richard Bartholomew, 'Publishing, Celebrity, and the Globalisation of Conservative Protestantism', *Journal of Contemporary Religion* 21:1 (2006), pp. 1-13.

[9] George Ritzer, *The McDonaldization of Society. An Investigation into the Changing Character of Contemporary Social Life* (Thousand Oaks, CA: Pine Forge Press, 1996).

Alpha brand. And like a corporate brand, Alpha is protected by its guardians at Holy Trinity, Brompton, who have used copyright law and their marketing capital to control the public image of Alpha and all it represents. The extraordinary wealth of HTB and the Alpha organisation has allowed them to advertise their product on billboards and on the side of city buses, so that Christianity has achieved a fresh visibility in our largely secularized Britain. Their successful use of marketing strategies has also engendered a standardization of the Christian message, in this case closely following the specific form of charismatic evangelicalism fostered in Holy Trinity. In this respect Alpha functions as a *normalizing force* within global Christianity, teaching, embodying and uncritically endorsing a form of evangelicalism that is presented as the true path to faith. In so far as Alpha has also successfully reinvigorated local congregations – its resources unsurprisingly embraced as a fresh and accessible source of teaching and spiritual guidance both within the evangelical world and beyond – it is increasingly triggering a standardization of congregational cultures. Like a business franchise, Alpha offers churches new opportunities for enrichment, but only if the brand is comprehensively endorsed, and this comes at a price.

Given the apparently ubiquitous influence of market forces, it is tempting to endorse Jeremy Carrette and Richard King's argument that economics is replacing science as the dominant discourse of our society and that the 'ideologies of consumerism and business enterprise are now infiltrating more and more aspects of our lives'.[10] Whether the co-opting of such ideologies into evangelical Christianity fosters social and political conservatism – encouraging individuals to remain compliant consumers rather than challenging the status quo – is a question for a different book to this one. What is striking is the extent to which such forces appear to have found a home within the evangelical movement and to have occupied a place from which they may increasingly infiltrate the life of evangelical congregations.

There are theological resources within Christian tradition that may be drawn from in justifying the legitimacy of social networks. The idea of the church being the body of Christ highlights common commitment to and relationship with Jesus as the basis of Christian fellowship, rather than geographical location or institutional affiliation as such. Indeed, this understanding is particularly popular among evangelicals, reflecting their passion for personal faith, a key identity marker distinguishing them from those more wedded to the Anglican parish system, or to institutions of priesthood or sacrament. Hence, dispersed networks lend themselves particularly well to the evangelical worldview and find a natural legitimacy among its affiliates. Their apparent flexibility also appeals to the passion for ecclesiological innovation at the heart of evangelical tradition and their dependence upon intersubjective engagement resonates with charismatic notions of the Spirit, flowing through the body of Christ as an organic phenomenon, rather than within bricks and mortar. These factors may lie behind Pete Ward's positive appraisal of networks as

---

[10] Jeremy Carrette and Richard King, *Selling Spirituality. The Silent Takeover of Religion* (Abingdon: Routledge, 2005), p. 4.

ideal contexts for a 'liquid church' which, to be a 'true expression of the kingdom', needs to embody the forms of community that have emerged in late modernity.[11] Indeed, the affinity between such deep-seated evangelical themes and the fluid, more malleable forms of community popular in late modern culture invite serious questions about the propensity of the evangelical movement to thrive in the contemporary world. Those wishing to move beyond the assumptions of the traditional secularization paradigm might appeal to this affinity in developing a fresh theoretical framework for addressing issues of growth and decline.

But what does the importance of networks mean for the theoretical debates presented as central to the preceding analysis? Heelas and Woodhead argue that, in recent years, the resilience and adaptability of secondary institutions, such as small groups, new spiritual outlets and the institutions of 'soft' capitalism, suggest the clear distinction between primary and secondary institutions may be breaking down.[12] Both now appear central to the construction of identities in late modernity so that it is no longer meaningful to subordinate one to the other. I would concur with this argument, but wish to expand it by suggesting that the identity-defining power of primary institutions is also being challenged by networks and markets, so that religious identities are no longer primarily formed within churches, chapels or more informal home groups, but in relationship with a whole range of phenomena set above the level of the individual. While these include the traditional forms of community gathering mentioned here, they also include dispersed informal friendship groups, web-based discussion forums, national networks associated with festivals or conferences, and the various strands of the commercial evangelical market which generates a shared material culture circulating among a global populace.

The examples offered above provoke the question of whether evangelical networks and markets are now more powerful than denominations or local churches in defining evangelical identities, not to mention traditional authorities such as scripture or the reputable preacher. Indeed, these examples, while properly referred to as mediating structures (in so far as they shape the appropriation of evangelical tradition), are not *secondary* in any strict sense, for their relationship to evangelical communities is complex, and often axiomatic rather than ancillary as such. I would not suggest that the conventional structures of the congregation have been supplanted; evidence suggests the congregation will continue to be the axis of collective identity for most practising Christians for some time yet.[13] Rather, the evangelical congregation must be addressed not merely as a local Christian gathering, but as a potential site for the flow of ideas, products and behavioural conventions which circulate within a national, or even international, network. Future research will need to explore the

---

[11] Pete Ward, *Liquid Church* (Carlisle: Paternoster Press, 2002), pp. 10, 41.

[12] Paul Heelas and Linda Woodhead, 'Homeless Minds Today?', in Linda Woodhead (ed.), *Peter Berger and the Study of Religion* (London and New York: Routledge, 2000), p. 69.

[13] Mathew Guest, 'Reconceiving the Congregation as a Source of Authenticity', in Jane Garnet et al (eds.), *Redefining Christian Britain. Post-1945 Perspectives* (London: SCM Press, 2007), pp. 63-72.

extent to which congregations have become mere filters for forces operative at the level of the network, or whether networked relationships remain epiphenomenal to more regular and immediate encounters, supportive of congregationally driven values. If the former, then evangelical authority is unlikely to be as fixed or perhaps as accountable as it is often assumed to be, and congregational studies will need to address the extent to which this has a destabilising effect on congregational cultures, in deference to a more delocalised form of evangelical identity. Is the network overtaking the congregation as the dominant point of reference in the construction of evangelical identity, and what are the implications of this for the strength of the evangelical movement?

Here, Christian Smith's work may again be instructive, especially his argument that opportunities for evangelicals to struggle with the challenges of the wider culture do not engender secularization but foster vitality.[14] If evangelicals thrive on tension, difference and impassioned cultural engagement, as Smith suggests, might a transnational, dispersed network actually facilitate this more effectively than the traditional congregation? After all, to exist within such networks is to relinquish the comparatively enclosed boundaries of conventional congregational structures and participate in a larger, less predictable social field, occupied by a range of other discourses, some inimical to evangelical values. The network society arguably heightens awareness of the cultural and religious diversity that characterises our pluralistic world and, as such, offers a prime site for the struggles that Smith associates with the sustenance of evangelical vitality. Might networks foster growth, strength and empowerment? Might their global reference allow UK evangelicals to transcend the constraints of their post-Christian context? Smith's notion of 'engaged orthodoxy' opens up a whole range of possibilities for future analysis.

Subjectivity, Community and Culture

While the question of networks and the globalisation of evangelicalism cannot be sidestepped, community continues to be a key value for British evangelicals. That is, the experience of being in fellowship with other evangelicals is still an important identity marker of being evangelical and is central to a sense of being authentically Christian, a sense perhaps heightened by the siege mentality common among those who see themselves as a remnant of believers in an otherwise secularised culture. But if community is important, what kind of community is this? Some light is shed on this question by reflecting on wider sociological debates about the nature of community in the late modern age. While it is widely argued that the fragmentation of the modern condition generates longings for community, it is also often assumed that efforts to forge communities are doomed to failure because of the fragmentation of social life. This is an extreme position, based on Ferdinand Tönnies' notion of the

---

[14] Christian Smith, *American Evangelicalism. Embattled and Thriving* (Chicago, IL, and London: University of Chicago Press, 1998), p. 150.

Gemeinschaft as inversely related to the progression of modernisation.[15] However, it would be more consistent with the evidence to suggest a transformation or reinvention of community in the light of changing conditions. For example, Michel Maffesoli has spoken of 'neo-tribes', interest and lifestyle-based groups which emerge as a response to the heightened individualism of late modernity. They are unstable, maintained through shared beliefs and consumption practices rather than by conventional ascriptions such as class or regional identities.[16] His description suggests some affinity with the fledgling alternative worship network were it not for its local links with churches and the undeniably middle class status of its constituency. Moreover, as the example of *Visions* demonstrates, the relative isolation of groups can generate a particular kind of structure, characterised by tight boundaries and a close-knit membership. They have forged a community for themselves and thus escaped postmodern fragmentation, but their esoteric and elusive project has demanded its own logic and language, and both have emerged and been sustained among a relatively consistent core group with its own evangelical subculture, a point to which we shall later return.

To take a different example, the St Michael's home groups show less inwardness due to their being embedded in a larger structure, which assists in the provision of leadership, organisation and materials. Members participate in a larger, but proximate, culture while resolving questions and problems through face-to-face dialogue. In offering places in which the individual can be felt to 'be known', they arguably go some way towards making up for what Peter Berger once described as the 'underinstitutionalised' state of the private sphere.[17] But home groups function in the middle ground, as secondary institutions, and it is this which grants their distinctiveness. While sufficiently private to foster intimacy and familiarity, they are sufficiently public to allow communality and a *sharing of subjectivities*. Examples from the Alpha course in chapter 7 demonstrate how this sharing process includes references to external links – embedded in the networks and markets described in the previous section – and that this enhances a sense of legitimacy and belonging among participants. They are not merely members of a home group, but participants in a home group network, co-searchers on the Alpha journey and channels for the wisdom and knowledge generated from past experience and encounters with the spiritual.

Indeed, it is such a network of interactive contexts which may best characterise the community offered within St Michael's. While the *experience* of being fostered is seen in terms of a meeting of subjective needs, the medium through which this occurs is an overlapping network of meetings, interest groups, services and friendship circles. As with the *Visions* group, these have an affinity with a particular set of social interests, catering to the middle class socialities of its membership. But the huge scale of St Michael's means that community is inevitably mediated by

---

[15] Ferdinand Tönnies, *Community and Association* (London: Routledge and Kegan Paul, 1955).

[16] Michel Maffesoli, *The Time of the Tribes. The Decline of Individualism in Mass Society* (London: Sage, 1996).

[17] Berger *et al*, *The Homeless Mind*, p. 167.

diffuse networks and the choices individuals make about which church meetings best suit their needs. In this way the networks addressed in the previous section play an important part in fostering the intersubjectivity that is at the heart of evangelical community.

This phenomenon was explored in detail in chapter 5, where the culturally driven *subjective turn* was explored in relation to the charismatic movement. For many evangelical Christians, this gradual sea change has set human relationships within a new framework, rendering existing relational dynamics pregnant with spiritual meaning while generating new styles of devotional practice and novel forms of power. This complex development has led to a variety of innovations across the evangelical world, the charismatic framing the collapse of hard boundaries dividing church from the therapeutic world on the one hand, while the Toronto Blessing and its successors have intensified the performative aspects of congregational life and caused some significant upheaval.

While different churches have embraced the charismatic renewal movement to different degrees, it is fair to say that the movement has nonetheless paralleled a transformation in evangelical culture of which it was partially, at least, the cause. This transformation, which had its axis in the 1960s, was characterised by a celebration of subjective experience coupled with a newfound willingness to embrace movements and media from the wider culture as resources co-opted into the job of promoting the gospel message. This led to the blurring and in some cases tearing down of boundaries which were previously sacrosanct, and opened the evangelical movement more radically to cultural influence. Culture was befriended as a potential ally and, eventually, as a family member who could no longer be conveniently left at the church door each Sunday. As Donald Miller's work on new paradigm churches in the US has demonstrated, such developments are often born out of a passion for evangelism, but foster an enculturation of evangelicalism that has far-reaching consequences for congregational life.[18] As worship, social justice, business ethics, leisure, sport, music, are all allowed beneath the evangelical sacred canopy as channels of the gospel and legitimate aspects of church life, so they foster a rich subculture which, because of the movement's constituency, shares many affinities with middle class lifestyles and values: expressivism, harmony, mutual support, tolerance, equality, acceptance of the religious 'other', enthusiasm for notable speakers and authors, and a sympathy with a reflective, embodied appreciation of human experience not unlike that driving the alternative therapy industry. Alongside this, the more counter-cultural dimension to evangelical identity has often been veiled behind a congenial public face, keen to affirm an expressive, tactile hospitality which sits uncomfortably with the combative tones of yesteryear.

Given these developments, in asking what evangelicals now affirm as their dominant mode of cultural engagement, it is tempting to speak of harnessing cultural affinities rather than the drawing of battle lines. The contemporary cynicism

---

[18] Donald E. Miller, *Reinventing American Protestantism. Christianity in the New Millennium* (Berkeley and Los Angeles, CA: University of California Press, 1997).

towards the more intensely performative aspects of charismatic spirituality, described in chapter 5, has also been accompanied by a reversion to more inclusive, holistic, altogether more tempered manifestations of the Holy Spirit. Even the Toronto Airport Christian Fellowship, once the global hub of the 'Blessing', has in recent years embraced more sedate forms of charismatic practice, embodied less in exuberance and open theatrics, more in a gentle tranquillity that reflects a turn towards a healing ministry with a decidedly therapeutic flavour.[19] It seems the ritualised performance of charismatic spirituality might take different forms over time, changing largely, perhaps, in response to shifting perceptions of power and authority. However, the enculturation of evangelicalism, which was urged on by charismatic renewal, has for the most part followed a consistent trajectory, i.e., more and more aspects of everyday life have been actively incorporated into the evangelical world as spiritually significant.

What is also clear from the foregoing analysis is that identity boundaries are continually negotiated in accordance with the needs of congregations and this is inevitably informed by the cultural identities of members. In certain respects, religion endorses the social order of the group's membership, or minimally that which allows members to affirm their social identity using religious means. Joseph Tamney makes a similar observation with respect to conservative Protestant congregations in the USA. Arguing against Dean Kelley's famous argument, which explains the success of conservative churches with reference to the strict, clear and exacting demands they make of their members, Tamney claims that 'when people need meaning, they do not automatically seek out a costly religion, but commit to one that is consistent with their ongoing values and beliefs'.[20] Within St Michael's, this is clear from the control of public discourse in sermons and in words of knowledge. Issues likely to cause conflict are evaded while members are given the means with which to affirm their existing values and conventions, and work through their worries. The value system of the church sits most comfortably with the social constituency of its congregation, so that career advancement, education, the nuclear family and issues of personal emotional struggle are absorbed into the divine plan and then projected as ordained priorities into the faith-lives of individual members. One hypothesis as to why this occurs may refer to how middle-class values are diffused throughout British culture, but lack an ordering framework. Within an

---

[19] See Martyn Percy, 'Adventure and Atrophy in a Charismatic Movement: Returning to the "Toronto Blessing"', *Journal of Contemporary Religion* 20:1 (2005), pp. 71-90. A recent example of this shift is what the Toronto Fellowship call 'soaking events', which appeal to images of immersion and tranquillity to describe an experience of the Holy Spirit that emphasises a quiet, invigorating encounter with God's presence, manifested in falling or in long periods of lying on the floor. According to the Fellowship's website, 'To "soak" in God's presence is to rest in His love rather than to "strive" in prayer'. See http://www.tacf.org/tacforghome/CatchTheFireMinistries/SoakingPrayerCenters/, accessed 1 August 2007.

[20] Joseph B. Tamney, *The Resilience of Conservative Religion. The Case of Popular, Conservative Protestant Congregations* (Cambridge: CUP, 2002), p. 227.

increasingly amoral, media-driven, fast-paced western society, moral order is elusive, a special concern among uprooted middle-class families with young children. St Michael's appears to skate that fine line between accommodating to a theologically diverse congregation while providing ample space for the expression and exploration of traditional understandings of moral order. The peculiar way in which moral teaching is dealt with, discussed in chapter 4, brings this out most clearly. To refer back to Berger, 'homeless minds' are provided with solace and a place in which to share their homelessness, but the spiritual homes provided are flexible enough to be able to adapt to individual needs and theological diversity.

Heelas and Woodhead employ a similar argument in explaining the popularity of the holistic milieu, including alternative therapies, spiritualities and the wellbeing culture. These phenomena successfully cater to the subjective turn that characterises contemporary western culture by affirming, cultivating and often even sacralising the subjective lives of individuals.[21] While charismatic evangelical churches would typically distance themselves from such expressions of the New Age Movement, they nevertheless embody this broader cultural shift. Of course, when asked about authority, they more often than not turn to scripture, but in terms of everyday practice, there is a discernible freedom with which human experience, in its mundane and spectacular forms, is attributed with spiritual meaning.

Changes at the Margins

It would be a mistake to conclude that this evolved subjectivisation always fosters a healthy inclusivism among evangelicals. The same dynamics sometimes work towards the exclusion of those who fail to find meaning within a particular set of cultural affinities. It was the recognition of this which triggered the emergence of what became the *Visions* group. Reaching out to those for whom conventional church was anathema, they broke out of the bonds of the evangelical subculture from whence they came. They embodied the dance culture in an attempt to preach the gospel in a way that was culturally authentic to the clubbers. In effect, they established their own subculture with its own set of boundaries. *Visions* found itself on the margins, between evangelicalism and secular culture. It has continued to embody this liminal identity, even if the social capital that once connected them with the clubbers has subsequently diminished, the group instead focusing largely on its own needs rather than those of any single target audience. The markers of the dance culture have become the *Visions* culture, absorbing group interests, artistic preferences and shared grievances along the way. In this respect members also affirm their own social identities through their religious practice.

Because of its small scale and peripheral status in relation to St Michael's and the rest of the church, *Visions* has developed a peculiar combination of open, exploratory theology within a close-knit micro-culture. Most strikingly, they are

---

[21] Paul Heelas and Linda Woodhead, *The Spiritual Revolution. Why Religion is Giving Way to Spirituality* (Oxford: Blackwell, 2005), p. 81.

social separatists by inclination, preferring to mix with others of a like-mind and often feeling alienated from mainstream evangelicalism and those affiliated to it. Thus, while St Michael's has arguably extended its affinities with contemporary middle class culture, *Visions* has adopted a hard set of social boundaries against it. Indeed, this sometimes issues in open expression during worship. During a service run by *Visions* but held in St Michael-le-Belfrey, one *Visions* member performed a 'rant', a diatribe against the superficiality of consumerism and the evils of the branding and designer-label culture. When discussing this event with me, one St Michael's member took exception to the rant, claiming that he had friends who had to buy designer clothes because of their jobs. They felt the accusation of exclusivism could be levelled at the *Visions* group, especially when they make people feel a bit too 'straight'.

This is one of the main reasons why an appeal to postmodernity alone – with the associations of deregulation that it implies – is insufficient for an understanding of alternative worship groups such as *Visions*. While embracing a multi-media technology that appears to undermine traditional parameters of meaning, these groups largely exist as *marginalised enclaves*. As such, they rely on oppositional relationships for a sense of identity, whether their nemesis is consumer culture, free market capitalism or the mainstream church. Moreover, the cultural resources upon which they draw in defining their identities are inevitably shaped by traditional social factors, particularly gender, class, generation and ecclesiastical background. The innovations of postmodernity take place within the confines of localised conditions.

In recent years, the status of the movement to which *Visions* belongs has changed, and these changes have arguably compromised the sense of marginality previously so important to those post-evangelicals seeking solace within the alt.worship network. On the one hand, there remains an important distinction between the more theologically radical, long-standing alt.worship groups, and those opting into its brand as a means of promoting multi-media worship within an otherwise fairly mainstream evangelical tradition, and this distinction is upheld by those wishing to maintain a sense of post-evangelical credibility. The same tension is replicated in the US, where Emergent Village, the network of mission-focused Christians committed to an open-ended, critical reappraisal of Christianity for a new era, find themselves sharing the 'emerging' label with young evangelicals keen to wear the clothes and speak the language of contemporary culture, but who also show no signs of challenging their existing theological assumptions.[22] However, at the same time, many groups that were considered radical and cutting edge during the 1990s have been absorbed more comfortably into the mainstream, and this has been driven by a number of factors. Much has to do with the gradual fading of what Steve Bruce has called the 'radical impetus'.[23] Many alt.worship groups have shrunk in size and lost momentum and their public profile has diminished, with the more

---

[22] See Andy Crouch, 'The Emerging Mystique', *Christianity Today* 48:11 (2004), pp. 36-43.

[23] Steve Bruce, *God is Dead. Secularization in the West* (Oxford: Blackwell, 2002), p. 24.

successful groups, like *Sanctus 1* in Manchester, depending to some degree on formal links with church structures. At the same time, the more successful, and less radical, youth events, such as Soul Survivor, have become the public face of youth Christianity, eclipsing more experimental initiatives that rarely enjoy the same financial backing. As alt.worship groups have sought new direction, those within the mainstream church have shown themselves to be more receptive to their innovations. Memories of the ignominy of the Nine O'Clock Service have faded and church leaders have softened their perspective on progressive forms of worship. Indeed, the 'fresh expressions' initiative of the Church of England has attempted to embrace alt.worship as a legitimate and valued expression of Christian community.

Influential figures within the alt.worship movement have also grown older, perhaps less rebellious, and many have found themselves in positions of institutional leadership. Indeed, it could be argued that alt.worship groups have been highly effective in fostering leadership skills in their long-standing members, and have perhaps facilitated the spiritual maturation necessary for responsible ministry. Dave Tomlinson claims that, during the 1990s, he was one of five regulars at Holy Joe's, the alternative church held in a London pub, who went on to be ordained.[24] Interestingly, around the same number have emerged from St Michael-le-Belfrey in recent years to pursue the same ambition. Clearly, for some, alt.worship has not been a last chance saloon on the way out of the church, nor a one-way retreat to the margins, but has been a source of spiritual reinvigoration and vocational renewal. Several of these individuals have published books about alt.worship, the pragmatics of doing it and its underlying theology, and, together with the literary efforts of their American and Australasian associates, these have issued the movement with its own body of literature,[25] filtering into teaching, worship and the informal discussions through which emerging identities are constructed and explored. Still more individuals maintain an open and evolving dialogue with an international constituency through their online blogs.

These developments have placed one-time radicals in what are almost establishment positions and they are now more likely to be encouraging, or even leading, gentle reform of the church than railing against it, or lamenting its mainstream mediocrity. At the same time, the ideas and resources once the preserve of the marginal have become accessible and desirable to a much wider audience, some based in churches which identify with the fresh expressions label, or who have felt affirmed following the *Mission Shaped Church* Report. Effectively, as labels like

---

[24] Heather Webb, 'Continuing the Journey: A Conversation with Dave Tomlinson', *Mars Hill Review* 18 (2001), p. 75.

[25] The emerging church literature has been sustained and nurtured in large part by the sizeable US market and particularly by the Zondervan publishing house, based in Grand Rapids, Michigan. In recent years, Zondervan have been responsible for publishing books by a wide range of well-known luminaries within the emerging church world, including Kester Brewin, Dan Kimball, Brian McLaren, Doug Pagitt, Steve Taylor and Robert Webber. They also published the revised US editions of Jonny Baker's *Alternative Worship* in 2004 and Dave Tomlinson's *The Post-Evangelical* in 2003.

'fresh expressions', 'alt.worship' and 'emerging church' have become common among mainstream Christians,[26] their meaning has become destabilised and as innovation in worship and community has become more acceptable, these Christians have a ready, flexible language with which to describe their activities. There has been a convergence of cultural capital, as the resources and ideas previously particular to mainstream evangelicals on the one hand, and progressives on the other, have merged to form a single, complex repertoire at the general disposal of the church. The artistic exuberance of the charismatic movement has evolved to a point where it has dissolved previously important boundaries between evangelicals of different shades, and has expanded and redefined the mainstream body of the movement.[27]

Conservative Resurgence

However, the situation is not so simple, or so monochrome, and as mainstream evangelicals find their numbers expanded, so others are content to be pushed even further to the edges, where more rigid boundaries of identity remain normative. This is especially the case for those elements of the movement who see contemporary culture as something from which the church should be clearly distinguished, lest it be tainted by it. For such conservative elements of the evangelical world, the church is inevitably presented as an a-cultural entity, the pure remnant around which all aspects of our aberrant society need to be gathered in order to be appropriately cleansed. Interestingly, the most well-known British representatives of this outlook – the organisations of Reform and Christian Voice – both present the mission of the church in national terms, as a quest to rescue England from its 'desperate spiritual and moral condition'.[28] Hence their immediate missional focus is culture and cultural problems, but these are conceived as entirely separate from the church, which retains a quasi-sectarian purity. This stands in stark contrast to the perspective implicit within the post-evangelicalism of the alt.worship movement, for whom culture is ontologically prior when it comes to matters of identity and, as such, is to be

---

[26] Peter Brierley claims that, by 2006, there were around 25,000 individuals in England attending 420 churches that referred to themselves as a 'fresh expression'. See Peter Brierley, *Pulling Out of the Nosedive. A Contemporary Picture of Churchgoing* (London: Christian Research, 2006), p. 37.

[27] In noting increasing internal diversity and the enthusiasm of evangelical congregations in offering a range of activities for their members, David Hilborn identifies symptoms of the same trend. He presents this as evidence that mainstream evangelicalism has absorbed postmodern ideas to a greater degree than many commentators care to admit, especially those who would present postmodernity as the preserve of those occupying the radical margins of the movement. See David Hilborn, *Picking up the Pieces. Can Evangelicals Adapt to Contemporary Culture?* (London: Hodder and Stoughton, 1997), pp. 48-51.

[28] Revd David Holloway, vicar of Jesmond Parish Church and a key spokesperson for the Reform group, cited in Martyn Percy, 'A Blessed Rage for Order: Exploring the Rise of "Reform" in the Church of England', *Journal of Anglican Studies* 3:1 (2005), p. 43.

respected and affirmed, rather than denied. While this position is a radical one, it is consistent with the dominant trend in present-day British evangelicalism in so far as culture is generally treated as a positive opportunity rather than a threat.

Having said this, the distinctively conservative – rather than charismatic – emphases of Reform and Christian Voice do reflect a discernible British resurgence in recent years of a conservative form of evangelicalism. At the congregational level, one could refer to Jesmond Parish Church, whose vicar, David Holloway, has strong links with Reform. Jesmond Parish Church is a well-known successful centre of conservative evangelicalism in the North East of England and now claims to attract around 1,000 individuals to its Sunday services. As such, it is achieving a popularity that even surpasses St Michael-le-Belfrey and reflects a trend across the North East that is partially propelled by the Emmanuel Schools Foundation, directed by wealthy car dealer and prominent evangelical Peter Vardy. The Foundation has overseen the establishment of three privately sponsored schools in Gateshead, Doncaster and Middlesborough, all of which enjoy significant autonomy due to their status as a city technology college, in the case of Emmanuel College Gateshead, or as City Academies, in the case of the other two. Repeatedly accused of incorporating creationism into biology classes,[29] these secondary schools are openly governed according to an evangelical Christian ethos, which informs staff recruitment, pupil admissions and some aspects of the curriculum.

A further noteworthy development is the appearance in recent years of Christianity Explored, an introductory course on Christianity designed by the Revd Rico Tice, a Chilean educated in Africa, who joined the staff of All Soul's, Langham Place as an associate minister in 1994. The course follows a virtually identical format to Alpha: there are ten weekly meetings involving a shared meal, DVD or video of a talk by Rico Tice, followed by discussion. Also like Alpha, it promotes itself as an opportunity for those interested in Christianity to ask the 'big' questions in a pressure-free, relaxed environment. However, the course differs from Alpha in organising sessions around a week-by-week study of Mark's Gospel, with the emphasis on 'who Jesus was, what his aims were, and what it means to follow him'.[30] While not as successful on anywhere near the same scale as Alpha, Christianity Explored is nevertheless branded and packaged for distribution and application in local congregations across the globe. It has established itself as an alternative to Alpha – the charismatic element is absent, and the substantive focus is more explicitly biblical – and is openly embraced by such flag-ship evangelical churches as Christ Church Fulwood, near Sheffield, and Jesmond Parish Church.

The emerging conservative strand does not take the same form as the anti-charismatic evangelicalism of the 1960s and 70s. Indeed, the austerity and severity of expression, coloured by a bookish articulacy and rather British concern for discipline

---

[29] See Joachim Allgaier and Richard Holliman, 'The Emergence of the Controversy Around the Theory of Evolution and Creationism in UK Newspaper Reports', *The Curriculum Journal* 17:3 (September, 2006), pp. 263-79.

[30] Taken from the Christianity Explored website – http://www.seeking.org.uk/, accessed 3 August 2007.

and proper conduct, appears to have been overtaken by a more relaxed, relational tone which characterises the bulk of the evangelical movement. In this, 'charismaticisation', as Dave Tomlinson has called it, does indeed reflect a sea change, evident also in the widespread entrepreneurialism with which evangelicals deploy cultural resources in the name of the gospel. But while a strict separatism is rarely evident in practice, those representing a conservative resurgence do affirm a more intense suspicion of contemporary culture, painting modern day Britain in fairly dark shades, emphasising moral and spiritual bankruptsy. The consequent quest for clearer boundaries of belief and practice is also reflected in a determination to appear more explicitly biblical than their forebears and, perhaps especially, than their charismatic cousins. This is apparent in the Christianity Explored course, which takes the form of an extended Bible study, albeit one aimed at the unchurched; in the activities of the Proclamation Trust, which, through its conferences, aims to equip leaders with biblical knowledge in the way that New Wine attempts to equip leaders with spiritual gifts; and in the material produced by Anglican Mainstream, a coalition of evangelical activist groups that fiercely advocates 'traditional biblical teaching on marriage, the family and human sexuality'.[31] It is also a trend that is particularly strong within some of the popular university Christian Unions, for whose members biblical obedience involves an obligation to live by a strict moral code, an effective identity marker within an environment characterised by youthful abandon and often hedonistic indulgence.

Evangelicals have gravitated to this more conservative position for a variety of reasons. Some seek out the more firmly established historical roots of traditional liturgy in preference to the saccharine tones of the charismatic chorus, eventually finding charismatic renewal modish to the point of being transient, superficial or capricious. Some have grown utterly disillusioned with the charismatic following the intensity of the Toronto Blessing. Others, perhaps like the St Michael's staff member whose outlook was described at the beginning of chapter 4, associate the charismatic with a certain wooliness and absence of doctrinal rigour. According to this viewpoint, an emphasis upon human experience as a site for divine activity has allowed emotion, immediacy, intuition and performance to overshadow responsible, rational and concerted reflection upon the nature of Christian truth.

Whatever the reasons for this intriguing change in the evangelical landscape, it raises important questions about the future of the movement: for unity, conflict, and also for its capacity to successfully negotiate patterns of cultural change. The tendency of conservative elements to fan the flames of cultural dissent and highlight points of difference, especially on moral issues, may foster the kind of evangelical tension that Christian Smith views as crucial to the vitality of the movement. If this argument holds, then the future of evangelicalism may depend on such factions periodically calling on Christians to bridle their accommodation to cultural trends. But what for some are prophetic voices are, for others, forces of retrenchment which

---

[31] Taken from the Anglican Mainstream website, http://www.anglican-mainstream.net/?page_id=216, accessed 13 August 2007.

impede the mission of the church by isolating it from the wider society and alienating its less conservative members. This is not just an issue of competing ideologies; as was demonstrated in chapter 7, evangelical congregations are shaped not merely by the values they profess, but also by the community structures they adopt as media for their expression. Moreover, the embodied and practical expression of collective identity may actually be weakened by the affirmation of a conservative agenda. This is illustrated nicely through a consideration of human relationships within evangelical congregations, and we turn again to the case of St Michael's as a useful case study.

Whatever the belief structures of this church might be – and the foregoing analysis suggests they are complex to say the least – what appears most striking about why members value being a part of St Michael's is the provision of an effective support network. The class and occupational profile of the congregation reflects this priority and their projects very much centre on the forging of affective relationships. Members rely on one another for mutual support, moral guidance and emotional nurture. According to the welcome cards which were distributed to newcomers at the time of my original research, St Michael's is

> ... a fellowship of Christian believers who believe seriously in the life-changing power of God's mercy and truth. We are a church where you can experience friendship, fellowship and acceptance as we grow together in our love and commitment to Jesus Christ.

The emphases here are telling: no reference to scripture, no use of 'evangelical', no mention of 'authority', 'sound teaching', 'Bible' or 'scripture', 'judgement' or even 'salvation'. Instead, the description emphasises this-worldly experience of God, alongside affirming qualities of 'friendship' and 'acceptance'. This is indicative of two things: the ubiquitous diplomacy of public discourse and the prioritisation of inter-personal support and intimacy. The latter feature in particular appears to be a key characteristic across the evangelical world; indeed, Stephen Hunt, working from a national UK survey, has discovered this to be central to the appeal of the Alpha course.[32] Given what Hunt also discovers about who attends these courses – chiefly existing churchgoers rather than unchurched 'seekers' - Alpha may be viewed less as a context of Christian evangelism, more as a window on to the aspirations of already committed Christians, these being focused on the exploration of faith and spirituality *in relationship with others.*

What is important here is not just the availability of support, but the availability of opportunities to adopt supportive roles. St Michael's offers a supportive and extensive community of like-minded friends, a context for the transmission of 'sound family values' of love and responsibility (especially appealing to those with small children), and opportunities for authority and empowerment consonant with one's own organisational, pastoral or pedagogical skills. It is these factors that appear to

---

[32] Stephen Hunt, *The Alpha Enterprise. Evangelism in a Post-Christian Era* (Aldershot: Ashgate, 2004), p. 182.

elicit continued commitment and enthusiastic involvement from parishioners. Of course, in addition to this is the reputation and spiritual pedigree of the church, which enhances feelings of status and of participating in an *effective* evangelical fellowship. If anything, St Michael's is saturated with the notion that this is a church which *actually works* – it lives out the gospel in ways which are socially visible and members cling on to this with pride and an almost tangible enthusiasm.

Given the apparent importance of relationships for the life of churches like St Michael's, as both channels of open spiritual expression and inter-personal support, and as a means of lay empowerment, it is interesting to reflect on how such dynamics might proceed within congregations committed to the more conservative evangelicalism described earlier. Such churches often combine a thoroughgoing biblicism with a more hierarchical model of leadership than that common within charismatic churches. Access to positions of power is more heavily curtailed, especially for women, with groups like Reform remaining strongly against the legitimacy of women's headship. Teaching is also more likely to take a direct, prescriptive form, and while the format of Christianity Explored indicates a willingness to foster an informal, exploratory context for seekers, norms of authority *within* the congregation are more likely to be structured around consistency and obedience, perhaps extending to the expectation of regular tithing. This style of evangelicalism does not present a bar to lay empowerment or strong support networks, but it does foster a very different kind of congregational culture to that described in the preceding chapters. Contemporary culture is treated with far greater suspicion, doctrinal orthodoxy is more likely to be policed and authority sustained as a preserve of the few. In such an environment, the expansive enculturation that St Michael's have managed to sustain alongside a firm sense of evangelical identity, and which has arguably been instrumental to its creativeness and success, is less likely to emerge and be encouraged. There are also more likely to be tensions between the cultural capital of educated middle-class evangelicals and the conservative positions they are expected to adopt, perhaps unquestioningly. It is difficult to understand the strength and vitality of largely middle-class evangelical churches apart from the cultural capital of many middle-class Christians: their theological articulacy, professional status and abilities, family orientation and disposable income. But there have to be channels for the expression of this capital; otherwise, one can see how disempowerment might emerge and become a force for stagnation.

On the other hand, when an open and more organic spirituality is reined in by a more rigidly defined moral-religious framework, issuing 'clear and exacting demands', it is understandable that evangelicals who yearn for a more bounded, morally trenchant Christianity would find this model attractive. That many appear to do so suggests empowerment of the kind described above is not essential for all evangelicals and perhaps, as Dean Kelley implies in his work, the chief mode of engagement among Christians seeking order in a postmodern world is not empowerment, but a form of submission. Moreover, the relationship between a strict, hierarchical evangelicalism and the empowerment of women is more complex than is often assumed, as Brenda Brasher has demonstrated within the USA,[33] and future research would do well to examine how congregations which teach a traditionalist line on gender roles nevertheless provide a context in which empowering and supportive relationships among women may emerge.

Evangelical Growth and Vitality

The argument that evangelical community is often embodied within discrete networks, and that these networks are especially suited to meeting the subjective needs of evangelical identities, is perhaps most applicable to large, middle-class churches, in which there is a high turnover of members, hence a high premium on support and high levels of mobile cultural capital. While such features appear to be conducive to fostering a dynamic and thriving congregation, powerful sociological arguments to the contrary remain. Specifically, do high levels of activism alongside a high turnover come at the expense of community cohesion, and hence durability? The question remains as to whether this arrangement leads to an inevitable *weakening of commitment*, on the grounds that a focus on meeting subjective needs compromises the cohesiveness of congregations as communities. This is a serious question, and one that might be answered in the affirmative by leaders of the conservative churches described above, who would probably associate doctrinal consistency with communal strength. Moreover, while my earlier stress upon communicative cultures highlights how the relationship between subjectivisation and fragmentation is not simple or uniform, decline has nevertheless emerged as a decisive trend within the apparently thriving church of St Michael-le-Belfrey. Indeed, while maintaining high levels of commitment, St Michael's is not managing to retain as many committed members as it used to. As charted in chapter 3, by the turn of the millennium, attendance levels had experienced a steady decline since 1993, fewer people were involved in home groups than before and financial giving had declined in real terms. St Michael's was not enjoying the same levels of success which it intermittently sustained during the 1970s and 80s. Why might this be so? Several possibilities can be suggested, and they are worth addressing in turn as they illuminate factors often overlooked in discussions of church growth and decline in the UK.

First, the generation which committed to David Watson's ministry in the 1960s are growing older and dying. Following H. Richard Niebuhr's classic argument about how sects evolve into denominations, it is possible that subsequent generations are less committed on account of not choosing but inheriting their membership, and some are not remaining within the church.[34] St Michael's is not a sect of course, but the success of the late 1960s was certainly accountable in large part to the charisma and initiatives of an inspiring leader. A subsequent fading of commitment and

---

[33] Brenda Brasher, *Godly Women. Fundamentalism and Female Power* (New Brunswick, NJ, and London: Rutgers University Press, 1998).

[34] H. Richard Niebuhr, *The Social Sources of Denominationalism* (New York: Meridian, 1962).

momentum is not just attributable to the fact that such original enthusiasm is by definition episodal and transient; it is also connected to the fact that David Watson has been a difficult act to follow. Succeeding clergy have been measured against his reputation – Watson often being idolised, especially after his death – and this has contributed to internal conflict and disappointment. Similar patterns can be found in other churches associated with a long-standing, charismatic leader, and Donald Miller has written of the fascinating problems the Vineyard Church faced after John Wimber's death in 1997.[35] However, in St Michael's, periods of decline have not occurred at times which support this theory, and very high levels of attendance continued well after Watson's departure. It is possible that any disillusionment may have taken some years before its effects were fully realised, especially given the overlap between Watson's and Graham Cray's ministry. Perhaps the honeymoon period extended well into the 1980s because Watson's influence was still clearly felt, not least in the deputy who succeeded him.

A more plausible, but not unrelated, explanation might refer to the narrowing of spirituality in the early 1990s. The introduction of the Toronto Blessing and the accompanying heightened and dramatised use of charismatic gifts, which were foregrounded in church life to the exclusion of other, less expressivist, forms of spirituality, provoked feelings of alienation and some disinvolvement. Indeed, as argued in chapter 5, this counter reaction to the third wave of charismatic renewal may well have been characteristic of evangelical churches across the UK. At the same time, some parishioners were less than comfortable with public teaching which affirmed conservative views on authority and morality. While attendance statistics do not suggest a mass exodus, they do support the possibility that fewer new members stayed within the church than they used to, or perhaps long-term members continued to leave in small clusters throughout the 1990s. As several of the long-term members who left were apparently involved in church leadership, it is also possible that they prompted others to act similarly. If this argument holds, then it counts firmly against Peter Berger's position, i.e. that the most thriving religious groups are those which erect successful boundaries against modern influence, as an attempt to steer church life in a more strictly dogmatic, counter-cultural direction, appears to have provoked decline and division rather than vitality. Additionally, it would stand against Dean Kelley's claim about conservative churches growing, as it was a switch from a more liberal to a more conservative position that coincided with a period of decline in church attendance.[36]

---

[35] Donald E. Miller, 'Routinizing Charisma: The Vineyard Christian Fellowship in the Post-Wimber Era', *Pneuma* 25.2 (Fall, 2003), pp. 216-39.

[36] Paul Chambers' recent research among congregations in Wales has also explored how evangelicalism itself can generate fragmentation and decline, especially when introduced into a community unused to this tradition. Chambers charts how the importation of an evangelical perspective by a new incumbent caused serious dissent among local parishioners because it disrupted established norms of social, as well as religious, order. See Paul Chambers, 'The Effects of Evangelical Renewal on Mainstream

Third, an external factor may relate to growth among independent evangelical churches in the immediate locality. In his otherwise comprehensive study of church attendance, Robin Gill does not have figures for these[37] so it is impossible to make precise comparisons, although insider estimates provided in 2002 do suggest significant pockets of growth. To take one example, at this time, The Rock Church, situated just a few streets away from St Michael's, consistently enjoyed attendances of over 300 with midweek small groups of up to sixty. According to church leaders, these levels had been as high as this for two to three years, so it is possible that decline in St Michael's is at least in part due to potential new members – many of them students – worshipping elsewhere. Also significant in the early 1990s was the North Yorkshire Vineyard Church, planted by David Watson's widow, Anne, and initially populated by former St Michael's members. At its peak, it was attracting around 120 individuals. After Watson left, it quickly fell into decline and eventually shut down after the congregation shrank to around twenty and could no longer support its pastor. While this church is no longer competing with St Michael's for members, it is possible that those who joined but then left have not returned to St Michael-le-Belfrey, perhaps going elsewhere, perhaps remaining faithful to the Vineyard and seeking out one of their other churches in the North of England.

Finally, and this returns to the point about community discussed earlier, it could be the case that St Michael's caters to its target audience a little too well. To expand, the leadership recognises that much of its congregational body is made up of students and elective parochials, who will probably move on within the space of a few years. While some are aware of the limitations which this engenders (see the quotation from one of the leadership team in chapter 3), the church appears to have adapted its outlook so as to cater to these people. This was made clear during small group sessions, where former members were remembered and prayed for without any degree of regret or disappointment. That many would move into and among the church's structures for a temporary period before moving on was accepted as inevitable. But as Wuthnow has argued with respect to small groups, this outlook allows bonding to remain temporary and commitment becomes attenuated.[38] There is a sense in which expectations of commitment have acclimatised to the mobile predicament of elective parochials so that the authentic member is no longer one who commits to a home group, attends services every Sunday and comes to the monthly prayer meeting. Rather, the authentic member is one who attends, maybe sporadically, occasionally, or who focuses their commitment on special occasions. Those gravitating to special events rather than committing to regular Sunday attendance may be described, using

---

Congregational Identities: A Welsh Case Study', in M. Guest *et al* (eds.), *Congregational Studies in the UK*, pp. 57-69.

[37] Robin Gill, *The Empty Church Revisited* (Aldershot: Ashgate, 2003).

[38] Robert Wuthnow, *Sharing the Journey. Support Groups and America's New Quest for Community* (New York, London, Toronto, Sydney, Singapore: The Free Press, 1996), p. 25.

Simon Coleman's term, as 'conference people',[39] seeking occasions of heightened experience rather than a long-term commitment to a single church. This may reflect a tendency replicated across the English churches, given Peter Brierley's 2005 Church Census finding that occasional attendees are more likely to attend a growing church,[40] and it would be interesting to explore whether other large evangelical churches maintain a comparable contingent of irregular participants. This shift in orientation mirrors the increase in elective parochialism and offers an illuminating example of how demographic trends inform changes in religious practice.

The segmentation of church life into a series of available meetings and services may also, paradoxically, contribute to a weakening of commitment. Individuals simply associate membership with participation (i.e., at whichever service or meeting is convenient) rather than with attendance at a prescribed series of gatherings. Therefore, there is a possibility that as expectations of long-term commitment have lowered, or at least a more attenuated commitment has become more acceptable, fewer occasional participants have made the transition to becoming a full member by involving themselves in an extended range of regular church activities. One dimension of this change relates to the status of home groups, which in recent years have become increasingly popular, suggesting a possible shift in the understanding of where the social axis of evangelical identity actually lies (see Epilogue).

If valid, this argument would endorse Steve Bruce's claim that liberalised religious groups have less chance of growing than consistently conservative or strict ones. However, a qualification needs to be made. Bruce, it would seem, is right to highlight the consequences of insufficiently emphasising the difference between membership and non-membership,[41] and this problem is highlighted in the diverse spectrum of commitment represented within the congregation of St Michael-le-Belfrey. However, I would challenge the simple correlation between a liberal outlook and a propensity to decline. According to Bruce, liberal churches are more likely to decline than conservative ones because the diffuseness of their beliefs makes them unstable as social institutions.[42] According to my analysis, the beliefs of the evangelicals in St Michael's are significantly liberalised and on some issues diverse. Yet decline has set in at points in its recent history when *conservative* reforms have been introduced into an already liberalised, or at least liberalising, church, threatening to rein in a broadening theological vision or inclusive understanding of spiritual legitimacy. As I argued in chapter 4, St Michael's has developed a method for managing its internal diversity by controlling public utterance and evading issues likely to cause fracture. Moreover, issues most likely to mobilise discontent appear

---

[39] Simon Coleman, *The Globalisation of Charismatic Christianity. Spreading the Gospel of Prosperity* (Cambridge: CUP, 2000), pp. 108-9.

[40] Brierley, *Pulling Out of the Nosedive*, pp. 199-200.

[41] Steve Bruce, *A House Divided. Protestantism, Schism and Secularization* (London: Routledge, 1989), pp. 152-3.

[42] Steve Bruce, *God is Dead. Secularization in the West* (Oxford: Blackwell, 2002), p. 239.

to be those which invoke a narrow, conservative approach to the faith prone to exclusion and open judgement.

What is more likely to have contributed to long-term decline is not the development of a liberalised, more tolerant set of beliefs as such, but the church's accommodation to a particular target audience, i.e., mobile, middle-class evangelicals. In this respect the development of a liberalised collection of beliefs needs to be analytically distinguished from an accommodating orientation towards a specific cultural grouping. While the two may go hand in hand, this is not necessarily the case, and, as demonstrated earlier, liberalisation is inevitably filtered by local factors, which may allay as well as quicken trends in growth or decline.

If an adaptation to elective parochials has been instrumental in causing decline, then it is the church's fame which has been its undoing. Its reputation has secured a steady supply of students, visitors and mobile newcomers to the area and it is in adapting to their needs that the church has adjusted the expectations it has of its members. As it has tempered its demands and accepted the legitimacy of a more attenuated commitment, so membership has fallen, with some participants preferring to attend a series of churches rather than commit to a single one.

Of course, there may be other salient factors at play, particularly to do with the local religious economy. Because of its long-term success and the way in which its reputation and attendance levels tower above those of its ecclesiastical neighbours, the status of St Michael's is not contested. If it was, or had to contend with a significant presence of New Age spirituality or other faith communities in its locality, then it might have responded by affirming harder group boundaries. Alternatively, it might have liberalised more rapidly and more extensively. However, it would be pure speculation to suggest that either of these responses would have necessarily engendered decline or growth. As I hope I have demonstrated in earlier chapters, responses to culture are not simple or unidirectional, but are negotiated within the congregational cultures of specific church communities. Evangelicals have been most keen to embrace this process for their own as a theological priority, grounded in mission, and as such, their attempts to negotiate their way through contemporary culture, far from signalling decline and attrition, often reflect the richness of life within the evangelical movement.

Epilogue

St Michael-le-Belfrey Revisited in 2006

In his presentation of the 2005 English Church Attendance Survey, Peter Brierley reflects on what attracts people to large or growing churches, commenting that often a 'sense of purposefulness',[1] that a church knows where it is going, can be instrumental in attracting people. In 2000, the St Michael-le-Belfrey Parochial Church Council met over a weekend to develop a shared vision for the church, which they articulated in the logo 'bring in, build up, send out' – a pithy, dynamic expression of their established focus on people and mission, empowerment and movement, expansion and dissemination. Five years later, they met again to reflect on how far they had met the targets set for themselves in 2000 and to set further targets for the next twelve months, three years and five years. A strong sense of purposefulness is conveyed in glossy church pamphlets, which outline this shared vision and list the church's targets, inviting others to join them in their 'commitment, prayer and sacrificial giving'. If, in 1999, the identity of St Michael's was most frequently articulated with reference to a shared history, rich and largely bound up in evangelical folklore, by 2005, its identity was professionally emblazoned across its material culture, using the slick tools of contemporary marketing. Before, there was a sense that it did not have to proclaim what it stood for beyond the established conventions of church services, meetings and functions, for its identity was well known and its pedigree securely established. By 2006, the mission-led ethos of its leadership had engendered a more transparent approach, characterised by the setting of concrete, realisable targets, in accordance with a clear and public statement of identity. It is useful to use the church's new threefold logo as a framework with which to think through its development post-2000, for its mission heart reveals points of both continuity with the past and significant innovation.

Bringing In ...

Evangelism remains at the heart of the Revd Roger Simpson's ministry and the various projects he has instigated are all in some way related to an effort to draw more people into the church. The problems associated with elective parochialism which were highlighted by the leader cited in chapter 3 were also identified by the

---

[1] Peter Brierley, *Pulling Out of the Nosedive. A Contemporary Picture of Churchgoing* (London: Christian Research, 2006), p. 200.

new vicar, who noticed a pattern to the flow of people coming through the doors of his new church. As he commented to me in October 2006,

> I felt we had a huge revolving door, 'cause we had lots of people coming in, but lots of people leaving, so they weren't staying ... and we weren't holding them and I thought to myself, I had a bit of a crisis actually, after I'd been here about six months, I thought, yipes, if St Michael-le-Belfrey, which is, you know, one of the ... best churches, Anglican churches, probably in the country, can't hold people, who can hold them? And it set up a huge sort of, like a fear actually, I had this sort of feeling of, we're gonna lose this, you know ... we're in danger of going under.

The famous St Michael-le-Belfrey was not showing the signs of success which were so central to its mythology and which had formed Simpson's prior impressions of the church, shaped also by his early meeting with David Watson. Seeing a need for change, he made it a priority to expand the church in a variety of ways, to bring in more people from the local area and from farther a field, to realise again the evangelistic potential of this church that had once been a flagship of growth and vitality, and an inspiration to so many evangelicals across the western world. But how successful have his efforts been? What do the available figures tell us?

Taking the highest attendances recorded in the service register for October of each year, St Michael's has actually declined by 31% between 2000 and 2005, gradually slipping from 356 to 244. However, this may indicate not a general haemorrhaging of participants, but a tendency for individuals to spread themselves more evenly among the various St Michael's services available. Aside from mid-week meetings, there are now six services held each Sunday: 9am, 11am and 7pm remain, augmented by a service aimed at the local Chinese community (attracting a congregation of twenty-five in 2005) and 'G2', a service held in a local gym aimed at offering Christian community in a setting more culturally familiar to the unchurched. In addition, *Visions* now hold weekly services and attendances there have increased in recent years, although not by a consistent pattern. The argument that participants have not left but simply occupy different places within the congregational structure is supported by figures for the diocesan count, which gauges attendances at all of St Michael's services in October of each year. For the last five years, figures have for the most part remained well above 500 and the 2005 figure was 645. Indeed, for the same period, the electoral roll has remained almost exactly the same (366 in 2005) and the address list retains names exceeding 700.

The emerging picture is one of consistency rather than significant numerical growth. St Michael's retains a general pool of participants who affiliate themselves with the church and this larger community amounts to between 700 and 900 individuals. A smaller group within that community form a committed core who invest a greater amount of time and energy in church related activities. Statistics gathered by the St Michael's leadership suggest that this core may actually be shrinking, with the percentage of the congregation participating in regular church events, special events and contributing to the church by standing order, decreasing between 2003 and 2005. However, Simpson's innovations have succeeded in harnessing significant energy at the centre and he has used this to launch creative new initiatives. In this, there is a discernible increase in focus, and a building up of a sense of collective identity and cohesion.

Building Up ...

It is perhaps odd to view St Michael-le-Belfrey as a church that needs building up at all given that, within the UK context, it appears to be a highly successful church by every criterion that comes to mind. And yet the preceding discussion of the culture of the church around the turn of the millennium reveals an impetus to build on past strengths while also coping with ongoing difficulties, as charted in chapters 4 and 5. Moreover, when I interviewed Roger Simpson in 2006, he recalled that his first impressions of St Michael's in 1999 were that the congregation was actually struggling and depressed:

> Actually when I got here, I found a church that was divided, lost a lot of its hope, people were unhappy. There was a sort of sadness, actually, I felt about the place and I think what God had been doing was humbling the church, 'cause it had been so famous and so well known ... That was my sense.

Roger did not confide in me these impressions when we first met, and this is unsurprising given his desire to instil an atmosphere of optimism in his new church. What is interesting, examining this account from a 2006 perspective, is how he interprets the state of St Michael's at that time in terms of an ongoing spiritual narrative, explaining contemporary woes with reference to past successes, and attributing this to God's own grand plan for the church. This interpretation is also used to endorse his own orientation to his new ministry, which has been pro-active, mission focused and dynamic, and to justify the new innovations that he has put in place. For Roger, St Michael's needed 'building up' in 1999, and he has pursued this challenge by introducing a number of fresh initiatives into the life of the congregation.

Most significant has been the introduction of a cell church structure, following the well-known model pioneered in the work of Ralph Neighbour and Lawrence Singlehurst.[2] Launched under Roger Simpson's leadership in 2001, the principles behind cell groups have gradually been embraced by the congregation. As more and more home groups have begun to function as cells, brand new cells have been established as old ones have multiplied. By 2003, St Michael's had thirty-five cells which together had 354 members; by 2006, there were 495 members occupying fifty-two cells, with the church leadership aiming to increase this to 100 groups within the following three years. Simpson is emphatic about the radical changes that this has brought about in the church, and in the extent to which the cell church principles – now emblazoned on an impressive public display erected in the church

---

[2] E.g., see Ralph Neighbour, *Where Do We Go From Here? A Guidebook for the Cell Group Church* (Houston, TX: Touch Publications, 2000).

nave – have changed his approach to his ministry. As he commented to me, '... [this] has completely transformed my view of church over the last seven years and it's given me probably more hope than anything else'.

Taking further the values at the heart of many small groups that were already functioning in St Michael's, cells cater to the need for face-to-face contact and a more intimate sense of community. In achieving this, so Roger Simpson argues, cells communicate and foster the kind of faith experience that individuals in contemporary British society find most meaningful: '... it meets the needs of people in our culture, who are very tired of institutions, and they're tired of institutional faith, but they're hungry for relationships'. Cells also reflect the church's commitment to mission and foster a sense of momentum and dynamism. There are contrasts with old style home groups, which were a surrogate for the close-knit community relationships people felt were increasingly lacking in modern British life; instead, cells seek always to multiply and move onwards, building relationships before encouraging members to move on and forge new ones. This inevitably opens up more opportunities for lay leadership, as regular members of cells are called upon to strike out on their own and lead a new group. Cell groups also perpetuate the focus on relationships described in chapter 7, as individual participants are asked to take part in a dynamic vision of Christian community that makes use of human connectedness in communicating faith, offering support and engaging in evangelism as they build new cells up alongside existing co-members and non-Christian friends.

There is also a possibility that, in addition to serving the purpose of attracting new members, cells also act as a surrogate form of congregational involvement. 25% of those listed as participating in a St Michael's cell group in 2006 – some 124 individuals – were not listed on the church address list, the standard, inclusive list of those involved in the life of the church. Is the cell beginning to serve as the primary social form of church for a significant number? Do these individuals see themselves on the margins of St Michael's, perhaps moving inwards to the centre as time goes by, or do they see their allegiance as primarily to their cell and are happy for things to remain that way? It is too early to tell, but the latter possibility raises important questions about the shape the church is taking in our post-institutional age. The cell structure – deferring relative autonomy to individual cells and encouraging them to move and grow – allows more individuals to forge their own mode of attachment and this includes the notion of cells becoming a form of church in their own right. There has been some effort to control cell activity from the centre, and the ministerial leadership of St Michael's regularly issue a package of written materials that all cell leaders are invited to download from the web and use in their weekly meeting. Lessons from Alpha may have been learnt here, as technology is deployed to construct a programme of study, acting as a normalising force among a diverse collection of home-based groups.

Moreover, Wuthnow's concerns about small groups still loom large: do cells encourage a commitment that is temporary and partial, precisely by appealing to those passing through the locality and by fostering a sense that the cell itself is an impermanent entity? Does a cell structure thereby hasten church decline, rather than encourage growth, as its advocates intend? Again, it is still early days, and while figures suggest the take up of cells among St Michael's congregants has seen steady growth, the very structure of cells makes it difficult to ascertain whether they foster net congregational growth or a periphery of temporary participation among an at present steady flow of interested but marginal individuals.

Another key development in recent years has seen the spiritual diversity of St Michael's further recognised and fostered. This has been achieved through the establishment of more regular services, an innovation which has effectively reconceived – or at least formalised – the identity of St Michael's in terms of multiple congregations. The establishment of G2 and the Chinese congregation reflects the church's mission focus in offering 'niche' congregations. This is presented as a way of tackling the scale of the church as a whole, offering a smaller-scale stratum to which members more immediately relate as the communal focus of their Christian identity. Simpson is highly supportive of this and is not worried about encouraging internal difference, arguing that it reflects a healthy diversity within the church body. He refers to a time when the leadership were praying about the launch of these new services, when one staff member received a 'picture' of a glass lighthouse filled with layers of coloured sand, like the ones marketed to tourists on the Isle of Wight. As he comments,

> ... we thought about it and reflected and it seemed like the Lord was saying, go for something multi-coloured ... for some churches, very big churches, go for uniformity. They have the same preacher, the same style. We've gone for great diversity, which I think also fits well in our culture, because ... I think spirituality is a very diverse thing. It's to do with personality, age, temperament, and I think to push everybody through the same ringer doesn't work, and I think at different stages in your life, you want different things ...

Such diversity is balanced, of course, with a sense on the part of the leadership that there remains a strong Anglican charismatic evangelical identity at the heart of St Michael's although, as detailed in the preceding chapters, this is interpreted in a variety of ways. The vicar is confident that this spiritual core remains firmly intact across the St Michael's community, but he is aware of the problems of balkanisation that could emerge in the wake of his new multi-congregational structure. He does not want the church to fragment or fall apart. In response to this, the leadership has encouraged cell groups to recruit from across the different congregations, so that they serve as a means of integrating those of diverse spiritual styles into cohesive and supportive groups. There are some dissenters, and some congregations prefer to remain fairly self-contained, including *Visions*, but Simpson is not worried, commenting that St Michael's is a big ship, so as long as all of these people are on the ship, that's fine.

His generous attitude extends to his feelings about the *Visions* group, whom he has grown to love and be proud of, especially for their creativity and emphasis on creation in worship. In turn, his eagerness to embrace diversity and empower the church is welcomed by the group itself, with Rebecca Wilson herself feeling

Epilogue 227

empowered as a consequence. Her status has also changed in that she was recently ordained into the Church of England and admits that she has been treated differently since then, invited to be more involved in St Michael's events. She has welcomed this, and comments on how her introduction of novel elements into St Michael's worship has happened alongside a shift towards more creative worship across its services generally. This was reflected in a Christmas service I attended in 2006, which involved a confession ritual, during which the associate minister encouraged each member of the congregation to reflect on their 'fears', 'doubts' and 'bad relationships', or 'whatever it is that God has put into your heart'. They were then invited to come to the front of the church and throw a pile of dirt into a hole situated at the foot of a large wooden cross, thus symbolising their act of handing over these negative feelings to Jesus. Such use of material symbolism, active participation and emphasis on personal worries, rather than guilt and culpability, reflect in so many ways the ritual and theology conveyed by the *Visions* group around the turn of the millennium, and demonstrates how what was once radical often subsequently gravitates inwards to become mainstream.

The *Visions* group itself has grown in numbers and become more active; by 2006 it had been holding weekly services for three years and was consistently attracting around twenty-five participants. According to one core member, growth has brought with it a less tightly cohesive core group and an expanded centre, and there are now fewer obvious differences between the group and the rest of St Michael's. At least one service each month involves discussion, sometimes focused on the group's engagement with the 'emerging church' literature, and as this covers the need for teaching more effectively, small group meetings have come to focus more on service planning and sharing meals together. In September 2006, I asked Rebecca Wilson what she felt holds *Visions* together now. She was not sure, but did comment that growth in membership has meant there is a greater diversity of perspectives within the group, with some, for example, much more committed to social justice campaigning than others. She said she senses that *Visions* is in a transitional stage, moving from an emphasis on deconstruction (knowing what they don't want) to a sense of what they do want, and articulates this in terms of an emphasis on sharing stories, walking alongside people on their spiritual journey. In this, they affirm significant continuity with what I encountered in 2000, and it is fair to say that their parent church has accommodated their innovative approaches without *Visions* having to radically adjust its ethos; perhaps a comment on how the evangelical mainstream has broadened its boundaries in recent years.

Sending Out ...

As discussed in chapter 7, St Michael's has for a long time struggled with the precise role of its home groups. Their initial focus on building up relationships of mutual support and fellowship was instrumental in fostering an ethos that was essential to the church's success, and yet this same focus arguably produced home groups which were by the late 1970s stagnant, inward looking and unfocused. There were also problems with the precise nature of leadership, with elders and home group leaders alike stuck between a sense of being empowered by position, and an experience of remaining spiritually dependent on David Watson. These problems found their way into the report on St Michael's issued by the Archbishop's Council on Evangelism (ACE) in 1977, which refers to the problem of 'dependence':

> The dependence to which I refer accounts for your apparent strength hitherto because it has been possible to organise a very tight-knit Christian community amenable to control from the centre. Potentially, however, this is your downfall because dependence overdone makes impossible growth into maturity, and that sort of growth is part of the divine will for the body.[3]

The strengths of having a close-knit, cohesive community were off-set by a tendency for that community to focus too much on its own needs and on preserving its own culture; it failed to engage with the outside world, an essential prerequisite for church growth. Its respect for and dependency on a strong spiritual leader also prevented the congregation from feeling empowered to break with this established tradition.

St Michael-le-Belfrey has travelled some distance since the ACE report, although church documents suggest it has faced the same set of problems on several occasions since then. Indeed, it is only in the past five years that it has fully embraced, and apparently seen through to success, a strategy that has overhauled the home group system in a way that seeks to address the problems of leadership, community momentum and growth alluded to above. In addition to this, St Michael's has publicly reaffirmed its identity as a mission-focused church, with clear mission targets that include enhancing the existing resources of the church and extending its mission projects. In 2004, the staff were housed in a newly refurbished 'parish centre', situated in rented offices immediately to the rear of the St Michael-le-Belfrey church building. I looked around the offices when I re-visited St Michael's in October 2006, and they are indeed impressive: spacious, bright, and conveying a general impression of busyness and slick professionalism. While my interviews with Roger Simpson in 1999 and 2000 were held in his compact office in the awkward converted interior of the St Cuthbert's building, in 2006 we were chatting in a comfortably furnished and highly spacious conference room. This shift in premises is symbolic of a broader shift in orientation: altogether more ambitious, more explicit and more creative in its initiatives as a force for Christian mission.

Projects popular six years before are still in evidence but have been adjusted to add novelty and push the agenda that little bit further. Student outreach projects have remained active in local schools and on the streets of York. Alpha continues to be central, but has been extended into more annual courses, with extra ones taking Alpha into local businesses and an Alpha conference held in 2003. St Michael's has

---

[3] 'Report from the Archbishop's Council on Evangelism Team which had studied the life of the Congregation of St Michael-le-Belfrey Church, York, in November 1977', p. 1. A copy of the report was kindly made available to the author by the St Michael-le-Belfrey leadership.

responded to the fact that a vast number of visitors wonder into the church building on a regular basis, appointing a visitor's co-ordinator to engage with them and offer a personal welcome. The vicar's report for the 2004 Annual Parochial Church Meeting reports that over 40,000 people had visited St Michael's since access to the church had been made more open to the public just a few years before. Evangelistic barbeques were held around York in 2003 and, in the same year, it was announced that the Alpha North office was to be based in the soon to be vacated St Cuthbert's building. The church's pamphlet stating its 'Vision Targets' also mentions long-term goals of increasing cells and the number of regular contributions *via* standing order, although as detailed earlier, these have met with mixed success.

Roger Simpson remains ambitious and commented to me that, before he moves on from St Michael's, he has three or four more churches he wants to plant, including one in the local cinema, one in the church building local to his own house, and one in St Cuthbert's itself. Strikingly, he says all will be led by the laity. While clergy may offer valuable support, his conviction is that such mission projects succeed because lay people feel empowered, and this has shaped his approach to leadership over the past six years: '... the more you give ministry away, the more the people grow ...' Indeed, this is reflected in the approaches adopted in establishing and developing new congregations: launch them with the human resources at the church's disposal, then allow those energies to come into their own by freeing people to lead and do ministry themselves.

In addition, recent mission strategies have acknowledged more explicitly the need to adopt styles of expression familiar to the unchurched, in order that the gospel be embodied in ways that are meaningful to a larger audience. In the establishment of G2, of cells, and of the 'hub' – a new evening gathering aimed at the student population – St Michael's is embracing a variety of forms of church, premised on the notion that in order to appeal to non-Christians, the church needs to adopt the forms of the secular culture. This is most clearly affirmed in G2, which is effectively a café-style church that takes place in a local gym. Reflecting on where people tend to be on a Sunday morning, the St Michael's leadership decided to take church to them, moving to a less alien environment and adopting a lower key, discussion-based format. In one sense, they are using the same language *Visions* did in the late 1980s and early 90s, although their cultural target was more specific. So it is interesting to explore both why St Michael's has embraced this more creative approach to mission and community, and how they make it a success, apparently exceeding *Visions*, at least in terms of regular attendance figures. The latter question leads us to issues of capital, both social (there are more people involved in running G2), cultural (like St Michael's, it speaks a language that middle-class professionals can relate to in contexts they are likely to be), and economic (according to the APCM vicar's report in 2005, the diocese have contributed £20,000 over three years to support the establishment of G2). Aside from issues of resource, St Michael's is here reflecting a broader trend in the British evangelical world whereby that which was radical and innovative fifteen years ago is now warmly embraced as mainstream. Instrumental here has been the Church of England's *Mission Shaped Church* Report, which – not insignificantly – was written principally by Graham Cray, now Bishop of Maidstone. The report affirms and encourages 'fresh expressions' of church which attempt to re-conceive church using the resources of contemporary culture, and names alternative worship groups as an example of how this has been successfully done in recent years. The radical innovations of groups like NOS, the Late Late Service and *Visions* are now not so marginal and represent a certain creativity that is readily embraced by more mainstream evangelical churches that are keen to explore new avenues for evangelism. In this sense, the boundaries of ecclesiological and evangelistic acceptability have been broadened still, although they are inevitably filtered through established norms and practical constraints, and this is certainly the case in St Michael's. What is clear, however, is that whatever the numerically measurable success of their mission projects, in recent years, their development along creative lines has enhanced the empowerment of the core congregation, offering new opportunities for leadership and innovation. In this way, the culture of St Michael's has been rendered more colourful, and has fostered a bright hope for the future, whatever that may hold.

APPENDIX 1

Research Methods

The bulk of the research upon which this book is based was conducted as ethnographic fieldwork over a twelve month period during 1999-2000. For a large part of this time I was resident in York, less than 30 minutes' walk from St Michael-le-Belfrey. Numerous visits were made subsequent to this exercise, right up until the final drafting of this manuscript in 2006, in order to supplement the data and explore unresolved issues.

Immersion and Observation

Penny Becker has argued that worship and religious education are the 'keys to reproducing a religious tradition'.[1] As I was interested in the ongoing tradition of St Michael's, the most obvious initial focus of my observation was the Sunday service, or in this case, the four Sunday services. Worship had also been the basis of my initial interest in the church, during my provisional visits to the field, and I wished to develop my emerging impressions. From my arrival in York, I began attending all three services at St Michael's – at 9.15am, 11am and 7pm – as well as the *Visions* services later in the evening. Sometimes the two evening services clashed and I either left the St Michael's services early or else spent the whole evening assisting the *Visions* group in the preparation and set-up of their own service. Soon into fieldwork, I discovered that time before and after services was just as important as the services themselves. The coffee sessions in the church hall on Sunday mornings were an especially fruitful source of data and a useful context in which to make new contacts.

In addition to Sunday worship, I regularly attended the recently established mid-week service, an entire Alpha course, and a series of home group meetings. I also made an effort to attend as many occasional church meetings as I practically could, including the monthly church prayer meeting. As the *Visions* group held their own home group meetings each week, I also attended these whenever possible. Indeed, the way in which these meetings were used for a variety of purposes – from service planning, to prayer, to socialising – enabled me to achieve a perspective on the group from a series of different angles.

---

[1] Penny Edgell Becker, *Congregations in Conflict: Cultural Models of Local Religious Life* (Cambridge: CUP, 1999), p. 55.

I made an effort to engage in conversation with as many people as I possibly could, while also attempting to remain aloof enough not to be seen to be an intrusive presence. I was intent on treading softly and listening carefully,[2] in order to achieve a fair understanding of the life of the congregation. But in addition to this, I found myself learning a great deal through physical participation. Drawing from Bourdieu, Judith Okely notes how the body can be a site of learning in the field, and that we acquire knowledge through practical labour.[3] In reflecting upon the extent and character of my practical engagement in church events, I was able to draw inferences about my acceptance, subjectivity and about the demands of participation made upon regular members.

It was my intention to observe the congregation – or more accurately congregations – of St Michaels in as many different contexts as possible. This approach was grounded in my desire to question how the expression of religious identity is conditioned by contextual factors. In this way I aimed to move beyond many recent studies of Christianity in the UK, which rely on singular forms of data, or upon secondary sources rather than primary observation. Adopting a multi-contextual focus meant that much of the data was drawn from informal conversations with congregational members. These took place after church services and at social occasions to which I was increasingly invited as I became more familiar to the congregation. They proved to be an invaluable resource for information not only on current trends, but also on the past history of the church since its evangelical revival during the 1960s.

I typically took notes privately, following each meeting or significant encounter, in order to maintain some sensitivity towards informants and so that my presence would remain as unobtrusive as possible. I would sometimes make hand-written notes at the earliest opportunity, but most notes would be made at my computer back at the house. In addition to this, I kept a regular field journal, recording more personal reflections and ideas, which eventually ran to four volumes. At first I attempted to record everything, from the layout of the church to the style of dress of church leaders, but later focused more on dialogue as I became accustomed to the physical aspects of the church buildings and as I learned to recognise names and people. I maintained this strategy throughout the fieldwork period, and although my note taking improved over this time, it still proved a demanding and exhausting exercise. This approach was particularly taxing on my memory, and conversations with congregants soon became experiences of significant mental labour, as I simultaneously attempted to achieve meaningful communication, probe for interesting angles, and memorise items that might constitute useful data. I soon learned that I could only take on two substantial meetings each day, as each required

---

[2] R. Stephen Warner, *New Wine in Old Wineskins. Evangelicals and Liberals in a Small-town Church* (Berkeley, Los Angeles, CA, and London: University of California Press, 1988), p. 69.

[3] Okely, Judith, 'Anthropology and Autobiography: Participatory Experience and Embodied Knowledge', in Judith Okely and Helen Callaway (eds.), *Anthropology and Autobiography* (London: Routledge, 1992), pp. 1-28.

intense concentration and an extended period of recollection and note-taking afterwards.

Although recording conversations in this unobtrusive manner remained a challenge throughout the fieldwork, capturing the subtleties of church services was made less problematic because of helpful assistance from the church leaders. The St Michael's office produce official orders of service – including lists of songs, Bible readings and details of role allocation – for the benefit of service leaders. A couple of weeks into my fieldwork, the church co-ordinator offered to post a copy of the order for each service to me in advance each week. In addition to this, each evening service sermon given at St Michael's is tape recorded and maintained in a library, for the benefit of congregants who might have missed the service but who would like to benefit from the teaching. I made a note of each sermon that was particularly illuminating and the church office kindly sent me copies.

My store of observational data rapidly grew and I was able to follow up areas of interest by continually reviewing my notes and field journals. However, I soon became aware of the need to conduct formal, recorded interviews. Ad hoc note-taking was a useful strategy, and had the advantage of remaining relatively unobtrusive, but I was unable to generate quotable data in this way. I was becoming increasingly intrigued by the differing styles of spoken discourse, as represented by the people of St Michael's and by the *Visions* group, but had no way of capturing this. I was also becoming aware of the often disorderly way in which conversations were developing. Although I could direct responses with my questions, an interview context would be far more suited for the gathering of issue-specific data.

Interviews

I began to interview congregants in early December 1999, approaching people informally at first, and often only requesting a formal, recorded interview after initial meetings had helped me establish rapport and familiarity. I was faced with a difficult issue of sampling: how could I go about selecting appropriate people for interview within such a large and diverse church? My sample of interviewees would, for practical reasons, be inevitably small, perhaps twenty-five or thirty people at the most. This amounted to a mere 3% of the entire congregational body. I was conscious that I could easily be faced with an unrepresentative sample, expressing a minority position on key issues, and consequently misconstrue the attitudes of the congregation in so far as they could be presented as a generic whole. I attempted to overcome this problem by making a selection of potential interviewees that reflected the largest variety of spiritual style, church background, service preference and age group that I could possibly identify. This process was of course contingent upon my knowledge of the congregation, and in some ways reflected the friendship networks that I had established in the field. But my familiarity with these people was necessary if this sample was to be authentically representative of the diversity of the congregation. Familiarity was also necessary for a sense of mutual trust and for a genuinely naturalistic rapport. Certain individuals were also interviewed not for reasons of representativeness, but for their valuable perspective on life in St Michael's, including several members of *Visions* (within its core and at its periphery), one former *Visions* member who had re-entered St Michael's, several former members of the church, several long-term members (including some who had been worshipping there since the 1960s), and several of the church leaders, including the vicar, associate minister, curate and one of the lay readers.

By the conclusion of the fieldwork period, I had enjoyed detailed informal conversations in and around church events with over 100 members of the congregation. I had also conducted a total of thirty-three formal interviews, twelve with women and twenty-one with men. This gender bias was not intentional, although several interviewees were members of the church staff or leadership, which was male dominated. Eighteen of these were recorded on dictaphone, subject to prior consent, and transcribed after the fieldwork period had elapsed. The remainder were recorded in note form, either during or after the interview had taken place. This was not generally because of any reluctance of the part of the interviewee, but was due to other factors, usually because sensitive subjects were being addressed, in which case requesting a tape recording would have been inappropriate.

Interviews took place in a variety of locations. I attempted to conduct as many as possible in the homes of interviewees in order to gain some appreciation of their attitudes and life-style as expressed in their domestic context. When this was not possible, I would agree to whichever location was suggested, often a local café, pub or, for some, my own residence in York. Interviews varied considerably in length; the shortest was little more than thirty minutes, the longest was well over two hours. Topics addressed also varied, although I did have a series of issues that I felt needed to be addressed each time, in accordance with the emerging key questions of the project. The following series of questions was used as a basic framework. Because of time constraints, not all of the questions were always covered, and some failed to elicit much of a response. I have highlighted those questions which were prioritised in bold type.

St Michael's: Interview Framework

1. General themes/background:
Tell me a little bit about your life history.
How did you come to faith?
How did you come to be involved in St Michael's? What is your Christian background?
What do you like most about being a part of St Michael's?
What, to you, have been the most significant changes in St Michael's since you arrived?
What do you think it means to be a Christian? How are we saved?
What will happen to those who are not Christians/not saved?

Appendix 1

2. The Bible:
What role does the Bible play in your life?
Is the whole of the Bible to be taken as absolutely true?
How do you deal with conflicts or contradictions in the Bible? Does it contradict the findings of science [evolution?] and if so, how do you deal with this?
What do you struggle with most when reading the Bible?
Can God be found outside of the biblical texts?

3. Worship:
What do you like most about the St Michael's services? When do you feel closest to God?
What is good worship? When does worship become problematic?
What is your view of the worship that occurs at *Visions*?
Do you find the use of charismatic gifts such as tongues or prophecy helpful? If so, how? If not, why not?

4. The World:
What do you think is the most serious problem in the world at the moment?
What is the place of the Christian within our wider culture?
Do you think the church relates well to our wider culture?

5. Morality:
Where, or to whom, do you first turn for moral guidance?
Is it necessary to be a Christian to be a moral person?
Do Christians have political and moral responsibilities as well as spiritual ones? What are they?
What does the word 'evil' describe to you? Where does evil come from?

6. The Church:
In what sense do you consider yourself to be a member of the church?
What is the biggest problem within the church at the present time?
How do you think St Michael's could change for the better in the future?
What do you think poses the biggest threat to the church today?

A slightly adjusted version of this framework was applied to interviewees from the *Visions* group, adding questions about the history of *Visions* and about its relationship with the rest of the St Michael's community.

While this framework served its purpose, i.e., to focus the interviews on a series of key questions, some interviewees clearly had their own sense of what were the important issues. This produced data on a multitude of topics, and all respondents were keen to include lengthy accounts of the history of St Michael's, particularly in relation to changes in clergy, and were also elaborate in their personal testimonies. In this respect their deviations from the interview structure produced useful data, and

I did not attempt to steer the conversation back around to my own questions on these occasions. I also made sure I questioned each interviewee on their perceptions of the relationship between St Michael's and *Visions*. Interviews were transcribed and then used alongside other forms of data in the discernment of patterns of value within both groups.

Document Resources

As fieldwork progressed and I became more and more aware of the rich history of St Michael-le-Belfrey, I also learned of the extensive collection of printed documents which could provide important insights into the life of the church. The church office staff were most generous in their assistance and I made repeated visits to pick up copies of internal reports, old issues of church magazines and newsletters, statistical data, attendance figures, address lists and numerous other invaluable resources. The *Visions* group had also kept an extensive file of notes and reports relating to their own activities over the years and kindly allowed me to photocopy this in its entirety. I also used church documents to build up a demographic profile of the church as a whole. Further data on the rise and fall in attendance levels was provided in archive form by the Borthwick Institute of the University of York, and I was also allowed to note down recent figures in the current service register.

Given its status and reputation, it is unsurprising that St Michael-le-Belfrey has been under the microscope before, and there are several published accounts of its life and work, although this is the first dispassionate, sociological analysis. David Watson's books often reflected on his ministry in York in developing theological arguments, and his autobiography *You Are My God* is particularly illuminating, offering a glimpse of his public life and private struggles.[4] Further essays reflecting on Watson's life and work appear in *David Watson. A Portrait by His Friends*,[5] including a revealing essay on sharing leadership by his parochial successor, Graham Cray. Teddy Saunders and Hugh Sansom's biography of David Watson has been particularly useful, based on rigorous research into his life, including accounts of his time at St Michael's which draw from testimonies from friends, family and fellow parishioners.[6] The church office was also kind enough to send me copies of some important reports written on St Michael's by external observers, including some journalistic accounts and the report composed by the Archbishops' Council on Evangelism after their study of St Michael-le-Belfrey in 1977. In my use of these sources, and of the various other essays published on St Michael's and its leaders, I have sought to be critical but sensitive, reading published accounts alongside personal narratives confided to me whilst conducting this research.

---

[4] David Watson, *You Are My God. An Autobiography* (Seven Oaks: Hodder and Stoughton, 1983).

[5] Edward England (ed.), *David Watson. A Portrait by his Friends* (Crowborough: Highland Books, 1985).

[6] Teddy Saunders and Hugh Sansom, *David Watson. A Biography* (London, Sydney, Auckland: Hodder and Stoughton, 1992).

Appendix 1

The Questionnaire Survey

My questionnaire survey of the St Michael-le-Belfrey congregation was administered in May 2000. The aim of the survey was to explore the religious and moral values of the community, the Christian background of members, and the active expression of Christian belief within the context of behaviour and church involvement. The desired outcome was a general portrait of the community and of the value differences within it. Strong claims about the community are not based on the survey data alone, but are informed by the survey, as it has been interpreted in the light of qualitative data gathered during the fieldwork period. In this way I follow Peter Berger's comment that quantitative methods have a role, 'as long as they are used to clarify the meanings operative in the situation being studied'.[7]

I was hoping that the survey would produce a representative picture of the St Michael-le-Belfrey community and selected a congregational sample, targeting them as respondents. The leadership of the church agreed to finance the printing of 200 questionnaires, approximately one quarter of the total community. As I was unable to finance the printing of any larger number, or deal with the processing of a larger sample of data, the target sample was set at 200.

The sample was based on the address list of the church. Long-standing attendees are already on this list, and newcomers are invited, at each service, to fill in a 'welcome' form should they wish to make St Michael's their home church. Those who fill in the form are then added to the address list. The address list is distributed to all those included on it each year and lists names alphabetically, also providing a postal address and contact telephone number for each individual. Consequently, the gender distribution of the community can be calculated on the basis of this list. In order to get a more detailed picture of the demographic spread of the community, I asked three independent, long-standing members to look through the list with me, including the church co-ordinator, providing the approximate age and occupation of each person on the list. In this way, I was able to piece together a reasonably accurate picture of the community, according to factors of gender, age and social class (gauged according to occupation).

Once the list had been adjusted in the light of recent departures, it ran to a total of 738 names. Although some teenagers are listed, the general policy is to include only adults on the list. (Young children and youths are included instead on the youth groups' prayer list, also distributed annually.) On the basis of the age and gender distribution of the congregation (summarised in chapter 3), a stratified random sample of names was selected from the address list. Certain individuals on the list had to be excluded from the sample. These individuals fell into one of two groups. First, those individuals who belong to the *Visions* group, that I originally intended to survey as a separate community at a later date, using an adjusted version of the questionnaire. Second, a group of thirty individuals who had recently been targeted as

---

[7] Quoted in Robert Wuthnow *et al*, *Cultural Analysis. The Work of Peter L. Berger, Mary Douglas, Michel Foucault and Jurgen Habermas* (London, Boston, Melbourne and Henley: Routledge and Kegan Paul, 1984), p. 74.

respondents for an internally distributed questionnaire on church growth. I was advised by the church that any attempt to approach these individuals for a second time could be seen as pastorally insensitive. Consequently, when any of these names was selected randomly, I passed over them in favour of the following randomly selected name.

The questionnaires were sealed together with a covering letter and an addressed return envelope. They were individually labelled and left for parishioners to pick up from their pigeonholes in the church narthex on Sunday 28 May 2000. Respondents were informed in the enclosed instructions to either take completed questionnaires to the church office, or alternatively place them in a marked box situated in the narthex of the church. The questionnaires were left in the pigeonholes for a period of four weeks. At this point, the remaining questionnaires were kindly posted on directly to respondents by the church co-ordinator.

I kept in touch with the church co-ordinator over the summer months in order to gauge the gradual return of the questionnaires. By mid August, at which point it appeared that a peak response level had been achieved, I returned to York to collect the completed questionnaires. A total of sixty-seven had been returned, amounting to a 34% response rate. The gender distribution of the collected sample was 36% males, 60% female, while 4.5% gave no answer. Fortunately, this showed no significant divergence from the 60:40 divide that was the initial target of the survey. The age distribution of the return sample was less in line with the congregational trends, with the '20s' cohort particularly under-represented and the 70s+ category over represented. This may have been because some students were not attending church so regularly during their exam period, or perhaps could not find time to complete the questionnaire. Whatever the reason, it was subsequently impossible to make strong claims about the '20s' age group on the basis of survey data alone

The survey data was dealt with in two ways. Quantifiable data was inputted into the SPSS programme and frequency and cross-tabulation analysis was used to explore patterns in member attitudes. Discursive data was analysed separately, but still in conjunction with individual profiles.

It was my original intention to also use a postal questionnaire to survey the *Visions* group. This would have used similar questions to the St Michael's questionnaire, for comparative purposes, but would also have included questions specific to the *Visions* group. Subsequently, I decided not to survey the group for several reasons. First, by the time I left the field, I already had a vast amount of data on the group, and many of the issues addressed in the questionnaire had been explored with individual *Visions* members through informal conversation and interviews. Second, part of the reason for administering the St Michael's questionnaire amounted to an attempt to deal with the size of the congregation. This was not an issue with the *Visions* group and I had got to know most of its ten or so core members fairly well during my stay in the field. Third, and most importantly, following my departure, the *Visions* group entered a difficult phase in its development. Several members who had been involved since its inception left the group following a change in employment. With the group showing few signs of recruiting new committed members, numbers were seriously depleted. This was a sensitive time for *Visions*, and certain indications suggested that further interference from distanced outsiders, including myself, would only exacerbate existing frustrations. It was consequently out of respect and sensitivity to the group, whose efforts and time were already stretched to the limit, that I decided not to ask them to complete survey questionnaires.

Ethics

It is a testimony to the confidence and generosity of the St Michael-le-Belfrey congregation that I was allowed free and welcome access to most meetings. Similarly, few members expressed any discomfort with my being among them and no sense of suspicion was directed at my work. Even so, throughout the fieldwork period and in subsequent work, I have made the utmost effort to respect the ongoing life of the church and the privacy of church members. I secured permission from the vicar and church co-ordinator before embarking on the study, and discussed my findings with them whenever possible. They were also given prior copies of the questionnaire for purposes of consent and feedback. As a means of sharing my findings, I also compiled a summary of questionnaire data for use by the church leadership. Once my findings had been written up, several members of the church read through various sections, either of my original PhD thesis, or of the manuscript of this book. I am most grateful for their feedback, which helped me refine my interpretation and alerted me to errors I had overlooked.

I remained completely open during the research period about my intentions as a sociological researcher, though this was confided in informal conversation. I did not announce my plans to the congregation because I wished to engage the trust of individuals on a face-to-face basis and the church leadership expressed no desire for me to make an announcement of this kind.

It was decided that the church would be named for several reasons. First, St Michael's being such a well-known church, to disguise the church but not its location would be futile. And to disguise its location would preclude the discussion of illuminating factors of context. Second, to disguise the church would rule out any presentation of crucial historical factors which are necessary to any full account of the church's growth and development. Thirdly, St Michael's itself – both leaders and parishioners – expressed no discomfort whatsoever with the notion of their church being named. Indeed, their sense of pride and evangelistic passion meant that many would be disappointed if it were not. However, the names of individuals have all been changed in order to protect their privacy. With the consent of the church leadership, I have named the church and, in doing this, have removed any point to disguising the identities of its incumbents. Hence the names of its four most recent vicars, covering the last forty years, are explicitly associated with the various developments that occurred during their incumbencies.

When addressing contentious topics, I have deliberately sought out a variety of perspectives and advice from leaders, in order that a balanced and fair portrayal of events might be presented. When I have been privy to confidential information I have kept it so.

APPENDIX 2

Visions Sung Creed[1]

I believe in God
I believe in Christ,
Who died to save us.
I believe in the Spirit's power
The Giver of all Life. (x2)

I don't believe in apathy
I don't believe in war.
I don't believe in bigotry
Or homophobia.
I don't believe in sexism
Or racism or hate.
I believe in the coming
Of the Heaven-on-Earth You'll make.

I don't believe in money,
And I don't believe in hype.
I don't believe an instant product
Will make the world right.
I don't believe that taking pills
Will bring you happiness
I don't believe to crush the poor
Will make you a success.

I believe in God
I believe in Christ,
Who died to save us.
I believe in the Spirit's power
The Giver of all Life. (x2)

---

[1] Reproduced here with the kind permission of Sue Wallace, on behalf of the *Visions* group.

I believe in God.
I believe in a
Passionate Creator
I believe in Jesus
Who's Humanity Divine. (x2)

I believe in God.
I believe in the Planet of the Future.
I believe in the coming
Of our resurrected life. (x2)

Bibliography

Abercrombie, Nicholas *et al*, 'Superstition and Religion: The God of the Gaps', in David Martin and Michael Hill (eds) *A Sociological Yearbook of Religion in Britain* (London: SCM Press, 1970), pp. 93-129.

Allgaier, Joachim and Richard Holliman, 'The Emergence of the Controversy Around the Theory of Evolution and Creationism in UK Newspaper Reports', *The Curriculum Journal* 17:3 (September, 2006), pp. 263-279.

Ammerman, Nancy T. *et al*, *Congregation and Community* (New Brunswick, NJ: Rutgers University Press, 1997).

Baker, Jonny, Doug Gay with Jenny Brown, *Alternative Worship* (London: SPCK, 2003).

Balmer, R.H., *Mine Eyes Have Seen the Glory. A Journey into the Evangelical Subculture in America*, (Oxford: OUP, 2000).

Bartholomew, Richard, 'Publishing, Celebrity, and the Globalisation of Conservative Protestantism', *Journal of Contemporary Religion* 21:1 (2006), pp. 1-13.

Bates, Stephen, 'Children should be 'told of Hell': Liberals twitch as Evangelicals turn to Fire and Brimstone', *The Guardian* 15 April 2000, p. 9.

Bauman, Zigmunt, *Intimations of Postmodernity* (London and New York: Routledge, 1992).

— *Postmodernity and its Discontents* (Cambridge: Polity, 1997).

— *Community. Seeking Safety in an Insecure World* (Cambridge: Polity, 2001).

Baumann, Gerd, *Contesting Culture. Discourses of Identity in Multi-Ethnic London*, (Cambridge, New York and Melbourne: CUP, 1996).

Baumgartner, M.P., *The Moral Order of a Suburb* (New York: OUP, 1988).

Beall, Patricia, 'A Place to Grow', in Jeane Hinton (ed.) *Renewal. An Emerging Pattern* (Poole: Celebration Publishing, 1980), pp. 142-147.

Beaudoin, Tom, *Virtual Faith. The Irreverent Spiritual Quest of Generation X* (San Francisco: Jossey Bass Inc., 1998).

Bebbington, David, *Evangelicalism in Modern Britain - A History from the 1730s to the 1980s* (London: Unwin Hyman, 1989).

— 'Evangelical Social Influence in North Atlantic Societies', in M.A. Noll, D.W. Bebbington and G.A. Rawlyk (eds), *Evangelicalism. Comparative Studies of Popular Protestantism in North America, the British Isles, and Beyond, 1700-1990* (New York and Oxford: OUP, 1994), pp. 113-136.

— 'Evangelicalism in its Settings: the British and American Movements since 1940', in M.A. Noll, D.W. Bebbington and G.A. Rawlyk (eds), *Evangelicalism. Comparative Studies of Popular Protestantism in North America, the British Isles, and Beyond, 1700-1990* (New York and Oxford: OUP, 1994), pp 365-88.

— 'The Decline and Resurgence of Evangelical Social Concern: 1918-1980', in John Wolffe (ed.), *Evangelical Faith and Public Zeal. Evangelicals and Society in Britain 1780-1980* (London: SPCK, 1995), pp. 175-197.

Beck, Ulrich, *Risk Society. Towards a New Modernity* (London: Sage, 1992).

Becker, Penny Edgell, *Congregations in Conflict. Cultural Models of Local Religious Life* (Cambridge: CUP, 1999).

Beckford, James A. *Religion and Advanced Industrial Society* (London: Unwin Hyman, 1989).

— 'Religion, Modernity and Postmodernity', in Bryan R. Wilson (ed.), *Religion. Contemporary Issues, the All Souls Seminars in the Sociology of Religion* (London: Belew Publishing, 1992), pp. 11-23.

Bellah, Robert *et al*, *Habits of the Heart. Individualism and Commitment in American Life* (Berkeley, Los Angeles and London: University of California Press, 1985).

Berger, Peter L., *The Sacred Canopy. Elements of a Sociological Theory of Religion* (Garden City, NY: Doubleday and Co., Inc, 1967).

— *A Rumour of Angels. Modern Society and the Rediscovery of the Supernatural* (London: Penguin, 1969).

— *The Heretical Imperative. Contemporary Possibilities of Religious Affirmation* (London: Collins, 1980).

— *A Far Glory. The Quest for Faith in an Age of Credulity* (New York: The Free Press, 1992).

— 'The Desecularization of the World. A Global Overview', in P. Berger (ed.), *The Desecularization of the World. Essays on the Resurgence of Religion in World Politics* (Washington: Ethics and Public Policy Centre; Grand Rapids: William B. Eerdmans, 1999), pp. 1-18.

Berger, Peter L. and Thomas Luckmann, *The Social Construction of Reality. A Treatise in the Sociology of Knowledge* (London, Fakenham and Reading: Penguin, 1967).

Berger, Peter L., Brigitte Berger and Hansfried Kellner, *The Homeless Mind. Modernization and Consciousness* (New York: Vintage Books, 1974).

Beyer, Peter, *Religion and Globalization* (London, Thousand Oaks, New Delhi: Sage Publications, 1994).

Bosch, David, *Transforming Mission. Paradigm Shifts in Theology of Mission* (New York: Orbis, 1991).

Brasher, Brenda, *Godly Women. Fundamentalism and Female Power* (New Brunswick, NJ and London: Rutgers University Press, 1998).

Brierley, Peter, *Christian England. What the 1989 English Church Census Reveals* (London: MARC Europe, 1991).

— *The Tide is Running Out. What the English Church Attendance Survey Reveals* (London: Christian Research, 2000).

— *Turning the Tide. The Challenge Ahead; Report of the 2002 Scottish Church Census* (London: Christian Research, 2003).

— *Pulling Out of the Nosedive. A Contemporary Picture of Churchgoing* (London: Christian Research, 2006).
— *Religious Trends 6* (London: Christian Research, 2006).
Brierley, Peter and Heather Wraight (eds), *UK Christian Handbook, 1996/7 Edition* (Bromley: Christian Research, 1995).
Briers, Stephen J., 'Negotiating with Babylon: Responses to Modernity within a Restorationist Community' (PhD thesis, University of Cambridge, 1993).
Brown, Callum, *The Death of Christian Britain* (London and New York: Routledge, 2001).
Bruce, Steve, *Firm in the Faith* (Aldershot: Gower, 1984).
— *A House Divided. Protestantism, Schism and Secularization* (London: Routledge, 1989).
— *Religion in Modern Britain* (Oxford: OUP, 1995).
— *Fundamentalism* (Cambridge: Polity, 2000).
— *God is Dead. Secularization in the West* (Oxford and Malden, MA: Blackwell, 2002).
Calver, Clive, 'Afterword: Hope for the Future', in Wolffe (ed.) *Evangelical Faith and Public Zeal*, pp. 198-210.
Capon, John, *... And There Was Light. Story of the Nationwide Festival of Light* (London: Lutterworth Press, 1972).
— *Evangelicals Tomorrow. A Popular Report of Nottingham '77, the National Evangelical Anglican Congress* (Glasgow: Fount Paperbacks, 1977).
Carrette, Jeremy and Richard King, *Selling Spirituality. The Silent Takeover of Religion* (Abingdon: Routledge, 2005).
Cartledge, Mark J., 'The Future of Glossolalia: Fundamentalist or Experientialist?', *Religion* 28 (1998), pp. 233-44.
Castells, Manuel, *The Information Age. Economy, Society and Culture, Vol. III: End of Millennium* (Malden, Massachusetts and Oxford: Blackwell, 1998).
Chambers, Paul, 'Factors in Church Growth and Decline (with Reference to the Secularisation Thesis)' (PhD thesis, University of Wales, 1999).
— 'The Effects of Evangelical Renewal on Mainstream Congregational Identities: A Welsh Case Study', in M. Guest, K. Tusting and L. Woodhead (eds), *Congregational Studies in the UK. Christianity in a Post-Christian Context* (Aldershot: Ashgate, 2004), pp. 57-69.
— *Religion, Secularization and Social Change in Wales. Congregational Studies in a Post-Christian Society* (Cardiff: University of Wales Press, 2005).
Churches Information for Mission, *Faith in Life. A Snapshot of Church Life at the Beginning of the 21st Century* (London: Churches Information for Mission, 2001).
Cohen, Anthony P., *The Symbolic Construction of Community* (Chichester: Ellis Horwood, 1985).
Coleman, Simon, 'Words as Things: Language, Aesthetics and the Objectification of Protestant Evangelicalism', *Journal of Material Culture* 1 (1) (1996), pp. 107-28.
— *The Globalisation of Charismatic Christianity. Spreading the Gospel of Prosperity* (Cambridge: CUP, 2000).

Coleman, Simon and Peter Collins, 'The 'Plain' and the 'Positive': Ritual, Experience and Aesthetics in Quakerism and Charismatic Christianity', *Journal of Contemporary Religion* 15:3 (2000), pp. 317-329.

Collins, Peter, 'Congregations, Narratives and Identity: A Quaker Case Study', in M. Guest, K. Tusting and L. Woodhead (eds), *Congregational Studies in the UK. Christianity in a Post-Christian Context* (Aldershot: Ashgate, 2004), pp. 99-112.

Coser, Lewis, *The Functions of Social Conflict* (New York: The Free Press, 1956).

Coupland, Douglas, *Generation X. Tales for An Accelerated Culture* (London: Abacus, 1991).

Cox, Harvey, *Fire from Heaven. The Rise of Pentecostal Spirituality and the Reshaping of Religion in the Twenty-First Century* (London: Cassell, 1996).

Cray, Graham, 'A Renewed Community as a Sign of the Kingdom: Lessons from St Michael-le-Belfrey, York, England', in Bill Burnett (ed.), *By My Spirit. Renewal in the Worldwide Anglican Church* (London, Sydney, Auckland, Toronto: Hodder & Stoughton, 1988), pp. 127-52.

— et al, *The Post-Evangelical Debate* (London: SPCK, 1997).

Crouch, Andy, 'The Emerging Mystique', *Christianity Today* 48:11 (2004), pp. 36-43.

Csordas, Thomas J., 'Genre, Motive, and Metaphor: Conditions for Creativity in Ritual Language', *Cultural Anthropology* 2:4 (1987), pp. 445-469.

— *Language, Charisma and Creativity. The Ritual Life of a Religious Movement* (Berkeley: University of California Press, 1997).

Dandelion, Pink, *A Sociological Analysis of the Theology of Quakers. The Silent Revolution* (Lewiston, Queenston, Lampeter: Edwin Mellen Press, 1996).

Davie, Grace, *Religion in Britain Since 1945. Believing Without Belonging* (Oxford: Blackwell, 1994).

— *Religion in Modern Europe. A Memory Mutates* (Oxford: OUP, 2000).

Doctrine Commission of the Church of England, *The Mystery of Salvation. The Story of God's Gift* (London: Church House Publishing, 1997).

Douglas, Mary, *Purity and Danger. An Analysis of the Concepts of Pollution and Taboo* (London: Routledge, 1966).

Dowie, Al, *Interpreting Culture in a Scottish Congregation* (New York: Lang, 2002).

Durkheim, Emile, *The Elementary Forms of Religious Life* (trans. with an introduction by Karen E. Fields), (New York: The Free Press, 1995 [orig. 1912]).

Edwards, David L., *The Futures of Christianity. An Analysis of Historical, Contemporary and Future Trends within the Worldwide Church* (London, Sydney, Auckland and Toronto: Hodder & Stoughton, 1987).

— *Essentials. A Liberal-Evangelical Dialogue* (London: Hodder & Stoughton, 1988).

Ellwood, Robert S., *The Sixties Spiritual Awakening. American Religion Moving from Modern to Postmodern* (New Brunswick, NJ: Rutgers University Press, 1994).

England, Edward (ed.), *David Watson. A Portrait by his Friends* (Crowborough: Highland Books, 1985).
Eisenstadt, S.N., *Fundamentalism, Sectarianism and Revolution. The Jacobin Dimension of Modernity* (Cambridge: CUP, 1999).
Evangelical Alliance, *The Nature of Hell* (Carlisle: Acute, 2000).
Evans-Pritchard, E.E., *Witchcraft, Oracles and Magic Among the Azande* (Oxford: Clarendon Press, 1976).
Fine, Gary Alan, 'Small Groups and Culture Creation: The Idioculture of Little League Baseball Teams', *American Sociological Review* 44 (1979), pp. 733-745.
Finke, Roger and Rodney Stark, *The Churching of America 1776-1990. Winners and Losers in Our Religious Economy* (New Brunswick, NJ: Rutgers University Press, 1992).
Flory, Richard and Donald E. Miller (eds), *GenX Religion* (New York and London: Routledge, 2000).
Fox, Matthew, *Original Blessing. A Primer in Creation Spirituality Presented in Four Paths, Twenty-six Themes, and Two Questions* (Santa Fe, NM: Bear & Co., 1983).
Francis, Leslie J., 'Evangelical Identity Among Young People', *Anvil* 15 (4), pp. 254-67.
Francis, Leslie J. and David W. Lankshear, 'The Comparative Strength of Evangelical and Catholic Anglican Churches in England', *Journal of Empirical Theology* 9:1 (1996), pp. 5-22.
Francis, Leslie J., David W. Lankshear and Susan H. Jones, 'The Influence of the Charismatic Movement on Local Church Life: A Comparative Study Among Anglican Rural, Urban and Suburban Churches', *Journal of Contemporary Religion* 15 (1) (2000), pp. 121-30.
Frith, Simon, *Performing Rites. Evaluating Popular Music* (Oxford and New York: OUP, 1996).
Garfinkel, Harold, *Studies in Ethnomethodology* (Cambridge: Polity Press, 1984).
Geertz, Clifford, 'Ethos, World View, and the Analysis of Sacred Symbols', in *The Interpretation of Cultures* (New York: Basic Books, 1973), pp. 126-141.
— *Works and Lives. The Anthropologist as Author* (Cambridge: Polity Press, 1988).
Gehlen, Arnold, *Man in the Age of Technology* (New York: Columbia University Press, 1980).
Gibbs, Eddie and Ryan K. Bolger, *Emerging Churches. Creating Christian Community in Postmodern Cultures* (London: SPCK, 2006).
Giddens, Anthony, *The Consequences of Modernity* (Cambridge: Polity Press, 1990).
— *Modernity and Self Identity. Self and Society and the Late Modern Age* (Oxford: Polity, 1991).
Gill, Robin, *The Myth of the Empty Church* (London: SPCK, 1993).
— *Churchgoing and Christian Ethics* (Cambridge: CUP, 1999).
— *The Empty Church Revisited* (Aldershot: Ashgate, 2003).

Gilliat-Ray, Sophie, 'The Fate of the Anglican Clergy and the Class of '97: Some Implications of the Changing Sociological Profile of Ordinands', *Journal of Contemporary Religion* 16:2 (2001), pp. 209-225.

Gledhill, R. 'Blessed by the Spirit', *The Times*, 24 February 1996.

Goldthorpe, J. and G. Marshall, 'The Promising Future of Class Analysis: A Response to Recent Critiques', *Sociology* 26 (3), pp. 381-400.

Grenz, Stanley J. and Roger E. Olson, *20th Century Theology. God and the World in a Transitional Age* (Carlisle: Paternoster, 1992).

Guest, Mathew, '"Alternative Worship": Challenging the Boundaries of the Christian Faith', in E. Arweck and M. Stringer (eds), *Theorising Faith. The Insider/Outsider Problem in the Study of Ritual* (Birmingham: University of Birmingham Press, 2002), pp. 35-56.

— 'Negotiating Community: An Ethnographic Study of an Evangelical Church' (PhD thesis, Lancaster University, 2002).

— '"Friendship, Fellowship and Acceptance": The Public Discourse of a Thriving Evangelical Congregation', in M. Guest, K. Tusting and L. Woodhead (eds), *Congregational Studies in the UK. Christianity in a Post-Christian Context* (Aldershot: Ashgate, 2004), pp. 71-84.

— 'Reconceiving the Congregation as a Source of Authenticity', in Jane Garnet *et al* (eds), *Redefining Christian Britain. Post-1945 Perspectives* (London: SCM Press, 2007), pp. 63-72.

— 'In Search of Spiritual Capital: The Spiritual as a Cultural Resource', in K. Flanagan and P. Jupp (eds), *A Sociology of Spirituality* (Aldershot: Ashgate, 2007), pp. 181-200.

Guest, Mathew and Steve Taylor, 'The Post-Evangelical Emerging Church: Innovations in New Zealand and the UK', *International Journal for the Study of the Christian Church* 6:1 (2006), pp. 49-64.

Guest, Mathew, Karin Tusting and Linda Woodhead (eds), *Congregational Studies in the UK. Christianity in a Post-Christian Context* (Aldershot: Ashgate, 2004).

Gumbel, Nicky, *A Life Worth Living* (Eastborne: Kingsway Publications, 1994).

— *Questions of Life* (London: Kingsway, 2001).

Hall, Ian R., 'The Current Evangelical Resurgence: An Analysis and Evaluation of the Growth of Contemporary Evangelicalism in Britain and the USA' (PhD thesis, University of Leeds, 1994).

Harvey, David, 'Cell Church: Its Situation in British Evangelical Culture', *Journal of Contemporary Religion* 18:1 (2003), pp. 95-109.

Hastings, Adrian, *A History of English Christianity, 1920-1985* (London: Fount Paperbacks, 1987).

Hatch, Nathan, *The Democratisation of American Christianity* (New Haven, CT: Yale University Press, 1989).

Heelas, Paul, *The New Age Movement. The Celebration of the Self and the Sacralization of Modernity* (Oxford: Blackwell, 1996).

— 'Introduction: On Differentiation and Dedifferentiation', in P. Heelas (ed.), *Religion, Modernity and Postmodernity* (Oxford: Blackwell, 1998), pp. 1-18.

Heelas, Paul and Linda Woodhead, 'Homeless Minds Today?', in Linda Woodhead (ed.), *Peter Berger and the Study of Religion* (London and New York: Routledge, 2000), pp. 43-72.
Heelas, Paul and Linda Woodhead (with Benjamin Seel, Bronislaw Szerszynski and Karin Tusting), *The Spiritual Revolution. Why Religion is Giving Way to Spirituality* (Malden, MA, Oxford and Carlton, Victoria: Blackwell, 2005).
Heelas, Paul, Scott Lash and Paul Morris (eds), *Detraditionalization. Critical Reflections on Authority and Identity* (Oxford: Blackwell, 1996).
Hetherington, Kevin, *Expressions of Identity. Space, Performance, Politics* (London: Sage, 1998).
Hilborn, David, *Picking Up the Pieces. Can Evangelicals Adapt to Contemporary Culture?* (London: Hodder & Stoughton, 1997).
Hinton, Michael, *The Anglican Parochial Clergy. A Celebration* (London, SCM Press, 1994).
Hirst, Rob, 'Social Networks and Personal Beliefs: An Example from Modern Britain', in G. Davie, P. Heelas and L. Woodhead (eds), *Predicting Religion. Christian, Secular and Alternative Futures* (Aldershot: Ashgate, 2003), pp. 86-94.
Hoover, Stewart, *Mass Media Religion. The Social Sources of the Electronic Church* (Newbury Park, CA: Sage, 1988).
Hopewell, James F., *Congregation. Stories and Structures* (London: SCM Press, 1988).
Howard, Roland, *The Rise and Fall of the Nine O'Clock Service* (London: Mowbray, 1996).
Hunt, Stephen, 'The "Toronto Blessing": A Rumour of Angels?', *Journal of Contemporary Religion* 10 (3) (1995), pp. 257-272.
— *The Alpha Enterprise. Evangelism in a Post-Christian Era* (Aldershot: Ashgate, 2004).
Hunter, James D., 'The New Religions: Demodernization and the Protest Against Modernity', in B.R. Wilson (ed.), *The Social Impact of New Religious Movements* (Barrytown, NY: Unification Theological Seminary, 1981), pp. 1-19.
— 'Subjectivisation and the New Evangelical Theodicy', *Journal for the Scientific Study of Religion* 20: 1 (1982), pp. 39-47.
— *American Evangelicalism. Conservative Religion and the Quandary of Modernity* (New Brunswick, NJ: Rutgers University Press, 1983).
— *Evangelicalism. The Coming Generation* (Chicago, IL, and London: University of Chicago Press, 1987).
— *Culture Wars. The Struggle to Define America* (New York: Basic Books, 1991).
Jensen, Lori, 'When Two Worlds Collide: Generation X Culture and Conservative Evangelicalism', in Richard Flory and Donald E. Miller (eds), *GenX Religion* (New York and London: Routledge, 2000), pp. 139-162.
Johnson, Douglas, *Contending for the Faith. A History of the Evangelical Movement in the Universities and Colleges* (Leicester: Inter-Varsity Press, 1979).
Jowell, Roger et al, *British Social Attitudes, the 16th Report. Who Shares New Labour Values?* (Aldershot: Ashgate, 1999).

— *British Social Attitudes, the 17th Report. Focusing on Diversity* (London, Thousand Oaks, New Delhi: Sage, 2000).
Kelley, Dean, *Why Conservative Churches are Growing* (New York: Harper and Row, 1972).
Kemp, Daren, 'The Christaquarians? A Sociology of Christians in the New Age' (PhD thesis, King's College, London, 1999).
Kepel, Gilles, *The Revenge of God. The Resurgence of Islam, Christianity and Judaism in the Modern World* (University Park, PA: Pennsylvania State University Press, 1994).
Kimball, Dan, *The Emerging Church. Vintage Christianity for New Generations* (Grand Rapids, MI: Zondervan, 2003).
Luckmann, Thomas, *The Invisible Religion. The Problem of Religion in Modern Society* (New York: Macmillan, 1967).
Lynch, Gordon, *After Religion. Generation X and the Search for Meaning* (London: Darton, Longman and Todd, 2002).
Lyon, David, *Jesus in Disneyland. Religion in Postmodern Times* (Cambridge: Polity, 2000).
Lyotard, Jean-Francois, *The Postmodern Condition* (Manchester: Manchester University Press, 1984).
Maffesoli, Michel, *The Time of the Tribes. The Decline of Individualism in Mass Society* (London: Sage, 1996).
Marcuse, Herbert, 'Repressive Tolerance', in R.P. Wolff, B. Moore and H. Marcuse (eds), *A Critique of Pure Tolerance* (London: Jonathan Cape, 1969), pp. 95-137.
Marsden, George, 'Evangelicalism and Fundamental Christianity', in Mircea Eliade (ed.), *The Encyclopedia of Religion, Vol. 5* (New York: Macmillan, 1987), pp. 190-197.
Martin, Bernice, 'From Pre- to Post-Modernity in Latin America: The Case of Pentecostalism', in P. Heelas (ed.), *Religion, Modernity and Postmodernity* (Oxford: Blackwell, 1998), pp. 102-146.
Martin, David, *A Sociology of English Religion* (London: SCM, 1967).
— *A General Theory of Secularisation* (London: Basil Blackwell, 1978).
— *Tongues of Fire. The Explosion of Protestantism in Latin America* (Oxford: Blackwell, 1990).
— *Pentecostalism. The World their Parish* (Oxford: Blackwell, 2002).
— 'Evangelical Christianity: A Review', in *Christian Language and its Mutations. Essays in Sociological Understanding* (Aldershot: Ashgate, 2002), pp. 187-205.
Matheson, Jill and Carol Summerfield (eds), *Social Trends, no. 31* (London: The Stationery Office, 2001).
Mayo, Simon and Martin Wroe, 'Put Young People at Risk, Please', *Church Times* 18 February 2000, p. 8.
McConkey, Dale, 'Whither Hunter's Culture War? Shifts in Evangelical Morality, 1988-1998', *Sociology of Religion* 62:2 (2001), pp. 149-174.
McGuire, Meredith, *Pentecostal Catholics. Power, Charisma and Order in a Religious Movement* (Philadelphia, PA: Temple University Press, 1982).

McLaren, Brian, *A Generous Orthodoxy* (Grand Rapids, MI: Zondervan, 2004).
McLeod, Hugh, *The Religious Crisis of the 1960s* (Oxford: OUP, 2007).
McLuhan, Marshall, *Understanding Media. the Extensions of Man* (London: Routledge, 2001 [original 1964]).
McPhee, Arthur, *Friendship Evangelism. The Caring Way to Share Your Faith* (Eastbourne: Kingsway, 1978).
Medhurst, Kenneth and George Moyser, *Church and Politics in a Secular Age* (Oxford: Clarendon Press, 1988).
Mestrovic, Stjepan G., *Postemotional Society* (London, Thousand Oaks, New Delhi: Sage, 1997).
Miller, Donald E., *The Case for Liberal Christianity* (London: SCM Press, 1981).
— *Reinventing American Protestantism. Christianity in the New Millennium* (Berkeley and Los Angeles, CA: University of California Press, 1997).
— 'Routinizing Charisma: The Vineyard Christian Fellowship in the Post-Wimber Era', *Pneuma* 25:2 (Fall, 2003), pp. 216-239.
Mission Shaped Church. Church Planting and Fresh Expressions of Church in a Changing Context (London: Church House Publishing, 2004).
Neighbour, Ralph, *Where Do We Go From Here? A Guidebook for the Cell Group Church* (Houston, TX: Touch Publications, 2000).
Niebuhr, H. Richard, *Christ and Culture* (London: Faber, 1952).
— *The Social Sources of Denominationalism* (New York: Meridian, 1962).
Noll, Mark A., 'The Historical Maturity of the Sociology of Religion', *Evangelical Studies Bulletin* 6 (2) (1989), pp. 1-5.
— *The Scandal of the Evangelical Mind* (Grand Rapids, MI: Eerdmans, 1994).
— *American Evangelical Christianity. An Introduction* (Oxford, UK and Malden, MA: Blackwell, 2001).
Noll, Mark A., David W. Bebbington and George A. Rawlyk (eds), *Evangelicalism. Comparative Studies of Popular Protestantism in North America, the British Isles, and Beyond, 1700-1990* (New York and Oxford: OUP, 1994).
Okely, Judith, 'Anthropology and Autobiography: Participatory Experience and Embodied Knowledge', in Judith Okely and Helen Callaway (eds), *Anthropology and Autobiography* (London: Routledge, 1992), pp. 1-28.
Packer, J.I., 'Keswick and the Reformed Doctrine of Sanctification', *Evangelical Quarterly* 27 (1955), pp. 153-167.
— *The Evangelical Anglican Identity Problem. An Analysis* (Oxford: Latimer House, 1978).
Penning, James M. and Corwin E. Smidt, *Evangelicalism. The Next Generation* (Grand Rapids, MI: Baker Academic, 2002).
Percy, Martyn, *Words, Wonders and Power. Understanding Contemporary Fundamentalism and Revivalism* (London: SPCK, 1996).
— 'Review Article: The Post-Evangelical', *Journal of Contemporary Religion* 11:3 (1996), p. 357-60.
— *Power and the Church. Ecclesiology in an Age of Transition* (London: Cassell, 1998).

— 'A Place at High Table? Assessing the Future of Charismatic Christianity', in G. Davie, P. Heelas and L. Woodhead (eds), *Predicting Religion. Christian, Secular and Alternative Futures* (Aldershot: Ashgate, 2003), pp. 95-108.
— 'A Blessed Rage for Order: Exploring the Rise of 'Reform' in the Church of England', *Journal of Anglican Studies* 3:1 (2005), pp. 33-52.
— 'Adventure and Atrophy in a Charismatic Movement: Returning to the 'Toronto Blessing'', *Journal of Contemporary Religion* 20 (1) (2005), pp. 71- 90.
Porter, Matthew, *David Watson. Evangelism, Renewal, Reconciliation* (Cambridge, Grove, 2003).
Poulton, John, 'St Michael-le-Belfrey', in Edward England (ed.), *David Watson. A Portrait by his Friends* (Crowborough: Highland Books, 1985), pp. 119-136.
Quebedeaux, Richard, *The Worldly Evangelicals* (San Francisco: Harper and Row, 1978).
Riddell, Mike, Mark Pierson and Cathy Kirkpatrick, *The Prodigal Project. Journey into The Emerging Church* (London: SPCK, 2000).
Ritzer, George, *The McDonaldization of Society. An Investigation into the Changing Character of Contemporary Social Life* (Thousand Oaks: Pine Forge Press, 1996).
Roberts, Paul, *Alternative Worship in the Church of England* (Cambridge: Grove, 1999).
Robinson, John A.T., *Honest to God* (London: SCM, 1963).
Ronson, Jon, 'Catch Me If You Can', *The Guardian Weekend*, 21 October 2000, p. 19.
Roof, Wade Clark, *Community and Commitment. Religious Plausibility in a Liberal Protestant Church* (New York: Elsevier, 1978).
— *A Generation of Seekers. The Spiritual Journeys of the Baby Boomer Generation* (New York: HarperCollins, 1993).
Ruthven, Jonathan, 'Back to the Future for Pentecostal/Charismatic Evangelicals in North America and World Wide: Radicalizing Evangelical Theology and Practice', in Craig Bartholomew *et al* (eds), *The Futures of Evangelicalism. Issues and Prospects* (Leicester: Inter-Varsity Press, 2003), pp. 302-315.
Saliba, John A., *Christian Responses to the New Age Movement. A Critical Assessment* (London: Cassell, 1999).
Saunders, Teddy and Hugh Sansom, *David Watson. A Biography* (Sevenoaks: Hodder & Stoughton, 1992).
Saward, Michael, *The Anglican Church Today. Evangelicals on the Move* (Oxford: Mowbrays, 1987).
Schneider, Floyd, *Friendship Evangelism* (Eastbourne: Monarch, 1989).
Schwarz, Christian, *Natural Church Development* (Churchsmart Resources, 1996).
Scotland, Nigel, 'Evangelicalism and the Charismatic Movement (UK)', in Craig Bartholomew *et al* (eds), *The Futures of Evangelicalism. Issues and Prospects* (Leicester: Inter-Varsity Press, 2003), pp. 271-301.
Sheppard, David, *Bias to the Poor* (London: Hodder & Stoughton, 1983).

Shibley, Mark, *Resurgent Evangelicalism in the United States. Mapping Cultural Change since 1970* (Columbia: University of South Carolina Press, 1996).
— 'Contemporary Evangelicals: Born Again and World Affirming', *Annals of the American Academy of Political and Social Science* 558 (1998), pp. 67-87.
Sider, Ronald, *Rich Christians in an Age of Hunger* (London: Hodder & Stoughton, 1997 [orig. 1977]).
Simmel, Georg, *Conflict and the Web of Group Affiliations* (trans. by Kurt H. Wolff and Reinhard Bendix) (Glencoe, IL: Free Press, 1955).
— *Essays on Religion* (New Haven and London: Yale University Press, 1997).
Sinclair, Christopher, 'Evangelical Belief in Contemporary England', *Archives de Sciences Sociales des Religions* 82 (1993), pp. 169-181.
Smith, Christian, *American Evangelicalism. Embattled and Thriving* (Chicago, IL, and London: University of Chicago Press, 1998).
— *Christian America? What Evangelicals Really Want* (Berkeley and London: University of California Press, 2000).
Smith, David, *Transforming the World? The Social Impact of British Evangelicalism* (Carlisle: Paternoster Press, 1998).
Smith, Richard J. and Tim Maughan, 'Youth Culture and the Making of the Post-Fordist Economy: Dance Music in Contemporary Britain', *Journal of Youth Studies* 1:2 (1998), pp. 211-228.
Soper, J. Christopher, *Evangelical Christianity in the United States and Great Britain. Religious Beliefs, Political Choices* (Washington Square, NY: New York University Press, 1994).
Steer, Roger, *Church on Fire. The Story of Anglican Evangelicals* (London, Sydney and Auckland: Hodder & Stoughton, 1998).
Stott, John, *Issues Facing Christians Today* (Basingstoke: Marshall Morgan & Scott, 1984).
Stringer, Martin D., 'Towards a Situational Theory of Belief', *Journal of the Anthropological Society of Oxford* 27:2 (1996), pp. 217-234.
— *On the Perception of Worship. The Ethnography of Worship in Four Christian Congregations in Manchester* (Birmingham: University of Birmingham Press, 1999).
Sweet, Leonard, *Postmodern Pilgrims* (Nashville, TN: Broadman and Holman, 2000).
Tamney, Joseph B., *The Resilience of Conservative Religion. The Case of Popular, Conservative Protestant Congregations* (Cambridge: CUP, 2002).
Taylor, Charles, *Sources of the Self* (Cambridge: CUP, 1989).
— *The Ethics of Authenticity* (Cambridge, MA and London: Harvard University Press, 1991).
Tipton, Steven M., *Getting Saved from the Sixties. Moral Meaning in Conversion and Cultural Change* (Berkeley and Los Angeles: University of California Press, 1982).
Tomlinson, Dave, *The Post-Evangelical* (London: SPCK, 1995).

— *The Post-Evangelical* (revised North American edition) (Grand Rapids, MI: Zondervan, 2003).
Tönnies, Ferdinand, *Community and Association* (London: Routledge and Kegan Paul, 1955).
Toulis, Nicole R., *Believing Identity. Pentecostalism and the Mediation of Jamaican Ethnicity and Gender in England* (Oxford and New York: Berg, 1997).
Towler, Robert and Anthony Coxon, *The Fate of the Anglican Clergy. A Sociological Study* (London: Macmillan, 1979).
Troeltsch, Ernst, *Protestantism and Progress. A Historical Study of the Relation of Protestantism to the Modern World* (Boston: Beacon Press, 1966).
van Maanen, John, *Tales of the Field. On Writing Ethnography* (Chicago, IL: University of Chicago Press, 1988).
Wacker, Grant, *Heaven Below. Early Pentecostals and American Culture* (Cambridge, MA and London: Harvard University Press, 2001).
Walker, Andrew, *Restoring the Kingdom - The Radical Christianity of the House Church Movement* (2nd edition) (London: Hodder & Stoughton, 1989).
— 'Thoroughly Modern: Sociological Reflections on the Charismatic Movement from the End of the Twentieth Century', in S. Hunt, M. Hamilton and T. Walter (eds), *Charismatic Christianity. Sociological Perspectives* (Basingstoke and London: Macmillan, 1997), pp. 17-42.
Wallis, Jim, *The New Radical* (Nashville, TN: Abingdon Press, 1983).
Wallis, Roy, *The Elementary Forms of the New Religious Life* (London: Routledge and Kegan Paul, 1984).
Wallis, Roy and Steve Bruce, 'Religion: The British Contribution', *British Journal of Sociology* 40 (3) (1989), pp. 493-520.
Walter Tony, 'Being Known: Mutual Surveillance in the House Group', *Archives de Science Sociales des Religions* 89 (1995), pp. 113-126.
Ward, Pete, 'Christian Relational Care', in Pete Ward (ed.), *Relational Youthwork. Perspectives on Relationships in Youth Ministry* (Oxford: Lynx, 1995), pp. 13-40.
— 'Alpha: The McDonaldization of Religion?' *Anvil* 15:4 (1998), pp. 279-286.
— *Liquid Church* (Carlisle: Paternoster, 2002).
Warner, R. Stephen, *New Wine in Old Wineskins. Evangelicals and Liberals in a Small-town Church* (Berkeley, Los Angeles, CA, and London: University of California Press, 1988).
— 'Work in Progress Toward a New Paradigm for the Sociological Study of Religion in the United States', *American Journal of Sociology* 98:5 (1993), pp. 1044-93.
Warner, Rob, 'Autonomous Conformism: the Paradox of Entrepreneurial Protestantism (Spring Harvest: a case study)', in L. Woodhead and A. Day (eds) *Religion and the Individual* (Aldershot: Ashgate, forthcoming).
Watson, David, *Discipleship* (London: Hodder & Stoughton, 1981).
— *You Are My God. An Autobiography*, (Seven Oaks: Hodder & Stoughton, 1983).

Webb, Heather, 'Continuing the Journey: A Conversation with Dave Tomlinson', *Mars Hill Review* 18 (2001), pp. 65-77.
Webber, Robert, *Ancient-Future Faith* (Grand Rapids, MI: Baker, 1999).
Weber, Max, *The Protestant Ethic and the Spirit of Capitalism* (New York: Scribner's, 1958).
— *The Sociology of Religion* (Boston: Beacon Press, 1963).
— *From Max Weber. Essays in Sociology* (ed. by H.H. Gerth and C. Wright-Mills) (London: Routledge and Kegan Paul, 1967).
Widdecombe, Sue and Robin Wooffitt, *The Language of Youth Subcultures. Social Identity in Action* (London: Harvester Wheatsheaf, 1995).
Williams, Raymond, *Keywords. A Vocabulary of Culture and Society* (London: Fontana, 1976).
Wilson, Bryan R., *Religion in Secular Society. A Sociological Comment* (Harmondsworth: Penguin, 1966).
— 'An Analysis of Sect Development', in B.R. Wilson (ed.) *Patterns of Sectarianism. Organisation and Ideology in Social and Religious Movements* (London: Heinemann, 1967), pp. 22-45.
— 'Sects', in Paul Barry Clarke and Andrew Linzey (eds), *Dictionary of Ethics, Theology and Society* (London and New York: Routledge, 1996), pp. 743-47.
Wimber, John, *Power Evangelism. Signs and Wonders Today* (London, Sydney, Auckland, Toronto: Hodder & Stoughton, 1985).
Wraight, Heather, *Eve's Glue. The Role Women Play in Holding the Church Together* (Carlisle: Paternoster, 2001).
Wuthnow, Robert, 'Religion as Sacred Canopy', in J.D. Hunter and S.C. Ainlay (eds), *Making Sense of Modern Times. Peter L. Berger and the Vision of Interpretive Sociology* (London and New York: Routledge and Kegan Paul, 1986), pp. 121-142.
— *Sharing the Journey. Support Groups and America's New Quest for Community* (New York, London, Toronto, Sydney, Singapore: The Free Press, 1996).
Wuthnow, Robert, James Davison Hunter, Albert Bergesen and Edith Kurzweil, *Cultural Analysis. The Work of Peter L. Berger, Mary Douglas, Michel Foucault and Jürgen Habermas* (London: Routledge, 1984).

Index

abortion 99
Abundant, London 138
accommodation 35, 80, 163, 197
Acomb Christian Fellowship 201
affirmation 188, 191
Aitken, Jonathan 46
All Soul's, Langham Place, London 35, 59, 213
Alpha course xxvi, 45-47, 51, 52, 54, 60, 61, 70, 72, 117, 166, 170, 175, 176, 179, 193, 196, 202, 203, 206, 213, 215, 225, 228, 229, 231
Alphalink 175, 176
alternative worship (or alt.worship) xxiv, 44, 45, 50, 52, 136, 137, 138, 139, 147, 157, 164, 210, 211, 212
Ammerman, Nancy T. 18
Anglican Evangelical Group Movement, the 34
Anglican Mainstream 214
Anglicanism 165
Anglicans 31, 44, 51, 54, 64, 65, 86, 226
Anglo-Catholicism 165
Anglo-Catholics 28, 29
anti-Catholicism 16
Archbishop's Council on Evangelism 64, 68, 69, 73, 74, 228
Augustine 155
authoritarianism 100
autonomy 19, 100, 191

baptism 67, 68, 175
Baptists 30, 44, 51, 55
Barth, Karl 34, 87
base communities 162
Baughan, Michael 59
Bauman, Zigmunt 6, 8, 9
Baumann, Gerd 97
Be Real, Nottingham 138

Beaudoin, Tom 146, 184
Bebbington, David 11, 20, 24, 32, 34, 81, 98, 134, 163
Becker, Penny E. 104, 173, 175, 184, 194, 195, 231
Beckford, James A. 49, 165
Bellah, Robert 108
Berger, Birgitte 3, 4, 5, 6, 18
Berger, Peter 1, 3, 4, 5, 6, 7, 8, 9, 12, 13, 14, 15, 16, 17, 18, 85, 96, 119, 133, 174, 192, 197, 198, 206, 209, 218
Bergesen, Albert 197
biblicism 81
black Pentecostal churches 112
Blanch, Stuart 26
Brain, Chris 43
Brasher, Brenda 217
Brethren 164
Brewin, Kester
  211
Brierley, Peter 24, 27, 28, 30, 63, 64, 65, 71, 220, 222
British Council of Churches 35
broad church 28, 30, 31, 82
broad theology 188
Brown, Callum 24
Bruce, Frederick Fyvie 25
Bruce, Steve 8, 96, 210, 220
Brunner, Emil 87
Buddhism 90, 108
bureaucracy 192
Buzz 42

Calvary Chapel 12
Calvary networks 164
Calver, Clive 27, 110
CARE for the Family 39
Carey, George 27
Carrette, Jeremy 203
Castells, Manuel 8
catholics 28, 29, 30

cell groups 163, 225
Celtic Christianity 161
Celtic tradition xxiv, 165
cessationists 111
Chalke, Steve 202
Chambers, Paul 218
charisma 188
charismata 121, 129, 130, 131
charismatic churches 128, 130
charismatic experience 81
charismatic gifts 61, 121, 122, 129, 131, 158, 159, 218
charismatic movement 12, 42, 109, 112, 113, 131, 147, 207, 212
charismatic prophecy 102
charismatic renewal/revival xxiv, xxv-xxvi, 28, 36, 54, 62, 74, 109, 111, 114, 214, 218
charismatic revivalism 116
charismatic ritual(s) 128, 129
charismatic theology 107, 109, 112
charismatic tradition 122, 128
charismatic worldview 178
charismatic worship xxv, 60, 70
charismaticisation 110
charismatics 30, 31, 56, 59, 68. 105, 106, 109, 110, 117, 126, 130, 132, 135, 142, 146, 160, 161, 163, 188, 194, 203, 209, 226
Christ Church Fulwood 213
Christian Unions 25, 214
Christian Voice 201, 212, 213
Christianity Explored 213, 216
church growth xxiv
Church of England xviii, 26, 27, 28, 30, 34, 49, 50, 52, 55, 63, 64, 67, 68, 98, 109, 138, 160, 203, 211, 223, 227, 229
Church Pastoral Aid Society 59
Coates, Gerald 202
Coggan, Donald 26
Cohen, Anthony P. 19, 20
Coleman, Simon 220
Collins, John 56, 58, 109
communalism 7
congregational studies 17-20
Congress on World Evangelization, Lausanne (1974) 36, 38

conservatism 102
conservatives 2
Contemporary Christian Music 42
conversion 40, 107, 116, 136, 153
conversionism 73, 88, 98
Coser, Lewis 104
Coupland, Douglas 190
Cray, Graham 39, 59, 60, 61, 62, 136, 137, 166, 171, 183, 218, 230, 236
Creation Spirituality xxiv
crucicentrism 81, 88
Csordas, Thomas J. 117, 122, 128, 230
cultural accommodation 9, 10, 37
Cupitt, Don 49

Dandelion, 'Ben' Pink 96, 97, 102
Darwinism 37
decade of evangelism 45
democratisation 146, 188
denominationalism 44
denominations 8, 11, 204
detraditionalisation 135, 167
discipleship 47
Douglas, Mary 50, 90
Dowie, Al 18
Durkheim, Emile 1, 3, 122
Dylan, Bob 42

Eastern orthodoxy 165
ecclesiology 12, 28, 49, 51
ecology 17, 18
ecumenism 10, 35-36, 38, 79
egalitarianism 8, 34, 93, 188
elders 59
Ellwood, Robert S. 33, 34
Emergent Village 210
emerging church 21, 171, 211, 227
emerging church network 162, 164
Emmanuel College, Gateshead 213
Emmanuel Schools Foundation 213
Emmaus course 47
enculturation 166, 207, 208, 216
Enlightenment, the 49
entrepreneurialism 16, 163, 214
equality 207
ethnography xxv, 21, 128

Index

euthanasia 100
Evangelical Alliance Relief (TEAR) Fund, the 37, 38, 40
Evangelical Alliance, the 24, 27, 39, 40, 52, 53, 110, 201
Evangelical Christians for Racial Justice 38
Evangelical Coalition for Urban Missions 38
evangelical piety 35
evangelical revival 74, 232
evangelical spirituality 77
evangelical tradition 163, 169, 203, 204
evangelicalism xix, xxiv, xxv, 1, 2, 3, 6, 7, 9, 10, 11, 12, 13, 14, 15, 16, 17, 19, 20, 23, 24, 25, 30, 31, 32-35, 38, 42, 44, 45, 50, 52, 58, 62, 74, 75, 76, 77, 78, 79, 80, 82, 83, 88, 89, 91, 92, 95, 98, 101, 105, 106, 107, 108, 109, 110, 134, 135, 142, 143, 146, 151, 152, 154, 160, 163, 164, 166, 169, 170, 171, 182, 185, 188, 191, 194, 196, 197, 199, 200, 201, 202, 203, 205, 207, 208, 209, 210, 212, 213, 214, 216, 217, 220, 221, 226
evangelicalism, marks of 20
evangelicals 10, 16, 17, 18, 21, 26, 27, 28, 29, 30, 32, 35, 36, 37, 38, 39, 42, 45, 48, 50, 51, 55, 59, 64, 65, 66, 67, 68, 78, 82, 91, 94, 112, 131, 146, 152, 156, 160, 161, 163, 169, 177, 194, 197, 200, 205, 209, 210, 214, 216, 221, 223, 230
evangelism 35, 37-41, 45, 47, 52, 59, 61, 62, 72, 73, 74, 79, 136, 142, 144, 160, 166, 200, 215, 225, 230
Evans-Pritchard, E.E. 117
experimentalism 135
expressivism 191, 194, 207

Festival of Light 34
Finke, Roger 16
Forster, Roger 41

Fountain Trust, the 109
Fox, Matthew 155
Fox, Samantha 46
Free Churches 30, 55
Fuller Theological Seminary 14, 113, 201
Fuller, Charles 14
fundamentalism 13, 14, 83, 94
fundamentalist separatism 14
fundamentalists 8, 14

Garfinkel, Harold 145
Gehlen, Arnold 5, 192
gender 7, 96, 210
Generation X 186, 187
GenX churches 164
Gill, Robin 55, 64, 65, 83, 218
glossolalia 109, 121, 122, 123, 129, 130, 131, 133
Graham, Billy 14, 24, 36
Greater London Crusade, Harringay (1954) 24
Greenbelt 25, 39, 42, 44, 135, 136, 138
Gumbel, Nicky 27, 45, 46, 176, 179

Hall, Ian Rodney 11, 109
Harper, Michael 109
Hastings, Adrian 28
healing 59, 95
Heelas, Paul 105, 106, 127
Henry, Carl F.H. 14
heterodoxy 189
higher biblical criticism 37
Hilborn, David 163, 212
Hinduism 90, 91
Hindus 56
Hirst, Rob 199
holism 148, 151, 156, 160
holistic worship 45
Holloway, David 213
Holy Joes 50
Holy Trinity, Brompton 28, 46, 53, 175, 176, 203
home groups 58, 73, 173
homosexuality 16, 92, 100, 154
Hopewell, James F. 18, 115
House Church Movement 201

House Churches 109
humanitarian egalitarianism 155
Hunt, Stephen 46, 72, 215
Hunter, James Davison 9, 10, 11, 14, 16, 39, 51, 74, 77, 78, 79, 81, 87, 88, 91, 94, 101, 107, 156, 197

Icthus Fellowship 41
inclusivism 135
Independents 86
individualisation 174
individualism 7, 8, 19, 33, 52, 74, 105, 108, 206
intellectualism 188
International Society for Krishna Consciousness, the 108
Inter-Varsity Fellowship (IVF) 25, 37
Inter-Varsity Press (IVP) 26, 202
Islam 90
Islamic fundamentalism 3, 7

Jehovah's Witnesses 90
Jenkins, Jerry B. 202
Jesmond Parish Church 213
Jesus Army, the 108
Jews 56
Joy, Oxford 138
Jubilee Centre 39

Keele Statement, the 50
Kelley, Dean 8, 9, 11, 15, 208, 216, 218
Kellner, Hansfried 3, 4, 5, 6, 18
Kendrick, Graham 110
Kepel, Gilles 8
Keswick Convention 37
Kimball, Dan 211
King, Richard 203
Kingsway 202
Kurzweil, Edith 197

LaHaye, Tim 202
Late Late Service, Glasgow 137, 230
Lausanne Covenant (1974) 41
lay ministry 58
laying on of hands 181
legitimation 191
Lewis, Clive Staples 87, 201

liberal Christianity 39, 49
liberal modernism 8
liberal Protestants 14
liberal scholarship 48
liberalisation 11, 14, 15, 74, 78, 81, 86, 87, 94, 95, 96, 101, 103, 104, 197, 198, 220, 221
liberalism xxiv, 78-81, 89, 91, 97, 100, 102, 103, 144, 156
liberals 2, 14, 28, 30, 47, 82
Link, the 141
liturgy 45
Lloyd-Jones, David Martyn 35
low church 28
Luckmann, Thomas 4, 129
Lyon, David 179

Maffesoli, Michel 206
Mair, Henry 179
Marcuse, Herbert 146
marriage 92, 100, 214
Mars Hill, Michigan 164
Martin, Bernice 1, 2
Martin, David 1
Marx, Karl 3
Marxism 34
Maughan, Tim 150
McConkey, Dale 95
McDonaldization 4, 47, 166, 202
McLaren, Brian 164, 211
McLeod, Hugh 32
McLuham, Marshall 5
McPhee, Arthur 40
Mestrovic, Stjepen G. 132
Methodists 30, 34, 44, 51, 55
millennialism 37, 38
Miller, Donald E. 12, 13, 49, 146, 147, 188, 192, 207, 218
miracles 37
mission 25, 36, 41, 163, 169, 170, 221, 222
Mission England (1984) 24
modern liberalism 49
modernisation 19, 94
modernity 5, 6, 7, 13, 14, 15, 16, 19, 23, 77, 78, 94-95, 192, 204
Monday Night Group, the 136, 171, 181

Index 261

moral libertarianism 7
moral pluralism 33
moral relativism 16
morality 91, 100, 102, 160
Mormons 90
Muslims 90, 152
Mustard Seed café 58
mystery 152

National Association of Evangelicals 14
National Evangelical Anglican Congress (NEAC) 26, 50, 51
National Evangelical Council 36
Nationwide Festival of Light (1971) 25
Neighbour, Ralph 171, 224
neo-evangelicalism 14
New Age xxv, 49, 56
New Age Movement 44, 105, 107, 134, 156, 161, 165, 178, 209
New Age spirituality 167, 191, 221
New Agers 47
New Christian Right 13
New Churches 30
New Wine 200, 214
New Wine Networks 201
Niebuhr, H. Richard 7, 79, 217
Nine O'Clock Service (NOS) xxiv, 43, 44, 112, 136, 137, 138, 140, 147, 157, 182, 200, 211, 230
Noll, Mark A. 23
non-conformity 35
non-evangelicals 30, 65
North Yorkshire Vineyard Church 219

Oak Hill Theological College, London 60
obscurism 190
Okely, Judith 232
original sin 155
Orthodoxy xxiv
orthodoxy 205
Oxford Group Movement, the 162
Oxford Youth Works 41

Packer, James I. 34, 51

Pagitt, Doug 211
parochialisation 191
Peale, Norman Vincent 87
Peck, Scott 87
Penning, James M. 11, 13
Pentecostalism 1, 109, 110, 111, 112, 163
Pentecostals 30, 31, 55, 111
Percy, Martyn 48
personalism 184
Plass, Adrian 202
pluralism 48, 79, 107, 192
post-catholics 50
post-evangelicalism 21, 45, 47-50, 158, 194, 212
post-evangelicals 47, 52, 80, 210
post-liberals 50
postmodern Christians 138
postmodern philosophy 52
postmodernism xxiv, 8, 50, 135, 136, 151, 163, 167, 189
postmodernity 5, 47, 48, 136, 163, 164, 165, 167, 210, 216
Poulton, John 64
Powell, Enoch 33
power evangelism 114, 146
pragmatism 163
premillennialism 202
Presbyterianism 140, 148
priesthood 203
primary institutions 192
primitivism 163
privatisation 101, 120
Proclamation Trust 214
prophecy 121, 125, 128, 129
proselytising 40
Protestant Ethic, the 5
Protestantism xxvi, 1, 2, 10, 32, 146, 188
Protestants 15, 24, 29
Pytches, David 200, 201

Quakerism 55, 199
Quakers 96, 97, 102
Quebedeaux, Richard 10, 39

radical community xxvi
rationalisation 8

Rave in the Nave 139
Reform (Anglican campaign group) 52, 201, 212, 213, 216
relativism 48
religious pluralism 33
Renewal 109
Restorationist churches 109, 110
Restorationists 102, 120
restorationism 39
re-traditionalisation 102
revival 132
revivalism 1, 132
Richard, Cliff 42
Riding Lights Theatre Company 58
ritual language 128
ritualisation 129-131, 178
rituals 129-131
Ritzer, George 4, 47
Roberts, Paul 138
Robinson, John A.T. 34, 162
Rock Church, The 219
Roman Catholic Church 182
Roman Catholicism xxiv, 53, 55, 162
Roman Catholics 14, 28, 29, 36, 38, 86, 117, 130, 146
Romero, Oscar xxii

sacrament(s) 45, 203
sanctification 37
Sanctus 1 211
Sansom, Hugh 236
Saunders, Teddy 236
Schneider, Floyd 40
secondary institutions 192
secularisation xxvi, 11, 15, 18, 23, 40, 204
sex 91
sexual equality 7
sexuality 10, 214
Shaftesbury Project, the 37
Sheppard, David 38, 56, 58
Shibley, Mark 11
Sider, Ronald 38
signs and wonders 111, 200
Sikhs 56
Simpson, Roger xviii, xix, xxv, 59, 61, 62, 76, 77, 95, 97 98, 102, 103, 121, 123, 134, 184, 222, 223, 224, 225, 226, 228, 229
Singlehurst, Lawrence 171, 224
Smidt, Corwin E. 11, 13
Smith, Christian 14, 15, 16, 17, 19, 20, 53, 205, 214
Smith, David 11
Smith, Richard J. 150
social action 37-41, 200
social activism xxiv
social reform 37
socialization 198
societalisation 8
Soul Survivor 201, 211
South America 1
southernization 12
spiritual warfare 113
spirituality 74, 105, 108, 165, 171, 181, 183, 215
Spring Harvest 25, 39, 110
St Aldates, Oxford 28
St Andrew's, Chorleywood 200
St Anthony's Hall, York 57
St Cuthbert's, York 56, 57, 58, 64, 70, 112, 170, 228, 229
St James's, Piccadilly 44
St John's College, Nottingham 61
St Mark's, Gillingham 56, 58, 109
St Paul and St George's, Edinburgh 61
St Thomas's, Crookes, Sheffield 43
Stark, Rodney 16
Stott, John R.W. 26, 27, 35, 36, 59, 61, 87, 170, 179, 201, 202
Stringer, Martin D. 86
Student Christian Movement 25
subcultural identity theory 17, 19
subjectivisation 5, 120, 167, 197, 198
substitutionary atonement 98, 107, 152
supernaturalism 132
symbolism 227
symbols 19

Tamney, Joseph B. 208
Taylor, Steve 211
technology 192, 198

Themelios 26
Third Sunday Service, Bristol 138
third wave (of charismatic renewal) 112, 132
Third Way 39
Third World, the 100
Tice, Rico 213
Time of Our Lives 139
Tipton, Steven 181
tolerance 74, 146, 197, 207
Tomlinson, Dave 47-50, 80, 87, 110, 135, 142, 146, 154, 164, 211, 214
Tomorrow Today! 39
Tönnies, Ferdinand 205
Toronto Airport Church 111, 208
Toronto Blessing, the xxvi, 60, 111, 114, 131, 207, 208, 214, 218
translocalism 149
Troeltsch, Ernst 1

unemployment 100
United Reformed Churches 55
Universities and Colleges Christian Fellowship (UCCF) 25, 26, 55, 200
USA 2, 12, 14, 50, 78, 79, 102, 104, 117, 163, 164, 172, 173, 208, 217

Vardy, Peter 213
Vineyard Church 218
Vineyard churches 12, 110, 111, 113, 114, 128
Vineyard network 146, 147, 164
Visions group xx-xxiv, xxv, 21, 60, 70, 74, 82, 102, 135, 136, 138, 139, 140, 141, 142, 143, 144, 145, 146, 147, 148, 149, 150, 151, 152, 153, 154, 155, 156, 157, 158, 159, 160, 161, 162, 163, 165, 166, 167, 169, 171, 173, 174, 175, 181, 182, 183, 184, 185, 186, 187, 189, 190, 191, 192, 193, 194, 195, 196, 198, 206, 209, 210, 223, 226, 227, 230, 231, 233, 234, 236, 237, 238

Wacker, Grant 163
Wakeman, Rick 42
Walker, Andrew 110
Wallis, Jim 38, 39
Walter, Tony 192
Ward, Pete 41, 47, 203
Warehouse Community/Project, the 60, 136, 137, 138, 139, 140, 141, 156, 157, 166, 169, 182
Warner, R. Stephen 9, 15, 54, 98
Watson, Anne 56, 219
Watson, David 27, 36, 56, 57, 58, 59, 60, 61, 62, 65, 77, 87, 88, 112, 113, 147, 168, 170, 171, 201, 217, 218, 219, 223, 228, 236
Webber, Robert 211
Weber, Max 1, 3, 4, 142
Wesley, John 201
Westminster Chapel, London 35
White, David 60, 61, 62, 77, 102, 114
Whitefield, George 201
Whitehouse, Mary 34
Wilson, Bryan 7, 8, 33, 199
Wimber, John 58, 60, 87, 111, 113, 128, 131, 132, 200, 201
witchcraft 117
women 61, 92, 93, 102, 154, 216, 217, 218
Wood, Maurice 26
Woodhead, Linda 105, 106, 127
words of knowledge 109, 121, 123, 125, 126, 127, 129, 130, 131, 133
World Council of Churches 35
World Development Movement 156
World Vision 201
Worlock, Derek 38
Wuthnow, Robert 172, 173, 179, 181, 184, 190, 192, 197

York Minster 56, 57
Youth for Christ 40

Studies in Evangelical History and Thought

(All titles uniform with this volume)
Dates in bold are of projected publication

Andrew Atherstone
Oxford's Protestant Spy
The Controversial Career of Charles Golightly
Charles Golightly (1807–85) was a notorious Protestant polemicist. His life was dedicated to resisting the spread of ritualism and liberalism within the Church of England and the University of Oxford. For half a century he led many memorable campaigns, such as building a martyr's memorial and attempting to close a theological college. John Henry Newman, Samuel Wilberforce and Benjamin Jowett were among his adversaries. This is the first study of Golightly's controversial career.
2006 / 1-84227-364-7 / approx. 324pp

Clyde Binfield
Victorian Nonconformity in Eastern England
Studies of Victorian religion and society often concentrate on cities, suburbs, and industrialisation. This study provides a contrast. Victorian Eastern England—Essex, Suffolk, Norfolk, Cambridgeshire, and Huntingdonshire—was rural, traditional, relatively unchanging. That is nonetheless a caricature which discounts the industry in Norwich and Ipswich (as well as in Haverhill, Stowmarket and Leiston) and ignores the impact of London on Essex, of railways throughout the region, and of an ancient but changing university (Cambridge) on the county town which housed it. It also entirely ignores the political implications of such changes in a region noted for the variety of its religious Dissent since the seventeenth century. This book explores Victorian Eastern England and its Nonconformity. It brings to a wider readership a pioneering thesis which has made a major contribution to a fresh evolution of English religion and society.
2006 / 1-84227-216-0 / approx. 274pp

John Brencher
Martyn Lloyd-Jones (1899–1981) and Twentieth-Century Evangelicalism
This study critically demonstrates the significance of the life and ministry of Martyn Lloyd-Jones for post-war British evangelicalism and demonstrates that his preaching was his greatest influence on twentieth-century Christianity. The factors which shaped his view of the church are examined, as is the way his reformed evangelicalism led to a separatist ecclesiology which divided evangelicals.
2002 / 1-84227-051-6 / xvi + 268pp

Jonathan D. Burnham
A Story of Conflict
The Controversial Relationship between Benjamin Wills Newton and John Nelson Darby

Burnham explores the controversial relationship between the two principal leaders of the early Brethren movement. In many ways Newton and Darby were products of their times, and this study of their relationship provides insight not only into the dynamics of early Brethrenism, but also into the progress of nineteenth-century English and Irish evangelicalism.

2004 / 1-84227-191-1 / xxiv + 268pp

Grayson Carter
Anglican Evangelicals
Protestant Secessions from the Via Media, c.1800–1850

This study examines, within a chronological framework, the major themes and personalities which influenced the outbreak of a number of Evangelical clerical and lay secessions from the Church of England and Ireland during the first half of the nineteenth century. Though the number of secessions was relatively small—between a hundred and two hundred of the 'Gospel' clergy abandoned the Church during this period—their influence was considerable, especially in highlighting in embarrassing fashion the tensions between the evangelical conversionist imperative and the principles of a national religious establishment. Moreover, through much of this period there remained, just beneath the surface, the potential threat of a large Evangelical disruption similar to that which occurred in Scotland in 1843. Consequently, these secessions provoked great consternation within the Church and within Evangelicalism itself, they contributed to the outbreak of millennial speculation following the 'constitutional revolution' of 1828–32, they led to the formation of several new denominations, and they sparked off a major Church–State crisis over the legal right of a clergyman to secede and begin a new ministry within Protestant Dissent.

2007 / 1-84227-401-5 / xvi + 470pp

J.N. Ian Dickson
Beyond Religious Discourse
Sermons, Preaching and Evangelical Protestants in Nineteenth-Century Irish Society

Drawing extensively on primary sources, this pioneer work in modern religious history explores the training of preachers, the construction of sermons and how Irish evangelicalism and the wider movement in Great Britain and the United States shaped the preaching event. Evangelical preaching and politics, sectarianism, denominations, education, class, social reform, gender, and revival are examined to advance the argument that evangelical sermons and preaching went significantly beyond religious discourse. The result is a book for those with interests in Irish history, culture and belief, popular religion and society, evangelicalism, preaching and communication.

2005 / 1-84227-217-9 / approx. 324pp

Neil T.R. Dickson
Brethren in Scotland 1838–2000
A Social Study of an Evangelical Movement

The Brethren were remarkably pervasive throughout Scottish society. This study of the Open Brethren in Scotland places them in their social context and examines their growth, development and relationship to society.

2003 / 1-84227-113-X / xxviii + 510pp

Crawford Gribben and Timothy C.F. Stunt (eds)
Prisoners of Hope?
Aspects of Evangelical Millennialism in Britain and Ireland, 1800–1880

This volume of essays offers a comprehensive account of the impact of evangelical millennialism in nineteenth-century Britain and Ireland.

2004 / 1-84227-224-1 / xiv + 208pp

Khim Harris
Evangelicals and Education
Evangelical Anglicans and Middle-Class Education in Nineteenth-Century England

This ground breaking study investigates the history of English public schools founded by nineteenth-century Evangelicals. It documents the rise of middle-class education and Evangelical societies such as the influential Church Association, and includes a useful biographical survey of prominent Evangelicals of the period.

2004 / 1-84227-250-0 / xviii + 422pp

Mark Hopkins
Nonconformity's Romantic Generation
Evangelical and Liberal Theologies in Victorian England
A study of the theological development of key leaders of the Baptist and Congregational denominations at their period of greatest influence, including C.H. Spurgeon and R.W. Dale, and of the controversies in which those among them who embraced and rejected the liberal transformation of their evangelical heritage opposed each other.
2004 / 1-84227-150-4 / xvi + 284pp

Don Horrocks
Laws of the Spiritual Order
Innovation and Reconstruction in the Soteriology of Thomas Erskine of Linlathen
Don Horrocks argues that Thomas Erskine's unique historical and theological significance as a soteriological innovator has been neglected. This timely reassessment reveals Erskine as a creative, radical theologian of central and enduring importance in Scottish nineteenth-century theology, perhaps equivalent in significance to that of S.T. Coleridge in England.
2004 / 1-84227-192-X / xx + 362pp

Kenneth S. Jeffrey
When the Lord Walked the Land
The 1858–62 Revival in the North East of Scotland
Previous studies of revivals have tended to approach religious movements from either a broad, national or a strictly local level. This study of the multifaceted nature of the 1859 revival as it appeared in three distinct social contexts within a single region reveals the heterogeneous nature of simultaneous religious movements in the same vicinity.
2002 / 1-84227-057-5 / xxiv + 304pp

John Kenneth Lander
Itinerant Temples
Tent Methodism, 1814–1832
Tent preaching began in 1814 and the Tent Methodist sect resulted from disputes with Bristol Wesleyan Methodists in 1820. The movement spread to parts of Gloucestershire, Wiltshire, London and Liverpool, among other places. Its demise started in 1826 after which one leader returned to the Wesleyans and others became ministers in the Congregational and Baptist denominations.
2003 / 1-84227-151-2 / xx + 268pp

Donald M. Lewis
Lighten Their Darkness
The Evangelical Mission to Working-Class London, 1828–1860
This is a comprehensive and compelling study of the Church and the complexities of nineteenth-century London. Challenging our understanding of the culture in working London at this time, Lewis presents a well-structured and illustrated work that contributes substantially to the study of evangelicalism and mission in nineteenth-century Britain.
2001 / 1-84227-074-5 / xviii + 372pp

Herbert McGonigle
'Sufficient Saving Grace'
John Wesley's Evangelical Arminianism
A thorough investigation of the theological roots of John Wesley's evangelical Arminianism and how these convictions were hammered out in controversies on predestination, limited atonement and the perseverance of the saints.
2001 / 1-84227-045-1 / xvi + 350pp

Lisa S. Nolland
A Victorian Feminist Christian
Josephine Butler, the Prostitutes and God
Josephine Butler was an unlikely candidate for taking up the cause of prostitutes, as she did, with a fierce and self-disregarding passion. This book explores the particular mix of perspectives and experiences that came together to envision and empower her remarkable achievements. It highlights the vital role of her spirituality and the tragic loss of her daughter.
2004 / 1-84227-225-X / xxiv + 328pp

Don J. Payne
The Theology of the Christian Life in J.I. Packer's Thought
Theological Anthropology, Theological Method, and the Doctrine of Sanctification
J.I. Packer has wielded widespread influence on evangelicalism for more than three decades. This study pursues a nuanced understanding of Packer's theology of sanctification by tracing the development of his thought, showing how he reflects a particular version of Reformed theology, and examining the unique influence of theological anthropology and theological method on this area of his theology.
2005 / 1-84227-397-3 / approx. 374pp

Ian M. Randall
Evangelical Experiences
A Study in the Spirituality of English Evangelicalism 1918–1939
This book makes a detailed historical examination of evangelical spirituality between the First and Second World Wars. It shows how patterns of devotion led to tensions and divisions. In a wide-ranging study, Anglican, Wesleyan, Reformed and Pentecostal-charismatic spiritualities are analysed.
1999 / 0-85364-919-7 / xii + 310pp

Ian M. Randall
Spirituality and Social Change
The Contribution of F.B. Meyer (1847–1929)
This is a fresh appraisal of F.B. Meyer (1847–1929), a leading Free Church minister. Having been deeply affected by holiness spirituality, Meyer became the Keswick Convention's foremost international speaker. He combined spirituality with effective evangelism and socio-political activity. This study shows Meyer's significant contribution to spiritual renewal and social change.
2003 / 1-84227-195-4 / xx + 184pp

James Robinson
Pentecostal Origins
Early Pentecostalism in Ireland in the Context of the British Isles
Harvey Cox describes Pentecostalism as 'the fascinating spiritual child of our time' that has the potential, at the global scale, to contribute to the 'reshaping of religion in the twenty-first century'. This study grounds such sentiments by examining at the local scale the origin, development and nature of Pentecostalism in Ireland in its first twenty years. Illustrative, in a paradigmatic way, of how Pentecostalism became established within one region of the British Isles, it sets the story within the wider context of formative influences emanating from America, Europe and, in particular, other parts of the British Isles. As a synoptic regional study in Pentecostal history it is the first survey of its kind.
2005 / 1-84227-329-1 / xxviii + 378pp

Geoffrey Robson
Dark Satanic Mills?
Religion and Irreligion in Birmingham and the Black Country
This book analyses and interprets the nature and extent of popular Christian belief and practice in Birmingham and the Black Country during the first half of the nineteenth century, with particular reference to the impact of cholera epidemics and evangelism on church extension programmes.
2002 / 1-84227-102-4 / xiv + 294pp

Roger Shuff
Searching for the True Church
Brethren and Evangelicals in Mid-Twentieth-Century England
Roger Shuff holds that the influence of the Brethren movement on wider evangelical life in England in the twentieth century is often underrated. This book records and accounts for the fact that Brethren reached the peak of their strength at the time when evangelicalism was at it lowest ebb, immediately before World War II. However, the movement then moved into persistent decline as evangelicalism regained ground in the post war period. Accompanying this downward trend has been a sharp accentuation of the contrast between Brethren congregations who engage constructively with the non-Brethren scene and, at the other end of the spectrum, the isolationist group commonly referred to as 'Exclusive Brethren'.
2005 / 1-84227-254-3 / xviii+ 296pp

James H.S. Steven
Worship in the Spirit
Charismatic Worship in the Church of England
This book explores the nature and function of worship in six Church of England churches influenced by the Charismatic Movement, focusing on congregational singing and public prayer ministry. The theological adequacy of such ritual is discussed in relation to pneumatological and christological understandings in Christian worship.
2002 / 1-84227-103-2 / xvi + 238pp

Peter K. Stevenson
God in Our Nature
The Incarnational Theology of John McLeod Campbell
This radical reassessment of Campbell's thought arises from a comprehensive study of his preaching and theology. Previous accounts have overlooked both his sermons and his Christology. This study examines the distinctive Christology evident in his sermons and shows that it sheds new light on Campbell's much debated views about atonement.
2004 / 1-84227-218-7 / xxiv + 458pp

Kenneth J. Stewart
Restoring the Reformation
British Evangelicalism and the Réveil at Geneva 1816–1849
Restoring the Reformation traces British missionary initiative in post-Revolutionary Francophone Europe from the genesis of the London Missionary Society, the visits of Robert Haldane and Henry Drummond, and the founding of the Continental Society. While British Evangelicals aimed at the reviving of a foreign Protestant cause of momentous legend, they received unforeseen reciprocating emphases from the Continent which forced self-reflection on Evangelicalism's own relationship to the Reformation.
2006 / 1-84227-392-2 / approx. 190pp

Martin Wellings
Evangelicals Embattled
Responses of Evangelicals in the Church of England to Ritualism, Darwinism and Theological Liberalism 1890–1930
In the closing years of the nineteenth century and the first decades of the twentieth century Anglican Evangelicals faced a series of challenges. In responding to Anglo-Catholicism, liberal theology, Darwinism and biblical criticism, the unity and identity of the Evangelical school were severely tested.
2003 / 1-84227-049-4 / xviii + 352pp

James Whisenant
A Fragile Unity
Anti-Ritualism and the Division of Anglican Evangelicalism in the Nineteenth Century
This book deals with the ritualist controversy (approximately 1850–1900) from the perspective of its evangelical participants and considers the divisive effects it had on the party.
2003 / 1-84227-105-9 / xvi + 530pp

Haddon Willmer
Evangelicalism 1785–1835: An Essay (1962) and Reflections (2004)
Awarded the Hulsean Prize in the University of Cambridge in 1962, this interpretation of a classic period of English Evangelicalism, by a young church historian, is now supplemented by reflections on Evangelicalism from the vantage point of a retired Professor of Theology.
2006 / 1-84227-219-5 / approx. 350pp

Linda Wilson
Constrained by Zeal
Female Spirituality amongst Nonconformists 1825–1875

Constrained by Zeal investigates the neglected area of Nonconformist female spirituality. Against the background of separate spheres, it analyses the experience of women from four denominations, and argues that the churches provided a 'third sphere' in which they could find opportunities for participation.

2000 / 0-85364-972-3 / xvi + 294pp

Paternoster
9 Holdom Avenue,
Bletchley,
Milton Keynes MK1 1QR,
United Kingdom
Web: www.authenticmedia.co.uk/paternoster

www.ingramcontent.com/pod-product-compliance
Lightning Source LLC
Chambersburg PA
CBHW061433300426
44114CB00014B/1662